P9-BJN-757

"A labor of love . . . King knows what things scare people and he has a pretty good idea of why. He connects the content of horror stories with the real terrors of everyday life. . . . Those who have never seen a horror film or read one of the books he discusses can still come away from Danse Macabre with a sense of pleasure and enlightenment." —Washington Star

"Highly entertaining . . . King knows what he's talking about when the subject is horror . . . considered by many to be our best current horror writer."
—Dallas Times Herald

"Sent me off to the libraries and book stores searching for the books under discussion that I hadn't read; it made me re-read the ones I was familiar with. (The irritating thing about Stephen King is that he can't discuss anything without offering new insights that force you to re-think your opinions.) There's plenty in Danse Macabre to keep any horror fan satisfied." —Jackson, Miss. Sun

"One of the best books on American popular culture in the late 20th century."
—Philadelphia Inquirer

"[Danse Macabre] succeeds on any number of levels, as pure horror memorabilia for longtime ghoulie groupies; as a bibliography for younger addicts weaned on King; and as an insightful non-credit course for would-be writers of the genre." —Baltimore Sun

"King is a real pro, guiding us through the fright factory as only an insider can . . ." —Birmingham News

"Danse Macabre is a conversation with Stephen King. . . . It's comfortable and easygoing. At the same time it's perceptive and knowledgeable, a visit with a craftsman who has honed his skills to an edge that cuts clean and sparkles with brilliance." —Milwaukee Journal

"King knows the horror genre—from film monsters with zipper suits to book monsters with seamlessly haunting presences. . . . King opens up the best of the horror world . . . he conducts a lively tour of the deadly inhabitants of the obscure byways of horror." —Des Moines Register

"A search for the place where we live at our most primitive level."
—Chelsea, Mich. Standard

"King has taken time off from weaving ghoulish yarns—at which he is this decade's master—to present us with a textbook of the macabre."
—Philadelphia Bulletin

STEPHEN KING

DANSE
MACABRE

G

Gallery Books
New York London Toronto Sydney

G Gallery Books
A Division of Simon & Schuster, Inc.
1230 Avenue of the Americas
New York, NY 10020

This book is a work of fiction. Names, characters, places, and incidents
either are products of the author's imagination or are used fictitiously.
Any resemblance to actual events or locales or persons, living or dead,
is entirely coincidental.

Copyright © 1981 by Stephen King
Portions of this book have appeared in *Playboy* magazine.
Originally published in hardcover by Everest House.

All rights reserved, including the right to reproduce this book or
portions thereof in any form whatsoever. For information address
Pocket Books Subsidiary Rights Department,
1230 Avenue of the Americas, New York, NY 10020.

This Gallery Books trade paperback edition February 2010

GALLERY and colophon are registered trademarks
of Simon & Schuster, Inc.

For information about special discounts for bulk purchases,
please contact Simon & Schuster Special Sales at
1-866-506-1949 or business@simonandschuster.com.

"What's Scary" was originally published in *Fangoria* magazine
No. 289–290 (January-February 2010).

The Simon & Schuster Speakers Bureau can bring authors
to your live event. For more information or to book an event contact
the Simon & Schuster Speakers Bureau at 1-866-248-3049 or visit our
website at www.simonspeakers.com.

Designed by William Ruoto

Manufactured in the United States of America

10   9   8   7   6   5

Library of Congress Cataloging-in-Publication Data is available.

ISBN 978-1-4391-7098-4
ISBN 978-1-4391-7116-5 (ebook)

It's easy enough—perhaps too easy—to memorialize
the dead. This book is for six great writers
of the macabre.

ROBERT BLOCH

JORGE LUIS BORGES

RAY BRADBURY

FRANK BELKNAP LONG

DONALD WANDREI

MANLY WADE WELLMAN

Enter, Stranger, at your Riske: Here there be Tygers.

"What was the worst thing you've ever done?"
"I won't tell you that, but I'll tell you the worst thing
that ever happened to me . . . the most dreadful thing . . ."
—PETER STRAUB, *Ghost Story*

"Well we'll really have a party but we gotta
post a guard outside . . ."
—EDDIE COCHRAN, "Come On Everybody"

Contents

What's Scary: A Forenote to the 2010 Edition   xi
Forenote to the Original Edition   xxxiii
Forenote to the 1983 Edition   xxxix

   I. October 4, 1957, and an Invitation to Dance   1
  II. Tales of the Hook   16
 III. Tales of the Tarot   50
 IV. An Annoying Autobiographical Pause   85
  V. Radio and the Set of Reality   113
 VI. The Modern American Horror Movie—
     Text and Subtext   137
VII. The Horror Movie as Junk Food   212
VIII. The Glass Teat, or, This Monster Was Brought
     to You by Gainesburgers   231
 IX. Horror Fiction   264
  X. The Last Waltz—Horror and Morality,
     Horror and Magic   413

Afterword   437
Appendix 1: The Films   439
Appendix 2: The Books   445
Index   449

What's Scary:
A Forenote to the 2010 Edition

A ll my life I've been going to see scary movies, beginning with 1950s black-and-white monsterfests like *The Black Scorpion* and *Earth vs. the Flying Saucers* (where the alien invaders look very much like the prawns in *District 9*), and although much has changed in my life since the days when it cost a quarter to get in and the butter on the popcorn was real, I find myself asking the same three questions.

First, why do so many so-called horror movies, even those with big budgets (maybe *especially* those with big budgets) not work? Second, why do genre fans such as myself so often go in with high hopes and come out feeling unsatisfied . . . and, worse, unscared? Third, and most important, why is it that others—sometimes those most unheralded others, with teensy budgets and unknown, untried actors—*do* work, surprising us with terror and amazement?

Oh, and here's a bonus question: Why do I care? What part of me feels driven to see another remake of *The Hills Have Eyes* (not very good) or *The Last House on the Left* (brilliant)? I'm sixty-three and my hair is graying. Shouldn't I have left all this childish crap behind?

Apparently not. Hell, I don't even want to.

In *Danse Macabre*, a book I wrote almost thirty years ago, I argued that people attracted to stories about monsters and mayhem are essentially pretty healthy (if sometimes morbid). Critics of the book—and there were quite a few—responded predictably: "Yeah, sure, what else are you gonna say? That you're all a bunch of sick canines?"

Well, we probably *are,* but we also have an overload of imagination (sometimes a blessing; sometimes—especially when it's late at night and you still can't sleep—a curse). One of the accessories you get when the Bureau of Genetics supersizes you in the imagination department is more worries than the average Joe or Jill has to deal with. So while Ma and Pa are downstairs, watching *American Idol,* chowing on Doritos and worrying that their favorite warbler may get voted off the show, their over-imaginative little sonny boy (or baby girl) is upstairs, listening to Slipknot and wondering if Doritos give you cancer.

The imaginative person has a clearer fix on the fact of his/her fragility; the imaginative person realizes that *anything* can go disastrously wrong, at *any time.* The imaginative person doesn't believe that serial killers only happen to other people; he or she understands that guys like Henry *are actually out there,* and running into one is a lot more likely than winning $350 million in the Powerball lottery. And there are a lot of other serial killers out there. They have names like cancer, stroke, or meeting a vodka-fueled alcoholic traveling southbound in the northbound lane of the turnpike—*your* lane—at 110 miles an hour, fantasizing that his crappy little Honda Accord is the *Millennium Falcon.* In a case like that, decapitation and instant death might be the best-case scenario. Worst case? You wind up a quadriplegic pissing into a bag on your hip for twenty-five years or so. *And the person with the supersize-me imagination knows it.*

I'd argue that people whose entertainment needs can be satisfied with *American Idol* on the old tube-ola, or a wild and crazy night out to watch the Cornpatch Players put on *The Sound of Music,* are afflicted with imaginative myopia. Those of us who feel more (and see in darker spectrums) may be sick puppies, but we're also *lively* puppies. *Brave* puppies, too, because we keep on trucking in the face of everything we *know* can go wrong. For us, horror movies are a safety valve. They are a kind of dreaming awake, and when a movie about ordinary people living ordinary lives skews off into some blood-soaked nightmare, we're able to let off the pressure that might otherwise build up until it blows us sky-high like the boiler that explodes and tears apart the Overlook Hotel in *The Shining* (the book, I mean; in the movie everything freezes solid—how dorky is that?).

We take refuge in make-believe terrors so the real ones don't overwhelm us, freezing us in place and making it impossible for us to function in our day-to-day lives. We go into the darkness of a movie theater *hoping* to dream badly, because the world of our normal lives looks ever so much better when the bad dream ends. If we keep this in mind, it becomes easier to understand why the good horror movies work (even if they do so, as is often the case, completely by accident) and why the hundreds of bad ones just don't.

Expensive CGI FX, elaborate makeup jobs, and exploding blood bags won't scare anybody over the age of fourteen (three years younger than you have to be to get into an R-rated movie). The kids have seen it all before. It's *borrr*-ing. If a horror movie is going to work, there has to be something in it beyond splatter. Either by pure chance (Tobe Hooper's *The Texas Chainsaw Massacre*) or by pure genius (Sam Raimi, Steven Spielberg), some filmmakers are able to reach that something; they grope into our subconscious minds, find the things so terrible we can't even articulate them (unless you've got the money and the inclination to spend twenty years or so on a psychiatrist's couch, that is) and allow us to confront them. Not directly, though; few of us are able to look straight into the eyes of the gorgon. Humans deal better with symbols—the cross equals Christianity, the swastika equals Nazism (or "Nawzi-ism," if you're Brad Pitt in *Inglourious Basterds*), a #3 decal on the back window of your pickup says you still miss Dale Earnhardt.

That being the case, the central thesis of *Danse Macabre*, written all those years ago, still holds true: A good horror story is one that functions on a symbolic level, using fictional (and sometimes supernatural) events to help us understand our own deepest real fears. And notice I said "understand" and not "face." I think a person who needs help *facing* his/her fears is a person who isn't strictly sane. If I assume most horror readers are like me—and I do—then we're as sane or saner as those who read *People,* their daily newspapers, and a few blogs, and then call themselves good to go. My friends, a vicarious obsession with celebrities and a few dearly held political opinions is not a useful life of the imagination; that's the life of a beetle that just happens to have opposable thumbs and the ability to count to ten.

I'm sure a lot of the so-called realists who run the world think we're cracked, pervo, and possibly ready to shoot up the local high school when they see us paying for a magazine with a decomposing monster on the cover . . . but that's their problem. I don't know about you, but as far as I'm concerned, everything's cool with the kid. I'm all for make love, not war . . . as long as I can have Jason and Freddy. The *American Idol* folks can collect all the Care Bears they want; I like my Fear Bears.

Besides, how can you not love a genre where a movie (*The Blair Witch Project*) made for under $100,000 can scare the bejabbers out of the whole world and gross a mind-boggling $250 million? That's either pure democracy or pure anarchy. Pick the term you like best; I think they're both beautiful. Here is a case where the low budget and unknown acting troupe became integral parts of the film's success. There's nothing hyped up and phony about *Blair Witch* (the way all the *Saw* movies after the original and *Saw II* are hyped up and phony—the cinematic equivalent of Thanksgiving Day Parade floats). One thing about *Blair Witch*: *the damn thing looks real.* Another thing about *Blair Witch: the damn thing **feels** real.* And because it does, it's like the worst nightmare you ever had, the one you woke from gasping and crying with relief because you thought you were buried alive and it turned out the cat jumped up on your bed and went to sleep on your chest.

Horror, like comedy, looks easy. In one, you throw a pie in someone's face and roll the camera. In the other, you throw blood in the person's face and roll it. Gotta work, right?

Actually, wrong. Horror's not a delicate genre—there's

nothing delicate or refined about movies where people turn into bubbling goo when some extraterrestrial plague starts eating them alive—but it's mysterious. What works one time (that final hand-from-the-grave scare in *Carrie,* for instance) often won't work again . . . at least until it does. What worked in a super-low-budget flick like *Blair Witch* may not work on a higher budget (the sequel, *Book of Shadows: Blair Witch 2,* for instance—I loved it, but I was pretty much alone on that one).

Making a successful horror movie is like catching lightning in a bottle, and even the most talented filmmakers may only be able to do it once or twice. When Sam Raimi finally returned to his roots with *Drag Me to Hell,* he created a movie that's terrific fun . . . but not particularly scary. If you want scary, you have to go back to *The Evil Dead* (or *Curse of the Demon,* the British film that inspired *Hell*), and even that may be a wasted trip by now. A good horror movie is in many ways like a good joke: Revisit the punch line too many times, and it wears out.

When you've been around horror movies awhile, you become aware that the same themes and bogeymen come up again and again (and the bogeymen often wear the same hockey masks). This is partly because we have a tendency to return to what scares us (in real life we call this need obsessive-compulsive disorder), and partly because—hey, let's face it—horror is the home turf of cinematic quick-buck artists and con men. Studios and indie producers have a tendency to green-light the same idea over and over again, running the money-pressing machinery until every last buck has been squeezed out of it.

The squeezing results in clear cycles that fans of the genre have seen again and again: Genius gives birth to genius perfected; genius perfected gives birth to unenlightened imitation (think of any direct-to-video haunted-house flick or made-for-TV demon-kid movie that ever bored you to death); unenlightened imitation gives birth to comedy, after which the basic idea lies still for a time before coming back to life again (like a vampire in his coffin). Here are three specific examples, beginning with *The Blair Witch Project.*

The first time I saw *Blair Witch* was in a hospital room about twelve days after a careless driver in a minivan smashed the shit out of me on a country road. I was, in a manner of speaking, the perfect viewer: roaring with pain from top to bottom, high on painkillers, and looking at a poorly copied bootleg videotape on a portable TV. (How did I get the bootleg? Never mind how I got it.) Around the time the three would-be filmmakers (Heather Donahue, Joshua Leonard, and Michael Williams, who, coincidentally, happen to be played by Heather Donahue, Joshua Leonard, and Michael Williams) start discovering strange Lovecraftian symbols hanging from the trees, I asked my son, who was watching with me, to turn the damn thing off. It may be the only time in my life when I quit a horror movie in the middle because I was too scared to go on. Some of it was the jerky quality of the footage (shot with a Hi-8 handheld and 16-millimeter shoulder-mounted camcorders), some of it was the dope, but basically I was just freaked out of my mind. Those didn't look like Hollywood-location woods; they looked like an actual forest in which actual people could actually get lost.

I thought then that *Blair Witch* was a work of troubling, accidental horror, and subsequent viewings (where I actually finished the film) haven't changed my mind. The situation is simplicity itself: The three kids, who start out making a documentary about a clearly bogus witch legend, get lost while making their movie. We know they are never going to get out; we're told on the title card that opens the movie that, to date, they have never been found. Only the jumpy, disconnected, haunting footage they shot remains.

The idea is complete genius, and a big budget would have wrecked it. Shot on a shoestring (a *ragged* one), this docu-horror movie gained its punch not in spite of the fact that the "actors" hardly act at all, but because of it. We become increasingly terrified for these people—even the annoying, overcontrolling Heather, who never shuts up and continues to insist everything is totally OK long after her two male companions (and everybody in the audience) knows it's not. Her final scene—

an excruciating close-up where she takes responsibility as one tear lingers on the lashes of her right eye—packs a punch that few Hollywood films, even those made by great directors, can match. The Fearless Girl Director who confidently proclaimed "I know *exactly* where we're going" has been replaced by a terrified woman on the brink of madness. And, sitting in a darkened tent after six nights in the woods, with the Hi-8 camcorder held up to her own face, we understand that she knows it.

Blair Witch, it seems to me, is *about* madness—because what is that, really, except getting lost in the woods that exist even inside the sanest heads? The footage becomes increasingly jerky, the cuts weirder, the conversations increasingly disconnected from reality. As the movie nears the end of its short course (at just eighty minutes and change, it's like a jury-rigged surface-to-surface missile loaded with dynamite), the video actually *disappears* for long stretches, just as rationality disappears from the mind of a man or a woman losing his/her grip on the real world. We are left with a mostly dark screen, panting, elliptical lines of dialogue (some we can understand, some we can only guess at), noises from the woods that might or might not be made by human beings, and occasional blurry flashes of image: a tree trunk, a jutting branch, the side of a tent in a close-up so intense that the cloth looks like green skin.

"Hungry, cold, and hunted," Heather whispers. "I'm scared to close my eyes, and I'm scared to open them." Watching her descent into irrationality, I felt the same way.

The movie climaxes when Heather and Michael find a decaying house deep in the woods. Shot almost completely in 16mm black-and-white at this point, the movie confronts us with a series of images that are simultaneously prosaic and almost too awful to bear—the wreckage inside seems to *glare*. Still carrying the camera, Heather bolts up the stairs. At this point, her two friends seem to be calling from everywhere, and the camera's randomly shifting eye flows past the handprints of the children who have almost certainly been murdered in this house. There's no dramatic music here or anywhere else; *Blair Witch* needs no such cinematic steroids. The only sounds are shuffling footsteps, yelling voices (from everywhere!) and Heather's escalating moans of terror.

Finally, she plunges down to the basement, where one of the hokey stories they were told before their rash entry into the woods turns out not to be bullshit after all. Michael (or is it Josh?) stands in the corner, dumbly waiting for the thing from the woods to do what it will. There is a thud as that unseen thing falls on Heather from behind. The camera drops, showing a blurred nothing. The film ends. And if you're like me, you watch the credits and try to escape the terrified ten-year-old into whom you have been regressed.

There have been fewer imitators of *Blair Witch*'s documentary style than you might expect, given its absurd box-office numbers. I believe that's because mainstream Hollywood moguls find something inherently offensive about amateurs playing with cameras, and they certainly don't want to look like amateurs themselves. In one *Blair Witch* sequence, you can hear a plane droning overhead, and even though it works in the context of the film, I can't think of a single Hollywood producer who wouldn't tear his toupee off in the screening room when he heard it. Or how about the studio exec who wouldn't be able to restrain himself from saying, "These kids are *nowhere*. Can we replace them? Who's hot at Disney right now?"

The mainstream faux docs I can think of—*Cloverfield, Quarantine* (the remake of the Spanish [*Rec*]), *Diary of the Dead*—are all pretty good, but only George A. Romero's *Diary* approaches the purity of *Blair Witch*. Not until *District 9* do we find genius perfected. It's not "pure," if we take that to mean absolute adherence to the idea of amateurs with cameras—and, of course, *D9*'s not a pure horror movie, either—but the technique allows the film to achieve a sense of reality that's seldom seen in the old monsters-from-space genre. With its use of mixed media—documentary footage, fake news reports, even what looks like home movies—*District 9* is closer to Orson Welles's radio version of *War of the Worlds* than it is to an entertaining but ultimately disposable big-budget flick like *Independence Day*.

Even the *D9* mother ship feels real. Instead of an awe-inspiring, almost heavenly apparition, like the mother ship in *Close Encounters of the Third Kind,* this baby looks like a stalled-out tractor-trailer rig that the driver, probably drunk, left in a no-parking zone. *D9* is nothing like *Blair Witch* in terms of its subtext—Neill Blomkamp's film is about xeno-phobia rather than madness—but I'd argue that without *Blair Witch, D9* wouldn't exist . . . at least not in its current form. And before leaving *Blair Witch,* I want to recommend Daniel Myrick's most recent film, *The Objective.* It isn't as successful as *Blair Witch,* but it's remarkably ambitious and has the same creepy vibe.

The comedy/horror-doc hasn't come along yet, but I'm confident there are at least three in development. In any case, enough with the pagan symbols and crumbling houses hidden deep in the woods: let's talk zombies.

They've been around in the movies for a long time. *I Walked with a Zombie* (great title, not-so-great flick) came out in 1943. *Macumba Love*—a panting engine of sexuality featuring the large and delectable breasts of June Wilkinson—shambled into double-bill theaters in 1960. Getting warmer, but still no genius. Romero's *Night of the Living Dead* followed in 1968. It was a groundbreaking horror movie for sure—fans can tell you to this day where they were when they realized that Bar-bara's brother Johnny really *was* coming to get her—but the true genius was Romero's follow-up, *Dawn of the Dead,* with its uniquely American situation: survivors of the original plague trapped in a mall surrounded by the living dead. The all-American shoppers' heaven becomes a glittering chrome-and-plastic hell; the consumers become the consumed. Released in 1979, around the time that mall multiplexes were becoming not just common but de rigueur, it was the perfect fright film at the perfect time, and one of the few unrated movies to suc-ceed commercially.

Genius perfected would be Zack Snyder's 2004 *Dawn* re-make, which begins with one of the best opening sequences of a horror film ever made. Ana (the gifted actress and director

Sarah Polley) is relaxing in bed with her husband, Luis, when they are visited by the cute little skate-girl who lives next door in their suburban Milwaukee development. When Luis goes to see what she wants, cute little skate-girl tears his throat open, turning him into a zombie . . . and in the Snyder version, the zombies move *fast*. (Romero never liked that part, but it works.) Through a miracle of inspired editing (just when did she pick up those car keys, for instance?), Ana is able to escape, first into a neighborhood that's become a slaughterhouse, and finally into the countryside (with a handy mall nearby).

I'd argue that the most effective terror sequences are either the result of instinct or pure accident rather than screenwriting or direction, and that's the case here. Polley is a Canadian actress whose face was largely unknown to American audiences in 2004 (her main claim to fame was getting fired by Disney after refusing to remove her peace-sign necklace at an awards ceremony when she was twelve—you go with your bad self, Sarah). If we saw an actress like Julia Roberts or Charlize Theron as Ana, we'd know she's going to live. Because it's Polley, we root for her to escape . . . but we're not sure she will. Those first nine minutes are a sonata of anxiety.

The opening action ends with Ana crashing her car against a tree (and once again, witness the miracles that can be accomplished in the editing room: the car runs at the tree on the driver's side, but in the next shot hits dead center). The credits that follow, set to Johnny Cash's "The Man Comes Around," are accompanied by documentary and faux-documentary footage (there's that *Blair Witch* influence again) that's supposed to show us the onset of the zombie plague. But the first shot shows something entirely different, and it's here that Snyder shows us exactly what this inspired remake is about and how well he knew what was driving our fear-engines at that particular point in time.

What we see in that brief black-and-white shot is what looks like a thousand devout Muslim worshippers, bowing toward Mecca in unison—an image of mass belief that most Americans found troubling. By 2004, only three years downriver from

9/11, rampant consumerism was the last thing on our minds. What haunted our nightmares was the idea of suicide bombers driven by an unforgiving (and unthinking, most of us believed) ideology and religious fervor. You could beat 'em or burn 'em, but they'd just keep coming, the news reports assured us. They would keep on coming until either we were dead or they were. The only way to stop them was a bullet in the head.

Remind you of anything?

And don't accuse me of racism or religious prejudice, either. We're not talking about political, religious, or intellectual concepts here; we're talking about terror, and that's exactly what Snyder's zombies are, it seems to me: fast-moving terrorists who never quit. You can't debate with them, you can't parley with them, you can't even threaten their homes and families with reprisals. All you can do is shoot them and then steer clear of the twitchers. Remember that their bite is worse than fatal.

"Are they dead?" one of the mall survivors asks Steve, the repulsive rich guy.

His response: "Dead-*ish*."

Man, *that's* scary.

Yet some of the terror in *Dawn* transcends subtext and goes straight to the id. The movie's most frightening moment has nothing to do with politics. One of the mall survivors (Kenneth, played by Ving Rhames), has been communicating with another survivor (Andy, played by Bruce Bohne) who is stranded on a nearby roof. They flash chess moves at each other on restaurant dry-erase boards and note zombies who resemble celebrities (Andy, a dead shot, then picks them off). After being bitten by a ghoul, the dying (or already dead) Andy flashes one final sign: not words but a jagged smear of blood. In that single three-second shot, Snyder tells us all we need to know about the insatiate hunger that lives in the decaying interior of an undead brain.

In the end, the survivors—those who haven't been killed by zombies or each other—set sail on the loathsome Steve's booze-cruise boat, heading for an unnamed island where they hope to find safety. The final credits suggest that hope is probably vain. It's not a cheery conclusion, but it didn't hurt the movie's grosses (*Dawn* dethroned Mel Gibson's *The Passion of the Christ* at the box office, suggesting that John Lennon was wrong—zombies, not the Beatles, turned out to be more popular than Jesus). And that ending probably reflected the audience's deepest underlying fear: How can you escape terrorists who don't care about dying?

There's no need for us to list the dozens of imitations; comedy follows imitation as day follows night: *Shaun of the Dead* (brilliant), *Black Sheep* (amiably absurd but in the last analysis not up to much) and *Zombieland,* which I haven't seen at this writing. That one looks hopeful—I mean, hey, Woody Harrelson plays a stench-killing gunslinger named Tallahassee, you gotta like that—but I have my doubts. Partly because it looks like a slam dunk, mostly because I don't like seeing my beloved monsters dressed up in clown suits and made mock of. I like mine raw and mean and still bleeding.

Which brings us to the best horror movie of the new century, Dennis Iliadis's brilliant revisiting of *The Last House on the Left.* The engine driving this movie is the most powerful the genre has to offer: fear of the Homicidal Other. There have been hundreds—perhaps even thousands—of these in the long history of the fright film, and most have the same underlying premise: You meet the Homicidal Other either as karmic retribution for doing something wrong (think of Janet Leigh in *Psycho,* who never would have been showering at the Bates Motel if she hadn't embezzled a bunch of money from the Phoenix business where she worked) or—this is worse—because you just happen to be in the wrong place at the wrong time.

There are very few Homicidal Other sequels that I care for (*Saw II* is one of the few exceptions to the rule), because they trade on a moral ambiguity that makes me uneasy. In *A Nightmare on Elm Street,* Freddy Krueger is flat-out evil—no question about it. We hate him and fear him from the get-go, and why not? He's a pedophile, a murderer, and a disfigured psycho from beyond the grave. But seven sequels later, he has become, grotesque but true, a kind of pal.

By the time *Freddy vs. Jason* rolled around in 2003, we were no longer expected to root for the nominal good guys (teenagers without an ounce of fat on them). What we were rooting for as the sequels plodded on and on was a high body count. These sequels are basically snuff movies. I go, hoping to see something new, and rarely find it. You can argue for Rob Zombie's excellent reimagining of *Halloween* if you want to refute the point, but I'd note that Zombie's take on Michael Myers—an inspired collaboration, for sure—isn't a sequel but a remake. Which brings us back to the Iliadis version of *Last House*, the best horror redux in modern times.

The Collingwood family—Emma, John, and daughter Mari—are on vacation at their lake house, which is marked by an ominously inverted sign reading LAKE ENDS IN THE ROAD. Mari (played with courage and grace by Sara Paxton) borrows the family car to go to town and visit her friend Paige (Martha MacIsaac), who works in the local grocery store. While they're talking, a young man named Justin (Spencer Treat Clark) tries to buy a pack of cigarettes with a bloodstained twenty-dollar bill. When Paige won't sell to him—he has no ID—Justin offers to trade them some good pot, which is back at the motel where he's staying with his family.

It's this chance meeting that leads to the terrible events that follow, but it's also where Iliadis begins to spring the film's surprises. Clark, whom some of you may remember as Silent Ray in *Mystic River*, gives a nuanced performance as the son of a homicidal maniac (Krug, played by Garret Dillahunt). We identify Clark's disturbing thousand-yard stare as the look of a dangerous psycho, but it's actually the numbed-out shock of an abused child who is more his father's victim than his son.

Mari and Paige are taken captive by Krug, Krug's girlfriend Sadie (Riki Lindhome), and his brother Francis (Aaron Paul, of *Breaking Bad* fame). After a botched escape attempt by the girls, Paige is stabbed to death, Mari is raped (Krug does it himself after Justin refuses his father's invitation to go first and "be a man") and then shot as she tries to swim across the lake to the house where her parents are awaiting her return. It's in this house that Krug and his devil's band seek shelter from a sudden summer storm—a coincidence, but a believable one, since Mari has purposely directed them toward it. So the Homicidal Others are given lodging for the night by the kindly parents of the very girl they have violated.

Justin, who has taken Mari's necklace, leaves it where he knows the parents will find it. At roughly the same time Emma Collingwood spots it curled around the base of a coffee cup, she and John hear an irregular banging sound coming from outside. It's Mari, badly wounded but still alive (in the original, she's killed after being raped). She has dragged herself from the lake and crawled up onto the porch, and is pushing a rocking chair against the side of the house.

What follows is a carnival of parental revenge. Mom half drowns Francis in the kitchen sink, then stuffs his arm down the garbage disposal and turns it on; Sadie is shot to death in the bathroom; Krug has his head exploded in the microwave oven after the outraged surgeon father has paralyzed him from the neck down. This last touch is the film's only false move—partly because it's presented in a clumsy flashback as the family crosses the lake to safety, partly because it's the only place where *Last House* looks like "just another horror movie," and partly because—dammit—*you can't run a microwave with the door open!*

The 2009 *Last House* is the most brutal and uncompromising film to play American movie theaters since *Henry, Portrait of a Serial Killer* (which didn't play many; the MPAA initially gave it an X rating, and it was finally released unrated). The murder of Paige and the rape of Mari in the woods are particularly excruciating, because there's a sense of filthy reality about these crimes that the depredations of Michael Myers and Jason Voorhees can't match. There's zero audience-rooting going on for the bad guys here; when Mari finally loses the struggle to keep her plain cotton underwear on and we know it's really going to happen, we are filled with rage and sorrow (and if there's an emotion more foreign to a *Friday the 13th* movie than sorrow, I don't know what it is). Our identification is all with the victim. The villains are bad people, and they deserve what's coming to them. What they do *not* deserve is a sequel where they become our *buddies*.

The very effectiveness of some horror movies—the ones that show us the Homicidal Other with all his masks thrown aside—dooms them when they come before the critics (Owen Gleiberman of *Entertainment Weekly*, a magazine I write for on a triweekly basis, gave *Last House* an F rating), and this one, like Michael Haneke's jolting American remake of his German film *Funny Games*, took a predictably vigorous pasting. Only Roger Ebert seemed to partially get it, praising the performances (Dillahunt, he points out, isn't just acting scary; he creates a character) but neglecting to note that great performances rise from stories where the motivations are believable and the things that happen have an air of inevitability.

The original 1972 *Last House on the Left*, written and directed by Wes Craven, is so bad it rises to the level of absurdity—call it *Abbott and Costello Meet the Rapists*. The bad guys are cartoons, the glare lighting is Early American Pornography, Mari's mom (in this version named Estelle and played by Cynthia Carr) looks suspiciously like Loretta Lynn and the cops are a couple of bumbling stereotypes out of a 1930s Dead End Kids comedy. The chainsaw climax, set in what appears to be a pine-paneled rumpus room (it may have belonged to one of the producers), is hilarious. The soundtrack is a wonder: This may be the only movie about rape, murder, and kidnapping to be set to a cheerful ricky-ticky public-domain soundtrack. There's even a kazoo, a musical instrument I do not associate with terror. The one positive thing you can say about the original is that Craven must have had an extremely steep learning curve, because he started his career deep in negative territory.

The Iliadis version is to the original what a mature artist's painting is to the drawing of a child who shows some gleams of talent. From the opening shot—a dream glide through the nighttime woods—the cinematography of Sharone Meir is a work of beauty and a study in contrasts; from Krug's brutal murder of the cops who were transporting him to prison, we jump to a serene underwater world where Mari floats beneath a cloud of silver exhaled bubbles. There is a similar ballet—a more nerve-wracking one—in the kitchen of the Collingwood cottage as Mari's mother makes subtle, enticing advances toward the odious Francis, trying to get him to let his guard down enough for her to use a butcher knife on him. The analogous scene in the 1972 version, where Mama attempts to bite off the bad guy's dingus, is just grotesque. Worse, it's funny.

I maintain that if the recent *Last House* hadn't come trailing the baggage of its infamous predecessor—and if it had been a foreign film that came equipped with subtitles—it would have been a critical success on the level of *Repulsion, Diabolique* or *An Occurrence at Owl Creek Bridge* (the short film by Robert Enrico that was telecast on CBS as a *Twilight Zone* episode). To some degree, *Last House* suffered from its own refusal to compromise, and I think it also paid a price for *all* its infamous predecessors, not just the original source material. But there's something else, too. Horror movies produce nerve-music rather than head-music. Because most critics (Ebert has always been an exception) tend to be creatures of the head rather than the heart, they can be amused (in a patronizing sort of way) by fright flicks that are too outlandish to be taken seriously, but they have a tendency to react with anger and outrage to the ones that operate successfully in the deep fathoms of primal fear. *Last House,* like Hitchcock's great film about the Homicidal Other, does exactly that. And, like the Iliadis film, *Psycho* was originally greeted with a chorus of largely negative reviews.

Sadly, not many scare-and-splatter films are worthy of even such light analysis as I've given those I've addressed in this essay, but that doesn't mean there aren't others that are worth viewing (or re-viewing). Here are some others that have worked for me over the last fifteen years or so:

From Dusk Till Dawn: Robert Rodriguez's furious horror/action picture, starring George Clooney and Quentin Tarantino. Although it was released in the mid-nineties, Clooney and Tarantino play seventies-style bad guys who find themselves hiding out in a strip club populated by vampires. *Twilight* looks pretty thin compared to this.

Scream: A knowing, funny/frightening sendup of the slasher genre, featuring a psycho in an Edvard Munch *Scream* mask. Written by Kevin Williamson, *Scream* alternates laughs with authentic scares. Especially notable for the *When a Stranger Calls* riff that opens the movie. Not Drew Barrymore's finest hour, but certainly her finest *horror* hour.

Mimic: Guillermo del Toro's first American film, and a work of brilliance and complexity. It plays on our fear of dark places, environmental mutation, science out of control . . . and killer insects that can look like people. Perversely believable, with great FX and great performances by Charles S. Dutton and Mira Sorvino.

Event Horizon: Basically a Lovecraftian terror tale in outer space with a *The Quartermass Xperiment* vibe, done by the Brits. The plot's messy, but the visuals are stunning and there's an authentic sense of horrors too great to comprehend just beyond the eponymous (I always knew I'd eventually get to use that word) event horizon.

Pi: Made on a shoestring by director Darren Aronofsky, this film about a theoretical mathematician descending into madness (he thinks he has found a 216-digit number that can somehow make him a fortune on the stock market) is a clear precursor of *The Blair Witch Project.* I left the theater not entirely sure of what I'd seen, but filled with feelings of deep unease. This one gets inside you.

Bride of Chucky: Naah! Just kidding!

Deep Blue Sea: Directed by the ever-popular Renny Harlin, who could probably turn *Heidi* into an action flick ("Give up the secret formula or the goat dies!"), this movie about genetically engineered sharks, you could say, isn't up to very much . . . until, at the most unexpected point of the film, one of the supermakos rears up and bites Samuel L. Jackson in half! *Yessss!* I screamed out loud, and I treasure any horror movie that can make me do that.

Stir of Echoes: Writer/director David Koepp should be declared a national treasure. His adaptation of Richard Matheson's 1958 novel is an unsettling exploration of what happens when an ordinary blue-collar guy (Kevin Bacon) starts to see ghosts, thanks to a hypnotic suggestion.

Final Destination: I love all these movies, with their elaborate Rube Goldberg setups—it's like watching R-rated splatter versions of those old Road Runner cartoons—but only the first is genuinely scary, with its grim insistence that you can't beat the Reaper; when your time is up, it's up.

Jeepers Creepers: Victor Salva is a troubling, erratic director with a troubling, erratic history—including a conviction for sexual molestation of a child—but this tightly focused film about a brother and sister who run across a supernatural serial killer in northern Florida is relentlessly terrifying, playing as it does on our feelings of claustrophobia (the pipe scene is pure genius). If you haven't seen it, watch it. If you have, watch it again. But steer clear of the teenage-Spam-in-a-bus sequel. It's for shit.

The Mothman Prophecies: Richard Gere adds weight and unease to this story of a reporter trying to recover from the loss of his wife (and trying to understand the strange drawings she made shortly before the tumor in her brain killed her). He is drawn to a West Virginia town where all sorts of strange phenomena have been reported, including sightings of an otherworldly being called the Mothman. Good scary movies sometimes work on us like those ominous dreams from which we wake just before they can plunge us into full-out nightmares. Gere's character never actually meets the Mothman, which isn't such a bad thing; he—or *it*—is scarier in the shadows. This movie reminded me of Val *(Cat People)* Lewton's best work.

Eight-Legged Freaks: Not really so scary, but great fun. Giant spiders that run fast and kill everyone they can. The actors look like they're having as much fun as the audience. Probably should have been titled *It Came from the Drive-in*.

28 Days Later: A furious (and sometimes infuriating) zombie film, shot on digital video in hey-look-at-me style by Danny Boyle, most notable for its opening sequences in an eerily deserted London after clueless animal rights activists have loosed a living-dead–type plague on the world. In its documentary feel, we can again see the influence of *The Blair Witch Project*.

Shaun of the Dead: I know it's a send-up, but this Simon Pegg/Edgar Wright giggle fest has a few genuinely frightening moments (a few good gross-outs, too). The best sequence combines humor and horror in a pleasantly disgusting soufflé as Shaun fails to notice the zombie uprising that has begun to happen all around him. *We* see it, but poor Shaun just keeps missing the guy who gets bitten while he's mowing his lawn, etc., etc.

Red Lights (Feux rouges): In this French import, an alcoholic husband (Jean-Pierre Darroussin) and his long-suffering wife (Carole Bouquet) have a fight and split up while driving back from the summer camp where they left their kids. What follows on a darkened country road is a kind of double horror movie, as fascinating to watch as Spielberg's *Duel*.

Saw: You know about this, but watch it again and you'll see that it also works as a really superior mystery story. The same is true of *Saw II*.

The Jacket: Adrien Brody is terrific (those long-suffering eyes!) in this story of a war veteran who becomes the subject of a mad doctor's experiments. He's locked in a morgue drawer and catapulted fifteen years into the future. This movie has a remarkable, chilly intensity and a sense of impending tragedy.

Pan's Labyrinth: Ofelia's harsh reality (the Spanish Civil War) and her retreat into a fantasy world populated by fauns and monsters are perfectly blended in Guillermo del Toro's exceptional movie. Once you see it, you never forget the pale, eyeless creature (every kid's nightmare) that almost catches Ofelia and eats her before she's able to escape back—for a while, anyway—into the real world.

The Descent: If I were to pick another movie to analyze closely, it would be this remarkable story of six women who go on a caving expedition and encounter a race of subhumans (who resemble del Toro's Pale Man, now that I think about it). What gives the movie its resonance is how the women play against each other—their very real resentments (and secrets) allow us to believe the monsters in a way that most horror movies do not. I never tire of saying this: In successful creepshows, it's not the FX, and mostly not even the monsters, that scare us. If we invest in the *people,* we invest in the movie . . . and in our own essential decency.

Snakes on a Plane: Just my opinion, but if you didn't love this movie, what the hell are you doing reading this?

The Hitcher (2007): Rutger Hauer in the original will never be topped, but this is that rarity, a reimagining that actually works. And Sean Bean is great in the role Hauer originated. Do we really need this film? No. But it's great to have it, and the existential theme of many great horror films—terrible things can happen to good people, and at any time—has never been so clearly stated.

1408: John Cusack gives a bravura performance as a cynical debunker of the supernatural who discovers there really *is* an invisible world out there, one full of horrors beyond imagining. As a one-man depiction of madness, it stands alone. And Room 1408 in the fictional Dolphin Hotel is scarier than all the rooms of Stanley Kubrick's Overlook put together. In overlooking Cusack's performance, the Academy of Motion Picture Arts and Sciences once more proved that great work is almost never rewarded if it's done in a horror movie. Kathy Bates in *Misery* is the exception that proves the rule.

The Mist: The ending will tear your heart out . . . but so will life, in the end. Frank Darabont's vision of hell is completely uncompromising. If you want sweet, the Hollywood establishment will be pleased to serve you at the cineplex, believe me, but if you want something that feels real, come here. Darabont could have made a higher-budget film if he'd added a cheerful "It's all OK, kiddies" ending, but he refused. His integrity and courage shine in every scene.

Funny Games: Already discussed, but if you love the genre and haven't seen this, you should—for the simple reason that it turns the genre on its head. When things don't go according to the psycho bad guys' plans, one of them just . . . well, see for yourself. Suffice it to say that it outrages the rules of reality, and that's always a good thing.

The Ruins: The Scott B. Smith–scripted adaptation of his novel isn't quite as creepy as the book, but the sense of dismay and disquiet grows as the viewer begins to sense that no one's going to get away. With its cast of mostly unknowns, this would play well on a double Halloween bill with Snyder's *Dawn* remake.

The Strangers: An orchestration of growing disquiet and horror as a young couple (Liv Tyler and Scott Speedman) are set upon by a trio of masked psychotics. It starts slowly and builds from unease to terror to horror. In the same class as *Jeepers Creepers,* but a little more existential: Why is this happening? Just because it is. Like cancer, stroke, or someone going the wrong way on the turnpike at 110 miles an hour.

These may not be your favorites, because none of us have quite the same fear receptors. What I'm trying to say—and to show by example—is that cinematic horror is a potent art form, and there's a lot more going on under the surface than immediately meets the eye. Therein lies its many dark pleasures. And the next time your parents or your significant other ask you why you want to go and see that crap, tell them this: Stephen King sent me. He told me to look for the good ones, because they're the ones that speak to what's good in the human heart.

And, of course, to what isn't. Because those are the things you have to look out for.

Forenote to the Original Edition

This book is in your hands as the result of a telephone call made to me in November of 1978. I was at that time teaching creative writing and a couple of literature courses at the University of Maine at Orono and working, in whatever spare time I could find, on the final draft of a novel, *Firestarter*, which will have been published by now. The call was from Bill Thompson, who had edited my first five books (*Carrie, 'Salem's Lot, The Shining, Night Shift,* and *The Stand*) in the years 1974–1978. More important than that, Bill Thompson, then an editor at Doubleday, was the first person connected with the New York publishing establishment to read my earlier, unpublished work with sympathetic interest. He was that all-important first contact that new writers wait and wish for . . . and so seldom find.

Doubleday and I came to a parting of the ways following *The Stand,* and Bill also moved on—he became the senior editor at Everest House. Because we had become friends as well as colleagues over the years of our association, we stayed in touch, had the occasional lunch together . . . and the occasional drinking bout as well. The best one was maybe during the All-Star baseball game in July of 1978, which we watched on a big-screen TV over innumerable beers in an Irish pub somewhere in New York. There was a sign over the backbar which advertised an EARLY BIRD HAPPY HOUR, 8–10 A.M. with all drinks priced at fifty cents. When I asked the barkeep what sort of clientele wandered in at 8:15 A.M. for a rum collins or a gin rickey, he fixed me with a baleful smile, wiped his hands on his apron, and said: "College boys . . . like you."

But on this November night not long after Halloween, Bill called me and said, "Why don't you do a book about the entire horror phenomenon as you see it? Books, movies, radio, TV, the whole thing. We'll do it together, if you want."

The concept intrigued and frightened me at the same time. Intrigued because I've been asked time and time again why I write that stuff, why people want to read it or go to the flicks to see it—the paradox seeming to be, why are people willing to pay good money to be made extremely uncomfortable? I had spoken to enough groups on the subject and written enough words on the subject (including a rather lengthy foreword to my collection of short stories, *Night Shift*) to make the idea of a Final Statement on the subject an attractive one. Forever after, I thought, I could choke off the subject by saying: if you want to know what I think about horror, there's this book I wrote on the subject. Read that. It's my Final Statement on the clockwork of the horror tale.

It frightened me because I could see the work stretching out over years, decades, centuries. If one were to begin with Grendel and Grendel's mum and work up from there, even the Reader's Digest Condensed Book version would encompass four volumes.

Bill's counter was that I should restrict myself to the last thirty years or so, with a few side trips to explore the roots of the genre. I told him I would think about it, and I did. I thought about it hard and long. I had never attempted a book-length nonfiction project, and the idea was intimidating. The thought of having to tell the *truth* was intimidating. Fiction, after all, is lies and more lies . . . which is why the Puritans could never really get behind it and go with the flow. In a work of fiction, if you get stuck you can always just make something up or back up a few pages and change something around. With nonfiction, there's all that bothersome business of making sure your facts are straight, that the dates jibe, that the names are spelled right . . . and worst of all, it means being out front. A novelist, after all, is a hidden creature; unlike the musician or the actor, he may pass on any street unremarked. His Punch-and-Judy creations strut across the stage while he himself remains unseen. The writer of nonfiction is all too visible.

Still, the idea had its attractions. I began to understand how the loonies who preach in Hyde Park ("the nutters," as our British cousins call them) must feel as they drag their soapboxes into position and prepare to mount them. I thought of having pages and pages in which to ride all my hobbyhorses—"And to be *paid* for it!" he cried, rubbing his hands together and cackling madly. I thought of a lit class I would be teaching the following semester titled Themes in Supernatural Literature. But most of all I thought that here was an opportunity to talk about a genre I love, an opportunity few plain writers of popular fiction are ever offered.

As for my Themes in Supernatural Literature course: on that November night Bill called, I was sitting at the kitchen table with a beer, trying to dope out a syllabus for it . . . and musing aloud to my wife that I was shortly going to be spending a lot of time in front of a lot of people talking about a subject in which I had previously only felt my way instinctively, like a blind man. Although many of the books and films discussed in the pages which follow are now taught routinely in colleges, I read the books, saw the films, and formed my conclusions pretty much on my own, with no texts or scholarly papers of any type to guide my thoughts. It seemed that very shortly I would get to see the true color of my thoughts for the first time.

That may seem a strange phrase. Further along in this book I have written my belief that no one is exactly sure of what they mean on any given subject until they have written their thoughts down; I similarly believe that we have very little understanding of what we have thought until we have submitted those thoughts to others who are at least as intelligent as ourselves. So, yeah, I was nervous at the prospect of stepping into that Barrows Hall classroom, and I spent too much of an otherwise lovely vacation in St. Thomas that year agonizing over Stoker's use of humor in *Dracula* and the paranoia quotient of Jack Finney's *Body Snatchers.*

In the days following Bill's call, I began to think more and more that if my series of talks (I don't quite have balls enough to call them lectures) on the horror-supernatural-gothic field seemed well received—by myself as well as by my students—then perhaps writing a book on the subject would complete the circle. Finally I called Bill and told him I would try to write the book. And as you can see, I did.

All this is by way of acknowledging Bill Thompson, who created the concept of this book. The idea was and is a good one. If you like the book which follows, thank Bill, who thought it up. If you don't, blame the author, who screwed it up.

It is also an acknowledgment of those one hundred Eh-90 students who listened patiently (and sometimes forgivingly) as I worked out my ideas. As a result of that class, many of these ideas cannot even be said to be my own, for they were modified during class discussions, challenged, and, in many cases, changed.

During that class, an English professor at the University of Maine, Burton Hatlen, came in to lecture one day on Stoker's *Dracula,* and you will find that his insightful thoughts on horror as a potent part of a myth-pool in which we all bathe communally also form a part of this book's spine. So, thanks, Burt.

My agent, Kirby McCauley, a fantasy/horror fan and unregenerate Minnesotan, also deserves thanks for reading this manuscript, pointing out errors of fact, arguing conclusions . . . and most of all for sitting up with me one fine drunk night in the U.N. Plaza Hotel in New York and helping me to make up the list of recommended horror films during the years 1950–1980 which forms Appendix I of this book. I owe Kirby for more than that, much more, but for now that will have to do.

I've also drawn upon a good many outside sources during the course of my work in *Danse Macabre,* and have tried as conscientiously as I can to acknowledge these on a pay-as-you-go basis, but I must mention a few that were invaluable: Carlos Clarens's seminal work on the horror film, *An Illustrated History of the Horror Film;* the careful episode-by-episode rundown of *The Twilight Zone* in *Starlog; The Science Fiction Encyclopedia*, edited by Peter Nicholls, which was particularly helpful in making sense (or trying to, anyway) of the works of Harlan Ellison and of the TV program *The Outer Limits;* and countless other odd byways that I happened to wander down.

Lastly, thanks are due to the writers—Ray Bradbury, Harlan Ellison, Richard Matheson, Jack Finney, Peter Straub, and Anne Rivers Siddons among them—who were kind enough to answer my letters of enquiry and to provide information about the genesis of the works discussed here. Their voices provide a dimension to this work which would otherwise be sadly lacking.

I guess that's about it . . . except I wouldn't want to leave you with any idea whatsoever that I believe what follows even approaches perfection. I suspect plenty of errors still remain in spite of careful combing; I can only hope that they are not too serious or too many. If you find such errors, I hope you'll write to me and point them out, so I can make corrections in any future editions. And, you know, I hope you have some fun with this book. Nosh and nibble at the corners or read the mother straight through, but enjoy. That's what it's for, as much as any of the novels. Maybe there will be something here to make you think or make you laugh or just make you mad. Any of those reactions would please me. Boredom, however, would be a bummer.

For me, writing this book has been both an exasperation and a deep pleasure, a duty on some days and a labor of love on others. As a result, I suppose you will find the course you are about to follow bumpy and uneven. I can only hope that you will also find, as I have, that the trip has not been without its compensations.

STEPHEN KING
Center Lovell, Maine

Forenote to the 1983 Edition

About two months after I had begun work on *Danse Macabre*, I told a West Coast friend of mine who also likes horror stories and horror movies what I was doing. I thought he'd be pleased. Instead, he fixed me with a look of absolute horror and told me I was crazy.

"Why?" I asked him.

"Buy me a beer and I'll tell you," he said.

I bought him a beer. He drank half of it and hunched over the table toward me, looking earnest.

"It's crazy because the fans will tear your ass to pieces," he said. "You'll get as many things wrong as you do right. And none of *those* guys will pat you on the head for what you got right; they'll just drive you nuts with the stuff you got wrong. Do you really think you're gonna be able to find research material on *The Texas Chainsaw Massacre*? Where you gonna look? *The New York Times*? Don't make me laugh."

"But—"

"Half the people you talk to will tell you one thing; the other half will tell you another. Good God, you could talk to Roger Corman about the people in the Roger Corman movies from the fifties, and *he'd* get most of it wrong, because he made most of those movies in three weeks!"

"But—"

"Tell you something else, too. Half the stuff you *read* will be wrong, because the people who love this genre are just like you and me. In a word, crazy."

"But—"

"And your own *memories* will play you false. Give it up. You'll screw up the waterworks righteously and the fans will chew your ass because that's why fans are fans. Give it up and write another novel. But first buy me another beer."

I bought him another beer, but I didn't give it up, as you can see. Remembering what he said, however, I included a cagey note in the first Forenote inviting fans to write to me and tell me what I'd gotten wrong. There weren't millions of replies, but my doomsaying friend wasn't entirely wrong; there *were* hundreds. Which brings me to Dennis Etchison.

Dennis Etchison is *another* West Coast horror fan. He is of medium height, usually bearded, and handsome in an anti-LA fashion that is relieving. He is also funny, gentle, and thoughtful. His reading in the field has been deep and wide, his experience of fright films both high and low is *very* wide, and his understanding is great. He is also one hell of a fiction writer, and if you have not read his volume of short stories, *The Dark Country*, you have missed one of the great volumes in our peculiar field (and no, it isn't covered in this book because it was issued after 1980). The stories are not just good; they are without exception exciting, and in some cases genuinely great, the way that Oliver Onion's "The Beckoning Fair One" is great. The hardcover was printed in a limited edition, but there *will* be a paperback soon, a Berkley paperback—and I advise you to run, not walk, to your nearest *emporium de bookstore* and pick up a copy of it as soon as it's available. And no, I was not paid for the plug; it comes from the heart.

Anyway, Kirby McCauley suggested Dennis would be the perfect guy to comb the errors out of *Danse Macabre* for the paperback edition. I asked Dennis if he would do it, and Dennis said he would. I shipped him my growing file of "you fucked up" letters that very day by Federal Express. And I think Dennis did me—and everyone who cares about accuracy in even such a dark dungeon as the field of horror fiction—proud. This edition is rather more accurate in a number of respects than the hardcover and Berkley's trade-paperback edition, and Dennis Etchison—assisted by a marching company of horror fans—is the reason why. I wanted you to know that, and I wanted to thank the man for tucking in my shirt and combing my hair for me.

Ladies and gentlemen, Dennis Etchison—give him a hand, would you? He sure as hell gave me one.

STEPHEN KING
June 1983

DANSE
MACABRE

CHAPTER I

October 4, 1957,
and an Invitation to Dance

For me, the terror—the real terror, as opposed to whatever demons and boogeys which might have been living in my own mind—began on an afternoon in October of 1957. I had just turned ten. And, as was only fitting, I was in a movie theater: the Stratford Theater in downtown Stratford, Connecticut.

The movie that day was and is one of my all-time favorites, and the fact that it—rather than a Randolph Scott western or a John Wayne war movie—was playing was also only fitting. The Saturday matinee on that day when the real terror began was *Earth vs. the Flying Saucers*, starring Hugh Marlowe, who at the time was perhaps best known for his role as Patricia Neal's jilted and rabidly xenophobic boyfriend in *The Day the Earth Stood Still*—a slightly older and altogether more rational science fiction movie.

In *The Day the Earth Stood Still*, an alien named Klaatu (Michael Rennie in a bright white intergalactic leisure suit) lands on The Mall in Washington, D.C., in a flying saucer (which, when under power, glows like one of those plastic Jesuses they used to give out at Vacation Bible School for memorizing Bible verses). Klaatu strides down the gangway and pauses there at the foot, the focus of every horrified eye and the muzzles of several hundred Army guns. It is a moment of memorable tension, a moment that is sweet in retrospect—the sort of moment that makes people like me simple movie fans for life. Klaatu begins fooling with some sort of gadget—it looked kind of like a Weed-Eater, as I recall—and a trigger-happy soldier-boy promptly shoots him in the arm. It turns out, of course, that the gadget was a gift for the President. No death ray here; just a simple interstellar cure for cancer.

That was in 1951. On that Saturday afternoon in Connecticut some six years later, the folks in the flying saucers looked and acted a good deal less friendly. Far from the noble and rather sad good looks of Michael Rennie as Klaatu, the space people in *Earth vs. the Flying Saucers* looked like old and extremely evil living trees, with their gnarled, shriveled bodies and their snarling old men's faces.

Rather than bringing a cure for cancer to the President like any new ambassador bringing a token of his country's esteem, the saucer people in *Earth vs. the Flying Saucers* bring death rays, destruction, and, ultimately, all-out war. All of this—most particularly the destruction of Washington, D.C.—was rendered with marvelous reality by the special effects work of Ray Harryhausen, a fellow who used to go to the movies with a chum named Ray Bradbury when he was a kid.

Klaatu comes to extend the hand of friendship and brotherhood. He offers the people of Earth membership in a kind of interstellar United Nations—always provided we can put our unfortunate habit of killing each other by the millions behind us. The saucerians of *Earth vs. the Flying Saucers* come only to conquer, the last armada of a dying planet, old and greedy, seeking not peace but plunder.

The Day the Earth Stood Still is one of a select handful—the real science fiction movies. The ancient saucerians of *Earth vs. the Flying Saucers* are emissaries of a much more common breed of film—the horror-show. No nonsense about "It was to be a gift for your President" here; these folks simply descend upon Hugh Marlowe's Operation Skyhook at Cape Canaveral and begin kicking ass.

It is in the space between these two philosophies that the terror was seeded, I think. If there is a line of force between such neatly opposing ideas, then the terror almost certainly grew there.

Because, just as the saucers were mounting their attack on Our Nation's Capital in the movie's final reel, everything just stopped. The screen went black. The theater was full of kids, but there was remarkably little disturbance. If you think back to the Saturday matinees of your misspent youth, you may recall that a bunch of kids at the movies has any number of ways of expressing its pique at the interruption of the film or its overdue commencement—rhythmic clapping; that great childhood tribal chant of "We-want-the-*show!* We-want-the-*show!* We-want-the-*show!*"; candy boxes that fly at the screen; popcorn boxes that become bugles. If some kid has had a Black Cat firecracker in his pocket since the last Fourth of July, he will take this opportunity to remove it, pass it around to his friends for their approval and admiration, and then light it and toss it over the balcony.

None of these things happened on that October day. The film hadn't broken; the projector had simply been turned off. And then the house-lights began to come up, a totally unheard-of occurrence. We sat there looking around, blinking in the light like moles.

The manager walked into the middle of the stage and held his hands up—quite unnecessarily—for quiet. Six years later, in 1963, I flashed on that moment when, one Friday afternoon in November, the guy who drove us home from school told us that the President had been shot in Dallas.

2

If there is any truth or worth to the danse macabre, it is simply that novels, movies, TV and radio programs—even the comic books—dealing with horror always do their work on two levels.

On top is the "gross-out" level—when Regan vomits in the priest's face or masturbates with a crucifix in *The Exorcist,* or when the raw-looking, terribly inside-out monster in John Frankenheimer's *Prophecy* crunches off the helicopter pilot's head like a Tootsie-Pop. The gross-out can be done with varying degrees of artistic finesse, but it's always there.

But on another, more potent level, the work of horror really is a dance—a moving, rhythmic search. And what it's looking for is the place where you, the viewer or the reader, live at your most primitive level. The work of horror is not interested in the civilized furniture of our lives. Such a work dances through these rooms which we have fitted out one piece at a time, each piece expressing—we hope!—our socially acceptable and pleasantly enlightened character. It is in search of another place, a room which may sometimes resemble the secret den of a Victorian gentleman, sometimes the torture chamber of the Spanish Inquisition . . . but perhaps most frequently and most successfully, the simple and brutally plain hole of a Stone Age cave-dweller.

Is horror art? On this second level, the work of horror can be nothing else; it achieves the level of art simply because it is looking for something beyond art, something that predates art: it is looking for what I would call phobic pressure points. The good horror tale will dance its way to the center of your life and find the secret door to the room you believed no one but you knew of—as both Albert Camus and Billy Joel have pointed out. The Stranger makes us nervous . . . but we love to try on his face in secret.

Do spiders give you the horrors? Fine. We'll have spiders, as in *Tarantula, The Incredible Shrinking Man,* and *Kingdom of the Spiders.* What about rats? In James Herbert's novel of the same name, you can feel them crawl all over you . . . and eat you alive. How about snakes? That shut-in feeling? Heights? Or . . . whatever there is.

Because books and movies are mass media, the field of horror has often been able to do better than even these personal fears over the last thirty years. During that period (and to a lesser degree, in the seventy or so years preceding), the horror genre has often been able to find national phobic pressure points, and those books and films which have been the most successful almost always seem to play upon and express fears which exist across a wide spectrum of people. Such fears, which are often political, economic, and psychological rather than supernatural, give the best work of horror a pleasing allegorical feel—and it's the one sort of allegory that most filmmakers seem at home with. Maybe because they know that if the shit starts getting too thick, they can always bring the monster shambling out of the darkness again.

We're going back to Stratford in 1957 before much longer, but before we do, let me suggest that one of the films of the last thirty years to find a pressure point with great accuracy was Don Siegel's *Invasion of the Body Snatchers*. Further along, we'll discuss the novel—and Jack Finney, the author, will also have a few things to say—but for now, let's look briefly at the film.

There is nothing really physically horrible in the Siegel version of *Invasion of the Body Snatchers;* no gnarled and evil star travelers here, no twisted, mutated shape under the facade of normality. The pod people are just a little different, that's all. A little vague. A little messy. Although Finney never puts this fine a point on it in his book, he certainly suggests that the most horrible thing about "them" is that they lack even the most common and easily attainable sense of aesthetics. Never mind, Finney suggests, that these usurping aliens from outer space can't appreciate *La Traviata* or *Moby Dick* or even a good Norman Rockwell cover on the *Saturday Evening Post*. That's bad enough, but—my God!—they don't mow their lawns or replace the pane of garage glass that got broken when the kid down the street batted a baseball through it. They don't repaint their houses when they get flaky. The roads leading into Santa Mira, we're told, are so full of potholes and washouts that

---

* There is in the Philip Kaufman remake, though. There is a moment in that film which is repulsively horrible. It comes when Donald Sutherland uses a rake to smash in the face of a mostly formed pod. This "person's" face breaks in with sickening ease, like a rotted piece of fruit, and lets out an explosion of the most realistic stage blood that I have ever seen in a color film. When that moment came, I winced, clapped a hand over my mouth ... and wondered how in the hell the movie had ever gotten its PG rating.

pretty soon the salesmen who service the town—who aerate its municipal lungs with the life-giving atmosphere of capitalism, you might say—will no longer bother to come.

The gross-out level is one thing, but it is on that second level of horror that we often experience that low sense of anxiety which we call "the creeps." Over the years, *Invasion of the Body Snatchers* has given a lot of people the creeps, and all sorts of high-flown ideas have been imputed to Siegel's film version. It was seen as an anti-McCarthy film until someone pointed out the fact that Don Siegel's political views could hardly be called leftish. Then people began seeing it as a "better dead than Red" picture. Of the two ideas, I think that second one better fits the film that Siegel made, the picture that ends with Kevin McCarthy in the middle of a freeway, screaming "They're here already! You're next!" to cars which rush heedlessly by him. But in my heart, I don't really believe that Siegel was wearing a political hat at all when he made the movie (and you will see later that Jack Finney has never believed it, either); I believe he was simply having fun and that the undertones . . . just happened.

This doesn't invalidate the idea that there is an allegorical element in *Invasion of the Body Snatchers;* it is simply to suggest that sometimes these pressure points, these terminals of fear, are so deeply buried and yet so vital that we may tap them like artesian wells—saying one thing out loud while we express something else in a whisper. The Philip Kaufman version of Finney's novel is fun (although, to be fair, not quite as much fun as Siegel's), but that whisper has changed into something entirely different: the subtext of Kaufman's picture seems to satirize the whole I'm-okay-you're-okay-so-let's-get-in-the-hot-tub-and-massage-our-precious-consciousness movement of the egocentric seventies. Which is to suggest that, although the uneasy dreams of the mass subconscious may change from decade to decade, the pipeline into that well of dreams remains constant and vital.

This is the real danse macabre, I suspect: those remarkable moments when the creator of a horror story is able to unite the conscious and subconscious mind with one potent idea. I believe it happened to a greater degree with the Siegel version of *Invasion of the Body Snatchers,* but of course both Siegel and Kaufman were able to proceed courtesy of Jack Finney, who sank the original well.

All of which brings us back, I think, to the Stratford Theater on a warm fall afternoon in 1957.

3

We sat there in our seats like dummies, staring at the manager. He looked nervous and sallow—or perhaps that was only the footlights. We sat wondering what sort of catastrophe could have caused him to stop the movie just as it was reaching that apotheosis of all Saturday matinee shows, "the good part." And the way his voice trembled when he spoke did not add to anyone's sense of well-being.

"I want to tell you," he said in that trembly voice, "that the Russians have put a space satellite into orbit around the earth. They call it . . . *Spootnik.*"

This piece of intelligence was greeted by absolute, tomblike silence. We just sat there, a theaterful of 1950s kids with crew cuts, whiffle cuts, ponytails, ducktails, crinolines, chinos, jeans with cuffs, Captain Midnight rings; kids who had just discovered Chuck Berry and Little Richard on New York's one black rhythm and blues station, which we could get at night, wavering in and out like a powerful jive language from a distant planet. We were the kids who grew up on Captain Video and Terry and the Pirates. We were the kids who had seen Combat Casey kick the teeth out of North Korean gooks without number in the comic books. We were the kids who saw Richard Carlson catch thousands of dirty Commie spies in *I Led Three Lives.* We were the kids who had ponied up a quarter apiece to watch Hugh Marlowe in *Earth vs. the Flying Saucers* and got this piece of upsetting news as a kind of nasty bonus.

I remember this very clearly: cutting through that awful dead silence came one shrill voice, whether that of a boy or a girl I do not know; a voice that was near tears but that was also full of a frightening anger: "Oh, go show the movie, you liar!"

The manager did not even look toward the place from which that voice had come, and that was somehow the worst thing of all. Somehow that proved it. The Russians had beaten us into space. Somewhere over our heads, beeping triumphantly, was an electronic ball which had been launched and constructed behind the Iron Curtain. Neither Captain Midnight nor Richard Carlson (who also starred in *Riders to the Stars;* and oh boy, the bitter irony in that) had been able to stop it. It was up there . . . and they called it Spootnik. The manager stood there for a moment longer, looking out at us as if he wished he had something else to say but could not think what it might be. Then he walked off and pretty soon the movie started up again.

4

So here's a question. You remember where you were when President Kennedy was assassinated. You remember where you were when you heard that RFK had taken a dive in some hotel kitchen as the result of another crazy. Maybe you even remember where you were during the Cuban missile crisis.

Do you remember where you were when the Russians launched Sputnik I?

Terror—what Hunter Thompson calls "fear and loathing"—often arises from a pervasive sense of disestablishment; that things are in the unmaking. If that sense of unmaking is sudden and seems personal—if it hits you around the heart—then it lodges in the memory as a complete set. Just the fact that almost everyone remembers where he/she was at the instant he/she heard the news of the Kennedy assassination is something I find almost as interesting as the fact that one nerd with a mail-order gun was able to change the entire course of world history in just fourteen seconds or so. That moment of knowledge and the three-day spasm of stunned grief which followed it is perhaps the closest any people in history has ever come to a total period of mass consciousness and mass empathy and—in retrospect—mass memory: two hundred million people in a living frieze. Love cannot achieve that sort of across-the-board hammerstrike of emotion, apparently. More's the pity.

I'm not suggesting that the news of Sputnik's launching had anywhere near the same sort of effect on the American psyche (although it was not without effect; see, for instance, Tom Wolfe's amusing narrative of events following the successful Russian launch in his superlative book about our space program, *The Right Stuff*,) but I am guessing that a great many kids—the war babies, we were called—remember the event as well as I do.

We were fertile ground for the seeds of terror, we war babies; we had been raised in a strange circus atmosphere of paranoia, patriotism, and national *hubris*. We were told that we were the greatest nation on earth and that any Iron Curtain outlaw who tried to draw down on us in that great saloon of international politics would discover who the fastest gun in the West was (as in Pat Frank's illuminating novel of the period, *Alas, Babylon*), but we were also told exactly what to keep in our fallout shelters and how long we would have to stay in there after we won the war. We had more to eat than any nation in the history of the world, but there were traces of Strontium-90 in our milk from nuclear testing.

We were the children of the men and women who won what Duke Wayne used to call "the big one," and when the dust cleared, America was on top. We had replaced England as the colossus that stood astride the world. When the folks got together again to make me and millions of kids like me, London had been bombed almost flat, the sun was setting every twelve hours or so on the British Empire, and Russia had been bled nearly white in its war against the Nazis; during the siege of Stalingrad, Russian soldiers had been reduced to dining on their dead comrades. But not a single bomb had fallen on New York, and America had the lightest casualty rate of any major power involved in the war.

Further, we had a great history to draw upon (all short histories are great histories), particularly in matters of invention and innovation. Every grade-school teacher produced the same two words for the delectation of his/her students; two magic words glittering and glowing like a beautiful neon sign; two words of almost incredible power and grace; and these two words were: PIONEER SPIRIT. I and my fellow kids grew up secure in this knowledge of America's PIONEER SPIRIT—a knowledge that could be summed up in a litany of names learned by rote in the classroom. Eli Whitney. Samuel Morse. Alexander Graham Bell. Henry Ford. Robert Goddard. Wilbur and Orville Wright. Robert Oppenheimer. These men, ladies and gentlemen, all had one great thing in common. They were all Americans simply bursting with PIONEER SPIRIT. We were and always had been, in that pungent American phrase, fastest and bestest with the mostest.

And what a world stretched ahead! It was all outlined in the stories of Robert A. Heinlein, Lester Del Rey, Alfred Bester, Stanley Weinbaum, and dozens of others! These dreams came in the last of the science fiction pulp magazines, which were shrinking and dying by that October in 1957 . . . but science fiction itself had never been in better shape. Space would be more than conquered, these writers told us; it would . . . it would be . . . why, it would be PIONEERED! Silver needles piercing the void, followed by flaming rockets lowering huge ships onto alien worlds, followed by hardy colonies full of men and women (*American* men and women, need one add) with PIONEER SPIRIT bursting from every pore. Mars would become our backyard, the new gold rush (or possibly the new rhodium rush) might well be in the asteroid belt . . . and ultimately, of course, the stars themselves would be ours—a glorious future awaited with tourists snapping Kodak prints of the six moons of Procyon IV and a Chevrolet JetCar assembly line on Sirius III. Earth itself would be transformed into a utopia that you could see on the cover of any '50s issue of *Fantasy and Science Fiction, Amazing Stories, Galaxy,* or *Astounding Science Fiction.*

A future filled with the PIONEER SPIRIT; even better, a future filled with the *AMERICAN* PIONEER SPIRIT. See, for example, the cover of the original Bantam paperback edition of Ray Bradbury's *Martian Chronicles*. In this artistic vision—a figment of the artist's imagination and not of Bradbury's; there is nothing so ethnocentric or downright silly in this classic melding of science fiction and fantasy—the landing space travelers look a great deal like gyrenes storming up the beach at Saipan or Tarawa. It's a rocket instead of an LST in the background, true, but their jut-jawed, automatic-brandishing commander might have stepped right out of a John Wayne movie: "Come on, you suckers, do you want to live forever? Where's your PIONEER SPIRIT?"

This was the cradle of elementary political theory and technological dreamwork in which I and a great many other war babies were rocked until that day in October, when the cradle was rudely upended and all of us fell out. For me, it was the end of the sweet dream . . . and the beginning of the nightmare.

The children grasped the implication of what the Russians had done as well and as quickly as anyone else—certainly as fast as the politicians who were falling all over themselves to cut the good lumber out of this nasty deadfall. The big bombers that had smashed Berlin and Hamburg in World War II were even then, in 1957, becoming obsolete. A new and ominous abbreviation had come into the working vocabulary of terror: ICBM. The ICBMs, we understood, were only the German V-rockets grown up. They would carry enormous payloads of nuclear death and destruction, and if the Russkies tried anything funny, we would simply blow them right off the face of the earth. Watch out, Moscow! Here comes a big, hot dose of the PIONEER SPIRIT for you, you turkeys!

Except that somehow, incredibly, the Russians were looking pretty good in the old ICBM department themselves. After all, ICBMs were only big rockets, and the Commies certainly hadn't lofted Sputnik I into orbit with a potato masher.

And in that context, the movie began again in Stratford, with the ominous, warbling voices of the saucerians echoing everywhere: *"Look to your skies . . . a warning will come from your skies . . . look to your skies . . ."*

5

This book is intended to be an informal overview of where the horror genre has been over the last thirty years, and not an autobiography of yours truly. The autobiography of a father, writer, and ex–high school teacher would make dull reading indeed. I am a writer by trade, which means that the most interesting things that have happened to me have happened in my dreams.

But because I am a horror novelist and also a child of my times, and because I believe that horror does not horrify unless the reader or viewer has been personally touched, you will find the autobiographical element constantly creeping in. Horror in real life is an emotion that one grapples with—as I grappled with the realization that the Russians had beaten us into space—all alone. It is a combat waged in the secret recesses of the heart.

I believe that we are all ultimately alone and that any deep and lasting human contact is nothing more nor less than a necessary illusion—but at least the feelings which we think of as "positive" and "constructive" are a reaching-out, an effort to make contact and establish some sort of communication. Feelings of love and kindness, the ability to care and empathize, are all we know of the light. They are efforts to link and integrate; they are the emotions which bring us together, if not in fact then at least in a comforting illusion that makes the burden of mortality a little easier to bear.

Horror, terror, fear, panic: these are the emotions which drive wedges between us, split us off from the crowd, and make us alone. It is paradoxical that feelings and emotions we associate with the "mob instinct" should do this, but crowds are lonely places to be, we're told, a fellowship with no love in it. The melodies of the horror tale are simple and repetitive, and they are melodies of disestablishment and disintegration . . . but another paradox is that the ritual outletting of these emotions seems to bring things back to a more stable and constructive state again. Ask any psychiatrist what his patient is doing when he lies there on the couch and talks about what keeps him awake and what he sees in his dreams. What do you see when you turn out the light? the Beatles asked; their answer: I can't tell you, but I know that it's mine.

The genre we're talking about, whether it be in terms of books, film, or TV, is really all one: make-believe horrors. And one of the questions that frequently comes up, asked by people who have grasped the paradox (but perhaps not fully articulated it in their own minds) is: Why do you want to make up horrible things when there is so much real horror in the world?

The answer seems to be that we make up horrors to help us cope with the real ones. With the endless inventiveness of humankind, we grasp the very elements which are so divisive and destructive and try to turn them into tools—to dismantle themselves. The term *catharsis* is as old as Greek drama, and it has been used rather too glibly by some practitioners in my field to justify what they do, but it still has its limited uses here. The dream of horror is in itself an out-letting and a lancing . . . and it may well be that the mass-media dream of horror can sometimes become a nationwide analyst's couch.

So, for the final time before we push on, October of 1957; now, absurd as it looks on the face of it, *Earth vs. the Flying Saucers* has become a symbolic political statement. Below its pulpy invaders-from-space storyline, it becomes a preview of the ultimate war. Those greedy, twisted old monsters piloting the saucers are really the Russians; the destruction of the Washington Monument, the Capitol dome, and the Supreme Court—all rendered with graphic, eerie believability by Harryhausen's stop-motion effects—becomes nothing less than the destruction one would logically expect when the A-bombs finally fly.

And then the end of the movie comes. The last saucer has been shot down by Hugh Marlowe's secret weapon, an ultrasonic gun that interrupts the electromagnetic drive of the flying saucers, or some sort of similar agreeable foolishness. Loudspeakers blare from every Washington street corner, seemingly: *"The present danger . . . is over. The present danger . . .*

is over. The present danger is over." The camera shows us clear skies. The evil old monsters with their frozen snarls and their twisted-root faces have been vanquished. We cut to a California beach, magically deserted except for Hugh Marlowe and his new wife (who is, of course, the daughter of the Crusty Old Military Man Who Died For His Country); they are on their honeymoon.

"Russ," she asks him, "will they ever come back?"

Marlowe looks sagely up at the sky, then back at his wife. "Not on such a pretty day," he says comfortingly. "And not to such a nice world."

They run hand in hand into the surf, and the end credits roll.

For a moment—just for a moment—the paradoxical trick has worked. We have taken horror in hand and used it to destroy itself, a trick akin to pulling one's self up by one's own bootstraps. For a little while the deeper fear—the reality of the Russian Sputnik and what it means—has been excised. It will grow back again, but that is for later. For now, the worst has been faced and it wasn't so bad after all. There was that magic moment of reintegration and safety at the end, that same feeling that comes when the roller coaster stops at the end of its run and you get off with your best girl, both of you whole and unhurt.

I believe it's this feeling of reintegration, arising from a field specializing in death, fear, and monstrosity, that makes the danse macabre so rewarding and magical . . . that, and the boundless ability of the human imagination to create endless dreamworlds and then put them to work. It is a world which a fine poet such as Anne Sexton was able to use to "write herself sane." From her poems expressing and delineating her descent into the maelstrom of insanity, her own ability to cope with the world eventually returned, at least for awhile . . . and perhaps others have been able to use her poems in their turn. This is not to suggest that writing must be justified on the basis of its usefulness; to simply delight the reader is enough, isn't it?

This is a world I've lived in of my own choosing since I was a kid, since long before the Stratford Theater and Sputnik I. I am certainly not trying to tell you that the Russians traumatized me into an interest in horror fiction, but am simply pointing out that instant when I began to sense a useful connection between the world of fantasy and that of what *My Weekly Reader* used to call Current Events. This book is only my ramble through that world, through all the worlds of fantasy and horror that have delighted and terrified me. It comes with very little plan or order, and if you are sometimes reminded of a hunting dog with a substandard nose casting back and forth and following any trace of interesting scent it happens to come across, that is fine with me.

But it's not a hunt. It's a dance. And sometimes they turn off the lights in this ballroom.

But we'll dance anyway, you and I. Even in the dark. Especially in the dark.

May I have the pleasure?

CHAPTER II

Tales of the Hook

The dividing line between fantasy and science fiction (for properly speaking, fantasy is what it is; the horror genre is only a subset of the larger genre) is a subject that comes up at some point at almost every fantasy or science fiction convention held (and for those of you unaware of the subculture, there are literally hundreds each year). If I had a nickel for every letter printed on the fantasy/sf dichotomy in the columns of the amateur magazines and the prozines of both fields, I could buy the island of Bermuda.

It's a trap, this matter of definition, and I can't think of a more boring academic subject. Like endless discussions of breath units in modern poetry or the possible intrusiveness of some punctuation in the short story, it is really a discussion of how many angels can dance on the head of a pin, and not really interesting unless those involved in the discussion are drunk or graduate students—two states of roughly similar incompetence. I'll content myself with stating the obvious inarguables: both are works of the imagination, and both try to create worlds which do not exist, cannot exist, or do not exist yet. There is a difference, of course, but you can draw your own borderline, if you want—and if you try, you may find that it's a very squiggly border indeed. *Alien,* for instance, is a horror movie even though it is more firmly grounded in scientific projection than *Star Wars. Star Wars* is a science fiction film, although we must recognize the fact that it's sf of the E. E. "Doc" Smith/Murray Leinster whack-and-slash school: an outer space western just overflowing with PIONEER SPIRIT.

Somewhere in between these two, in a buffer zone that has been little used by the movies, are works that seem to combine science fiction and fantasy in a nonthreatening way—*Close Encounters of the Third Kind*, for instance.

With such a number of divisions (and any dedicated science fiction or fantasy fan could offer a dozen more, ranging from Utopian Fiction, Negative Utopian Fiction, Sword and Sorcery, Heroic Fantasy, Future History, and on into the sunset), you can see why I don't want to open this particular door any wider than I have to.

Let me, instead of defining, offer a couple of examples, and then we'll move along—and what better example than *Donovan's Brain*?

Horror fiction doesn't necessarily have to be nonscientific. Curt Siodmak's novel *Donovan's Brain* moves from a scientific basis to outright horror (as did *Alien)*. It was adapted three times for the screen, and all versions enjoyed fair popular success. Both the novel and the films focus on a scientist who, if not quite mad, is certainly operating at the far borders of rationality. Thus we can place him in a direct line of descent from the original Mad Labs proprietor, Victor Frankenstein.* This scientist has been experimenting with a technique designed to keep the brain alive after the body has died—specifically, in a tank filled with an electrically charged saline solution.

In the course of the novel, the private plane of W. D. Donovan, a rich and domineering millionaire, crashes near the scientist's desert lab. Recognizing the knock of opportunity, the scientist removes the dying millionaire's skull and pops Donovan's brain into his tank.

So far, so good. This story has elements of both horror and science fiction; at this point it could go either way, depending on Siodmak's handling of the subject. One of the earlier versions of the film tips its hand almost at once: the removal operation takes place in a howling thunderstorm and the

---

* And on back to Faust? Daedalus? Prometheus? Pandora? A genealogy leading straight back into the mouth of hell if ever there was one!

scientist's Arizona laboratory looks more like Baskerville Hall. And none of the films is up to the tale of mounting terror Siodmak tells in his careful, rational prose. The operation is a success. The brain is alive and possibly even thinking in its tank of cloudy liquid. The problem now becomes one of communication. The scientist begins trying to contact the brain by means of telepathy . . . and finally succeeds. In a half-trance, he writes the name *W. D. Donovan* three or four times on a scrap of paper, and comparison shows that his signature is interchangeable with that of the millionaire.

In its tank, Donovan's brain begins to change and mutate. It grows stronger, more able to dominate our young hero. He begins to do Donovan's bidding, said bidding all revolving around Donovan's psychopathic determination to make sure the right person inherits his fortune. The scientist begins to experience the frailties of Donovan's physical body (now moldering in an unmarked grave): low back pain, a decided limp. As the story builds to its climax, Donovan tries to use the scientist to run down a little girl who stands in the way of his implacable, monstrous will.

In one of its film incarnations, the Beautiful Young Wife (no comparable creature exists in Siodmak's novel) rigs up lightning rods, which zap the brain in its tank. At the end of the book, the scientist attacks the tank with an ax, resisting the endless undertow of Donovan's will by reciting a simple yet haunting mnemonic phrase—*He thrusts his fists against the posts and still insists he sees the ghosts.* The glass shatters, the saline solution pours out, and the loathsome, pulsing brain is left to die like a slug on the laboratory floor.

Siodmak is a fine thinker and an okay writer. The flow of his speculative ideas in *Donovan's Brain* is as exciting to follow as the flow of ideas in a novel by Isaac Asimov or Arthur C. Clarke or my personal favorite in the field, the late John Wyndham. But none of those esteemed gentlemen has ever written a novel quite like *Donovan's Brain* . . . in fact, no one has.

The final tip-off comes at the very end of the book, when Donovan's nephew (or perhaps it was his bastard son, I'll be damned if I can remember which) is hanged for murder.* Three times the scaffold's trap-door refuses to open when the switch is thrown, and the narrator speculates that Donovan's spirit still remains, indomitable, implacable . . . and hungry.

For all its scientific trappings, *Donovan's Brain* is as much a horror story as M. R. James's "Casting the Runes" or H. P. Lovecraft's nominal science fiction tale, "The Colour Out of Space."

Now let's take another story, this one an oral tale of the sort that never has to be written down. It is simply passed mouth to mouth, usually around Boy Scout or Girl Scout campfires after the sun has gone down and marshmallows have been poked onto green sticks to roast above the coals. You've heard it, I guess, but instead of summarizing it, I'd like to tell it as I originally heard it, gape-mouthed with terror, as the sun went down behind the vacant lot in Stratford where we used to play scratch baseball when there were enough guys around to make up two teams. Here is the most basic horror story I know:

>"This guy and his girl go out on a date, you know? And they go parking up on Lover's Lane. So anyway, while they're driving up there, the radio breaks in with this bulletin. The guy says this dangerous homicidal maniac named The Hook has just escaped from the Sunnydale Asylum for the Criminally Insane. They call him The Hook because that's what he's got instead of a right hand, this razor-sharp hook, and he used to hang around these lover's lanes, you know, and he'd catch these people making out and cut their heads off with the hook. He could do that 'cause it was so sharp, you know, and when they caught him they found like fifteen or twenty heads in his refrigerator. So the news guy says to be on the lookout for any guy with a hook instead of a hand, and to stay away

---

* You can see why Donovan liked the kid enough to want to leave him his money, I think. Just a chip off the old block.

from any dark, lonely spots where people go to, you know, get it on.

"So the girl says, Let's go home, okay? And the guy—he's this real big guy, you know, with muscles on his muscles—he says, I'm not scared of that guy, and he's probably miles from here anyway. So she goes, Come on, Louie, I'm scared, Sunnydale Asylum isn't that far from here. Let's go back to my house. I'll make popcorn and we can watch TV.

"But the guy won't listen to her and pretty soon they're up on The Outlook, parked at the end of the road, makin' out like bandidos. But she keeps sayin' she wants to go home because they're the only car there, you know. That stuff about The Hook scared away everybody else. But he keeps sayin', Come on, don't be such a chicken, there's nothin' to be afraid of, and if there was I'd protectcha, stuff like that.

"So they keep makin' out for awhile and then she hears a noise—like a breakin' branch or something. Like someone is out there in the woods, creepin' up on them. So then she gets real upset, hysterical, crine and everything, like girls do. She's beggin' the guy to take her home. The guy keeps sayin' he doesn't hear anything at all, but she looks up in the rearview mirror and thinks she sees someone all hunkered down at the back of the car, just peekin' in at them, and grinnin'. She says if he doesn't take her home she's never gonna go out parkin' with him again and all that happy crappy. So finally he starts up the car and really peels out cause he's so jacked-off at her. In fact, he just about cracks them up.

"So anyway, they get home, you know, and the guy goes around to open her door for her, and when he gets there he just stands there, turnin' as white as a sheet, and his eyes are gettin' so big you'd think they was gonna fall out on his shoes. She says Louie, what's wrong? And he just faints dead away, right there on the sidewalk.

> "She gets out to see what's wrong, and when she slams
> the car door she hears this funny clinking sound and
> turns around to see what it is. And there, hanging from
> the doorhandle, is this razor-sharp hook."

The story of The Hook is a simple, brutal classic of horror. It offers no characterization, no theme, no particular artifice; it does not aspire to symbolic beauty or try to summarize the times, the mind, or the human spirit. To find these things we must go to "literature"—perhaps to Flannery O'Connor's story "A Good Man Is Hard to Find," which is very much like the story of The Hook in its plot and construction. No, the story of The Hook exists for one reason and one reason alone: to scare the shit out of little kids after the sun goes down.

One could jigger the story of The Hook to make him—it—a creature from outer space, and you could attribute this creature's ability to travel across the parsecs to a photon drive or a warp drive; you could make it a creature from an alternate earth à la Clifford D. Simak. But none of these conventions would turn the story of The Hook into science fiction. It's a flesh-crawler pure and simple, and in its direct point-to-point progress, its brevity, and its use of story only as a means to get to the effect in the last sentence, it is remarkably similar to John Carpenter's *Halloween* ("It *was* the bogey man," Jamie Lee Curtis says at the end of that film. "As a matter of fact," Donald Pleasence agrees softly, "it was.") or *The Fog*. Both of these movies are extremely frightening, but the story of The Hook was there first.

The point seems to be that horror simply *is*, exclusive of definition or rationalization. In a *Newsweek* cover story titled "Hollywood's Scary Summer" (referring to the summer of 1979—the summer of *Phantasm, Prophecy, Dawn of the Dead, Nightwing,* and *Alien)* the writer said that, during *Alien's* big, scary scenes, the audience seemed more apt to moan with revulsion than to scream with terror. The truth of this can't be argued; it's bad enough to see a gelatinous crab-thing spread over some fellow's face, but the infamous "chest-burster" scene which follows is a quantum leap in grue . . . and it happens at the dinner table, yet. It's enough to put you off your popcorn.

The closest I want to come to definition or rationalization is to suggest that the genre exists on three more or less separate levels, each one a little less fine than the one before it. The finest emotion is terror, that emotion which is called up in the tale of The Hook and also in that hoary old classic, "The Monkey's Paw." We actually *see* nothing outright nasty in either story; in one we have the hook and in the other there is the paw, which, dried and mummified, can surely be no worse than those plastic dogturds on sale at any novelty shop. It's what the mind sees that makes these stories quintessential tales of terror. It is the unpleasant speculation called to mind when the knocking on the door begins in the latter story and the grief-stricken old woman rushes to answer it. Nothing is there but the wind when she finally throws the door open . . . but what, the mind wonders, *might* have been there if her husband had been a little slower on the draw with that third wish?

As a kid, I cut my teeth on William M. Gaines's horror comics—*The Haunt of Fear, Tales from the Crypt, The Vault of Horror*—plus all the Gaines imitators (but like a good Elvis record, the Gaines magazines were often imitated, never duplicated). Those horror comics of the fifties still sum up for me the epitome of horror, that emotion of fear that underlies terror, an emotion which is slightly less fine, because it is not entirely of the mind. Horror also invites a physical reaction by showing us something which is physically wrong.

One typical E.C. screamer goes like this: The hero's wife and her boyfriend determine to do away with the hero so they can run away together and get married. In almost all the weird comics of the '50s, the women are seen as slightly overripe, enticingly fleshy and sexual, but ultimately evil: castrating, murdering bitches who, like the trapdoor spider, feel an almost instinctual need to follow intercourse with cannibalism. These two heels, who might have stepped whole and breathing from a James M. Cain novel, take the poor slob of a husband for a ride and the boyfriend puts a bullet between his eyes. They wire a cement block to the corpse's leg and toss him over a bridge into the river.

Two or three weeks later, our hero, a living corpse, emerges from the river, rotted and eaten by the fish. He shambles after wifey and her friend . . . and not to invite them back to his place for a few drinks, either, one feels. One piece of dialogue from this story which I've never forgotten is, "I am coming, Marie, but I have to come slowly . . . because little pieces of me keep falling off . . ."

In "The Monkey's Paw," the imagination alone is stimulated. The reader does the job on himself. In the horror comics (as well as the horror pulps of the years 1930–1955), the viscera are also engaged. As we have already pointed out, the old man in "The Monkey's Paw" is able to wish the dreadful apparition away before his frenzied wife can get the door open. In *Tales from the Crypt*, the Thing from Beyond the Grave is still there when the door is thrown wide, big as life and twice as ugly.

Terror is the sound of the old man's continuing pulsebeat in "The Tell-Tale Heart"—a quick sound, "like a watch wrapped in cotton." Horror is the amorphous but very physical "thing" in Joseph Payne Brennan's wonderful novella "Slime" as it enfolds itself over the body of a screaming dog.*

But there is a third level—that of revulsion. This seems to be where the "chest-burster" from *Alien* fits. Better, let's take another example from the E.C. file as an example of the Revolting Story—Jack Davis's "Foul Play" from "The Crypt of Terror" will serve nicely, I think. And if you're sitting in your living room right now, putting away some chips and dip or maybe some sliced pepperoni on crackers as you read this,

---

* No less a writer than Kate Wilhelm, the acclaimed mainstream and science fiction novelist (author of *Where Late the Sweet Birds Sang* and *The Clewiston Test*, among others), began her career with a short but gruesomely effective horror novel—a paperback original called *The Clone*, written in collaboration with Ted Thomas. In this story, an amorphous creature made of almost pure protein (more blob than clone, *The Science Fiction Encyclopedia* rightly points out) forms in the sewer system of a major city . . . around a nucleus of half-rotted hamburger, yet. It begins to grow, swallowing hundreds of people into its noxious self as it does. In one memorable scene, a little kid is yanked arm-first into the drain of the kitchen sink.

maybe you'd just better put the munchies away for awhile, because this one makes the chest-burster from *Alien* look like a scene from *The Sound of Music*. You'll note that the story lacks any real logic, motivation, or character development, but, as in the tale of The Hook, the story itself is little more than the means to an end, a way of getting to those last three panels.

"Foul Play" is the story of Herbie Satten, pitcher for Bayville's minor league baseball team. Herbie is the apotheosis of the E.C. villain. He's a totally black character, with absolutely no redeeming qualities, the Compleat Monster. He's murderous, conceited, egocentric, willing to go to any lengths to win. He brings out the Mob Man or Mob Woman in each of us; we would gladly see Herbie lynched from the nearest apple tree, and never mind the Civil Liberties Union.

With his team leading by a single run in the top of the ninth, Herbie gets first base by deliberately allowing himself to be hit by an inside pitch. Although he is big and lumbering, he takes off for second on the very next pitch. Covering second is Central City's saintly slugger, Jerry Deegan. Deegan, we are told, is "sure to win the game for the home team in the bottom of the ninth." The evil Herbie Satten slides into second with his spikes up, but saintly Jerry hangs in there and tags Satten out.

Jerry is spiked, but his wounds are minor . . . or so they appear. In fact, Herbie has painted his spikes with a deadly, fast-acting poison. In Central City's half of the ninth, Jerry comes to the plate with two out and a man in scoring position. It looks pretty good for the home team guys; unfortunately, Jerry drops dead at home plate even as the umpire calls strike three. Exit the malefic Herbie Satten, smirking.

The Central City team doctor discovers that Jerry has been poisoned. One of the Central City players says grimly: "This is a job for the police!" Another responds ominously, "No! Wait! Let's take care of him ourselves . . . our way."

The team sends Herbie a letter, inviting him to the ballpark one night to be presented with a plaque honoring his achievements in baseball. Herbie, apparently as stupid as he is evil, falls for it, and in the next scene we see the Central City nine on the field. The team doctor is tricked out in umpire's regalia. He is whisking off home plate . . . which happens to be a human heart. The base paths are intestines. The bases are chunks of the unfortunate Herbie Satten's body. In the penultimate panel we see that the batter is standing in the box and that instead of a Louisville Slugger he is swinging one of Herbie's severed legs. The pitcher is holding a grotesquely mangled human head and preparing to throw it. The head, from which one eyeball dangles on its stalk, looks as though it's already been hit over the fence for a couple of home runs, although as Davis has drawn it ("Jolly Jack Davis," as the fans of the day called him; he now sometimes does covers for *TV Guide*), one would not expect it to carry so far. It is, in the parlance of baseball players, "a dead ball."

The Crypt Keeper followed this helping of mayhem with his own conclusions, beginning with the immortal E. C. Chuckle: "Heh, heh! So that's my yelp-yarn for this issue, kiddies. Herbie, the pitcher, went to pieces that night and was taken out . . . of existence, that is . . ."

As you can see, both "The Monkey's Paw" and "Foul Play" are horror stories, but their mode of attack and their ultimate effect are light-years apart. You may also have an idea of why the comic publishers of America cleaned their own house in the early fifties . . . before the U.S. Senate decided to do it for them.

So: terror on top, horror below it, and lowest of all, the gag reflex of revulsion. My own philosophy as a sometime writer of horror fiction is to recognize these distinctions because they are sometimes useful, but to avoid any preference for one over the other on the grounds that one effect is somehow better than another. The problem with definitions is that they have a way of turning into critical tools—and this sort of criticism, which I would call criticism-by-rote, seems to me needlessly restricting and even dangerous. I recognize terror as the finest emotion (used to almost quintessential effect in Robert Wise's film *The Haunting*, where, as in "The Monkey's Paw," we are never allowed to see what is behind the door), and so I will try to terrorize the reader. But if I find I cannot terrify him/her, I will try to horrify; and if I find I cannot horrify, I'll go for the gross-out. I'm not proud.

When I conceived of the vampire novel which became *'Salem's Lot,* I decided I wanted to try to use the book partially as a form of literary homage (as Peter Straub has done in *Ghost Story,* working in the tradition of such "classical" ghost story writers as Henry James, M. R. James, and Nathaniel Hawthorne). So my novel bears an intentional similarity to Bram Stoker's *Dracula,* and after awhile it began to seem to me what I was doing was playing an interesting—to me, at least—game of literary racquet-ball: *'Salem's Lot* itself was the ball and *Dracula* was the wall I kept hitting it against, watching to see how and where it would bounce, so I could hit it again. As a matter of fact, it took some pretty interesting bounces, and I ascribe this mostly to the fact that, while my ball existed in the twentieth century, my wall was very much a product of the nineteenth. At the same time, because the vampire story was so much a staple of the E.C. comics I grew up with, I decided that I would also try to bring in that aspect of the horror story.*

Some of the scenes from *'Salem's Lot* which run parallel to scenes from *Dracula* are the staking of Susan Norton (corresponding to the staking of Lucy Westenra in Stoker's book), the drinking of the vampire's blood by the priest, Father Callahan (in *Dracula* it is Mina Murray Harker who is forced to take the Count's perverse communion as he croons those memorable, chilling lines, "My bountiful wine-press for a little while . . ."), the burning of Callahan's hand as he tries to enter his church to receive absolution (when, in *Dracula,* Van Helsing touches Mina's forehead with a piece of the Host to cleanse her of the Count's unclean touch, it flashes into fire, leaving

---

* The scene in *'Salem's Lot* which works best in the E.C. tradition—at least, as far as I'm concerned—is when the bus driver, Charlie Rhodes (who is a typical E.C.-type rotter in the best Herbie Satten tradition), awakes at midnight and hears someone blowing the horn of his bus. He discovers, after the bus doors have swung shut forever behind him, that his bus is loaded with children, as if for a school run . . . but they're all vampires. Charlie begins to scream, and perhaps the reader wonders why; after all, they only stopped by for a drink.

    Heh, heh.

a terrible scar), and, of course, the band of Fearless Vampire Hunters which forms in each book.

The scenes from *Dracula* which I chose to retool for my own book were the ones which impressed me the most deeply, the ones Stoker seemed to have written at fever pitch. There are others, but the one "bounce" that never made it into the finished book was a play on Stoker's use of rats in *Dracula*. In Stoker's novel, the Fearless Vampire Hunters—Van Helsing, Jonathan Harker, Dr. Seward, Lord Godalming, and Quincey Morris—enter the basement of Carfax, the Count's English house. The Count himself has long since split the scene, but he has left some of his traveling coffins (boxes full of his native earth), and another nasty surprise. Very shortly after the F.V.H.s enter, the basement is crawling with rats. According to the lore (and in his long novel, Stoker marshals a formidable amount of vampire lore), a vampire has the ability to command the lesser animals—cats, rats, weasels (and possibly Republicans, ha-ha). It is Dracula who has sent these rats to give our heroes a hard time.

Lord Godalming is ready for this, however. He lets a couple of terriers out of a bag, and they make short work of the Count's rats. I decided I would let Barlow—my version of Count Dracula—also use the rats, and to that end I gave the town of Jerusalem's Lot an open dump, where there are lots of rats. I played on the presence of the rats there several times in the first couple of hundred pages of the novel, and to this day I sometimes get letters asking if I just forgot about the rats, or tried to use them to create atmosphere, or what.

Actually, I used them to create a scene so revolting that my editor at Doubleday (the same Bill Thompson mentioned in the forenote to this volume) suggested strongly that I remove it and substitute something else. After some grousing, I complied with his wishes. In the Doubleday/New American Library editions of *'Salem's Lot*, Jimmy Cody, a local doctor, and Mark Petrie, the boy accompanying him, discover that the king vampire—to use Van Helsing's pungent term—is almost certainly denning in the basement of a local boarding house.

Jimmy begins to go downstairs, but the stairs have been cut away and the floor beneath littered with knives pounded through boards. Jimmy Cody dies impaled upon these knives in a scene of what I would call "horror"—as opposed to "terror" or "revulsion," the scene is a middle-of-the-roader.

In the first draft manuscript, however, I had Jimmy go down the stairs and discover—too late—that Barlow had called all the rats from the dump to the cellar of Eva Miller's boarding house. There was a regular HoJo for rats down there, and Jimmy Cody became the main course. They attack Jimmy in their hundreds, and we are treated (if that is the word) to a picture of the good doctor struggling back up the stairs, covered with rats. They are down his shirt, crawling in his hair, biting his neck and arms. When he opens his mouth to yell Mark a warning, one of them runs into his mouth and lodges there, squirming.

I was delighted with the scene as written because it gave me a chance to combine *Dracula*-lore and E.C.-lore into one. My editor felt that it was, to put it frankly, out to lunch, and I was eventually persuaded to see it his way. Perhaps he was even right.*

I've tried here to delineate some of the differences between science fiction and horror, science fiction and fantasy, terror and horror, horror and revulsion, more by example than by definition. All of which is very well, but perhaps we ought to examine the emotion of horror a little more closely—not in terms of definition but in terms of effect. What does horror do? Why do people want to be horrified . . . why do they *pay* to be horrified? Why an *Exorcist*? A *Jaws*? An *Alien*?

---

* Rats are nasty little buggers, aren't they? I wrote and published a rat story called "Graveyard Shift" in *Cavalier* magazine four years prior to *'Salem's Lot*—it was, in fact, the third short story I ever published—and I was uneasy about the similarity between the rats under the old mill in "Graveyard Shift" and those in the basement of the boarding house in *'Salem's Lot*. As writers near the end of a book, I suspect that they cope with weariness in all sorts of ways— and my response as I neared the end of *'Salem's Lot* was to indulge in this bit of self-plagiarism. And so, even though I suspect there's a disappointed rat-fan or two out there, I've got to say I believe Bill Thompson's judgment that the rats in *'Salem's Lot* should simply fade from the scene was the right one.

But before we talk about why people crave the effect, maybe we ought to spend a little time thinking about components—and if we do not choose to define horror itself, we can at least examine the elements and perhaps draw some conclusions from them.

2

Horror movies and horror novels have always been popular, but every ten or twenty years they seem to enjoy a cycle of increased popularity and visibility. These periods almost always seem to coincide with periods of fairly serious economic and/or political strain, and the books and films seem to reflect those free-floating anxieties (for want of a better term) which accompany such serious but not mortal dislocations. They have done less well in periods when the American people have been faced with outright examples of horror in their own lives.

Horror went through a boom period in the 1930s. When people hard-pressed by the Depression weren't ponying up at the box office to see a hundred Busby Berkeley girls dancing to the tune of "We're in the Money," they were perhaps releasing their anxieties in another way—by watching Boris Karloff shamble across the moors in *Frankenstein* or Bela Lugosi creep through the dark with his cape up over his mouth in *Dracula*. The '30s also marked the rise of the so-called "Shudder Pulps," which encompassed everything from *Weird Tales* to *Black Mask*.

We find few horror movies or novels of note in the 1940s, and the one great magazine of fantasy which debuted in that decade, *Unknown*, did not survive for long. The great Universal Studios monsters of the Depression days—Frankenstein's monster, the Wolf Man, the Mummy, and the Count—were dying in that particularly messy and embarrassing way that the movies seem to reserve for the terminally ill; instead of being retired with honors and decently interred in the moldy soil of their European churchyards, Hollywood decided to play them for laughs, squeezing every last quarter and dime admission possible out of the poor old things before letting them go. Hence, Abbott & Costello met the monsters, as did the Bowery Boys, not to mention those lovable eye-boinkers and head-knockers, the Three Stooges. In the '40s, the monsters themselves became stooges. Years later, in another post-war period, Mel Brooks would give us his version of *Abbott and Costello Meet Frankenstein, Young Frankenstein*—starring Gene Wilder and Marty Feldman instead of Bud Abbott and Lou Costello.

The eclipse of horror in fiction that began in 1939 lasted for twenty-five years. Oh, an occasional novel such as Richard Matheson's *Shrinking Man* or William Sloane's *Edge of Running Water* would pop up, reminding us that the genre was still there (although even Matheson's grim man-against-giant-spider tale, a horror story if there ever was one, was touted as science fiction), but the idea of a best-selling horror novel would have been laughed out of court along Publisher's Row.

As with the movies, the golden age of weird fiction had passed in the '30s, when *Weird Tales* was at the peak of its influence and quality (not to mention its circulation), publishing the fiction of Clark Ashton Smith, the young Robert Bloch, Dr. David H. Keller, and, of course, the twentieth-century horror story's dark and baroque prince, H. P. Lovecraft. I will not offend those who have followed weird fiction over a span of fifty years by suggesting that horror disappeared in the 1940s; indeed it did not. Arkham House had then been founded by the late August Derleth, and Arkham published what I regard as its most important works in the period 1939–1960—works including Lovecraft's *The Outsider* and *Beyond the Wall of Sleep*, Henry S. Whitehead's *Jumbee, The Opener of the Way* and *Pleasant Dreams*, by Robert Bloch . . . and Ray Bradbury's *Dark Carnival*, a marvelous and terrifying collection of a darker world just beyond the threshold of this one.

But Lovecraft was dead before Pearl Harbor; Bradbury would turn his hand more and more often to his own lyric blend of science fiction and fantasy (and it was only after he did so that his work began to be accepted by such mainstream magazines as *Collier's* and the *Saturday Evening Post);* Robert Bloch had begun to write his suspense stories, using what he had learned in his first two decades as a writer to create a powerful series of offbeat novels, which are only surpassed by the novels of Cornell Woolrich.

During and after the war years, horror fiction was in decline. The age did not like it. It was a period of rapid scientific development and rationalism—they grow very well in a war atmosphere, thanks—and it became a period which is now thought of by fans and writers alike as "the golden age of science fiction." While *Weird Tales* plugged grimly along, holding its own but hardly reaping millions (it would fold in the midfifties after a downsizing from its original gaudy pulp size to a digest form failed to effect a cure for its ailing circulation), the sf market boomed, spawning a dozen well-remembered pulps and making names such as Heinlein, Asimov, Campbell, and Del Rey, if not household words, at least familiar and exciting to an ever-growing community of fans dedicated to the proposition of the rocket ship, the space station, and the ever-popular death ray.

So horror languished in the dungeon until 1955 or so, rattling its chains once in a while but causing no great stir. It was around that time that two men named Samuel Z. Arkoff and James H. Nicholson stumbled downstairs and discovered a money machine rusting away unnoticed in that particular dungeon. Originally film distributors, Arkoff and Nicholson decided that, since there was an acute shortage of B-pictures in the early fifties, they would make their own.

Insiders predicted speedy economic ruin for the entrepreneurs. They were told they were setting to sea in a lead sailboat; this was the age of TV. The insiders had seen the future and it belonged to Dagmar and Richard Diamond, Private Detective. The consensus among those who cared at all (and there weren't many) was that Arkoff and Nicholson would lose their shirts very quickly.

But during the twenty-five years that the company they formed, American-International Pictures, has been around (it's now Arkoff alone; James Nicholson died several years ago), it has been the only major American film company to show a consistent profit, year in and year out. AIP has made a great variety of films, but all of them have taken dead aim on the youth market; the company's pictures include such dubious classics as *Boxcar Bertha, Bloody Mama, Dragstrip Girl, The Trip, Dillinger,* and the immortal *Beach Blanket Bingo.* But their greatest success was with horror films.

What elements made these AIP films shlock classics? They were simple, shot in a hurry, and so amateurish that one can sometimes see the shadow of a boom mike in the shot or catch the gleam of an air tank inside the monster suit of an underwater creature (as in *The Attack of the Giant Leeches*). Arkoff himself recalls that they rarely began with a completed script or even a coherent screen treatment; often money was committed to projects on the basis of a title that sounded commercial, such as *Terror from the Year 5000* or *The Brain Eaters,* something that would make an eye-catching poster.

Whatever the elements were, they worked.

3

Well, let all that go for the moment. Let's talk monsters.

Exactly what is a monster?

Begin by assuming that the tale of horror, no matter how primitive, is allegorical by its very nature; that it is symbolic. Assume that it is talking to us, like a patient on a psychoanalyst's couch, about one thing while it means another. I am not saying that horror is *consciously* allegorical or symbolic; that is to suggest an artfulness that few writers of horror fiction or directors of horror films aspire to. There has recently been a retrospective of AIP movies in New York (1979), and the idea of a retrospective suggests art, but at most they are trash art. The pictures have great nostalgia value, but those searching for culture may look elsewhere. To suggest that Roger Corman was unconsciously creating art while on a four-day shooting schedule and a budget of $10,000 is to suggest the absurd.

The element of allegory is there only because it is built-in, a given, impossible to escape. Horror appeals to us because it says, in a symbolic way, things we would be afraid to say right out straight, with the bark still on; it offers us a chance to exercise (that's right; not *exorcise* but *exercise*) emotions which society demands we keep closely in hand. The horror film is an invitation to indulge in deviant, antisocial behavior by proxy—to commit gratuitous acts of violence, indulge our puerile dreams of power, to give in to our most craven fears. Perhaps more than anything else, the horror story or horror movie says it's okay to join the mob, to become the total tribal being, to destroy the outsider. It has never been done better or more literally than in Shirley Jackson's short story "The Lottery," where the entire concept of the outsider is symbolic, created by nothing more than a black circle colored on a slip of paper. But there is no symbolism in the rain of stones which ends the story; the victim's own child pitches in as the mother dies, screaming "It's not fair! It's not fair!"

Nor is it an accident that the horror story ends so often with an O. Henry twist that leads straight down a mine shaft. When we turn to the creepy movie or the crawly book, we are not wearing our "Everything works out for the best" hats. We're waiting to be told what we so often suspect—that everything is turning to shit. In most cases the horror story provides ample proof that such is indeed the case, and I don't believe, when Katharine Ross falls prey to the Stepford Men's Association at the conclusion of *The Stepford Wives* or when the heroic black man is shot dead by the numbnuts sheriff's posse at the end of *Night of the Living Dead*, that anyone is really surprised. It is, as they say, a part of the game.

And monstrosity? What about that part of the game? What sort of handle can we get on that? If we don't define, can we at least exemplify? Here is a fairly explosive package, my friends.

What about the freaks in the circus? The carny aberrations observed by the light of naked hundred-watt bulbs? What about Cheng and Eng, the famous Siamese twins? A majority of people considered them monstrous in their day, and an even greater number no doubt considered the fact that each had his own married life even more monstrous. America's most mordant—and sometimes funniest—cartoonist, a fellow named Rodrigues, has rung the changes on the Siamese-twin theme in his Aesop Brothers strip in the *National Lampoon,* where we have our noses rubbed in almost every possible bizarre exingency of life among the mortally attached: the sex lives of, the bathroom functions of, the love lives, the sicknesses. Rodrigues provides everything you ever wondered about in regard to Siamese twins . . . and fulfills your darkest surmises. To say that all of this is in poor taste may be true, but it's still a futile and impotent criticism—the old *National Enquirer* used to run pictures of car-wreck victims in pieces and dogs munching happily away at severed human heads, but it did a land-office business in grue before lapsing back into a quieter current of the American mainstream.*

What about the other carny freaks? Are they classifiable as monstrosities? Dwarfs? Midgets? The bearded lady? The fat lady? The human skeleton? At one time or another most of us have been there, standing on the beaten, sawdust-strewn dirt with a chili dog or a paper of sweet cotton candy in one hand while the barker hucksters us, usually with one sample of these human offshoots standing nearby as a specimen—the fat lady in her pink little girl's tutu, the tattooed man with the tail of a dragon curled around his burly neck like a fabulous hangman's noose, or the man who eats nails and scrap metal and light bulbs. Perhaps not so many of us have surrendered to the urge to cough up the two bits or four bits or six bits to go inside and see them, plus such all-time favorites as The Two-Headed Cow or The Baby in a Bottle (I have been writing horror stories since I was eight, but have never yet attended a freak show), but most of us have surely felt the impulse. And at some carnivals, the

---

* And there is life in the old *Enquirer* yet. I buy it if there's a juicy UFO story or something about Bigfoot, but mostly I only scan it rapidly while in a slow supermarket checkout lane, looking for such endearing lapses of taste as the notorious autopsy photo of Lee Harvey Oswald or their photo of Elvis Presley in his coffin. Still, it is a far cry from the old MOM COOKS PET DOG AND FEEDS IT TO THE KIDS days.

most terrible freak of all is kept out back, kept in darkness like some damned thing from Dante's Ninth Circle of Hell, kept there because his performance was forbidden by law as long ago as 1910, kept in a pit and dressed in a rag. This is the geek, and for an extra buck or two you could stand at the edge of his pit and watch him bite off the head of a live chicken and then swallow it even as the decapitated bird fluttered in his hands.

There is something so attractive about freaks, yet something so forbidden and appalling, that the one serious effort to use them as the mainspring of a horror picture resulted in the film's quick shelving. The picture was *Freaks*, a Tod Browning film made in 1932 for MGM.

Freaks is the story of Cleopatra, the beautiful acrobat who marries a midget. In the best E.C. tradition (an E.C. that was almost twenty years unborn in 1932), she has a heart as black as midnight in a coal mine. It's not the midget she's interested in, it's his money. Like the mate-eating human trapdoor spiders of those comic-book stories yet to come, Cleo soon takes up with another man; in this case it's Hercules, the show's strongman. Like Cleopatra herself, Hercules is at least nominally okay, although it is with the freaks that our sympathies lie. These two heels begin a systematic poisoning program on Cleo's tiny husband. The other freaks discover what is going on and take an almost unspeakable revenge on the pair. Hercules is killed (there is a rumor that, as Browning originally conceived the film, the strongman was to be castrated) and the beautiful Cleopatra is turned into a bird-woman, feathered and legless.

Browning made the mistake of using real freaks in his film. We may only feel really comfortable with horror as long as we can see the zipper running up the monster's back, when we understand that we are not playing for keepsies. The climax of *Freaks*, as the Living Torso and the Armless Wonder and the Hilton Sisters—Siamese twins—among others, slither and flop through the mud after the screaming Cleopatra, was simply too much. Even some of MGM's tame exhibitors flatly refused to show it, and Carlos Clarens reports in his *Illustrated History of the Horror Film* (Capricorn Books: 1968) that at its one preview in San Diego "a woman ran screaming up the aisle." The film was exhibited—after a fashion—in a version so radically cut that one film critic complained that he had no idea what he was watching. Clarens further reports that the film was banned for thirty years in the U.K., the country that has brought us, among other things, Johnny Rotten, Sid Vicious, the Snivelling Shits, and the charming custom of "Paki-bashing."

Freaks is now sometimes exhibited on PTV stations and may at this writing have finally become available on videocassettes. But to this day it remains a source of heated discussion, comment, and conjecture among horror fans—and although many have heard of it, surprisingly few have actually seen it.

<u>4</u>

Leaving freaks entirely out of it for the moment, what else do we consider horrible enough to label with what surely must be the world's oldest perjorative? Well, there were all those bizarre Dick Tracy villains, perhaps best epitomized by Fly-face, and there was the archenemy of Don Winslow, The Scorpion, whose face was so horrible that he had to keep it constantly covered (although he would sometimes unveil it to minions who had failed him in some way—said minions would immediately drop dead of heart attacks, literally scared to death). So far as I know, the horrible secret of The Scorpion's physiognomy was never uncovered (pardon the pun, heh-heh), but the intrepid Commander Winslow did once succeed in unmasking The Scorpion's daughter, who had the slack, dead face of a corpse. This information was delivered to the breathless reader in italics—*the slack, dead face of a corpse!*—for added emphasis.

Perhaps the "new generation" of comic monsters is best epitomized by those created by Stan Lee's Marvel Comics, where for every superhero such as Spider-Man or Captain America, there seem to be a dozen freakish aberrations: Dr. Octopus (known to children all over the comic-reading world as Doc

Ock), whose arms have been augmented by what appear to be a waving forest of homicidal vacuum-cleaner attachments; The Sandman, who is a sort of walking sand dune; The Vulture; Stegron; The Lizard; and most ominous of all, Dr. Doom, whose appearance has been so badly maimed in his Twisted Pursuit of Forbidden Science that he now resembles a great, clanking cyborg who wears a green cape, peers through eye-holes like the archers' slits in a medieval castle, and who appears to be literally sweating rivets. Superheroes with elements of monstrosity in their makeup seem less enduring. My own favorite, Plastic Man (always accompanied by his wonderfully screwball sidekick, Woozy Winks), just never made it. Reed Richards of the Fantastic Four is a Plastic Man lookalike, and his cohort Ben Grimm (aka The Thing) looks like a hardened lava flow, but they are among the few exceptions to the rule.

So far, we've talked about carny freaks and the caricatures we sometimes find in the funnies, but let's come a trifle closer to home. You might ask yourself what you consider monstrous or horrible in daily life—you're exempted from this if you're a doctor or a nurse; these people see all the aberrations they can handle, and much the same can be said for policemen and bartenders.

But as for the rest of us?

Take fat. How fat does a person have to be before he or she passes over the line and into a perversion of the human form severe enough to be called monstrosity? Surely it is not the woman who shops Lane Bryant or the fellow who buys his suits in that section of the menswear store reserved for the "husky build"—or is it? Has the obese person reached the point of monstrosity when he or she can no longer go to the movies or to a concert because his/her buttocks will no longer fit between the fixed armrests of a single seat?

You will understand that I am not talking about how fat is too fat here, either in the medical or aesthetic sense, nor anyone's "right to be fat"; I am not talking about the lady you glimpsed crossing a country road to get her mail on a summer day, her gigantic butt encased in black slacks, cheeks whacking and wobbling together, belly hanging out of an untucked white blouse like slack dough; I am talking of a point where simple overweight has passed through the outermost checkpoints of normality and has become something that, regardless of morality or immorality, attracts the helpless eye and overwhelms it. I am speculating on your reaction—and my own—to those human beings so enormous that we wonder about how they may perform acts that we mostly take for granted: going through a door, sitting down in a car, calling home from a telephone booth, bending over to tie our shoes, taking a shower.

You may say to me, Steve, you're just talking carny again—the fat lady in her pink little girl's tutu; those humongous twins who have been immortalized in the Guinness Book of World Records riding away from the camera that clicked the picture on identical tiny motor scooters, their buttocks sticking out to either side like a dream of gravity in suspension. But in point of fact, I am not talking about such people, who, after all, exist in their own world where a different scale is applied to questions of normality; how freakish can you feel, even at five hundred pounds, in the company of dwarfs, Living Torsos, and Siamese twins? Normality is a sociological concept. There's an old joke about two African leaders getting together with JFK for a state meeting and then going home on a plane together. One of them marvels, "Kennedy! What a funny name!" In the same vein, there is the *Twilight Zone* episode, "Eye of the Beholder," about the horribly ugly woman whose plastic surgery has failed for the umpteenth time . . . and we only find out at the end of the program that she exists in a future where most people look like grotesquely humanoid pigs. The "ugly" woman is, by our standards, at least, extraordinarily beautiful.

I am talking about the fat man or woman in our society—the four-hundred-pound businessman, for example—who routinely buys two seats in tourist when he flies and kicks up the armrest between them. I am talking about the woman who cooks herself four hamburgers for lunch, eats them between eight slices of bread, has a quart of potato salad on the side topped with sour cream, and follows this repast with half a gallon of Breyer's ice cream spread over the top of a Table Talk pie like frosting.

On a business trip to New York in 1976, I observed a very fat man who had become trapped in a revolving door at the Doubleday Book Shop on Fifth Avenue. Gigantic and sweating in a blue pinstriped suit, he seemed to have been poured into his wedge of the door. The bookshop's security guard was joined by a city policeman, and the two of them pushed and grunted until the door began to move again, jerk by jerk. At last it moved enough to let the gentleman out. I wondered then and wonder now if the crowd that gathered to watch this salvage operation was much different from those crowds that form when the carny barker begins his spiel . . . or when, in the original Universal film, Frankenstein's monster arose from its laboratory slab and walked.

Are fat people monstrous? How about somebody with a harelip or a large facial birthmark? You couldn't get into any self-respecting carny in the country with one of those two— too common, so sorry. What about somebody with six fingers on one or both hands, or a total of six toes on both feet? There are a lot of those guys around, too. Or, getting down even further toward Your Block, U.S.A., what about someone with a really bad case of acne?

Of course ordinary pimples are no big deal; even the prettiest cheerleader on the squad is apt to get one on her forehead or near one corner of her kissable mouth once in a while, but ordinary fat is no big deal, either—I'm talking about the case of acne that has run absolutely apeshit, spreading like something out of a Japanese horror movie, pimple on pimples, and most of them red and suppurating.

Like the chest-burster in *Alien*, it's enough to put you off your popcorn . . . except this is *real*.

Perhaps I've not touched your idea of monstrosity in real life even yet, and perhaps I won't, but for just a moment consider such an ordinary thing as left-handedness. Of course, the discrimination against left-handed people is obvious from the start. If you've attended a college or high school with the more modern desks, you know that most of them are built for inhabitants of an exclusively right-handed world. More educational facilities will order a few left-handed desks as a token gesture, but that's all. And during testing or composition situations, lefties are usually segregated on one side of the lecture hall so they will not jog the elbows of their more normal counterparts.

But it goes deeper than discrimination. The roots of discrimination spread wide, but the roots of monstrosity spread both wide and deep. Left-handed baseball players are all considered screwballs, whether they are or not.* The French for left, bastardized from the Latin, is *la sinistre,* from which comes our word *sinister.* According to the old superstition, your right side belongs to God, your left side to that other fellow. Southpaws have always been suspect. My mother was a leftie, and as a schoolgirl, so she told my brother and me, the teacher would rap her left hand smartly with a ruler to make her change her pen to her right hand. When the teacher left she would switch the pen back again, of course, because with her right hand she could make only large, childish scrawls—the fate of most of us when we try to write with what New Englanders call "the dumb hand." A few of us, such as Branwell Brontë (the gifted brother of Charlotte and Emily), can write clearly and well with either hand. Branwell Brontë was in fact so ambidextrous that he could write two different letters to two different people *at the same time.* We might reasonably wonder if such an ability qualifies as monstrosity . . . or genius.

In fact, almost every physical and mental human aberration has been at some point in history, or is now, considered monstrous—a complete list would include widows' peaks (once considered a reliable sign that a man was a sorcerer), moles on the female body (supposed to be witches' teats), and extreme

---

* Take for instance Bill Lee, late of the Montreal Expos and the Boston Red Sox. Lee was dubbed "The Spaceman" by his colleagues and is remembered fondly by Boston fans for exhorting those who attended a rally following the Sox's pennant win in 1975 to pick up their trash when they left. Perhaps the strongest proof of his "leftiness" came when he referred to Red Sox manager Don Zimmer as "the designated gerbil." Lee moved to Montreal soon after.

schizophrenia, which on occasion has caused the afflicted to be canonized by one church or another.

Monstrosity fascinates us because it appeals to the conservative Republican in a three-piece suit who resides within all of us. We love and need the concept of monstrosity because it is a reaffirmation of the order we all crave as human beings . . . and let me further suggest that it is not the physical or mental aberration in itself which horrifies us, but rather the lack of order which these aberrations seem to imply.

The late John Wyndham, perhaps the best writer of science fiction that England has ever produced, summarized the idea in his novel *The Chrysalids* (published as *Rebirth* in America). It is a story that considers the ideas of mutation and deviation more brilliantly than any other novel written in English since World War II, I think. A series of plaques in the home of the novel's young protagonist offer stern counsel: ONLY THE IMAGE OF GOD IS MAN; KEEP PURE THE STOCK OF THE LORD; IN PURITY OUR SALVATION; BLESSED IS THE NORM; and most telling of all: WATCH THOU FOR THE MUTANT! After all, when we discuss monstrosity, we are expressing our faith and belief in the norm and watching for the mutant. The writer of horror fiction is neither more nor less than an agent of the status quo.

5

Having said all that, let's now return to the American-International pictures of the 1950s. In a little while we'll talk about the allegorical qualities of these films (you there in the back row, stop laughing or leave the room), but for now let's stick to the idea of monstrosity . . . and if we touch allegory at all, we'll touch it only lightly, by suggesting some of the things films were not.

Although they came along at the same time rock and roll broke the race barrier, and although they appealed to the same fledgling boppers, it's interesting to notice the sort of things that are altogether absent . . . at least in terms of "real" monstrosity.

We've noted already that the AIP pictures, and those of the other independent film companies that began to imitate AIP, gave the movie industry a much-needed shot in the arm during the ho-hum fifties. They gave millions of young viewers something they couldn't get at home on TV, and it gave them a place where they could go and make out in relative comfort. And it was the "indies," as *Variety* calls them, that gave a whole generation of war babies an insatiable jones for the movies, and perhaps prepared the way for the success of such disparate movies as *Easy Rider, Jaws, Rocky, The Godfather*, and *The Exorcist*.

But where are the monsters?

Oh, we've got fake ones by the score: saucer-men, giant leeches, werewolves, mole people (in a Universal picture), and dozens more. But what AIP didn't show as they tested these interesting new waters was anything that smacked of *real* horror . . . *at least as those war babies understood the term emotionally*. That is an important qualification, and I hope you'll come to agree with me that it warrants its italics.

These were—we were—children who knew about the psychic distress that came with The Bomb, but who had never known any real physical want or deprivation. None of the kids who went to these movies were starving or dying of internal parasites. A few had lost fathers or uncles in the war. Not many.

And in the movies themselves, there were no fat kids; no kids with warts or tics; no kids with pimples; no kids picking their noses and then wiping it on the sun visors of their hot rods; no kids with sexual problems; no kids with any visible physical deformity (not even such a minor one as vision that had been corrected by glasses—all the kids in the AIP horror and beach pictures had 20/20 vision). There might be an endearingly wacky teenager on view—of the sort often played by Nick Adams—a kid who was a bit shorter or did daring, kooky things such as wearing his hat backwards like a baseball catcher (and who had a name like Weirdo or Scooter or Crazy), but that was as far as it ever went.

The setting for most of these films was small-town America,

the scene the audience could best identify with . . . but all of these Our Towns looked eerily as if a eugenics squad had gone by the day before production actually began, removing everyone with a lisp, birthmark, limp, or potbelly—everyone, in short, who did not look like Frankie Avalon, Annette Funicello, Robert Young, or Jane Wyatt. Of course Elisha Cook, Jr., who appeared in a great many of these films, has always looked a bit weird, but he always got killed in the first reel, so I feel he really doesn't count.

Although both rock and roll and the new youth movies (everything from *I Was a Teenage Werewolf* to *Rebel Without a Cause*) burst upon an older generation, just beginning to relax enough to translate "their war" into myth, with all the unpleasant surprise of a mugger leaping out of a privet hedge, both the music and the movies were only preshocks of a genuine youthquake to come. Little Richard was certainly unsettling, and Michael Landon—who didn't even have enough school spirit to at least take off his high school jacket before turning into a man-wolf—was also unsettling, but it would still be miles and years to the Fish Cheer at Woodstock and Old Leatherface doing impromptu surgery with his McCulloch in *The Texas Chainsaw Massacre*.

It was a decade when every parent trembled at the spectre of juvenile delinquency: the mythic teenaged hood leaning in the doorway of the candy store there in Our Town, his hair bejeweled with Vitalis or Brylcreem, a pack of Luckies tucked under the epaulet of his motorcycle jacket, a fresh zit at one corner of his mouth and a brand-new switchblade in his back pocket, waiting for a kid to beat up, a parent to harass and embarrass, a girl to assault, or possibly a dog to rape and then kill . . . or maybe vice-versa. It is a once-dread image which has James Dean and/or Vic Morrow here, wait twenty years, and hey-presto! out pops Arthur Fonzarelli. But during the period, the newspapers and magazines of the popular press saw young jd's everywhere, just as these same organs of the fourth estate had seen Commies everywhere a few years before. Their chain-decked engineer boots and pegged Levis could be seen or imagined on the streets of Oakdale and Pineview and Centerville; in Mundamian, Iowa, and in Lewiston, Maine. The shadow of the dreaded jd stretched long. Marlon Brando had been first to give this empty-headed nihilist a voice, in a picture called *The Wild One*. "What are you rebelling against?" the pretty girl asks him. Answers Marlon: "What have you got?"

To some fellow in Asher Heights, North Carolina, who had somehow survived forty-one missions over Germany in the belly of a bomber and who now only wanted to sell a lot of Buicks with Power-Flite transmissions, that sounded like very bad news indeed; here was a fellow for whom the Jaycees held no charms.

But as there turned out to be fewer Communists and fifth columnists than was at first suspected, the Shadow of the Dread JD also proved to be rather overrated. In the last analysis, the war babies wanted what their parents wanted. They wanted driver's licences; jobs in the cities and homes in the suburbs; wives and husbands; insurance; underarm protection; kids; time payments which they would meet; clean streets; clear consciences. They wanted to be good. Years and miles between Senior Glee Club and the SLA; years and miles between Our Town and the Mekong Delta; and the only known fuzz-tone guitar track in existence was a technical mistake on a Marty Robbins country and western record. They adhered happily to school dress codes. Long sideburns were laughed at in most quarters, and a guy wearing stacked heels or bikini briefs would have been hounded unmercifully as a faggot. Eddie Cochran could sing about "those crazy pink pegged slacks" and kids would buy the records . . . but not the pants themselves. For the war babies, the norm was blessed. They wanted to be good. They watched for the mutant.

Only one aberration per picture was allowed in the early youthcult horror film of the fifties, one mutation. It was the parents who would never believe. It was the kids—who wanted to be good—who stood watch (most often from those lonely bluffs which overlook Our Town from the ends of lovers' lanes); it was the kids who stamped the mutant out, once more making the world safe for country club dances and Hamilton Beach blenders.

Horrors in the fifties, for the war babies, were mostly—except maybe for the psychic strain of waiting for The Bomb to fall—mundane horrors. And perhaps a conception of real horror is impossible for people whose bellies are full. The horrors the war babies felt were scale-model horrors, and in that light the movies that really caused AIP to take off, *I Was a Teenage Werewolf* and *I Was a Teenage Frankenstein,* become mildly interesting.

In *Werewolf,* Michael Landon plays an attractive but moody high school student with a quick temper. He's basically a good kid, but he's involved in one fight after another (like David Banner, the Hulk's alter-ego on TV, the Landon character actually provokes none of these fights) until it looks as though he will be suspended from school. He goes to see a psychiatrist (Whit Bissell, who also plays the mad descendant of Victor Frankenstein in *Teenage Frankenstein)* who turns out to be totally evil. Seeing Landon as a throwback to an earlier stage of human development—like back to the Alley Oop stage—Bissell uses hypnosis to regress Landon totally, in effect deliberately making the problem worse instead of trying to cure it.

Bissell's experiments succeed beyond his wildest dreams—or worst nightmares—and Landon becomes a ravening werewolf. For a 1957 high school or junior high school kid watching the transformation for the first time, this was *baaad* shit. Landon becomes the fascinating embodiment of everything you're *not* supposed to do if you want to be good . . . if you want to get along in school, join the National Honor Society, get your letter, and be accepted by a good college where you can join a frat and drink beer like your old man did. Landon grows hair all over his face, produces long fangs, and begins to drool a substance that looks suspiciously like Burma-Shave. He peeks at a girl doing exercises on the balance beam all by herself in the gymnasium, and one imagines him smelling like a randy polecat who just rolled in a nice fresh pile of coyote shit. No button-down Ivy League shirt with the fruit loop on the back here; here's a fellow who doesn't give a fart in a high wind for the Scholastic Aptitude Tests. He has gone absolutely, not apeshit, but wolfshit.

Undoubtedly part of the reason for the movie's meteoric takeoff at the box office had to do with the liberating, vicarious feelings the movie allowed these war babies who wanted to be good. When Landon attacks the pretty gymnast in the leotard, he is making a social statement on behalf of those watching. But those watching also react in horror, because on the psychological level, the picture is a series of object lessons on how to get along—everything from "shave before you go to school" to "never exercise in a deserted gym."

After all, there are beasts everywhere.

6

If *I Was a Teenage Werewolf* is, psychologically, that old dream of having your pants fall down when you stand up during homeroom period to salute the flag, taken to its most nightmarish extreme—the ultimate hirsute outsider menacing the peer groups at Our Town High—then *I Was a Teenage Frankenstein* is a sick parable of total glandular breakdown. It is a movie for every fifteen-year-old who ever stood in front of her or his mirror in the morning looking nervously at the fresh pimple that surfaced in the night and realizing glumly that even Stri-Dex Medicated Pads weren't going to solve the whole problem no matter what Dick Clark said.

I keep coming back to pimples, you may say. You are right. In many ways I see the horror films of the late fifties and early sixties—up until *Psycho,* let us say—as paeans to the congested pore. I've suggested that it may be impossible for a people whose bellies are full to feel real horror. Similarly, Americans have had to severely limit their conceptions of physical deformity—and that is why the pimple has played such an important part in the developing psyche of the American teenager.

Of course, there's probably a guy out there, a guy born with a congenital birth defect, who's muttering to himself: don't talk to *me* about deformity, you asshole . . . and it is certainly true that there are Americans with club feet, Americans without noses, amputee Americans, blind Americans (I've always wondered if the blind of America felt discriminated against by that McDonald's jingle that goes, "Keep your eyes on your fries . . ."). Beside such cataclysmic physical fuck-ups of God, man, and nature, a few pimples look about as serious as a hangnail. But I should also point out that in America, cataclysmic physical fuck-ups are (so far, at least) the exception rather than the rule. Walk down any ordinary street in America and count the serious physical defects you see. If you can walk three miles and come up with more than half a dozen, you're beating the average by a good country mile. Look for people under forty whose teeth have rotted right down to the gum line, children with the bloated bellies of oncoming starvation, folks with smallpox scars, and you will look in vain. You'll not find folks in the A & P with running sores on their faces or untreated ulcers on their arms and legs; if you set up a Head Inspection Station at the corner of Broad and Main, you could check a hundred heads and come up with only four or five really lively colonies of head lice. Incidence of these and other ailments rise in white rural areas and in the inner cities, but in the towns and suburbs of America, most people are looking good. The proliferation of self-help courses, the growing cult of personal development ("I'm going to be more assertive, if that's all right with you," as Erma Bombeck says), and the increasingly widespread hobby of navel-contemplation are all signs that, for the time being, great numbers of Americans have taken care of the nitty-gritty realities of life as it is for most of the world— the survival trip.

I can't imagine anyone with a severe nutritional deficiency caring much about *I'm OK—You're OK,* or anyone trying to scratch out a subsistence-level existence for himself, his wife, and his eight kids giving much of a toot about Werner Erhard's est course or Rolfing. Such things are for rich folks. Recently Joan Didion wrote a book about her own odyssey through the sixties, *The White Album.* For rich folks, I suppose it's a pretty interesting book: the story of a wealthy white woman who could afford to have her nervous breakdown in Hawaii—the seventies equivalent of worrying over pimples.

When the horizons of human experience shrink to HO scale, perspective changes. For the war babies, secure (except for The Bomb) in a world of six-month checkups, penicillin, and eternal orthodontics, the pimple became the primary physical deformity with which you were seen on the street or in the halls of your school; most of the other deformities had been taken care of. And say, having mentioned orthodontics, I'll add that many kids who had to wear braces during those years of heavy, almost suffocating peer pressure saw them as a kind of deformity—every now and then you would hear the cry of "Hey, metal-mouth!" in the halls. But most people saw them only as a form of treatment, no more remarkable than a girl with her arm in a sling or a football player wearing an Ace bandage on his knee.

But for the pimple there was no cure.

And here comes *I Was a Teenage Frankenstein*. In this film, Whit Bissell assembles the creature, played by Gary Conway, from the bodies of dead hot-rodders. The leftover pieces are fed to the alligators under the house—of course we have an idea early on that Bissell himself will end up being munched by the gators, and we are not disappointed. Bissell is a total fiend in this movie, reaching existential heights of villainy: "He's crying, even the tear ducts work! . . . You've got a civil tongue in your head. I know you have. Because I sewed it back myself."* But it is the unfortunate Conway who catches the eye and mainsprings the film. Like the villainy of Bissell, the physical deformity of Conway is so awful it becomes almost absurd . . . and he looks like nothing so much as a high school kid whose acne has run totally wild. His face is a lumpy bas-relief map of mountainous terrain from which one shattered eye bugs madly.

---

* Quoted in *An Illustrated History of the Horror Film*, by Carlos Clarens (New York: Capricorn Books, 1968).

And yet . . . and yet . . . somehow this shambling creature still manages to dig rock and roll, so he can't be all bad, can he? We have met the monster, and, as Peter Straub points out in *Ghost Story*, he is us.

We'll have more to say about monstrosity as we go along, and hopefully something of a more profound nature than is contained in the ore we can mine from *I Was a Teenage Werewolf* and *I Was a Teenage Frankenstein*, but I think it's important first to establish the fact that, even on their simplest level, these Tales of the Hook do a number of things without even trying to. Allegory and catharsis are both provided, but only because the creator of horror fiction is above all else an agent of the norm. This is true of horror's more physical side, and we'll find it's also true of works which are more consciously artistic, although when we turn our discussion to the mythic qualities of horror and terror, we may find some rather more disturbing and puzzling associations. But to reach that point, we need to turn our discussion away from film, at least for awhile, and to three novels which form most of the base on which the modern horror genre stands.

CHAPTER III

Tales of the Tarot

One of the most common themes in fantastic literature is that of immortality. "The thing that would not die" has been a staple of the field from Beowulf to Poe's tales of M. Valdemar and of the telltale heart, to the works of Lovecraft (such as "Cool Air"), Blatty, and even, God save us, John Saul.

The three novels I want to discuss in this chapter seem to have actually achieved that immortality, and I believe it's impossible to discuss horror in the years 1950–1980 with any real fullness of understanding unless we begin with these three books. All three live a kind of half-life outside the bright circle of English literature's acknowledged "classics," and perhaps with good reason. *Dr. Jekyll and Mr. Hyde* was written at white heat by Robert Louis Stevenson in three days. It so horrified his wife that Stevenson burned the manuscript in his fireplace . . . and then wrote it again from scratch in another three days. *Dracula* is a frankly palpitating melodrama couched in the frame of the epistolary novel—a convention that had been breathing its last gasps twenty years before when Wilkie Collins was writing the last of his great mystery/suspense novels. *Frankenstein,* the most notorious of the three, was penned by a nineteen-year-old girl, and although it is the best written of the three, it is the least read, and its author would never again write so quickly, so well, so successfully . . . or so audaciously.

In the most unkind of critical lights, all three can be seen as no more than popular novels of their day, with little to distinguish them from novels roughly similar—*The Monk,* by

M. G. Lewis, for instance, or Collins's *Armadale*—books largely forgotten except by teachers of Gothic fiction who occasionally pass them on to students, who approach them warily . . . and then gulp them down.

But these three are something special. They stand at the foundation of a huge skyscraper of books and films—those twentieth-century gothics which have become known as "the modern horror story." More than that, at the center of each stands (or slouches) a monster that has come to join and enlarge what Burt Hatlen calls "the myth-pool"—that body of fictive literature in which all of us, even the nonreaders and those who do not go to the films, have communally bathed. Like an almost perfect Tarot hand representing our lusher concepts of evil, they can be neatly laid out: the Vampire, the Werewolf, and the Thing Without a Name.

One great novel of supernatural terror, Henry James's *The Turn of the Screw*, has been excluded from this Tarot hand, although it would complete the grouping by supplying the best-known mythic figure of the supernatural, that of the Ghost. I have excluded it for two reasons: first, because *The Turn of the Screw*, with its elegant drawing-room prose and its tightly woven psychological logic, has had very little influence on the mainstream of the American mass cult. We would do better discussing Casper the Friendly Ghost in terms of the archetype. Secondly, the Ghost is an archetype (unlike those represented by Frankenstein's monster, Count Dracula, or Edward Hyde) which spreads across too broad an area to be limited to a single novel, no matter how great. The archetype of the Ghost is, after all, the Mississippi of supernatural fiction, and although we will discuss it when the time comes, we'll not limit its summing-up to a single book.

All of these books (including *The Turn of the Screw*) have certain things in common, and all of them deal with the very basis of the horror story: secrets best left untold and things best left unsaid. And yet Stevenson, Shelley, and Stoker (James, too) all promise to tell us the secret. They do so with varying degrees of effect and success . . . and none of them can be said to have really failed. Maybe that's what's kept the novels alive and vital. At any rate, there they stand, and it seems to me impossible to write a book of this sort without doing *something* with them. It's a matter of roots. It may not do you any good to know that your grandfather liked to sit on the stoop of his building with his sleeves rolled up and smoke a pipe after supper, but it may help to know that he emigrated from Poland in 1888, that he came to New York and helped to build the subway system. If it does nothing else, it may give you a new perspective on your own morning subway ride. In the same way, it is hard to fully understand Christopher Lee as Dracula without talking about that red-headed Irishman Abraham Stoker.

So . . . a few roots.

2

Frankenstein has probably been the subject of more films than any other literary work in history, including the Bible. The pictures include *Frankenstein*, *The Bride of Frankenstein*, *Frankenstein Meets the Wolf-Man*, *The Revenge of Frankenstein*, *Blackenstein*, and *Frankenstein 1970*, to name just a handful. In light of this, summary would seem almost unnecessary, but as previously pointed out, *Frankenstein* is not much read. Millions of Americans know the name (not as many as know the name of Ronald McDonald, granted; now there is a *real* culture hero), but most of them don't realize that Frankenstein is the name of the monster's creator, not the monster itself, a fact which enhances the idea that the book has become a part of Hatlen's American myth-pool rather than detracting from it. It's like pointing out that Billy the Kid was in reality a tenderfoot from New York who wore a derby hat, had syphilis, and probably back-shot most of his victims. People are interested in such facts, but understand intuitively that they aren't what's really important now . . . if indeed they ever were. One of the things that makes art a force to be reckoned with even by those who don't care for it is the regularity with which myth swallows truth . . . and without so much as a burp of indigestion.

Mary Shelley's novel is a rather slow and talky melodrama, its theme drawn in large, careful, and rather crude strokes. It is developed the way a bright but naive debate student might develop his line of argument. Unlike the films based upon it, there are few scenes of violence, and unlike the inarticulate monster of the Universal days ("the Karloff-films," as Forry Ackerman so charmingly calls them), Shelley's creature speaks with the orotund, balanced phrases of peer in the House of Lords or William F. Buckley disputing politely with Dick Cavett on a TV talk show. He is a cerebral creature, the direct opposite of Karloff's physically overbearing monster with the shovel forehead and the sunken, stupidly crafty eyes; and in all the book's pages there is nothing as chilling as Karloff's line in *The Bride of Frankenstein,* spoken in that dull, dead, and dragging tenor: "Yes . . . dead . . . I love . . . dead."

Ms. Shelley's novel is subtitled "The Modern Prometheus," and the Prometheus in question is Victor Frankenstein. He leaves hearth and home to go to university in Ingolstadt (and already we can hear the whirr of the author's grindstone as she prepares to sharpen one of the horror genre's most famous axes: There Are Some Things Mankind Was Not Meant To Know), where he gets a lot of crazy—and dangerous—ideas put into his head about galvanism and alchemy. The inevitable result, of course, is the creation of a monster with more parts than a J. C. Whitney automotive catalogue. Frankenstein accomplishes this creation in one long, delirious burst of activity—and it is in these scenes that Shelley offers us her most vivid prose.

On the grave robbery necessary to the task at hand:

> Who shall conceive the horrors of my secret toil as I dabbled among the unhallowed damps of the grave or tortured the living animal to animate the lifeless clay? My limbs now tremble, and my eyes swim with the remembrance. . . . I collected bones from charnel-houses and

> disturbed, with profane fingers, the tremendous secrets of the human frame. . . . I kept my workshop of filthy creation; my eyeballs were starting from their sockets in attending to the details of my employment.

On the dream which follows the completion of the experiment:

> I thought I saw Elizabeth, in the bloom of health, walking in the streets of Ingolstadt. Delighted and surprised, I embraced her, but as I imprinted the first kiss on her lips, they became livid with the hue of death; her features appeared to change, and I thought that I held the corpse of my dead mother in my arms; a shroud enveloped her form, and I saw the graveworms crawling in the folds of the flannel. I started from my sleep with horror; a cold dew covered my forehead, my teeth chattered, and every limb became convulsed; when, by the dim and yellow light of the moon, as it forced its way through the window shutters, I beheld the wretch—the miserable monster whom I had created. He held up the curtain of the bed; and his eyes, if eyes they may be called, were fixed on me. His jaws opened, and he muttered some inarticulate sounds, while a grin wrinkled his cheeks.

Victor responds to this vision as any sane man would; he runs shrieking into the night. The remainder of Shelley's story is a Shakespearean tragedy, its classical unity broken only by Ms. Shelley's uncertainty as to where the fatal flaw lies—is it in Victor's *hubris* (usurping a power that belongs only to God) or in his failure to take responsibility for his creation after endowing it with the life-spark?

The monster begins its revenge against its creator by killing Frankenstein's little brother, William. We are not terribly sorry to see William go, by the way; when the monster tries to befriend the boy, William replies: "Hideous monster! Let me go. My papa is a syndic—he is M. Frankenstein—he will punish you. You dare not keep me." This piece of rich-kid snottiness is Willy's last; when the monster hears the name of its creator on the boy's lips, he wrings the kid's bratty little neck.

A blameless servant in the Frankenstein household, Justine Moritz, is accused of the crime and is promptly hanged for it—thus doubling the unfortunate Frankenstein's load of guilt. The monster approaches his creator soon after and tells him the story.* The upshot of the matter is that he wants a mate. He tells Frankenstein that if his wish is granted, he will take his lady and the two of them will live out their span in some desolate wasteland (South America is suggested, as New Jersey had not yet been invented), removed from the eye and mind of man forever. The alternative, the monster threatens, is a reign of terror. He voices his existential credo—better to do evil than do nothing at all—by saying, "I will revenge my injuries; if I cannot inspire love, I will cause fear, and chiefly towards you, my arch-enemy, because my creator, do I swear inextinguishable hatred. Have a care; I will work at your destruction. . . . I will desolate your heart, so that you shall curse the hour of your birth."

At length, Victor agrees, and actually does make the woman. He accomplishes this second act of creation on a desolate island in the Orkney chain, and in these pages Mary Shelley creates an intensity of mood and atmosphere that nearly rivals the creation of the original. Doubts assail Frankenstein moments before he is to imbue the creature with life. He imagines the world desolated by the pair of them. Even worse, he imagines them as a hideous Adam and Eve of an entire race of monsters. A child of her times, Shelley apparently never considered the idea that for a man capable of creating life from moldering

---

* Much of the story is unintentionally hilarious. The monster hides in a shed adjacent to a peasant hut. One of the peasants, Felix, just happens to be teaching his girlfriend, a runaway Arabian noblewoman named Safie, his language; thus the monster learns how to talk. His reading primers are *Paradise Lost*, Plutarch's *Lives*, and *The Sorrows of Werter* [sic], books he has discovered in a cast-off trunk lying in a ditch. This baroque tale-within-a-tale is only rivaled in Defoe's *Robinson Crusoe*, when Crusoe strips naked, swims out to the foundering ship that has marooned him, and then, according to Defoe, fills his pockets with all sorts of goodies. My admiration for such invention knows no bounds.

spare parts, it would be child's play to create a woman without the capacity for conceiving a child.

The monster turns up immediately after Frankenstein has destroyed its mate, of course; he has several words for Victor Frankenstein and none of them are "happy birthday." The reign of terror he has promised takes place like a chain of exploding firecrackers (although in Ms. Shelley's sedate prose they are more like a roll of caps). Frankenstein's boyhood friend, Henry Clerval, is strangled by the monster for openers. Shortly thereafter the monster utters the book's most horrible innuendo; he promises Frankenstein, "I will be with you on your wedding night." The implications of this threat, for readers of Mary Shelley's time as well as our own, go beyond murder.

Frankenstein responds to this threat by almost immediately marrying his childhood sweetheart, Elizabeth—not one of the book's more believable moments, although hardly in a class with the abandoned trunk in the ditch or the runaway Arabian noblewoman. On their wedding night, Victor goes out to confront the creature, having naively assumed that the monster's threat is against himself. Meanwhile, the monster has broken into the small hut Victor and Elizabeth have taken for the night. Exit Elizabeth. Frankenstein's father goes next, a victim of shock and heartbreak.

Frankenstein pursues his demon creation relentlessly north, into the Arctic wastes, where he dies aboard the Polebound ship of Robert Walton, another scientist determined to crack open the mysteries of God and Nature . . . and the circle neatly closes.

3

So the question arises: How did it happen that this modest gothic tale, which was only about a hundred pages long in its first draft (Ms. Shelley's husband, Percy, encouraged her to flesh it out), became caught in a kind of cultural echo chamber, amplifying through the years until, a hundred and sixty-four years later, we have a cereal called Frankenberry (closely related to those two other favorites of the breakfast table, Count Chocula and Booberry); an old TV series called *The Munsters*, which has apparently gone into terminal syndication; Aurora Frankenstein model kits, which, when completed, delight the happy young modelmaker with a glow-in-the-dark creature lurching through a glow-in-the-dark graveyard; and a saying such as "He looked like Frankenstein" as a kind of apotheosis of ugly?

The most obvious answer to this question is, the movies. The movies did it. And this is a true answer, as far as it goes. As has been pointed out in film books *ad infinitum* (and possibly *ad nauseam*), the movies have been very good at providing that cultural echo chamber . . . perhaps because, in terms of ideas as well as acoustics, the best place to create an echo is in a large empty space. In place of the ideas that books and novels give us, the movies often substitute large helpings of gut emotion. To this American movies have added a fierce sense of image, and the two together create a dazzling show. Take Clint Eastwood in Don Siegel's *Dirty Harry,* for instance. In terms of ideas, the film is an idiotic mishmash. In terms of image and emotion—the young kidnap victim being pulled from the cistern at dawn, the bad guy terrorizing the busload of children, the granite face of Dirty Harry Callahan himself—the film is brilliant. Even the best of liberals walk out of a film like *Dirty Harry* or Peckinpah's *Straw Dogs* looking as if they have been clopped over the head . . . or run over by a train.

There *are* films of ideas, of course, ranging all the way from *Birth of a Nation* to *Annie Hall.* But until a few years ago these were largely the province of foreign filmmakers (the cinema "new wave" that broke in Europe from 1946 until about 1965), and these movies have always been chancy in America, playing at your neighborhood "art house" with subtitles, if they play at all. I think it's easy to misread the success of Woody Allen's later films in this regard. In America's urban areas, his films—and films such as *Cousin, Cousine*—generate long lines at the box office, and they certainly get what George (*Night of the Living Dead, Dawn of the Dead*) Romero calls "good ink," but in the sticks—the quad cinema in Davenport, Iowa, or the twin in Portsmouth, New Hampshire—these pictures play a fast week or two and then disappear. It is Burt Reynolds in *Smokey and the Bandit* that Americans really seem to take to; when Americans go to the films, they seem to want billboards rather than ideas; they want to check their brains at the box office and watch car crashes, custard pies, and monsters on the prowl.

Ironically, it took a foreign director, the Italian Sergio Leone, to somehow frame the archetypal American movie; to define and typify what most American filmgoers seem to want. What Leone did in *A Fistful of Dollars, For a Few Dollars More,* and most grandiosely in *Once Upon a Time in the West* cannot even properly be called satire. *O.U.A.T.I.T.W.* in particular is a huge and wonderfully vulgar overstatement of the already overstated archetypes of American film westerns. In this movie gunshots seem as loud as atomic blasts; close-ups seem to go on for minutes at a stretch, gunfights for hours; and the streets of Leone's peculiar little Western towns all seem as wide as freeways.

So when one asks who or what turned Mary Shelley's well-spoken monster with his education from *The Sorrows of Young Werther* and *Paradise Lost* into a pop archetype, the movies are a perfectly good answer. God knows the movies have turned unlikelier subjects into archetypes—scuzzy mountain-men matted with dirt and crawling with lice become proud and handsome symbols of the frontier (Robert Redford in *Jeremiah Johnson,* or pick the Sunn International picture of your choice), half-witted killers become representatives of American's dying free spirit (Beatty and Dunaway in *Bonnie and Clyde*), and even incompetency becomes myth and archetype, as in the Blake Edwards/Peter Sellers pictures starring the late Sellers as Inspector Clouseau. Seen in the context of such archetypes, the American movies have created their own Tarot deck, and most of us are familiar with the cards, cards such as the War Hero (Audie Murphy, John Wayne), the Strong and Silent Peace Officer (Gary Cooper, Clint Eastwood), the Whore with the Heart of Gold, the Crazed Hoodlum ("Top of the world, ma!"), the Ineffectual but Amusing Dad, the Can-Do Mom, the Kid from the Gutter Who Is On His Way Up, and a dozen others. That all of these creations are stereotypes developed with varying degrees of cleverness goes without saying, but even in the most inept hands, that reverberation, that cultural echo, seems to be there.

But we're not discussing the War Hero or the Strong, Silent Peace Officer here; we are discussing that ever-popular archetype, the Thing Without a Name. For surely if any novel spans the entire period of book-into-film-into-myth, *Frankenstein* is that book. It was the subject of one of the first "story" films ever made, a one-reeler starring Charles Ogle as the creature. Ogle's conception of the monster caused him to tease his hair and to apparently cover his face with partially dried Bisquick. That film was produced by Thomas Edison. The same archetype is on view today as the subject of the CBS television series *The Incredible Hulk,* which has managed to combine two of the archetypes we are discussing here . . . and to do so with a fair amount of success (*The Incredible Hulk* can be seen as a Werewolf story as well as a Thing story). Although I have to say that each transformation from David Banner into the Hulk leaves me wondering where the hell the guy's shoes go to and how he gets them back.*

So we begin with the movies—but what has turned *Frankenstein* into a movie not just once but again and again and again? One possibility is that the storyline, although constantly changed (perverted, one is tempted to say) by the filmmakers who have used (and abused) it, usually contains the wonderful dichotomy that Mary Shelley built into her story: on one hand the horror writer is an agent of the norm, he or she wants us to watch for the mutant, and we feel Victor Frankenstein's horror and disgust at the relentless, charnel creature he has made. But

---

* "Ole greenskin is back," my seven-year-old son Joe is apt to say comfortably when David Banner begins his shirt-ripping, pants-shredding transformation. Joe quite rightly sees the Hulk not as a frightening agent of chaos but as a blind force of nature fated only to do good. Oddly enough, the comforting lesson that many horror movies seem to teach the young is that fate is kind. Not a bad lesson at all for the little people, who so rightly see themselves as hostages to forces larger than themselves.

on the other hand, we grasp the fact of the creature's innocence and the author's infatuation with the *tabula rasa* idea.

The monster strangles Henry Clerval and promises Frankenstein he will "be with him on his wedding night," but the monster is also a creature of childlike pleasure and wonder, who beholds the "radiant form" of the moon rising above the trees; he brings wood to the poor peasant family like a good spirit in the night; he seizes the hand of the old blind man, falls on his knees, and begs him: "Now is the time! Save and protect me! . . . Do not desert me in the hour of trial!" The creature who strangles snotty William is also the creature who saves a little girl from drowning . . . and is rewarded with a charge of buckshot in the ass for his pains.

Mary Shelley is—let us bite the bullet and tell the truth—not a particularly strong writer of emotional prose (which is why students who come to the book with great expectations of a fast, gory read—expectations formed by the movies—usually come away feeling puzzled and let down). She's at her best when Victor and his creation argue the pros and cons of the monster's request for a mate like Harvard debaters—that is to say, she is at her best in the realm of pure ideas. So it's perhaps ironic that the facet of the book which seems to have insured its long attractiveness to the movies is Shelley's splitting of the reader into two people of opposing minds: the reader who wants to stone the mutation and the reader who feels the stones and cries out at the injustice of it.

Even so, no moviemaker has gotten all of this idea; probably James Whale came the closest in his stylish *Bride of Frankenstein,* where the monster's more existential sorrows (young Werther with bolts through his neck) are boiled down to a more mundane but emotionally powerful specific: Victor Frankenstein goes ahead and makes the female . . . but she doesn't like the original monster. Elsa Lanchester, looking like a latter-day Studio 54 disco queen, screams when he tries to touch her, and we are in perfect sympathy with the monster when he rips the whole rotten laboratory to pieces.

A fellow named Jack Pierce did Boris Karloff's makeup

in the original sound version of *Frankenstein,* creating a face as familiar to most of us (if slightly more ugly) as the uncles and cousins in a family photograph album—the square head, the dead-white, slightly concave brow, the scars, the bolts, the heavy eyelids. Universal Pictures copyrighted Pierce's makeup, and so when Britain's Hammer Films made their series of Frankenstein movies in the late fifties and early sixties, a different concept was used. It is probably not as inspired or as original as the Pierce makeup (in most cases the Hammer Frankenstein bears a closer resemblance to the unfortunate Gary Conway in *I Was a Teenage Frankenstein*), but the two have one thing in common: although in both cases the monster is horrible to look at, there is also something so sad, so miserable there that our hearts actually go out to the creature even as they are shrinking away from it in fear and disgust.*

As I've said, most directors who have tried their hands at a Frankenstein film (with the exception of those played exclusively for laughs) have sensed this dichotomy and tried to use it. Breathes there a moviegoer with soul so dead who never wished the monster would jump down from that burning windmill and stuff those torches right down the throats of those ignorant slobs so dedicated to ending its life? I doubt if there is such a moviegoer, and if there is, he must be hardhearted indeed. But I don't believe any director has caught the full pathos of the situation, and there is no Frankenstein movie that will bring tears to the eyes as readily as the final reel of *King Kong,* where the big ape straddles the top of the Empire State Building and tries to fight off those machine-gun-equipped biplanes as if they were the prehistoric birds of his native island. Like Eastwood in Leone's spaghetti westerns, Kong is the archetype of the archetype. We see the horror of being a monster in the eyes of Boris Karloff and, later, in those of Christopher Lee; in *King Kong* it is spread across the ape's entire face, due to the

---

* The greatest of the Hammer Frankenstein monsters was probably Christopher Lee, who went on to nearly eclipse Bela Lugosi as Count Dracula. Lee, a great actor, is the only man to approach Karloff's interpretation of the role, although Karloff was far more fortunate in matters of script and direction. All in all, Christopher Lee fared better as a vampire.

marvelous special effects of Willis O'Brien. The result is almost a cartoon of the friendless, dying outsider. It is one of the great fusions of love and horror, innocence and terror, the emotional reality which Mary Shelley only suggests in her novel. Even so, I suspect she would have understood and agreed with Dino De Laurentiis's remark on the great attraction of that dichotomy. De Laurentiis was speaking of his own forgettable remake of *King Kong,* but he could have been speaking about the hapless monster itself when he said, "Nobody cry when Jaws die." Well, we don't exactly cry when Frankenstein's monster dies— not the way audiences weep when Kong, that shanghaied hostage of a simpler, more romantic world, topples from his perch atop the Empire State—but we are, perhaps, disgusted at our own sense of relief.

4

Although the gathering which ultimately resulted in Mary Shelley's writing of *Frankenstein* took place on the shores of Lake Geneva, miles from British soil, it must still qualify as one of the maddest British tea parties of all time. And in a funny way, the gathering may have been responsible not only for *Frankenstein,* published that same year, but for *Dracula* as well, a novel written by a man who would not be born for another thirty-one years.

It was June of 1816, and the band of travelers—Percy and Mary Shelley, Lord Byron, and Dr. John Polidori—had been confined to quarters by two weeks of torrential rains. They began a joint reading of German ghost stories from a book called *Fantasmagoria,* and the gathering began to get decidedly weird. Things really culminated when Percy Shelley threw a kind of fit. Dr. Polidori noted in his diary: "After tea, 12 o'clock, really began to talk ghosts. Lord Byron read some verses of Coleridge's 'Christabel,' [the part about] the witch's breast; when silence ensued, Shelley, suddenly shrieking, and putting his hands to his head, ran out of the room with a candle. [I] Threw water in his face and after gave him ether. He was looking at Mrs. Shelley, and suddenly thought of a woman he had heard of who had eyes instead of nipples; which, taking hold of his mind, horrified him."

Leave it to the English.

An agreement was made that each member of the party would try his or her hand at creating a new ghost story. It was Mary Shelley, whose work as a result of the gathering would alone endure, who had the most trouble in setting to work. She had no ideas at all, and several nights passed before her imagination was fired by a nightmare in which "a pale student of unhallowed arts created the awful phantom of a man." It is the creation scene presented in chapters four and five of her novel (quoted from earlier).

Percy Bysshe Shelley produced a fragment entitled "The Assassins." George Gordon Byron produced an interesting macabre tale titled "The Burial." But it is John Polidori, the good doctor, who is sometimes mentioned as a possible link to Bram Stoker and *Dracula*. His short story was later expanded to novel length and became a great success. It was called "The Vampyre."

In point of fact, Polidori's novel isn't very good . . . and it bears an uncomfortable resemblance to "The Burial," the short story written by his immeasurably more talented patient, Lord Byron. There is perhaps a breath of plagiarism there. We do know that Byron and Polidori argued violently shortly after the interlude at Lake Geneva, and that their friendship ended. It is not entirely beyond supposition that the similarity between the two tales was the cause. Polidori, who was twenty-one at the time he wrote "The Vampyre," came to an unhappy end. The success of the novel he developed from his story encouraged him to retire from the doctoring profession and to become a full-time writer. He had little success at writing, although he was quite good at piling up gambling debts. When he felt his reputation had become irredeemably impugned, he behaved as we would expect of an English gentleman of the day and shot himself.

Stoker's turn-of-the-century horror novel *Dracula* bears only a slight resemblance to Polidori's *The Vampyre*—the field is a narrow one, as we will point out again and again, and exclusive of any willful imitation, the family resemblance is always there—but we can be sure that Stoker was aware of Polidori's story. One believes, after reading *Dracula,* that Stoker left no stone unturned as he researched the project. Is it so far-fetched to believe that he might have read Polidori's novel, have been excited by the subject matter, and determined to write a better book? I like to believe this might be so, much as I like to believe that Polidori really did crib his idea from Lord Byron. That would make Byron the literary grandfather of the legendary Count, who boasts early on to Jonathan Harker that he drove the Turks from Transylvania . . . and Byron himself died while aiding the Greek insurgents against the Turks in 1824, eight years after the gathering with the Shelleys and Polidori on the shores of Lake Geneva. It was a death of which the Count himself would have greatly approved.

5

All tales of horror can be divided into two groups: those in which the horror results from an act of free and conscious will—a conscious decision to do evil—and those in which the horror is predestinate, coming from outside like a stroke of lightning. The most classic horror tale of this latter type is the Old Testament story of Job, who becomes the human Astro-Turf in a kind of spiritual Superbowl between God and Satan.

The stories of horror which are psychological—those which explore the terrain of the human heart—almost always revolve around the free-will concept; "inside evil" if you will, the sort we have no right laying off on God the Father. This is Victor Frankenstein creating a living being out of spare parts to satisfy his own *hubris,* and then compounding his sin by refusing to take the responsibility for what he has done. It is Dr. Henry Jekyll, who creates Mr. Hyde essentially out of Victorian hypocrisy—he wants to be able to carouse and party-down without anyone, even the lowliest Whitechapel drab, knowing that he is anything but saintly Dr. Jekyll whose feet are "ever treading the upward path." Perhaps the best tale of inside evil ever written is Poe's "The Tell-Tale Heart," where murder is committed out of pure evil, with no mitigating circumstances whatever to tincture the brew. Poe suggests we will call his narrator mad because we must always believe that such perfect, motiveless evil is mad, for the sake of our own sanity.

Novels and stories of horror which deal with "outside evil" are often harder to take seriously; they are apt to be no more than boys' adventure yarns in disguise, and in the end the nasty invaders from outer space are repelled; or at the last possible instant the Handsome Young Scientist comes up with the gimmick solution . . . as when, in *Beginning of the End*, Peter Graves creates a sonic gun which draws all the giant grasshoppers into Lake Michigan.

And yet it is the concept of outside evil that is larger, more awesome. Lovecraft grasped this, and it is what makes his stories of stupendous, Cyclopean evil so effective when they are good. Many aren't, but when Lovecraft was on the money—as in "The Dunwich Horror," "The Rats in the Walls," and best of all, "The Colour Out of Space"—his stories packed an incredible wallop. The best of them make us feel the size of the universe we hang suspended in, and suggest shadowy forces that could destroy us all if they so much as grunted in their sleep. After all, what is the paltry inside evil of the A-bomb when compared to Nyarlathotep, the Crawling Chaos, or Shub-Niggurath, the Goat with a Thousand Young?

Bram Stoker's *Dracula* seems a remarkable achievement to me because it humanizes the outside evil concept; we grasp it in a familiar way Lovecraft never allowed, and we can feel its texture. It is an adventure story, but it never degenerates to the level of Edgar Rice Burroughs or *Varney the Vampyre*.

Stoker achieves the effect to a large degree by keeping the evil literally outside for most of his long story. The Count is onstage almost constantly during the first four chapters, dueling with Jonathan Harker, pressing him slowly to the wall ("Later there will be kisses for all of you," Harker hears him tell the three weird sisters as he [Harker] lies in a semiswoon) . . . and then he disappears for most of the book's three hundred or so remaining pages.* It is one of English literature's most remarkable and engaging tricks, a *trompe l'oeil* that has rarely been matched. Stoker creates his fearsome, immortal monster much the way a child can create the shadow of a giant rabbit on the wall simply by wiggling his fingers in front of a light.

The Count's evil seems totally predestinate; the fact that he comes to London with its "teeming millions" does not proceed from any mortal being's evil act. Harker's ordeal at Castle Dracula is not the result of any inner sin or weakness; he winds up on the Count's doorstep because his boss asked him to go. Similarly, the death of Lucy Westenra is not a deserved death. Her encounter with Dracula in the Whitby churchyard is the moral equivalent of being struck by lightning while playing golf. There is nothing in her life to justify the end she comes to at the hands of Van Helsing and her fiancé, Arthur Holmwood—her heart burst apart by a stake, her head chopped off, her mouth stuffed with garlic.

It is not that Stoker is ignorant of inside evil or the Biblical concept of free will; in *Dracula* the concept is embodied by that most engaging of maniacs, Mr. Renfield, who also symbolizes the root source of vampirism—cannibalism. Renfield, who is working his way up to the big leagues the hard way (he begins by snacking on flies, progresses to munching on spiders, then to dining on birds), invites the Count into Dr. Seward's madhouse knowing perfectly well what he is doing—but to suggest he is a large enough character to take responsibility for all the terrors that follow is to suggest the absurd. His character, though engaging, is just not strong enough to take that weight.

---

* The Count appears onstage another half-dozen times, most splendidly in Mina Murray Harker's bedroom. The men in her life burst into her room following the death of Renfield and are greeted with a scene worthy of Bosch: the Count clutching Mina, his face slathered with her blood. In an obscene parody of the marriage sacrament, he opens a vein in his own chest with one dirty fingernail and forces her to drink. Other glimpses of the Count are less powerful. We glimpse him once strolling along an avenue in a foppish straw hat, and once ogling a pretty girl like any run-of-the-mill dirty old man.

We assume that if Dracula hadn't gotten in by using Renfield, he would have gotten in another way.

In a way it was the mores of Stoker's day which dictated that the Count's evil should come from outside, because much of the evil embodied in the Count is a perverse sexual evil. Stoker revitalized the vampire legend largely by writing a novel which fairly pants with sexual energy. The Count doesn't ever attack Jonathan Harker; in fact he is promised to the weird sisters who live in the castle with him. Harker's one brush with these voluptuous but lethal harpies is a sexual one, and it is presented in his diary in terms that were, for turn-of-the-century England, pretty graphic:

> The girl went on her knees, and bent over me, simply gloating. There was a deliberate voluptuousness which was both thrilling and repulsive and as she arched her neck she actually licked her lips like an animal, till I could see in the moonlight the moisture shining on the scarlet lips and on the red tongue as it lapped the sharp white teeth. . . . There she paused, and I could hear the churning sound of her tongue as it licked her teeth and lips, and could feel the hot breath on my neck. . . . I could feel the soft, shivering touch of the lips on the supersensitive skin of my throat, and the hard dents of two sharp teeth, just touching and pausing there. I closed my eyes in a langourous ecstacy and waited—waited with beating heart.

In the England of 1897, a girl who "went on her knees" was not the sort of girl you brought home to meet your mother; Harker is about to be orally raped, and he doesn't mind a bit. And it's all right, *because he is not responsible.* In matters of sex, a highly moralistic society can find a psychological escape valve in the concept of outside evil: this thing is bigger than both of us, baby. Harker is a bit disappointed when the Count enters and breaks up this little tête-à-tête. Probably most of Stoker's wide-eyed readers were, too.

Similarly, the Count preys only on women: first Lucy, then

Mina. Lucy's reactions to the Count's bite are much the same as Jonathan's feelings about the weird sisters. To be perfectly vulgar, Stoker indicates in a fairly classy way that Lucy is coming her brains out. By day an ever-more-pallid but perfectly Apollonian Lucy conducts a proper and decorous courtship with her promised husband, Arthur Holmwood. By night she carouses in Dionysian abandon with her dark and bloody seducer.

In real life at this same time, England was experiencing a mesmerism fad—although Franz Mesmer, the father of what we now call hypnotism, had been dead for about eighty years. Like the Count, many of Mesmer's disciples preferred young girls, and these 19th-century Svengalis would put their subjects into a trance by stroking their bodies . . . all over. Many of the female subjects experienced "wonderful feelings that seemed to culminate in a burst of pleasure." It seems very likely that these "culminating bursts of pleasure" were in fact orgasms—but very few unmarried women of the day would have known an orgasm if it bit them on the nose, and the effect was simply seen as one of the pleasanter side effects of a scientific process. Many of these girls returned and begged to be mesmerized again; "The men don't know, but the little girls understand," as the Bo Diddley song goes. Anyway, the point made in regard to vampirism applies just as well to mesmerism: the "culminating burst of pleasure" was all right because it came from outside; she experiencing the pleasure could not be held responsible.

These strong sexual undertones are surely one reason why the movies have conducted such a long love affair with the Vampire, beginning with Max Schreck in *Nosferatu,* continuing through the Lugosi interpretation (1931), the Christopher Lee interpretation, right up to *'Salem's Lot* (1979), where Reggie Nalder's interpretation brings us full circle to Max Schreck's again.

When all else is said and done, it's a chance to show women in scanty nightclothes, and guys giving the sleeping ladies some of the worst hickeys you ever saw, and to enact, over and over, a situation of which movie audiences never seem to tire: the primal rape scene.

But maybe there's even more going on here sexually than first meets the eye. Early on I mentioned my own belief that much of the horror story's attraction for us is that it allows us to vicariously exercise those antisocial emotions and feelings which society demands we keep stoppered up under most circumstances, for society's good and our own. Anyway, *Dracula* sure isn't a book about "normal" sex; there's no Missionary Position going on here. Count Dracula (and the weird sisters as well) are apparently dead from the waist down; they make love with their mouths alone. The sexual basis of *Dracula* is an infantile oralism coupled with a strong interest in necrophilia (and pedophilia, some would say, considering Lucy in her role as the "bloofer lady"). It is also sex without responsibility, and in the unique and amusing term coined by Erica Jong, the sex in *Dracula* can be seen as the ultimate zipless fuck. This infantile, retentive attitude toward sex may be one reason why the vampire myth, which in Stoker's hands seems to say "I will rape you with my mouth and you will love it; instead of contributing potent fluid to your body, I will remove it," has always been so popular with adolescents still trying to come to grips with their own sexuality. The vampire appears to have found a short-cut through all the tribal mores of sex . . . and he lives forever, to boot.

6

There are other interesting elements in Stoker's book, all sorts of them, but it is the elements of outside evil and sexual invasion that seem to have powered the novel most strongly. We can see the legacy of Stoker's weird sisters in the wonderfully lush and voluptuous vampires in Hammer's 1960 film, *Brides of Dracula* (and also be assured in the best moralistic tradition of the horror movie that the wages of kinky sex are a stake through the heart while catching some z's in your coffin) and dozens of other movies both before and after.

When I wrote my own vampire novel, *'Salem's Lot,* I decided to largely jettison the sexual angle, feeling that in a society where homosexuality, group sex, oral sex, and even, God save us, water sports have become matters of public discussion (not to mention, if you believe the Forum column in *Penthouse,* sex with various fruits and vegetables), the sexual engine that powered much of Stoker's book might have run out of gas.

To some degree that is probably true. Hazel Court constantly falling out of the top of her dress (well . . . almost) in AIP's *The Raven* (1963) looks nearly comic today, not to mention Bela Lugosi's corny Valentino imitation in Universal's *Dracula,* which even hardened horror aficionados and cinema buffs cannot help giggling over. But sex will almost certainly continue to be a driving force in the horror genre; sex that is sometimes presented in disguised, Freudian terms, such as Lovecraft's vaginal creation, Great Cthulhu. After viewing this many-tentacled, slimy, gelid creature through Lovecraft's eyes, do we need to wonder why Lovecraft manifested "little interest" in sex?

Much of the sex in horror fiction is deeply involved in power tripping; it's sex based upon relationships where one partner is largely under the control of the other; sex which almost inevitably leads to some bad end. I refer you, for instance, to *Alien,* where the two women crew members are presented in perfectly nonsexist terms until the climax, where Sigourney Weaver must battle the terrible interstellar hitchhiker that has even managed to board her tiny space lifeboat. During this final battle, Ms. Weaver is dressed in bikini panties and a thin T-shirt, every inch the woman, and at this point interchangeable with any of Dracula's victims in the Hammer cycle of films in the sixties. The point seems to be, "The girl was okay until she got undressed."*

The business of creating horror is much the same as the

---

* I thought there was another extremely sexist interlude in *Alien,* one that disappoints on a plot level no matter how you feel about women's ability as compared to men's. The Sigourney Weaver character, who is presented as tough minded and heroic up to this point, steps *out* of character at the scriptwriters' whim by going after the ship's cat. Enabling the males in the audience, of course, to relax, roll their eyes at each other, and say either aloud or telepathically, "Isn't that just like a woman?" It is a plot twist which depends upon a sexist idea for its believability, and we might well answer the question asked above by asking in turn, "Isn't that just

business of paralyzing an opponent with the martial arts—it is the business of finding vulnerable points and then applying pressure there. The most obvious psychological pressure point is the fact of our own mortality. Certainly it is the most universal. But in a society that sets such a great store by physical beauty (in a society, that is, where a few pimples become the cause of psychic agony) and sexual potency, a deep-seated uneasiness and ambivalence about sex becomes another natural pressure point, one that the writer of the horror story or film gropes for instinctively. In the bare-chested sword-and-sorcery epics of Robert E. Howard, for instance, the female "heavies" are presented as monsters of sexual depravity, indulging in exhibitionism and sadism. As previously pointed out, one of the most tried-and-true movie poster concepts of all time shows the monster—whether it be a BEM (bug-eyed monster) from *This Island Earth* or the mummy for Hammer's 1959 remake of the Universal film—striding through the darkness or the smoking ruins of some city with the body of an unconscious lovely in its arms. Beauty and the beast. You are in my power. Heh-heh-heh. It's that primal rape scene again. And the primal, perverse rapist is the Vampire, stealing not only sexual favors but life itself. And best of all, perhaps, in the eyes of those millions of teenaged boys who have watched the Vampire take wing and then flutter down inside the bedroom of some sleeping young lady, is the fact that the Vampire doesn't even have to get it up to do it. What better news to those on the threshold of the sexual sphere, most of whom have been taught (as certainly they have been, not in the least by the movies themselves) that successful sexual relationships are based upon man's domination and woman's submission? The joker in this deck is that most fourteen-year-old boys who have only recently discovered their own sexual potential feel capable of dominating only the centerfold in *Playboy* with total success. Sex makes young adolescent boys feel many things, but one of them, quite frankly,

---

like a male chauvinist pig of a Hollywood scriptwriter?" This gratuitous little twist doesn't spoil the movie, but it's still sort of a bummer.

is scared. The horror film in general and the Vampire film in particular confirms the feeling. Yes, it says; sex *is* scary; sex *is* dangerous. And I can prove it to you right here and now. Sid-down, kid. Grab your popcorn. I want to tell you a story. . . .

7

Enough of sexual portents, at least for the time being. Let's flip up the third card in this uneasy Tarot hand. Forget Michael Landon and AIP for the time being. Gaze, if you dare, on the face of the *real* Werewolf. His name, gentle reader, is Edward Hyde.

Robert Louis Stevenson conceived *Dr. Jekyll and Mr. Hyde* as a shocker, pure and simple, a potboiler and, hopefully, a money machine. It so horrified his wife that Stevenson burned the first draft and rewrote it, injecting a little moral uplift to please his spouse. Of the three books under discussion here, *Jekyll and Hyde* is the shortest (it runs about seventy pages in close type) and undoubtedly the most stylish. If Bram Stoker serves us great whacks of horror in *Dracula,* leaving us, after Harker's confrontation with Dracula in Transylvania, the stak-ing of Lucy Westenra, the death of Renfield and the branding of Mina, feeling as if we have been hit square in the chops by a two-by-four, then Stevenson's brief and cautionary tale is like the quick, mortal stab of an icepick.

Like a police-court trial (to which the critic G. K. Chester-ton compared it), we get the narrative through a series of dif-ferent voices, and it is through the testimony of those involved that Dr. Jekyll's unhappy tale unfolds.

It begins as Jekyll's lawyer, Mr. Utterson, and a distant cousin, one Richard Enfield, stroll through London one morn-ing. As they pass "a certain sinister block of building" with "a blind forehead of discoloured wall" and a door which is "blistered and distained," Enfield is moved to tell Utterson a story about that particular door. He was on the scene one early morning, he says, when he observed two people approaching the corner from opposite directions—a man and a little girl.

They collide. The girl is knocked flat and the man—Edward Hyde—simply goes on walking, trampling the screaming child underfoot. A crowd gathers (what all of these people are doing abroad at three A.M. of a cold winter's morning is never explained; perhaps they were all discussing what Robinson Crusoe used for pockets when he swam out to the foundering ship), and Enfield collars Mr. Hyde. Hyde is a man of so loathsome a countenance that Enfield is actually obliged to protect him from the mob, which seems on the verge of tearing him apart: "We were keeping the women off as best we could, for they were as wild as harpies," Enfield tells Utterson. Moreover, the doctor who was summoned "turn[ed] sick and white with desire to kill him." Once again we see the horror writer as an agent of the norm; the crowd that has gathered is watching faithfully for the mutant, and in the loathsome Mr. Hyde they seem to have found the genuine article—although Stevenson is quick to tell us, through Enfield, that *outwardly* there appears to be nothing much wrong with Hyde. Although he's no John Travolta, he's certainly no Michael Landon sporting a pelt above his high school jacket, either.

Hyde, Enfield admits to Utterson, "carried it off like Satan." When Enfield demands compensation in the name of the little girl, Hyde disappears through the door under discussion and returns a short time later with a hundred pounds, ten in gold and a check for the balance. Although Enfield won't tell, we find out in due course that the signature on the check was that of Henry Jekyll.

Enfield closes his account with one of the most telling descriptions of the Werewolf in all of horror fiction. Although it describes very little in the way we usually think of description, it says a great deal—we all know what Stevenson means, and he knew we would, because he knew, apparently, that all of us are old hands at watching for the mutant:

> He is not easy to describe. There is something wrong with his appearance; something displeasing, something downright detestable. I never saw a man I so disliked,

and yet I scarcely know why. He must be deformed somewhere; he gives a strong feeling of deformity, although I
couldn't specify the point. He's an extraordinary looking man, and yet I can really name nothing out of the
way. . . . And it's not for want of memory; for I declare I
can see him this moment.

It was Rudyard Kipling, years later and in another tale, who
named what was bothering Enfield about Mr. Hyde. Wolfsbane and potions aside (and Stevenson himself dismissed the
device of the smoking potion as "so much hugger-mugger"), it
is very simple: somewhere upon Mr. Hyde, Enfield sensed what
Kipling called the Mark of the Beast.

8

Utterson has information of his own with which Enfield's tale
neatly dovetails (God, the construction of Stevenson's novel is
beautiful; it ticks smoothly away like a well-made watch). He
has custody of Jekyll's will and knows that Jekyll's heir is Edward Hyde. He also knows that the door Enfield has pointed
out stands at the back of Jekyll's townhouse.

A bit of a swerve off the main road here. *Dr. Jekyll and Mr.
Hyde* was published a good three decades before the ideas of
Sigmund Freud would begin to surface, but in the first two sections of Stevenson's novella the author gives us a startlingly apt
metaphor for Freud's idea of the conscious and subconscious
minds—or, to be more specific, the contrast between superego
and id. Here is one large block of buildings. On Jekyll's side,
the side presented to the public eye, it seems a lovely, grace-
ful building, inhabited by one of London's most respected
physicians. On the other side—but still a part of the same
building—we find rubbish and squalor, people abroad on ques-
tionable errands at three in the morning, and that "blistered
and distained door" set in "a blind forehead of discoloured
wall." On Jekyll's side, all things are in order and life goes its
steady Apollonian round. On the other side, Dionysus prances

unfettered. Enter Jekyll here, exit Hyde there. Even if you're an anti-Freudian and won't grant Stevenson's insight into the human psyche, you'll perhaps grant that the building serves as a nice symbol for the duality of human nature.

Well, back to business. The next witness of any real importance in the case is a maid who witnesses the murder which turns Hyde into a fugitive from the scaffold. It's the murder of Sir Danvers Carew, and as Stevenson sketches it for us we hear echoes of every nasty murder to hit the tabloids in our time: Richard Speck and the student nurses, Juan Corona, even the unfortunate Dr. Herman Tarnower. Here is the beast caught in the act of pulling down its weak and unsuspecting prey, acting not with cunning and intelligence but only with stupid, nihilistic violence. Can anything be worse? Yes, apparently one thing: his face is not so terribly different from the face you and I see in the bathroom mirror each morning.

> And then all of a sudden he broke out in a great flame of anger, stamping with his foot, brandishing the cane, and carrying on . . . like a madman. The old gentleman took a step back, with the air of one very much surprised and a trifle hurt; and at that Mr. Hyde broke out of all bonds and clubbed him to the earth. And next moment, with ape-like fury, he was trampling his victim under foot and hailing down a storm of blows, under which the bones were audibly shattered and the body jumped upon the roadway. At the horror of these sights and sounds, the maid fainted.

All that's really lacking here to make the tabloid picture complete is a scrawl of LITTLE PIGGIES or HELTER SKELTER on a nearby wall, written in the victim's blood. Stevenson further informs us that "The stick with which the deed had been done, although it was of some rare and very tough and heavy wood, had broken in the middle under the stress of this insensate cruelty; and one splintered half had rolled in the neighbouring gutter. . . ."

Stevenson, here and in other places, describes Hyde as "ape-like." He suggests that Hyde, like Michael Landon in *I Was a Teenage Werewolf,* is a step backward along the evolutionary scale, something vicious in the human makeup that has not yet been bred out . . . and isn't that what really frightens us in the myth of the Werewolf? This is inside evil with a vengeance, and it is no wonder that clergymen of Stevenson's day hailed his story. They apparently knew a parable when they read one, and saw Hyde's vicious caning of Sir Danvers Carew as the old Adam coming out full blast. Stevenson suggests that the Were-wolf's face is our face, and it takes some of the humor out of Lou Costello's famous comeback to Lon Chaney, Jr. in *Abbott and Costello Meet Frankenstein.* Chaney, playing the persecuted skin-changing Larry Talbot, mourns to Costello: "You don't understand. When the moon rises, I'll turn into a wolf." Costello replies: "Yeah . . . you and about five million other guys."

At any rate, Carew's murder leads the police to Hyde's Soho flat. The bird has flown the coop, but the Scotland Yard inspector in charge of the investigation is sure they'll get him, because Hyde has burned his checkbook. "Why, money's life to the man. We have nothing to do but wait for him at the bank, and get out the handbills."

But Hyde, of course, has another identity he can turn to. Jekyll, at last frightened back to reason, determines never to use the potion again. Then he discovers to his horror that the change has begun to occur spontaneously. He has created Hyde to escape the strictures of propriety, but has discovered that evil has its own strictures; in the end he has become Hyde's prisoner. The clergy hailed *Jekyll and Hyde* because they believed the book showed the grim results of allowing man's "baser nature" more than the shortest possible tether; modern readers are more apt to sympathize with Jekyll as a man looking for an escape route—if only for short periods—from the straitjacket of Victorian prudery and morality. Either way, when Utterson and Jekyll's butler, Poole, break into Jekyll's laboratory, Jekyll is dead . . . and it is the body of Hyde which they find. The worst horror of all has occurred; the man has died thinking like Jekyll and looking like Hyde, the secret sin (or the Mark of the Beast, if you prefer) which he hoped to conceal (or to Hyde, if you prefer) stamped indelibly on his face. He concludes his confession with the words, "Here then, as I lay down the pen and proceed to seal up my confession, I bring the life of that unhappy Dr. Jekyll to an end."

It's easy—too easy—to get caught up in the story of Jekyll and his ferocious alter ego as a religious parable told in penny-dreadful terms. It's a moral tale, sure, but it seems to me that it's also a close study of hypocrisy—its causes, its dangers, its damages to the spirit.

Jekyll is the hypocrite who falls into the pit of secret sin; Utterson, the book's real hero, is Jekyll's exact opposite. Because this seems important, not only to Stevenson's book but to the whole idea of the Werewolf, let me take a minute of your time to quote from the book again. Here's how he introduces Utterson to us on page one of *Dr. Jekyll and Mr. Hyde:*

> Mr. Utterson the lawyer was a man of rugged countenance that was never lighted by a smile; cold, scanty, and embarrassed in discourse; backward in sentiment; lean, long, dusty, dreary and yet somehow lovable.* . . . He was austere with himself; drank gin when he was alone to mortify a taste for vintages; and though he enjoyed the theater, had not crossed the doors of one for twenty years.

About the Ramones, an amusing punk-rock band that surfaced some four years ago, Linda Ronstadt is on record as saying, "That music's so tight it's hemorrhoidal." You could say the same thing for Utterson, who fulfills the function of court stenographer in the book and still manages to come off as the story's most engaging character. He's a Victorian prig of the first water, of course, and one would fear for a son or daughter brought up by the old man, but Stevenson's point is that there

---

* I must admit that, after reading Stevenson's description of Utterson, I found myself curious as to just *how* he was lovable!

is as little of the hypocrite in him as there is in any man living. ("We may sin in thought, word, or deed," the old Methodist credo goes, and I suppose that by thinking of fine vintages while he knocks off his gin-and-water, we could say that Utterson is a hypocrite in thought . . . but here we're entering a fuzzy gray area where the concept of free will seems harder to grasp: "The mind is a monkey," Robert Stone's protagonist muses in *Dog Soldiers,* and he is so right.)

The difference between Utterson and Jekyll is that Jekyll would only drink gin to mortify a taste for vintages in public. In the privacy of his own library he's the sort of man who might well drink an entire bottle of good port (and probably congratulate himself on not having to share it, or any of his fine Jamaican cigars, either). Perhaps he would not want to be caught dead attending a risqué play in the West End, but he is more than happy to go as Hyde. Jekyll does not want to mortify *any* of his tastes. He only wants to gratify them in secret.

2

What we're talking about here, at its most basic level, is the old conflict between id and superego, the free will to do evil or to deny it . . . or in Stevenson's own terms, the conflict between mortification and gratification. This old struggle is the cornerstone of Christianity, but if you want to put it in mythic terms, the twinning of Jekyll and Hyde suggests another duality: the aforementioned split between the Apollonian (the creature of intellect, morality, and nobility, "always treading the upward path") and the Dionysian (god of partying and physical gratification; the get-down-and-boogie side of human nature). If you try to take it any further than the mythic, you come damn close to splitting the body and mind altogether . . . which is exactly the impression Jekyll wants to give his friends: that he is a creature of pure mind, with no human tastes or needs at all. It's hard to picture the guy sitting on the jakes with a newspaper.

If we look at the Jekyll and Hyde story as a pagan conflict

between man's Apollonian potential and his Dionysian desires, we see that the Werewolf myth—in nominal disguise—runs through a great many modern horror novels and movies.

Perhaps the best example of all is Alfred Hitchcock's film *Psycho,* although in all deference to the master, the idea was there for the taking in Robert Bloch's novel. Bloch, in fact, had been honing this particular vision of human nature in a number of previous books, including *The Scarf* (which begins with those wonderful, eerie lines: "Fetish? You name it. All I know is that I've always had to have it with me . . .") and *The Deadbeat.* These books are not, at least technically, horror novels; there is nary a monster or supernatural occurrence on view. They are labeled "suspense novels." But if we look at them with that Apollonian/Dionysian conflict in mind, we see that they are very much honor novels; each of them deals with the Dionysian psychopath locked up behind the Apollonian facade of normality . . . but slowly, dreadfully emerging. In short, Bloch has written a number of Werewolf novels in which he has dispensed with the hugger-mugger of the potion or the wolfsbane. What happened with Bloch when he ceased writing his Lovecraftian stories of the supernatural (and he never has, completely; see the recent *Strange Eons)* was not that he ceased being a horror writer; he simply shifted his perspective from the outside (beyond the stars, under the sea, on the Plains of Leng, or in the deserted belfry of a Providence, Rhode Island, church) to the inside . . . to the place where the Werewolf is. It may be that someday these three novels, *The Scarf, The Deadbeat,* and *Psycho,* will be anthologized as a kind of unified triptych, as were James M. Cain's *The Postman Always Rings Twice, Double Indemnity,* and *Mildred Pierce*—for in their own way, the novels that Robert Bloch wrote in the 1950s had every bit as much influence on the course of American fiction as did the Cain "heel-with-a-heart" novels of the 1930s. And although the method of attack is radically different in each case, both the novels of Cain and Bloch are great crime novels; the novels of both adopt a naturalistic view of American life; the novels of both explore the idea of protagonist as antihero; and the novels of both point up the central Apollonian/Dionysian conflict and thus become Werewolf novels.

Psycho, the best known of the three, deals with Norman Bates—and as played by Anthony Perkins in the Hitchcock film, Norman is about as tight-assed and hemorrhoidal as they come. To the observing world (or that small part of it that would care to observe the proprietor of a gone-to-seed backwater motel), Norman is as normal as they come. Charles Whitman, the Apollonian Eagle Scout who went on a Dionysian rampage from the top of the Texas Tower, comes immediately to mind; Norman seems like such a nice fellow. Certainly Janet Leigh sees no reason to fear him in the closing moments of her life.

But Norman is the Werewolf. Only instead of growing hair, his change is effected by donning his dead mother's panties, slip, and dress—and hacking up the guests instead of biting them. As Dr. Jekyll keeps secret rooms in Soho and has his own "Mr. Hyde door" at home, so we discover that Norman has his own secret place where his two personae meet: in this case it is a knothole behind a picture, which he uses to watch the ladies undress.

Psycho is effective because it brings the Werewolf myth home. It is not outside evil, predestination; the fault lies not in our stars but in ourselves. We know that Norman is only outwardly the Werewolf when he's wearing Mom's duds and speaking in Mom's voice; but we have the uneasy suspicion that inside he's the Werewolf *all* the time.

Psycho spawned a score of imitators, most of them immediately recognizable by their titles, which suggested more than a few toys in the attic: *Straitjacket* (Joan Crawford does the ax-wielding honors in this gritty if somewhat overplotted film, made from a Bloch script), *Dementia-13* (Francis Coppola's first feature film), *Nightmare* (a Hammer picture), *Repulsion*. These are only a few of the children of Hitchcock's film, which was adapted for the screen by Joseph Stefano. Stefano went on to pilot television's *Outer Limits,* which we will get to eventually.

10

It would be ridiculous for me to suggest that all modern horror fiction, both in print and on celluloid, can be boiled down to these three archetypes. It would simplify things enormously, but it would be a false simplification, even with the Tarot card of the Ghost thrown in for good measure. It doesn't end with the Thing, the Vampire, and the Werewolf; there are other bogeys out there in the shadows as well. But these three account for a large bloc of modern horror fiction. We can see the blurry shape of the Thing Without a Name in Howard Hawks's *The Thing* (it turns out—rather disappointingly, I always thought—to be big Jim Arness tricked out as a vegetable from space); the Werewolf raises its shaggy head at Olivia de Havilland in *Lady in a Cage* and as Bette Davis in *What Ever Happened to Baby Jane?;* and we can see the shadow of the Vampire in such diverse films as *Them!* and George Romero's *Night of the Living Dead* and *Dawn of the Dead* . . . although in these latter two, the symbolic act of blood-drinking has been replaced by the act of cannibalism itself as the dead chomp into the flesh of their living victims.*

It is also undeniable that filmmakers seem to return again and again to these three great monsters, and I think that in large part it's because they really are archetypes; which is to say, clay that can be easily molded in the hands of clever children, which is exactly what so many of the filmmakers who work in the genre seem to be.

Before leaving these three novels behind, and any kind of in-depth analysis of nineteenth-century supernatural fiction with them (and if you'd like to pursue the subject further, may I recommend H. P. Lovecraft's long essay *Supernatural Horror in Literature?* It is available in a cheap but handsome and durable Dover paperback edition.), it might be wise to backtrack

---

* Romero's *Martin* is a classy and visually sensuous rendering of the Vampire myth, and one of the few examples of the myth consciously examined in film, as Romero contrasts the romantic assumptions so vital to the myth (as in the John Badham version of *Dracula*) with the grisly reality of actually drinking blood as it spurts from the veins of the vampire's chosen victim.

to the beginning and simply offer a tip of the hat to them for the virtues they possess as *novels.*

There always has been a tendency to see the popular stories of yesterday as social documents, moral tracts, history lessons, or the precursors of more interesting fictions which follow (as Polidori's *The Vampyre* foreran *Dracula,* or Lewis's *The Monk,* which in a way sets the stage for Mary Shelley's *Frankenstein*)— as anything, in fact, but novels standing on their own feet, each with its own tale to tell.

When teachers and students turn to the discussion of novels such as *Frankenstein, Dr. Jekyll and Mr. Hyde,* and *Dracula* upon their own terms—that is, as sustained works of craft and imagination—the discussion is often all too short. Teachers are more apt to focus on shortcomings, and students more apt to linger on such amusing antiquities as Dr. Seward's phonograph diary, Quincey P. Morris's hideously overdone drawl, or the monster's lucky grab-bag of philosophic literature.

It's true that none of these books approaches the great novels of the same period, and I will not argue that they do; you need only compare two books of roughly the same period— *Dracula* and *Jude the Obscure,* let's say—to make the point pretty conclusively. But *no* novel survives solely on the strength of an idea—nor on its diction or execution, as so many writers and critics of modern literature seem sincerely to believe . . . these salesmen and saleswomen of beautiful cars with no motors. While *Dracula* is no *Jude,* Stoker's novel of the Count continues to reverberate in the mind long after the more ghoulish and clamorous *Varney the Vampyre* has grown silent; the same is true of Mary Shelley's handling of the Thing Without a Name and Robert Louis Stevenson's handling of the Werewolf myth.

What the would-be writer of "serious" fiction (who would relegate plot and story to a place at the end of a long line headed by diction and that smooth flow of language which most college writing instructors mistakenly equate with style) seems to forget is that novels are engines, just as cars are engines; a Rolls Royce without an engine might as well be the world's most luxurious begonia pot, and a novel in which there is no story becomes nothing but a curiosity, a little mental game. Novels are engines, and whatever we might say about these three, their creators stoked them with enough invention to run each fast and hot and clean.

Oddly enough, only Stevenson was able to stoke the engine successfully more than once. His adventure novels continue to be read, but Stoker's later books, such as *The Jewel of Seven Stars* and *The Lair of the White Worm,* are largely unheard-of and unread except by the most rabid fantasy fans.* Mary Shelley's later gothics have similarly fallen into almost total obscurity.

Each of the three novels we've been discussing is remarkable in some way, not just as a horror tale or as a suspense yarn, but as an example of a much wider genre: that of the novel itself.

When Mary Shelley can leave off belaboring the philosophical implications of Victor Frankenstein's work, she gives us several powerful scenes of desolation and grim horror—most notably, perhaps, in the silent polar wastes as this mutual dance of revenge draws to its close.

Of the three, Bram Stoker is perhaps the most energetic. His book may seem overlong to modern readers, and to modern critics who have decided that one should not be expected to devote any more time to a work of popular fiction than one might devote to a made-for-TV movie (the belief seeming to be that the two are interchangeable), but during its course we are rewarded—if that's the right word—with scenes and images worthy of Doré: Renfield spreading his sugar with all the unflagging patience of the damned; the staking of Lucy; the beheading of the weird sisters by Van Helsing; the Count's final end, which comes in a hail of gunfire and a scary race against darkness.

Dr. Jekyll and Mr. Hyde is a masterpiece of concision—the verdict of Henry James, not myself. In that indispensable little

---

* In all fairness it must be added that Bram Stoker wrote some absolutely champion short stories—"The Squaw" and "The Judge's House" may be the best known. Those who enjoy macabre short fiction could not do better than his collection *Dracula's Guest,* which is stupidly out of print but remains available in the stacks of most public libraries.

handbook by Wilfred Strunk and E. B. White, *The Elements of Style*, the thirteenth rule for good composition reads simply: "Omit needless words." Along with Stephen Crane's *Red Badge of Courage*, Henry James's *The Turn of the Screw*, James M. Cain's *The Postman Always Rings Twice*, and Douglas Fairbairn's *Shoot*, Stevenson's economy-sized horror story could serve as a textbook example for young writers on how Strunk's Rule 13—the three most important words in all of the textbooks ever written on the technique of composition—is best applied. Characterizations are quick but precise; Stevenson's people are sketched but never caricatured. Mood is implied rather than belabored. The narrative is as chopped and lowered as a kid's hot rod.

We'll leave where we picked this up, with the wonder and terror these three great monsters continue to create in the minds of readers. The most overlooked facet of each may be that each succeeds in overleaping reality and entering a world of total fantasy. But we are not left behind in this leap; we are brought along and allowed to view these archetypes of Werewolf, Vampire, and Thing not as figures of myth but as figures of near reality—which is to say, we are brought along for the ride of our lives. And this, at least, surpasses "good."

Man . . . that's great.

CHAPTER IV

*An Annoying
Autobiographical Pause*

Early on, I mentioned that trying to deal successfully with the phenomenon of terror and horror as a media/cultural event during the last thirty years would be impossible without a slice of autobiography. It seems to me that the time to make good on that threat has now arrived. What a drag. But you're stuck with it, if only because I cannot divorce myself from a field in which I am mortally involved.

Readers who find themselves inclining toward some genre on a regular basis—western, private-eye stories, drawing-room mysteries, science fiction, or flat-out adventure yarns—seem rarely to feel the same desire to psychoanalyze their favorite writers' interests (and their own) as do the readers of horror fiction. Secretly or otherwise, there is the feeling that the taste for horror fiction is an abnormal one. I wrote a fairly long essay at the beginning of a book of mine *(Night Shift)*, trying to analyze some of the reasons why people read horror fiction and why I write it. I don't have any interest in reheating that hash here; if you're interested in pursuing that subject, I recommend the introduction to you; all my relatives loved it.

The question here is a more esoteric one: Why do people have such an interest in my interest—and in their own? I believe that, more than anything else, it's because we all have a postulate buried deep in our minds: that an interest in horror is unhealthy and aberrant. So when people say, "Why do you write that stuff?" they are really inviting me to lie down on the couch and explain about the time I was locked in the cellar for three weeks, or my toilet training, or possibly some abnormal sibling rivalry. Nobody wants to know if Arthur Hailey or Harold Robbins took an unusually long time learning to use the potty, because writing about banks and airports and How I Made My First Million are subjects which seem perfectly normal. There is something totally American in wanting to know how things work (which goes a long way toward explaining the phenomenal success of the *Penthouse Forum*, I think; what all those letters are really discussing is the rocketry of intercourse, the possible trajectories of oral sex and the how-to of various exotic positions—all as American as apple pie; *Forum* is simply a sexual plumbing manual for the enthusiastic do-it-yourselfer), but something unsettlingly alien about a taste for monsters, haunted houses, and the Thing that Crawled Out of the Crypt at Midnight. Questioners automatically turn into reasonable facsimiles of that amusing comic-strip psychiatrist Victor De Groot, ignoring the fact that making things up for money—which is what any writer of fiction does—is a pretty bizarre way to earn a living.

In March of 1979, I was invited to be one of three speakers on a panel discussing horror at an event known as the Ides of Mohonk (a once-yearly gathering of mystery writers and fans sponsored by Murder Ink, a nifty mystery-and-detection bookshop in Manhattan). During the course of the panel discussion I told a story that my mother had told me about myself—the event occurred when I was barely four, so perhaps I can be excused for remembering her story of it but not the actual event.

According to Mom, I had gone off to play at a neighbor's house—a house that was near a railroad line. About an hour after I left I came back (she said), as white as a ghost. I would not speak for the rest of that day; I would not tell her why I'd not waited to be picked up or phoned that I wanted to come home; I would not tell her why my chum's mom hadn't walked me back but had allowed me to come alone.

It turned out that the kid I had been playing with had been run over by a freight train while playing on or crossing the tracks (years later, my mother told me they had picked up the pieces in a wicker basket). My mom never knew if I had been near him when it happened, if it had occurred before I even arrived, or if I had wandered away after it happened. Perhaps she had her own ideas on the subject. But as I've said, I have no memory of the incident at all; only of having been told about it some years after the fact.

I told this story in response to a question from the floor. The questioner had asked, "Can you recall anything in your childhood that was particularly terrible?"—in other words, step right in, Mr. King, the doctor will see you now.

Robert Marasco, author of *Burnt Offerings* and *Parlor Games,* said he could not. I offered my train story mostly so the questioner wouldn't be totally disappointed, finishing just as I have here, by saying that I could not actually remember the incident. To which the third panel member, Janet Jeppson (who is a psychiatrist as well as a novelist), said: "But you've been writing about it ever since."

There was an approving murmur from the audience. Here was a pigeonhole where I could be filed . . . here was a by-God *motive.* I wrote *'Salem's Lot, The Shining,* and destroyed the world by plague in *The Stand* because I saw this kid run over by a slow freight in the days of my impressionable youth. I believe this is a totally specious idea—such shoot-from-the-hip psychological judgments are little more than jumped-up astrology.

Not that the past doesn't supply grist for the writer's mill; of course it does. One example: the most vivid dream I can recall came to me when I was about eight. In this dream I saw the body of a hanged man dangling from the arm of a scaffold on a hill. Rocks perched on the shoulders of the corpse, and behind it was a noxious green sky, boiling with clouds. This corpse bore a sign: ROBERT BURNS. But when the wind caused the corpse to turn in the air, I saw that it was my face—rotted and picked by the birds, but obviously mine. And then the corpse opened its eyes and looked at me. I woke up screaming, sure that that dead face would be leaning over me in the dark. Sixteen years later, I was able to use the dream as one of the central images in my novel *'Salem's Lot*. I just changed the name of the corpse to Hubie Marsten. In another dream—this is one which has recurred at times of stress over the last ten years—I am writing a novel in an old house where a homicidal madwoman is reputed to be on the prowl. I'm working in a third-floor room that's very hot. A door on the far side of the room communicates with the attic, and I know—I *know*—she's in there, and that sooner or later the sound of my typewriter will cause her to come after me (perhaps she's a critic for the *Times Book Review*). At any rate, she finally comes through the door like a horrid jack from a child's box, all gray hair and crazed eyes, raving and wielding a meat-ax. And when I run, I discover that somehow the house has exploded outward—it's gotten ever so much bigger—and I'm totally lost. On awakening from this dream, I promptly scoot over to my wife's side of the bed.

But we all have our bad dreams, and we all use them as best we can. Yet it is one thing to use the dream and quite another to suggest the dream is the cause in and of itself. That is to suggest the ridiculous about an interesting subfunction of the human brain that has little or no practical application to the real world. Dreams are only mind-movies, the scraps and remnants of waking life woven into curious little subconscious quilts by the thrifty human mind, which is loath to throw anything out. Some of these mind-movies are of the X-rated variety; some are comedies; some are horror movies.

I think that writers are made, not born or created out of dreams or childhood trauma—that becoming a writer (or a painter, actor, director, dancer, and so on) is a direct result of conscious will. Of course there has to be some talent involved, but talent is a dreadfully cheap commodity, cheaper than table salt. What separates the talented individual from the successful one is a lot of hard work and study; a constant process of honing. Talent is a dull knife that will cut nothing unless it is wielded with great force—a force so great that the knife is not really cutting at all but bludgeoning and breaking (and after two or three of these gargantuan swipes it may succeed in breaking itself... which may be what happened to such disparate writers as Ross Lockridge and Robert E. Howard). Discipline and constant work are the whetstones upon which the dull knife of talent is honed until it becomes sharp enough, hopefully, to cut through even the toughest meat and gristle. No writer, painter, or actor—no *artist*—is ever handed a sharp knife (although a few people are handed almighty big ones; the name we give to the artist with the big knife is "genius"), and we hone with varying degrees of zeal and aptitude.

I'm suggesting that, to be successful, the artist in any field has to be in the right place at the right time. The right time is in the lap of the gods, but any mother's son or daughter can work his/her way to the right place and wait.*

But what is the right place? That is one of the great, amiable mysteries of human experience.

I can remember going dowsing as a kid with my Uncle Clayton, a real old Mainer if one ever lived. We walked out, my Uncle Clayt and I, he in his red-and-black-checked flannel shirt and his old green cap, me in my blue parka. I was about twelve; he might have been in his late forties or his late sixties. He had his dowsing rod under one arm, a wishbone-shaped piece of applewood. Applewood was the best, he said, although birch would do in a pinch. There was also maple, but Uncle Clayt's scripture was that maple was the worst of the dowsing woods, because the grain wasn't true and it would lie if you let it.

At twelve, I was old enough not to believe in Santa Claus, the Tooth Fairy, or dowsing. One of the odd things about our culture is that many parents seem honor-bound to lay all such lovely stories to rest in their children's minds as soon as possible— Dad and Mom may not be able to find time enough to help their little ones with their homework or to read them a story in the evening (let them watch TV instead, TV's a great sitter, lotsa good stories, let 'em watch TV), but they go to great

---

* The thought is not original with me, but I'll be damned if I can remember who said it—so let me just credit that most prolific of writers, Mr. Author Unknown.

pains to discredit poor old Santa and such wonders as dowsing and stumpwater-witchcraft. There's enough time for *that*. Somehow such parents find the fairy tales told on *Gilligan's Island*, *The Odd Couple*, and *The Love Boat* more acceptable. God knows why so many adults have confused enlightenment with emotional and imaginational bank robbery, but they have; they cannot seem to rest content until the wonder has flickered and died out of their children's eyes. (He doesn't mean me, you're whispering to yourself right now—but sir or madam, I just might.) Most parents quite rightly recognize the fact that children are mad, in the classic sense of that word. But I'm not altogether sure that killing Santa Claus or the Tooth Fairy is the same thing as "rationality." For children, the rationality of madness seems to work remarkably well. For one thing, it keeps the thing in the closet at bay.

Uncle Clayt had lost very little of that sense of wonder. Among his other amazing talents (amazing to me, at least) was the ability to line bees—that is, to spot a honeybee bumbling at a flower and then follow it back to its hive, tramping through woods, splashing through bogs, scrambling over deadfalls—his ability to roll his own cigarettes with one hand (always giving them that final eccentric twirl before sticking them into his mouth and lighting them with Diamond matches kept in a small waterproof cannister), and his seemingly endless fund of lore and tales . . . Indian stories, ghost stories, family stories, legends, you name it.

On this day my mother had been complaining to Clayt and his wife, Ella, over dinner about how slowly the water was drawing in the sinks and the toilet tank. She was afraid the well was going dry again. In those days, along about 1959 or 1960, we had a shallow dug well, and it went dry every summer for a month or so. Then my brother and I and our cousin hauled water in a big old tank that another uncle (Uncle Oren, that one was—for many years the best damn carpenter and contractor in southern Maine) had welded together in his workshop. We would perch the tank on the tailgate of an old station wagon and then lug it down to the well in a relay, using big galvanized-steel milk cans. During that dry month or six weeks we drew our drinking water from the town pump.

So Uncle Clayt grabbed me while the women were washing up and told me we were going to dowse my mother a new well. At twelve, it was an interesting enough way to spend some time, but I was skeptical; Uncle Clayt might as well have told me he was going to show me where a flying saucer had landed behind the Methodist meeting hall.

He walked around, green cap tilted back on his head, one of his Bugler cigarettes jutting from the corner of his mouth, applewood stick held in both hands. He held it by the wishbone, wrists rotated outward, his big thumbs pressed firmly against the wood. We walked aimlessly around the back yard, the driveway, the hill where the apple tree stood (and still stands today, although new people live in that little five-room house). And Clayt talked . . . stories about baseball, about an attempt to form a copper-mining concern once upon a time in Kittery, of all places, about how Paul Bunyan was supposed to have turned the course of the Prestile Stream once upon a time to provide water for the logging camps.

And every now and then he would pause, and the rod of that applewood dowser would tremble just a little. He would pause in his story and wait. The trembling might increase to a steady vibration, and then fade out. "You got somethin there, Stevie," he'd say. "Somethin. Not too much." And I would nod wisely, convinced he was doing it all himself. Like the way it's parents, not Santa Claus, who put the presents under the tree, don't you know, or the way they take away the tooth under your pillow after you're asleep and replace it with a dime. But I went along with him. I came from an age of children who wanted to be good, remember; we were taught to "speak when spoken to," and to humor their elders no matter how nutty their ideas might be. This is not a bad way of initiating children into the more exotic realms of human behavior and human belief, by the way; the quiet child (and I was one) is often given walking tours through some extremely bizarre tracts of mental countryside. I did not believe it possible to dowse water with an applewood stick, but I was quite interested in seeing how the trick would be performed.

We walked around onto the front lawn, and the stick began to tremble again. Uncle Clayt brightened. "We got the real thing here," he said. "Look at this, Stevie! She's gonna dive, be damned if she ain't!"

Three steps further along, the applewood rod dove—it simply revolved in Uncle Clayt's hands and pointed straight down. It was a good trick, all right; I could actually hear the tendons in his wrists creak, and there was some strain on his face as he forced the straight part of the wishbone-shaped stick skyward again. As soon as he released the pressure, the stick whipped down at the ground again.

"Got plenty of water here," he said. "You could drink it until Judgment Day and it'd still run. It's close, too."

"Let me try it," I said.

"Well, you got to back off a little first," he said, and we did. We went back to the edge of the driveway.

He gave me the stick, showed me how to hold it with my thumbs cocked just so (wrists outward, thumbs pointing down—"Otherwise, that son of a whore is gonna break your wrists tryin to point when you get over that water," Clayt said), and then he gave me a little push on the ass.

"It don't feel like nothin' but a piece of wood right now, does it?" he asked.

I agreed that this was so.

"But when you start gettin' close to that water, you're gonna feel her come alive," he said. "I mean really *alive,* like it was still on the tree. Oh, applewood's good for dowsing. Nothing beats applewood when you're huntin' wellwater."

So some of what happened could well have been suggestion, and I'm not trying to convince you otherwise, although I've read enough since then to believe that dowsing really does work, at least at some times and for some people and for some crazy reason of its own.* I will say that Uncle Clayt had lulled me into that same state that I have tried again and again to lull the readers of my stories into—that state of believability where the ossified shield of "rationality" has been temporarily laid aside, the suspension of disbelief is at hand, and the sense of wonder is again within reach. And if that's the power of suggestion, it seems okay to me; better than cocaine for the brain.

I started walking toward the spot where Uncle Clayt had been when the rod dove, and I'll be damned if that applewood stick didn't seem to come alive in my hands. It got warm, and it began to move. At first it was a vibration that I could feel but not see, and then the tip of the rod began to jiggle around.

"It's working!" I screamed at Uncle Clayt. "I can *feel* it!"

Clayt got laughing. I got laughing, too—not a hysterical sort of laughter, but one of pure and utter delight. When I got over the spot where the dowsing rod dove for Uncle Clayt, it dove for me; at one moment it was upright, and at the next it was pointing straight down. I can remember two things very clearly about that moment. One was a sensation of weight— how *heavy* that wooden wishbone had become. It seemed I could barely hold it up. It was as if the water was inside the stick instead of in the ground; as if it were fairly *bloated* with water. Clayt had brought the stick up to its original position after it dove. I could not. He took it out of my hands, and as he did I felt the sensation of weight and magnetism break. It did not pass from me to him; it *broke*. It was there at one moment and at the next it was gone.

The other thing I remember is a combined feeling of certainty and mystery. The water was there. Uncle Clayt knew it and I knew it, too. It was down there in the earth, a river caught in rock, for all we knew. It was that feeling of having come to the right place. There are lines of power in the world,

---

* One of the more plausible explanations of the phenomenon is that the stick doesn't dowse the water; the person holding the stick does, and then imputes the ability to the stick. Horses can smell water twelve miles away if the wind is right; why should not a person be able to sense water fifty or a hundred feet underground?

you know—invisible but thrumming with a tremendous, scary load of energy. Every now and then someone will stumble over one and get fried, or grasp one in the right way and set it to work. But you have to find one.

Clayt drove a stake into the ground where we had felt the pull of the water. The well did indeed go dry—in July instead of August, as a matter of fact—and as there was no money for a new well that year, the water tank made its yearly summer appearance on the tailgate of the station wagon, and my brother, my cousin, and I made our round trips down to the old well with the milk cans of water again. We did the same the following summer. But around 1963 or '64, we had the artesian well drilled.

By then the stake Clayt had driven was long gone, but I remembered its location well enough. The well-drillers located their rig, that big red gadget that looked so much like some child's Erector Set vision of a praying mantis, within three feet of where the stake had been (and in my mind now I can still hear Mom moaning about the wet clay that was spewed all over our front lawn). They had to go down less than a hundred feet—and as Clayt had said on that Sunday when he and I walked out with the applewood rod, there was plenty of water. We could have drunk it until Judgment Day and it still would have kept running.

2

I'm working my way back to the main point, this main point being why it is useless to ask any writer what he writes about. You might as well ask the rose why it is red. Talent, like the water Uncle Clayt doused out under our lawn after dinner one Sunday afternoon, is there all along—except, instead of water, it's more like a big rude lump of ore. It can be refined—or honed, to return to an earlier image—and it can be set to work in an infinite number of ways. The honing and the setting-to-work are simple operations, completely under the control of the fledgling writer. Refining talent is merely a matter of exercise.

If you work out with weights for fifteen minutes a day over a course of ten years, you're gonna get muscles. If you write for an hour and a half a day for ten years, you're gonna turn into a good writer.*

But what's down there? That's the one great variable, the wild card in the deck. I don't think the writer has any control over that. When you drill a well and get the water, you send a sample to your state's Water Testing Agency and get back a readout—and the mineral content can vary amazingly. All H_2O is not created equal. Similarly, while Joyce Carol Oates and Harold Robbins are both writing English, they are really not writing the same language at all.

There is a certain fascination inherent in the discovery of talent (although it is a difficult thing to write well about, and something I will not attempt at all—"Leave it to the poets!" he cried. "The poets know how to talk about that, or at least they think they do, and it comes to the same; so leave it to the poets!"), that magical moment when the dowsing rod turns downward and you know that it is here, right *here*. There's also a certain fascination in the actual drilling of the well, refining the ore, honing the knife (also a difficult thing to write well about; one saga of the Heroic Struggle of the Young and Virile Writer that has always struck me well is Herman Wouk's *Youngblood Hawke*), but what I really want to spend a couple of minutes talking about is another kind of dowsing—not the actual discovery of talent, but that lightning stroke which occurs when you discover not talent itself, but the particular direction in which that talent will incline. It is the moment, if you will, when a Little Leaguer discovers, not that he or she can pitch (which he/she may have known for some time), but that she or he has a particular ability to throw the good live fastball or to

---

* But, I hasten to add, only if you have the talent there to begin with. You can spend ten years refining common earth and come out at the end with nothing but common earth, sifted flame. I have been playing guitar since the age of fourteen, and at the age of thirty-three I've not progressed much beyond where I was at sixteen, playing "Louie, Louie" and "Little Deuce Coupe" on rhythm guitar with a group called the MoonSpinners. I can play a little, and it sure cheers me up when I've got the blues, but I think Eric Clapton is still safe.

pop a curve that rises or dips outrageously. This is also a particularly fine moment. And all of this, I hope, will justify the bit of autobiography that follows. It doesn't try to explain my own interest in the danse macabre, or justify it, or psychoanalyze it; it only tries to set the stage for an interest that has proved to be lifelong, profitable, and pleasant . . . except, of course, when the madwoman pops out of her attic in that unpleasant dreamhouse in which my subconscious places me every four months or so.

3

My mother's people were named Pillsbury, and came originally (or so she said) from the same family that produced the Pillsburys who now make cake mixes and flour. The difference between the two branches of the family, Mom said, was that the flour-Pillsburys moved west to make their fortune, while our people stayed shirttail but honest on the coast of Maine. My grandmother, Nellie Pillsbury (née Fogg), was one of the first women ever to graduate from Gorham Normal School— the class of '02, I think. She died at age eighty-five, blind and bedridden, but still able to decline Latin verbs and name all of the presidents up to Truman. My maternal grandfather was a carpenter and, for a brief time, Winslow Homer's handyman.

My father's people came from Peru, Indiana, and much further back, from Ireland. The Pillsburys, of good Anglo-Saxon stock, were levelheaded and practical. My father apparently came from a long line of eccentrics; his sister, my aunt Betty, had mental fugues (my mother believed her to be a manic-depressive, but then, Mom never would have run for president of the Aunt Betty Fan Club), my paternal grandmother enjoyed frying half a loaf of bread in bacon fat for breakfast, and my paternal grandfather, who stood six feet six and weighed a cool three hundred and fifty pounds, dropped dead at the age of thirty-two while running to catch a train. Or so the story goes.

I've been saying that it's impossible to tell why one particular area strikes the mind with all the peculiar force of obsession, but that it's very possible to pinpoint that moment when the interest was discovered—the moment, if you will, when the dowsing rod turns suddenly and emphatically down toward hidden water. Put another way, talent is only a compass, and we'll not discuss why it points toward magnetic north; instead we'll treat briefly of that moment when the needle actually swings toward that great point of attraction.

It has always seemed peculiar to me that I owe that moment in my own life to my father, who left my mother when I was two and my brother, David, four. I don't remember him at all, but in the few pictures of him I've seen, he is a man of average height, handsome in a 1940s sort of way, a bit podgy, bespectacled. He was a merchant mariner during World War II, crossing the North Atlantic and playing German roulette with the U-boats. His worst fear, my mother said, was not of the submarines but of having his master's license revoked because of his poor eyesight—while on land, he had a habit of driving over curbs and through stoplights. My own eyesight is similar; they look like glasses, but sometimes I think they're a couple of Coke-bottle bottoms up there on my face.

Don King was a man with an itchy foot. My brother was born in 1945, I was born in 1947, and in 1949 my father was seen no more . . . although in 1964, during the troubles in the Congo, my mother insisted that she had seen him in a newsclip of white mercenaries fighting for one side or the other. I suppose it is just barely possible. By then he would have been in his late forties or early fifties. If it *was* so, I sure hope he had his lenses corrected in the interim.

After my father took off, my mother landed on her feet, scrambling. My brother and I didn't see a great deal of her over the next nine years. She worked at a succession of low-paying jobs: presser in a laundry, doughnut-maker on the night shift at a bakery, store clerk, housekeeper. She was a talented pianist and a woman with a great and sometimes eccentric sense of humor, and somehow she kept things together, as women before her have done and as other women are doing even now as we speak. We never had a car (nor a TV set until 1956), but we never missed any meals.

We hopscotched our way across the country during those nine years, always returning to New England. In 1958 we returned to Maine for good. My grandfather and grandmother were into their eighties, and the family hired my mother to care for them in their declining years.

This was in Durham, Maine, and while all these family ramblings may seem far from the point, we're getting near to it now. About a quarter of a mile away from the small house in Durham where my brother and I finished our growing up, there was a lovely brick house where my mother's sister, Ethelyn Pillsbury Flaws, and her husband, Oren, lived. Over the Flaws's garage was a lovely, long attic room with loose, rumbling boards and that entrancing attic smell.

At that time the attic connected with a whole complex of outbuildings, which in turn finally led to a great old barn—all of these buildings smelling intoxicatingly of sweet hay long departed. But there was a reminder of the days when animals had been kept in the barn. If one climbed to the third loft, one could observe the skeletons of several chickens that had apparently died of some strange disease up there. It was a pilgrimage I made often; there was something fascinating about those chicken skeletons, lying in a drift of feathers as ephemeral as moondust, some secret in the black sockets where their eyes had once been. . . .

But the attic over the garage was a kind of family museum. Everyone on the Pillsbury side of the family had stored things up there from time to time, from furniture to photographs, and there was just room for a small boy to twist and turn his way along narrow aisles, ducking under the arm of a standing lamp or stepping over a crate of old wallpaper samples that someone had wanted saved for some forgotten reason.

My brother and I were not actually forbidden the attic, but my Aunt Ethelyn frowned on our visits up there because the floorboards had only been laid, not nailed, and some were missing. It would have been easy enough, I suppose, to trip and go headfirst through a hole and down to the concrete floor below—or into the bed of my Uncle Oren's green Chevy pickup truck.

For me, on a cold fall day in 1959 or 1960, the attic over my aunt and uncle's garage was the place where that interior dowsing rod suddenly turned over, where the compass needle swung emphatically toward some mental true north. That was the day I happened to come on a box of my father's books . . . paperbacks from the mid-forties.

There was a lot of my mother and father's married life in the attic, and I can understand how, in the wake of his sudden disappearance from her life, she would want to take as many of his things as possible and put them away in a dark place. It was there, a year or two earlier, that my brother found a reel of movie film my father had taken on shipboard. Dave and I pooled some money we had saved (without my mother's knowledge), rented a movie projector, and watched it over and over again in fascinated silence. My father turned the camera over to someone else at one point and there he is, Donald King of Peru, Indiana, standing against the rail. He raises his hand, smiles, unknowingly waves to sons who were then not even conceived. We rewound it, watched it, rewound it, watched it again. And again. Hi, Dad; wonder where you are now.

In another box there were piles of his merchant marine manuals; in another, scrapbooks of stuff from foreign countries. My mother told me that while he would go around with a paperback western stuffed into his back pocket, his real interest was in science fiction and horror stories. He tried his own hand at a number of tales of this type, submitting them to the popular men's magazines of the day, *Bluebook* and *Argosy* among them. He ultimately published nothing ("Your father didn't have a great deal of stick-to-it in his nature," my mother once told me dryly, and that was about as close as she ever came to ranking him out), but he did get several personal rejection notes; "This-won't-do-but-send-us-more" notes I used to call them in my teens and early twenties, when I collected a good many of my own (during periods of depression I would sometimes wonder what it would be like to blow your nose on a rejection slip).

The box I found that day was a treasure trove of old Avon paperbacks. Avon, in those days, was the one paperback publisher committed to fantasy and weird fiction. I remember those books with great affection—particularly the shiny overcoating which all Avons bore, a material that was a cross between isinglass and Saran Wrap. When and if the story lagged, you could peel this shiny stuff off the cover in long strips. It made a perfectly wonderful noise. And although it wanders from the subject, I also remember the forties Dell paperbacks with love—they were all mysteries back then, and on the back of each was a luxurious map showing the scene of the crime.

One of those books was an Avon "sampler"—the word *anthology* was apparently considered too esoteric for readers of this sort of material to grasp. It contained stories by Frank Belknap Long ("The Hounds of Tindalos"), Zelia Bishop ("The Curse of Yig"), and a host of other tales culled from the early days of *Weird Tales* magazine. Two of the others were novels by A. Merritt—*Burn, Witch, Burn* (not to be confused with the later Fritz Leiber novel, *Conjure Wife*) and *The Metal Monster*.

The pick of the litter, however, was an H. P. Lovecraft collection from 1947 called *The Lurking Fear and Other Stories*. I remember the picture on the cover very well: a cemetery (somewhere near Providence, one assumes!) at night, and coming out from beneath a tombstone, a loathsome green thing with long fangs and burning red eyes. Behind it, suggested but not graphically drawn, was a tunnel leading down into the bowels of the earth. Since then I've seen literally hundreds of editions of Lovecraft, yet that remains the one which best sums up H.P.L.'s work for me . . . and I've no idea who the artist might have been.

That box of books wasn't my first encounter with horror, of course. I think that in America you would have to be blind and deaf not to have come in contact with at least one creature or bogey by the age of ten or twelve. But it was my first encounter with serious fantasy-horror fiction. Lovecraft has been called a hack, a description I would dispute vigorously, but whether he was or wasn't, and whether he was a writer of popular fiction or a writer of so-called "literary fiction" (depending on your critical bent), really doesn't matter very much in this context, because either way, the man himself took his work seriously. And it showed. So that book, courtesy of my departed father, was my first taste of a world that went deeper than the B-pictures which played at the movies on Saturday afternoon or the boys' fiction of Carl Carmer and Roy Rockwell. When Lovecraft wrote "The Rats in the Walls" and "Pickman's Model," he wasn't simply kidding around or trying to pick up a few extra bucks; he *meant* it, and it was his seriousness as much as anything else which that interior dowsing rod responded to, I think.

I took the books out of the attic with me. My aunt, who was a grammar school teacher and the soul of practicality down to her shoes, disapproved of them strenuously, but I held onto them. That day and the next, I visited the Plains of Leng for the first time; made my first acquaintance with that quaint pre-OPEC Arab, Abdul Alhazred (author of *The Necronomicon*, which, to the best of my knowledge, has never been offered to members of the Book-of-the-Month Club or the Literary Guild, although a copy was reputed to have been kept for years under lock and key in the Special Collections vault at Miskatonic University); visited the towns of Dunwich and Arkham, Massachusetts; and was, most of all, transported by the bleak and creeping terror of "The Colour Out of Space."

A week or two later all of those books disappeared, and I never saw them again. I've always suspected that my aunt Ethelyn might have been an unindicted co-conspirator in that case . . . not that it mattered in the long run. I was on my way. Lovecraft—courtesy of my father—opened the way for me, as he had done for others before me: Robert Bloch, Clark Ashton Smith, Frank Belknap Long, Fritz Leiber, and Ray Bradbury among them. And while Lovecraft, who died before the Second

World War could fulfill many of his visions of unimaginable horror, does not figure largely in this book, the reader would do well to remember that it is his shadow, so long and gaunt, and his eyes, so dark and puritanical, which overlie almost all of the important horror fiction that has come since. It is his eyes I remember best from the first photograph of him I ever saw . . . eyes like those in the old portraits which still hang in many New England houses, black eyes which seem to look inward as well as outward.

Eyes that seem to follow you.

4

The first movie I can remember seeing as a kid was *Creature from the Black Lagoon*. It was at the drive-in, and unless it was a second-run job I must have been about seven, because the film, which starred Richard Carlson and Richard Denning, was released in 1954. It was also originally released in 3-D, but I cannot remember wearing the glasses, so perhaps I did see a rerelease.

I remember only one scene clearly from the movie, but it left a lasting impression. The hero (Carlson) and the heroine (Julia Adams, who looked absolutely spectacular in a one-piece white bathing suit) are on an expedition somewhere in the Amazon basin. They make their way up a swampy, narrow waterway and into a wide pond that seems an idyllic South American version of the Garden of Eden.

But the creature is lurking—naturally. It's a scaly, batrachian monster that is remarkably like Lovecraft's half-breed, degenerate aberrations—the crazed and blasphemous results of liaisons between gods and human women (I told you it's difficult to get away from Lovecraft). This monster is slowly and patiently barricading the mouth of the stream with sticks and branches, irrevocably sealing the party of anthropologists in.

I was barely old enough to read at that time, the discovery of my father's box of weird fiction still years away. I have a vague memory of boyfriends in my mom's life during that period—from 1952 until 1958 or so; enough of a memory to be sure she had a social life, not enough to even guess if she had a sex life. There was Norville, who smoked Luckies and kept three fans going in this two-room apartment during the summer; and there was Milt, who drove a Buick and wore gigantic blue shorts in the summertime; and another fellow, very small, who was, I believe, a cook in a French restaurant. So far as I know, my mother came close to marrying none of them. She'd gone that route once. Also, that was a time when a woman, once married, became a shadow figure in the process of decision-making and bread-winning. I think my mom, who could be stubborn, intractable, grimly persevering and nearly impossible to discourage, had gotten a taste for captaining her own life. And so she went out with guys, but none of them became permanent fixtures.

It was Milt we were out with that night, he of the Buick and the large blue shorts. He seemed to genuinely like my brother and me, and to genuinely not mind having us along in the back seat from time to time (it may be that when you have reached the calmer waters of your early forties, the idea of necking at the drive-in no longer appeals so strongly . . . even if you have a Buick as large as a cabin cruiser to do it in). By the time the Creature made his appearance, my brother had slithered down onto the floor of the back and had fallen asleep. My mother and Milt were talking, perhaps passing a Kool back and forth. They don't matter, at least not in this context; nothing matters except the big black-and-white images up on the screen, where the unspeakable Thing is walling the handsome hero and the sexy heroine into . . . into . . . *the Black Lagoon*!

I knew, watching, that the Creature had become *my* Creature; I had bought it. Even to a seven-year-old, it was not a terribly convincing Creature. I did not know then it was good old Ricou Browning, the famed underwater stuntman, in a molded latex suit, but I surely knew it was some guy in some kind of a monster suit . . . just as I knew that, later on that night, he would visit me in the black lagoon of my dreams, looking much more realistic. He might be waiting in the closet when we got back; he might be standing slumped in the blackness of the bathroom at the end of the hall, stinking of algae and swamp rot, all ready for a post-midnight snack of small boy. Seven isn't old, but it is old enough to know that you get what you pay for. You own it, you bought it, it's yours. It is old enough to feel the dowser suddenly come alive, grow heavy, and roll over in your hands, pointing at hidden water.

My reaction to the Creature on that night was perhaps the perfect reaction, the one every writer of horror fiction or director who has worked in the field hopes for when he or she uncaps a pen or a lens: total emotional involvement, pretty much undiluted by any real thinking process—and you understand, don't you, that when it comes to horror movies, the only thought process really necessary to break the mood is for a friend to lean over and whisper, "See the zipper running down his back?"

I think that only people who have worked in the field for some time truly understand how fragile this stuff really is, and what an amazing commitment it imposes on the reader or viewer of intellect and maturity. When Coleridge spoke of "the suspension of disbelief" in his essay on imaginative poetry, I believe he knew that disbelief is not like a balloon, which may be suspended in air with a minimum of effort; it is like a lead weight, which has to be hoisted with a clean and a jerk and held up by main force. Disbelief isn't light; it's heavy. The difference in sales between Arthur Hailey and H. P. Lovecraft may exist because everyone believes in cars and banks, but it takes a sophisticated and muscular intellectual act to believe, even for a little while, in Nyarlathotep, the Blind Faceless One, the Howler in the Night. And whenever I run into someone who expresses a feeling along the lines of, "I don't read fantasy or go to any of those movies; none of it's real," I feel a kind of sympathy. They simply can't lift the weight of fantasy. The muscles of the imagination have grown too weak.

In this sense, kids are the perfect audience for horror. The paradox is this: children, who are physically quite weak, lift the weight of unbelief with ease. They are the jugglers of the invisible world—a perfectly understandable phenomenon when you consider the perspective they must view things from. Children deftly manipulate the logistics of Santa Claus's entry on Christmas Eve (he can get down small chimneys by making himself small, and if there's no chimney there's the letter slot, and if there's no letter slot there's always the crack under the door), the Easter Bunny, God (big guy, sorta old, white beard, throne), Jesus ("How do you think he turned the water into wine?" I asked my son Joe when he—Joe, not Jesus—was five; Joe's idea was that he had something "kinda like magic Kool-Aid, you get what I mean?"), the devil (big guy, red skin, horse feet, tail with an arrow on the end of it, Snidely Whiplash moustache), Ronald McDonald, the Burger King, the Keebler Elves, Dorothy and Toto, the Lone Ranger and Tonto, a thousand more.

Most parents think they understand this openness better than, in many cases, they actually do, and try to keep their children away from anything that smacks too much of horror and terror—"Rated PG (or G in the case of *The Andromeda Strain*), but may be too intense for younger children," the ads for *Jaws* read—believing, I suppose, that to allow their kids to go to a real horror movie would be tantamount to rolling a live hand grenade into a nursery school.

But one of the odd Döppler effects that seems to occur during the selective forgetting that is so much a part of "growing up" is the fact that almost *everything* has a scare potential for the child under eight. Children are literally afraid of their own shadows at the right time and place. There is the story of the four-year-old who refused to go to bed at night without a light on in his closet. His parents at last discovered he was frightened of a creature he had heard his father speak of often; this creature, which had grown large and dreadful in the child's imagination, was the "twi-night double-header."

Seen in this light, even Disney movies are minefields of terror, and the animated cartoons, which will apparently be released and re-released even unto the end of the world,* are usually the worst offenders. There are adults today, who, when questioned, will tell you that the most frightening thing they saw at the movies as children was Bambi's mother shot by the hunter, or Bambi and his father running before the forest fire. Other Disney memories which are right up there with the batrachian horror inhabiting the Black Lagoon include the marching brooms that have gone totally out of control in *Fantasia* (and for the small child, the real horror inherent in the situation is probably buried in the implied father-son relationship between Mickey Mouse and the old sorcerer; those brooms are making a terrible mess, and when the sorcerer/father gets home, there may be PUNISHMENT. . . . This sequence might well send the child of strict parents into an ecstasy of terror); the night on Bald Mountain from the same film; the witches in *Snow White* and *Sleeping Beauty,* one with her enticingly red poisoned apple (and what small child is not taught early to fear the idea of POISON?), the other with her deadly spinning wheel; this holds all the way up to the relatively innocuous *One Hundred and One Dalmatians,* which features the logical granddaughter of those Disney witches from the thirties and forties—the evil Cruella DeVille, with her scrawny, nasty face, her loud voice (grownups sometimes forget how terrified young children are of loud voices, which come from the giants of their world, the adults), and her plan to kill all the dalmatian puppies (read "children," if you're a little person) and turn them into dogskin coats.

---

* Dennis Etchison (see the Forenote to the 1983 Edition) writes: "Virtually all of the 3-D movies made in the fifties were made using the Polaroid process (the *only* exception I know of is *Robot Monster*). The Polaroid process did not use red-and-green (or red-and-blue) glasses, but clear gray leases; hence we were able to see many of (the films) in full Technicolor, since the glasses added no color of their own. The confusion arises because reissues of a select few *black and white films* (italics mine) in recent years have been in a single-strip, one-projector, red-and-green anaglyphic 3-D, a cheapjack simulation of the original process . . . every other 3-D film we remember from the fifties was originally shown as Polaroid with clear gray glasses."

Dennis further points out that 3-D is back with a vengeance *(Parasite, Friday the 13th Part III, Spacehunter: Adventures in the Forbidden Zone, Treasure of the Four Crowns).* He suggests that "bi-polarized permanent lenses are available for die-hard fans," but a theater manager suggested to me that a pair of off-the-rack Foster Grant polarized sunglasses—clip-on if you wear prescription specs—would do the trick nicely for under twelve bucks. Ain't modern technology wonderful?

Yet it is the parents, of course, who continue to underwrite the Disney procedure of release and rerelease, often discovering goosebumps on their own arms as they rediscover what terrified them as children . . . because what the good horror film (or horror sequence in what may be billed a "comedy" or an "animated cartoon") does above all else is to knock the adult props out from under us and tumble us back down the slide into childhood. And there our own shadow may once again become that of a mean dog, a gaping mouth, or a beckoning dark figure.

Perhaps the supreme realization of this return to childhood comes in David Cronenberg's marvelous horror film *The Brood*, where a disturbed woman is literally producing "children of rage" who go out and murder the members of her family, one by one. About halfway through the film, her father sits dispiritedly on the bed in an upstairs room, drinking and mourning his wife, who has been the first to feel the wrath of the brood. We cut to the bed itself . . . and clawed hands suddenly reach out from beneath it and dig into the carpeting near the doomed father's shoes. And so Cronenberg pushes us down the slide; we are four again, and all of our worst surmises about what might be lurking under the bed have turned out to be true.

The irony of all this is that children are better able to deal with fantasy and terror *on its own terms* than their elders are. You'll note I've italicized the phrase "on its own terms." An adult is able to deal with the cataclysmic terror of something like *The Texas Chainsaw Massacre* because he or she understands that it is all make-believe, and that when the take is done the dead people will simply get up and wash off the stage blood. The child is not so able to make this distinction, and *Chainsaw Massacre* is quite rightly rated R. Little kids do not need this scene, any more than they need the one at the end of *The Fury* where John Cassavetes quite literally blows apart. But the point is, if you put a little kid of six in the front row at a screening of *The Texas Chainsaw Massacre* along with an adult who was temporarily unable to distinguish between make-believe and "real things" (as Danny Torrance, the little boy in

The Shining puts it)—if, for instance, you had given the adult a hit of Yellow Sunshine LSD about two hours before the movie started—my guess is that the kid would have maybe a week's worth of bad dreams. The adult might spend a year or so in a rubber room, writing home with Crayolas.

A certain amount of fantasy and horror in a child's life seems to me a perfectly okay, useful sort of thing. Because of the size of their imaginative capacity, children are able to handle it, and because of their unique position in life, they are able to put such feelings to work. They understand their position very well, too. Even in such a relatively ordered society as our own, they understand that their survival is a matter almost totally out of their hands. Children are "dependents" up until the age of eight or so in every sense of the word; dependent on mother and father (or some reasonable facsimile thereof) not only for food, clothing, and shelter, but dependent on them not to crash the car into a bridge abutment, to meet the school bus on time, to walk them home from Cub Scouts or Brownies, to buy medicines with childproof caps, dependent on them to make sure they don't electrocute themselves while screwing around with the toaster or while trying to play with Barbie's Beauty Salon in the bathtub.

Running directly counter to this necessary dependence is the survival directive built into all of us. The child realizes his or her essential lack of control, and I suspect it is this very realization which makes the child uneasy. It is the same sort of free-floating anxiety that many air travelers feel. They are not afraid because they believe air travel to be unsafe; they are afraid because they have surrendered control, and if something goes wrong all they can do is sit there clutching air-sick bags or the inflight magazine. To surrender control runs counter to the survival directive. Conversely, while a thinking, informed person may understand intellectually that travel by car is much more dangerous than flying, he or she is still apt to feel much more comfortable behind the wheel, because she/he has control . . . or at least an illusion of it.

This hidden hostility and anxiety toward the airline pilots

of their lives may be one explanation why, like the Disney pictures which are released during school vacations in perpetuity, the old fairy tales also seem to go on forever. A parent who would raise his or her hands in horror at the thought of taking his/her child to see *Dracula* or *The Changeling* (with its pervasive imagery of the drowning child) would be unlikely to object to the baby sitter reading "Hansel and Gretel" to the child before bedtime. But consider: the tale of Hansel and Gretel begins with deliberate abandonment (oh yes, the stepmother masterminds that one, but she is the symbolic mother all the same, and the father is a spaghetti-brained nerd who goes along with everything she suggests even though he knows it's wrong—thus we can see her as amoral, him as actively evil in the Biblical and Miltonian sense), it progresses to kidnapping (the witch in the candy house), enslavement, illegal detention, and finally justifiable homicide and cremation. Most mothers and fathers would never take their children to see *Survive*, that quicky Mexican exploitation flick about the rugby players who survived the aftermath of a plane crash in the Andes by eating their dead teammates, but these same parents find little to object to in "Hansel and Gretel," where the witch is fattening the children up so she can eat them. We give this stuff to the kids almost instinctively, understanding on a deeper level, perhaps, that such fairy stories are the perfect points of crystallization for those fears and hostilities.

Even anxiety-ridden air travelers have their own fairy tales—all those *Airport* movies, which, like "Hansel and Gretel" and all those Disney cartoons, show every sign of going on forever . . . but which should only be viewed on Thanksgivings, since all of them feature a large cast of turkeys.

My gut reaction to *Creature from the Black Lagoon* on that long-ago night was a kind of terrible, waking swoon. The nightmare was happening right in front of me; every hideous possibility that human flesh is heir to was being played out on that drive-in screen.

Approximately twenty-two years later, I had a chance to see *Creature from the Black Lagoon* again—not on TV, with any kind of dramatic build and mood broken up by adverts for used cars, K-Tel disco anthologies, and Underalls pantyhose, thank God, but intact, uncut . . . and even in 3-D. Guys like me who wear glasses have a hell of a time with 3-D, you know; ask anyone who wears specs how they like those nifty little cardboard glasses they give you when you walk in the door. If 3-D ever comes back in a big way, I'm going to take myself down to the local Pearle Vision Center and invest seventy bucks in a special pair of prescription lenses: one red, one blue. Annoying glasses aside, I should add that I took my son Joe with me—he was then five, about the age I had been myself, that night at the drive-in (and imagine my surprise—my *rueful* surprise— to discover that the movie which had so terrified me on that long-ago night had been rated G by the MPAA . . . just like the Disney pictures).*

As a result, I had a chance to experience that weird doubling back in time that I believe most parents only experience at the Disney films with their children, or when reading them the Pooh books or perhaps taking them to the Shrine or the Barnum & Bailey circus. A popular record is apt to create a particular "set" in a listener's mind, precisely because of its brief life of six weeks to three months, and "golden oldies" continue to be played because they are the emotional equivalent of freeze-dried coffee. When the Beach Boys come on the radio singing "Help Me, Rhonda," there is always that wonderful second or two when I can reexperience the wonderful, guilty joy of copping my first feel (and if you do the mental subtraction from my present age of thirty-three, you'll see that I was a little backward in that respect). Movies and books do the same thing, although I would argue that the mental set, its depth

---

* In one of my favorite Arthur C. Clarke stories, this actually happens. In this vignette, aliens from space land on earth after the Big One has finally gone down. As the story closes, the best brains of this alien culture are trying to figure out the meaning of a film they have found and learned how to play back. The film ends with the words *A Walt Disney Production.* I have moments when I really believe that there would be no better epitaph for the human race, or for a world where the only sentient being absolutely guaranteed of immortality is not Hitler, Charlemagne, Albert Schweitzer, or even Jesus Christ—but is, instead, Richard M. Nixon, whose name is engraved on a plaque placed on the airless surface of the moon.

and texture, tends to be a little richer, a little more complex, when reexperiencing films, and a lot more complex when dealing with books.

With Joe that day I experienced *Creature from the Black Lagoon* from the other end of the telescope, but this particular theory of set identification still applied; in fact, it prevailed. Time and age and experience have all left their marks on me, just as they have on you; time is not a river, as Einstein theorized—it's a big fucking buffalo herd that runs us down and eventually mashes us into the ground, dead and bleeding, with a hearing-aid plugged into one ear and a colostomy bag instead of a .44 clapped on one leg. Twenty-two years later I knew that the Creature was really good old Ricou Browning, the famed underwater stuntman, in a molded latex suit, and the suspension of disbelief, that mental clean-and-jerk, had become a lot harder to accomplish. But I did it, which may mean nothing, or which may mean (I hope!) that the buffalo haven't got me yet. But when that weight of disbelief was finally up there, the old feelings came flooding in, as they flooded in some five years ago when I took Joe and my daughter Naomi to their first movie, a reissue of *Snow White and the Seven Dwarfs*. There is a scene in that film where, after Snow White has taken a bite from the poisoned apple, the dwarfs take her into the forest, weeping copiously. Half the audience of little kids was also in tears; the lower lips of the other half were trembling. The set identification in that case was strong enough so that I was also surprised into tears. I hated myself for being so blatantly manipulated, but manipulated I was, and there I sat, blubbering into my beard over a bunch of cartoon characters. But it wasn't Disney that manipulated me; I did it myself. It was the kid inside who wept, surprised out of dormancy and into schmaltzy tears . . . but at least awake for awhile.

During the final two reels of *Creature from the Black Lagoon*, the weight of disbelief is nicely balanced somewhere above my head, and once again director Jack Arnold places the symbols in front of me and produces the old equation of the fairy tales, each symbol as big and as easy to handle as a child's alphabet block. Watching, the child awakes again and knows that this is what dying is like. Dying is when the Creature from the Black Lagoon dams up the exit. Dying is when the monster gets you.

In the end, of course, the hero and heroine, very much alive, not only survive but triumph—as Hansel and Gretel do. As the drive-in floodlights over the screen came on and the projector flashed its GOOD NIGHT, DRIVE SAFELY slide on that big white space (along with the virtuous suggestion that you ATTEND THE CHURCH OF YOUR CHOICE), there was a brief feeling of relief, almost of resurrection. But the feeling that stuck longest was the swooning sensation that good old Richard Carlson and good old Julia Adams were surely going down for the third time, and the image that remains forever after is of the creature slowly and patiently walling its victims into the Black Lagoon; even now I can see it peering over that growing wall of mud and sticks.

Its eyes. Its ancient eyes.

CHAPTER V

Radio and the Set of Reality

Books and movies are all very well, and we'll come
back to them before long, but before we do I'd like
to talk a little about radio in the mid-fifties. I'll start
with myself, and from me, we can hopefully progress
to a more profitable general case.

I am of the last quarter of the last generation that remembers
radio drama as an active force—a dramatic art form with its
own set of reality. This is a true statement as far as it goes, but
of course it doesn't go anywhere near far enough. Radio's real
golden age ended around 1950, the year at which this book's
casual attempt at media history begins, the year I celebrated
my third birthday and began my first full year of doing it in
the potty. As a child of the media, I have been pleased to have
attended the healthy birth of rock and roll, and to have seen
it grow up fast and healthy . . . but I was also in attendance,
during my younger years, at the deathbed of radio as a strong
fictional medium.

Drama is still to be found on the radio, God knows—*CBS
Mystery Theater* is a case in point—and there is even comedy, as
every devoted follower of that abysmally inept superhero, Chickenman, knows. But the *Mystery Theater* seems oddly flat, oddly
dead; a curiosity only. There is none of the heavy emotional
zap that used to come out of the radio when *Inner Sanctum's*
creaking door swung open each week, or during *Dimension X,
I Love a Mystery,* or the early days of *Suspense.* Although I listen to *Mystery Theater* when I can (and happen to think that
E. G. Marshall does a great job as host), I don't particularly

recommend it; it is a fluke like a Studebaker that still runs—
poorly—or the last surviving auk. Even more than these, *CBS
Mystery Theater* is like an electrical power cable through which
a heavy, almost lethal, current used to run and which now lies
inexplicably cold and harmless. *The Adventures of Chickenman,*
a syndicated comedy program, works much better (but comedy, a naturally auditory as well as visual medium, often does),
but the intrepid, klutzy Chickenman is still something of an
acquired taste, like taking snuff or eating escargots. My own
favorite moment in Chickenman's career occurs when he gets
on the crosstown bus clad in boots, tights, and cape, only to
discover that, since he has no pockets, he doesn't have a dime
for the fare box.* And still, endearing as Chickenman seems as
he stumbles gamely from one abysmal situation to another—
with his Jewish mother always close behind, bearing advice and
chicken soup with *matzoh* balls—he is never quite in focus for
me . . . except maybe for that one priceless moment as he stands
slumped before the bus driver, cape between his legs. I smile at
Chickenman; I have occasionally even chuckled; but there are
never moments as gut-bustingly funny as the moments when
Fibber McGee, as unstoppable as Time itself, would approach
his closet or when Chester A. Riley would engage in long and
uneasy conversations with his next-door neighbor, a mortician
named Digger O'Dell ("He sure is swell").

Of the radio programs I remember with the most clarity,
the only one which properly belongs in the danse macabre was
Suspense, also presented by the CBS Radio Network.

My grandfather (the one who worked for Winslow Homer
as a young man) and I really presided at the death rattle of
radio together. He was fairly hale and fairly hearty at the age of
eighty-two, but incomprehensible because he had a heavy beard
and no teeth. He would talk—volubly at times—but only my

---

* And for some people, Chickenman doesn't work at all. My good friend Mac McCutcheon
once played an album of the Great Fowl's adventures to a group of friends who simply sat and
listened with polite, blank expressions on their faces. No one even chuckled. As Steve Martin
says in *The Jerk:* "Take those snails off her plate and bring her the toasted cheese sandwich like
I told you in the first place!"

mother could really understand what he was saying. "Gizzen-groppen fuzzwah grupp?" he might ask me as we sat listening to his old Philco table model. "That's right, Daddy Guy," I'd say, with not the slightest idea of what I'd agreed to. Nonetheless, we had the radio to unite us.

At this time—around 1958—my grandmother and grandfather lived together in a combination bed-sitting room that was a converted parlor, the biggest room in a small New England house. He was ambulatory—barely—but my grandmother was blind and bedridden and horribly corpulent, a victim of hypertension. Occasionally her mind would clear; mostly she would go into long, excited rants, telling us that the horse needed to be fed, the fires needed to be banked, that someone had to get her up so she could bake pies for the Elks supper. Sometimes she talked to Flossie, one of my mother's sisters. Flossie had died of spinal meningitis forty years ago. So the situation in that room was this: my grandfather was lucid but incomprehensible; my grandmother was comprehensible but far gone in senility.

Somewhere in between was Daddy Guy's radio.

On radio nights, I would bring in a chair and place it in my grandfather's corner of the room, and he would fire up one of his huge cigars. The gong would sound for *Suspense,* or Johnny Dollar would begin to spin that week's tale through the unique (so far as I know) device of itemizing his expense account, or the voice of Bill Conrad as Matt Dillon would come on, deep and somehow unutterably weary: "It makes a man watchful . . . and a little lonely." For me, the smell of strong cigar smoke in a small room brings up its own set of ghost referents: Sunday night radio with my grandfather. The creak of batwing doors, the jingle of spurs . . . or the scream at the end of that classic *Suspense* episode, "You Died Last Night."

They died, all right, one by one, that last handful of radio programs. *Gunsmoke* went first. TV audiences had associated the face of Matt Dillon, only imagined for the previous ten years or so, with that of James Arness, Kitty's with Amanda Blake, Doc's with Milburn Stone, and Chester's, of course, with the face of Dennis Weaver. Their faces and their voices eclipsed the voices which came from the radio, and even now, twenty years later, it is the eager, slightly whining voice of Weaver that I associate with Chester Good (or, as he was known on the radio series, Chester Proudfoot) as he comes hurrying up the Dodge City boardwalk with gimpy enthusiasm, calling, "Mr. Dillon! Mr. Dillon! There's trouble down t'the Long-branch!" *Johnny Dollar* went a year or so later; he totted up his last expense account and drifted away into whatever limbo waits for retired insurance investigators.

Suspense, the last of the grisly old horrors, died the same day as *Johnny Dollar*: September 30, 1962. By then TV had demonstrated its ability to produce its own horrors; like *Gunsmoke*, *Inner Sanctum* had made the jump from radio to video, the swinging door finally visible. And visible, it certainly was horrible enough—slightly askew, festooned with cobwebs—but it was something of a relief, just the same. Nothing could have looked as horrible as that door *sounded*. I'm going to avoid any long dissertation on just why radio died, or in what ways it was superior to television in terms of the imaginational requirements it imposed on the listener (although we will touch briefly on some of this when we talk about the great Arch Oboler), because radio drama has been rather overanalyzed and certainly overeulogized. A little nostalgia is good for the soul, and I think I have already indulged in mine.

But I do want to say something about imagination purely as a tool in the art and science of scaring the crap out of people. The idea isn't original with me; I heard it expressed by William F. Nolan at the 1979 World Fantasy Convention. Nothing is so frightening as what's behind the closed door, Nolan said. You approach the door in the old, deserted house, and you hear something scratching at it. The audience holds its breath along with the protagonist as she/he (more often she) approaches that door. The protagonist throws it open, and there is a ten-foot-tall bug. The audience screams, but this particular scream has an oddly relieved sound to it. "A bug ten feet tall is pretty horrible," the audience thinks, "but I can deal with a ten-foot-tall bug. I was afraid it might be a *hundred* feet tall."

Consider, if you will, the most frightening sequence in *The Changeling*. The heroine (Trish Van Devere) has rushed off to the haunted house her new friend (George C. Scott) has rented, thinking he may need help. Scott is not there at all, but a series of small, stealthy sounds leads her to believe that he is. The audience watches, mesmerized, as Trish climbs to the second floor, the third floor; and finally she negotiates the narrow, cob-webby steps leading to the attic room where a young boy has been murdered in particularly nasty fashion some eighty years before. When she reaches the room, the dead boy's wheelchair suddenly whirls around and pursues her, chasing her screaming down all three flights of stairs, racing along after as she runs down the hall, to finally overturn near the front door. The audience screams as the empty wheelchair chases the lady, but the real scare has already happened; it comes as the camera dwells on those long, shadowy staircases, as we try to imagine walking up those stairs toward some as-yet-unseen horror waiting to happen.

Bill Nolan was speaking as a screenwriter when he offered the example of the big bug behind the door, but the point applies to all media. What's behind the door or lurking at the top of the stairs is never as frightening as the door or the staircase itself. And because of this, comes the paradox: the artistic work of horror is almost always a disappointment. It is the classic no-win situation. You can scare people with the unknown for a long, long time (the classic example, as Bill Nolan also pointed out, is the Jacques Tourneur film with Dana Andrews, *Curse of the Demon*), but sooner or later, as in poker, you have to turn your down cards up. You have to open the door and show the audience what's behind it. And if what happens to be behind it is a bug, not ten but a hundred feet tall, the audience heaves a sigh of relief (or utters a scream of relief) and thinks, "A bug a hundred feet tall is pretty horrible, but I can deal with that. I was afraid it might be a *thousand* feet tall." The thing is—and a pretty good thing for the human race, too, with such neato-keeno things to deal with as Dachau, Hiroshima, the Children's Crusade, mass starvation in Cambodia, and what happened in Jonestown, Guyana—the human consciousness can deal with almost anything . . . which leaves the writer or director of the horror tale with a problem which is the psychological equivalent of inventing a faster-than-light space drive in the face of $E = MC^2$.

There is and always has been a school of horror writers (I am not among them) who believe that the way to beat this rap is to never open the door at all. The classic example of this—it even involves a door—is the Robert Wise version of Shirley Jackson's novel *The Haunting of Hill House.* The film and the book do not differ greatly in terms of plot, but they differ significantly, I think, in terms of thrust, point of view, and final effect. (We were talking about radio, weren't we? Well, we'll get back to it, I guess, sooner or later.) Later on we will have some converse of Ms. Jackson's excellent novel, but for now let's deal with the film. In it, an anthropologist (Richard Johnson) whose hobby is ghost hunting invites a party of three to summer with him at the infamous Hill House, where any number of nasty things have occurred in the past and where, from time to time, ghosts may (or may not) have been seen. The party includes two ladies who have previously experienced aspects of the invisible world (Julie Harris and Claire Bloom) and the happy-go-lucky nephew of the present owner (played by Russ Tamblyn, that old dancing fool from the film version of *West Side Story*).

The housekeeper, Mrs. Dudley, offers each her simple, bone-chilling catechism as they arrive: "No one lives any closer than town; no one will come any closer than that. So no one will hear you if you scream. In the night. In the dark."

Of course Mrs. Dudley is proved absolutely right, and that right early. The four of them experience a steadily escalating run of horrors, and happy-go-lucky Luke ends by saying that the property he has so looked forward to inheriting should be burned flat . . . and the ground seeded with salt.

For our purposes here, the interesting thing lies in the fact that we never actually see whatever it is that haunts Hill House. *Something* is there, all right. *Something* holds hands with the terrified Eleanor in the night—she thinks it's Theo, but finds out the next day that Theo hasn't even been close to her. *Something* knocks on the wall with a sound like cannonfire. And most apropos to where we are now, this same something causes a door to bulge grotesquely inward until it looks like a great convex bubble—a sight so unusual to the eye that the mind reacts with horror. In Nolan's terms, something is scratching at the door. In a very real way, in spite of fine acting, fine direction, and the marvelous black-and-white photography of David Boulton, what we have in the Wise film (title shortened to *The Haunting*) is one of the world's few radio horror movies. Something is scratching at that ornate, paneled door, something horrible . . . but it is a door Wise elects never to open.

Lovecraft would open the door . . . but only a crack. Here is the final entry of Robert Blake's diary in the story "The Haunter of the Dark," which was dedicated to Robert Bloch:

> Sense of distance gone—far is near and near is far. No light—no glass—see that steeple—that tower—window—can hear—Roderick Usher—am mad or going mad—the thing is stirring and fumbling in the tower—I am it and it is I—I want to get out . . . must get out and unify the forces . . . It knows where I am . . .
>
> I am Robert Blake, but I see the tower in the dark. There is a monstrous odor . . . senses transfigured . . . boarding at that tower window cracking and giving way . . . I'd . . . ngai . . . ygg . . .
>
> I see it—coming here—hell-wind—titan blur—black wings—Yog-Sothoth save me—the three-lobed burning eye . . .

So the tale ends, leaving us with only the vaguest intimations of what Robert Blake's haunter may have been. "I cannot describe it," protagonist after protagonist tells us. "If I did, you would go mad with fear." But somehow I doubt that. I think both Wise and Lovecraft before him understood that to open the door, in ninety-nine cases out of a hundred, is to destroy the unified, dreamlike effect of the best horror. "I can deal with that," the audience says to iself, settling back, and bang! you just lost the ballgame in the bottom of the ninth.

My own disapproval of this method—we'll let the door bulge but we'll never open it—comes from the belief that it is playing to tie rather than to win. There is (or may be), after all, that hundredth case, and there is the whole concept of suspension of disbelief. Consequently, I'd rather yank the door open at some point during the festivities; I'd rather turn my hole cards face-up. And if the audience screams with laughter rather than terror, if they see the zipper running up the monster's back, then you just gotta go back to the drawing board and try it again.

The exciting thing about radio at its best was that it bypassed the whole question of whether to open the door or leave it closed. Radio, by the very nature of the medium, was exempt. For the listeners during the years 1930 to 1950 or so, there were no visual expectations to fulfill in their set of reality.

What about this set of reality, then? Another example, for purposes of comparison and contrast, from the movies. One of the classic fright films that I consistently missed as a child was Val Lewton's *Cat People,* directed by Jacques Tourneur. Like *Freaks,* it is one of those movies that comes up when the conversation among fans turns to what makes a "great horror movie"—others would include *Curse of the Demon, Dead of Night,* and *The Creeping Unknown,* I suppose, but for now let's stick with the Lewton film. It's one that a great many people remember with affection and respect from their childhoods—one that scared the crap out of them. Two specific sequences from the film are always brought up; both involve Jane Randolph, the "good" girl, menaced by Simone Simon, the "bad" girl (who is, let's be fair, no more willfully evil than is poor old Larry Talbot in *The Wolf Man*). In one, Ms. Randolph is trapped in a deserted basement swimming pool while, somewhere nearby and getting closer all the time, a great jungle cat menaces her. In the other sequence, she is walking through Central Park and the cat is getting closer and closer . . . getting ready to spring . . . we hear a hard, coughing roar . . . which turns out only to be the airbrakes of an arriving bus. Ms. Randolph steps onto it, leaving the audience limp with relief and with the feeling that a horrible disaster has been averted by inches.

In terms of what it does psychologically, I wouldn't argue the thesis that *The Cat People* is a good, perhaps even a great, American film. It is almost certainly the best horror film of the forties. At the base of the myth of the cat people—werecats, if you like—is a deep sexual fear; Irena (Ms. Simon) has been convinced as a child that any outpouring of passion will cause her to change into a cat. Nevertheless, she marries Kent Smith, who is so smitten that he takes her to the altar even though we pretty much understand he'll be spending his wedding night—and many nights thereafter—sleeping on the couch. No wonder the poor guy eventually turns to Jane Randolph.

But to return to those two scenes: the one in the swimming pool works quite well. Lewton and his director Jacques Tourneur were, like Stanley Kubrick, masters of contest here, lighting the scene to perfection and controlling every variable. We feel the truth of that scene everywhere, from the tiled walls, the lap of the water in the pool, to that slightly flat echo when Ms. Randolph speaks (to ask that time-honored horror movie question, "Who's there?"). And I am sure the Central Park scene worked for audiences of the forties, but today it simply will not wash; even out in the sticks, audiences would hoot and laugh at it.

I finally saw the movie as an adult, and puzzled for some time over what all the shouting could have been about. I think I finally figured out why that Central Park stalking scene worked then but doesn't work now. It has something to do with what film technicians call "state of the art." But this is only the technician's way of referring to that thing I have called "visual set" or "the set of reality."

If you should get a chance to see *The Cat People* on TV or

at a revival house in or near your city, pay particular attention to that sequence where Irena stalks Jane Randolph as Ms.
Randolph hurries to catch her bus. Take a moment to look at
it closely and you'll see it is not Central Park at all. It's a set
built on a soundstage. A little thought will suggest a reason
why. Tourneur, who wanted to be in control of lighting at all
times,* didn't elect to shoot on set; he simply had no choice.
"The state of the art" in 1942 did not allow for night shooting
on location. So instead of shooting in daylight with a heavy
filter, a technique that shows up as even more glaringly faked,
Tourneur quite sensibly opted for the soundstage—and it is interesting to me that, some forty years later, Stanley Kubrick did
exactly the same thing with *The Shining*... and like Lewton
and Tourneur before him, Kubrick is a director who shows an
almost exquisite sensitivity to the nuances of light and shadow.

To theatrical audiences of the time there was no false note in
this; they were used to integrating movie sets into their imaginative processes. Sets were simply accepted, the way we might
accept a single piece of scenery or two in a play that calls (as
Thornton Wilder's *Our Town* does) for mostly "bare stage"—
this is an acceptance that the Victorian playgoer would simply
have balked at. He or she might accept the *principle* of the bare
stage, but emotionally the play would lose most of its effect and
its charm. The Victorian playgoer would be apt to find *Our
Town* outside her or his set of reality.

For me, the scene in Central Park lost its believability for
the same reason. As the camera moves with Ms. Randolph, everything surrounding her screams fake! fake! fake! to my eye.
While I was supposed to be worrying about whether or not
Jane Randolph was going to be attacked, I found myself worrying instead about that papier-mâché stone wall in the background. When the bus finally pulls up, the chuff of its airbrakes
miming the cat's cheated growl, I was wondering if it was hard

---

* William F. Nolan, mentioning this film, said that the memory which remained with him
most strongly from the Central Park sequence was the pattern of "light-shadow-light-shadow-
light-shadow" as the camera moves with Ms. Randolph—and it is indeed a fine, eerie effect.

getting that New York City bus onto a closed soundstage and if the bushes in the background were real or plastic.

The set of reality changes, and the boundaries of that mental country where the imagination may be fruitfully employed (Rod Serling's apt phrase for it, now a part of the American idiom, was the Twilight Zone) are in near-constant flux. By the 1960s, the decade when I saw more movies than I ever have since, the "state of the art" had advanced to a point where a set and soundstages had become nearly obsolete. New fast films had made available-light shooting perfectly possible. In 1942 Val Lewton could not shoot in Central Park by night, but in *Barry Lyndon* Stanley Kubrick shot several scenes by candlelight. This is a quantum technical leap which has this paradoxical effect: it robs the bank of imagination. Perhaps realizing the fact, Kubrick takes a giant step backward to the soundstage with his next film, *The Shining.**

All of this may seem far afield from the subject of radio drama and the question of whether or not to open the door on the monster, but we're really standing right next to both subjects. As movie audiences of the forties and fifties believed Lewton's Central Park set, so radio listeners believed what the announcers, the actors, and the soundmen told them. The visual set was there, but it was plastic, bound by very few hard and fast expectations. When you made the monster in your mind, there was no zipper running down its back; it was a perfect monster. Audiences of today listening to old tapes don't accept the Make-Believe Ballroom any more than I am able to accept Lewton's papier-mâché rock wall; we are simply hearing a 1940s deejay playing records in a studio. But to audiences of a different day, the Make-Believe Ballroom was more real than make-believe; you could imagine the men in their tuxedos, the

---

* Want more proof of how the set of reality changes, whether we want it to or not? Remember *Bonanza*, which ran on NBC for a thousand years or so? Check it out in syndication someday. Look at that Ponderosa set—the front yard, the big family room—and ask yourself how you ever believed it was "real." It seemed real because we were used to seeing TV series shot on soundstages up until 1965 or so; nowadays even TV producers don't use soundstages for exteriors. The state of the art has, for better or worse, moved on.

women in their gowns and smooth elbow-length gloves, the flaring wall sconces, and Tommy Dorsey, resplendent in white dinner jacket, conducting. Or in the case of the infamous Orson Welles broadcast of *The War of the Worlds*, a Mercury Theater Halloween presentation (and that was a trick-or-treat millions of Americans never forgot), you could broaden that country of the imagination enough to send people screaming into the streets. On TV it wouldn't have worked, but on the radio there were no zippers running down the Martians' backs.

Radio avoided the open-door/closed-door question, I think, because radio deposited to that bank of imagination rather than making withdrawals in the name of "state of the art." Radio made it real.

2

My first experience with real horror came at the hands of Ray Bradbury—it was an adaptation of his story "Mars Is Heaven!" on *Dimension X*. This would have been broadcast around 1951, which would have made me four at the time. I asked to listen, and was denied permission by my mother. "It's on too late," she said, "and it would be much too upsetting for a little boy your age."

At some other time Mom told me that one of her sisters almost cut her wrists in the bathtub during the Orson Welles *War of the Worlds* broadcast. My aunt was not going about it hastily; she could look out the bathroom window and had, she said later, no plans at all to make the cuts until she saw the Martian death machines looming on the horizon. I guess you could say my aunt had found the Welles broadcast too upsetting . . . and my mother's words echo down to me over the years like a voice in an uneasy dream that has never really ended: "Too upsetting . . . upsetting . . . upsetting . . ."

I crept down to the door to listen anyway, and she was right: it was plenty upsetting.

Space travelers land on Mars—only it isn't Mars at all. It's good old Greentown, Illinois, and it's inhabited by all the voyagers' dead friends and relatives. Their mothers are here, their sweethearts, good old Clancey the patrolman, Miss Henreys from the second grade. On Mars, Lou Gehrig is still pounding them over the fences for the Yankees.

Mars is heaven, the space travelers decide. The locals take the crew of the spaceship into their homes, where they sleep the sleep of those perfectly at peace, full of hamburgers and hot dogs and Mom's apple pie. Only one member of the crew suspects the unspeakable obscenity, and he's right. Boy, is he right! And yet even he has awakened to the realization of this deadly illusion too late . . . because in the night, these well-loved faces begin to drip and run and change. Kind, wise eyes become black tar pits of murderous hate. The rosy apple cheeks of Grandma and Grandpa lengthen and turn yellow. Noses elongate into wrinkled trunks. Mouths become gaping maws. It is a night of creeping horror, a night of hopeless screams and belated terror, because Mars isn't heaven after all. Mars is a hell of hate and deception and murder.

I didn't sleep in my bed that night; that night I slept in the doorway, where the real and rational light of the bathroom bulb could shine on my face. That was the power of radio at its height. The Shadow, we were assured at the beginning of each episode, had "the power to cloud men's minds." It strikes me that, when it comes to fiction in the media, it is television and movies which so often cloud that part of our minds where the imagination moves most fruitfully; they do so by imposing the dictatorship of the visual set.

If you view imagination as a mental creature of a hundred different possible forms (imagine, if you will, Larry Talbot not just condemned to turn into a wolf man at the full of the moon but into an entire bestiary on successive nights; everything from a wereshark to a wereflea), then one of the forms is that of a rampaging gorilla, a creature that is dangerous and totally out of control.

If this seems fanciful or melodramatic, think of your own children or the children of close friends (never mind your own childhood; you may remember events that took place then with some fidelity, but most of your memories of how the emotional weather was then will be utterly false), and of the times when they simply find themselves unable to turn off the second-floor light or go down into the cellar or maybe even bring a coat from the closet because they saw or heard something that frightened them—and not necessarily a movie or a TV program, either. I've mentioned the fearsome twi-night double-header already; John D. MacDonald tells the story of how for weeks his son was terrified of something he called "the green ripper." Mac-Donald and his wife finally figured it out—at a dinner party, a friend had mentioned the Grim Reaper. What their son had heard was *green ripper*, and later it became the title of one of MacDonald's Travis McGee stories.

A child may be frightened by such a wide sweep of things that adults generally understand that to worry about this over-much is to endanger all relations with the child; you begin to feel like a soldier in the middle of a minefield. Added to this is another complicating factor: sometimes we frighten our kids on purpose. *Someday*, we say, *a man in a black car may stop and offer you a sweet to take a ride with him. And that is a Bad Man* (read: the Bogeyman), *and if he stops for you, you must never, never, never . . .*

Or: *Instead of giving that tooth to the Tooth Fairy, Ginny, let's put it in this glass of Coke. Tomorrow morning that tooth will be all gone. The Coke will dissolve it. So think about it the next time you have a quarter and . . .*

Or: *Little boys who play with matches wet the bed, they just can't help it, so don't you . . .*

Or that all-time favorite: *Don't put that in your mouth, you don't know where it's been.*

Most children deal with their fears quite well . . . most of the time, anyway. The shape-changing of their imaginations is so wide, so marvelously varied, that the gorilla pops out of the deck only infrequently. Besides worrying about what might be in the closet or under the bed, they have to imagine themselves as firefighters and policemen (imagination as the Very Gentle Perfect Knight), as mothers and nurses, as superheroes of various stripes and types, as their own parents, dressed up in attic clothes and giggling hand in hand before a mirror which shows them the future in the most unthreatening way. They need to experience a whole range of emotions from love to boredom, to try them out like new shoes.

But every now and then the gorilla gets out. Children understand that this face of their imagination must be caged ("It's only a movie, that couldn't really happen, could it?" . . . Or as Judith Viorst writes in one of her fine children's books, "My mom says there are no ghosts, vampires, and zombies . . . but . . ."). But their cages are of necessity more flimsy than those their elders build. I do not believe there are people out there with no imagination at all—although I have come to believe that there are a few who lack even the most rudimentary sense of humor—but it sometimes seems that way . . . perhaps because some people seem to build not just cages for the gorilla but Chase Manhattan Bank-type safes. Complete with time locks.

I remarked to an interviewer once that most great writers have a curious childish look to their faces, and that this seems even more pronounced in the faces of those who write fantasy. It is perhaps most noticeable in the face of Ray Bradbury, who retains very strongly the look of the boy he was in Illinois—his face retains this indefinable look in spite of his sixty-plus years, his graying hair, his heavy glasses. Robert Bloch has the face of a sixth-grade cutup, the Klass Klown, don't you know, although he is past sixty (just how far past I would not venture to guess; he might send Norman Bates after me); it is the face of the kid who sits in the back of the classroom—at least until the teacher assigns him a place up front, which usually doesn't take long—and makes screeching sounds on the top of his desk with the palms of his hands. Harlan Ellison has the face of a tough inner-city kid, confident enough in himself to be kind in most cases, but more than able to fuck you over royally if you give him any shit.

But perhaps the look I'm trying to describe (or indicate; actual description is really impossible) is most visible on the face of Isaac Bashevis Singer, who, while regarded as a "straight" writer of literature by the critical establishment, has nonetheless made the cataloguing of devils, angels, demons, and *dybbuks* a good part of his career. Grab a Singer book and take a good look at the author photo (you can read the book, too, when you're done looking at Singer's picture, okay?). It is the face of an old man, but that is a surface so thin you could read a newspaper through it. The boy is beneath, stamped very clearly on his features. It's in his eyes, mostly; they are young and clear.

One of the reasons for these "young faces" may be that writers of fantasy rather like the gorilla. They have never taken the trouble to strengthen the cage, and as a result, part of them has never accomplished the imaginative going-away that is so much a part of growing up, of establishing the tunnel vision so necessary for a successful career as an adult. One of the paradoxes of fantasy/horror is that the writer of this stuff is like the lazy pigs who built their houses of straw and sticks—but instead of learning their lesson and building sensible brick houses like their oh-so-adult elder brother (memorialized in his engineer's cap forever in my memory by the Disney cartoon), the writer of fantasy/horror simply rebuilds with sticks and straw again. Because, in a crazy kind of way, he or she *likes* it when the wolf comes and blows it all down, just as he or she sorta likes it when the gorilla escapes from its cage.

Most people aren't fantasy writers, of course, but almost all of us recognize the need to feed the imagination some of the stuff from time to time. People seem to recognize that the imagination somehow needs a dose of it, like vitamins or iodized salt to avoid goiter. Fantasy is salt for the mind.

Earlier on I talked about the suspension of disbelief, Coleridge's classic definition of what the reader must provide when seeking a hot shot from a fantasy story, novel, or poem. Another way of putting this is that the reader must agree to let the gorilla out of its cage for a while, and when we see the zipper running up the monster's back, the gorilla goes promptly back into its cage. After all, by the time we get to be forty or so, it's been in there for a long time, and perhaps it's developed a bit of the old "institutional mentality." Sometimes it has to be prodded out with a stick. And sometimes it won't go at all.

Seen in these terms, the set of reality becomes a very difficult thing to manipulate. Of course it has been done in the movies; if it had not been, this book would be shorter by a third or more. But by detouring around the visual part of the set of reality, radio developed an awesome tool (perhaps even a dangerous one; the riot and national hysteria following *The War of the Worlds* broadcast suggests that it could have been so)* for picking the lock on the gorilla's cage. But in spite of all the nostalgia we might want to feel, it is impossible to go back and reexperience the creative essence of radio terror; that particular lock pick has been broken by the simple fact that, for better or worse, we now demand believable visual input as part of the set of reality. Like it or lump it, we seem to be stuck with it.

3

We're almost done with our brief discussion of radio now—I think that to do much more would be to risk droning along like one of those tiresome cinema buffs who want to spend the night telling you how Charlie Chaplin was the greatest screen actor who ever lived or that the Clint Eastwood spaghetti westerns stand at the apex of the Existential/Absurdist movement— but no discussion of the phenomenon of radio terror, no matter how brief, would be complete without some mention of the genre's prime *auteur*—not Orson Welles, but Arch Oboler, the first playwright to have his own national radio series, the chilling *Lights Out*.

Lights Out was actually broadcast in the forties, but enough of the programs were rebroadcast in the fifties (and even in the sixties) for me to feel I can justify their inclusion here.

---

* Or what about Hitler? Most of us associate him now with newsreel footage and forget that in the pretelevision thirties, Hitler used radio with a kind of malevolent brilliance. My guess is that two or three appearances on *Meet the Press* or maybe one you're-on-the-griddle *60 Minutes* segment with Mike Wallace would have cooked Hitler's goose quite effectively.

The one I remember most vividly from its rebroadcast on *Dimension X* was "The Chicken Heart That Ate the World." Oboler, like so many people in the horror field—Alfred Hitchcock is another prime example—are extremely alert to the humor implicit in horror, and this alertness was never on better view than in the Chicken Heart story, which made you giggle at its very absurdity even as the gooseflesh raced up and down your arms.

"You remember that only a few days ago you asked me my opinion on how the world would end?" the scholarly scientist who has unwittingly perpetrated the horror on an unsuspecting world solemnly tells his young protégé as they fly at 5,000 feet in a light plane over the ever-growing chicken heart. "You remember my answer? Oh, such a scholarly prophecy! Mighty-sounding theories about cessation of earth rotation . . . entropy . . . but now, this is reality, Louis! The end has come for humanity! Not in the red of atomic fusion . . . not in the glory of interstellar combustion . . . not in the peace of white, cold silence . . . but with *that*! That creeping, grasping flesh below us. It is a joke, eh, Louis? The joke of the cosmos! The end of mankind . . . because of a chicken heart."

"No," Louis gibbers. "No, I can't die. I'll find a safe landing place—"

But then, perfectly on cue, the comforting drone of a plane's engine in the background becomes a coughing stutter. "We're in a spin!" Louis screams.

"The end of all mankind," the doctor proclaims in stentorian tones, and the two of them fall directly into the chicken heart. We hear its steady beat . . . louder . . . louder . . . and then the sickly splash that ends the play. Part of Oboler's real genius was that when "Chicken Heart" ended, you felt like laughing and throwing up at the same time.

"Cue the bombers," an old radio bit used to run (drone of bombers in the background; the mind's eye visualizes a sky black with Flying Forts). "Drop the ice cream into Puget Sound," the voice continues (whining, hydraulic sound of bomb bays opening, a rising whistle followed by a gigantic splash). "All right . . . cue the chocolate syrup . . . the whipped cream . . . and . . . *drop the maraschino cherries!*" We hear a great liquid squishing sound as the chocolate syrup goes, then a huge hissing as the whipped cream follows. These sounds are followed by a heavy *plop* . . . *plop* . . . *plop* in the background. And, absurd as it may be, the mind responds to these cues; that interior eye actually sees a series of gigantic ice cream sundaes rising out of Puget Sound like strange volcanic cones—each with a maraschino cherry the size of Seattle's Kingdome on top of it. In fact we see those disgustingly red cocktail cherries raining down, plopping into all that whipped cream and leaving craters nearly the size of Great Tycho. Thank the genius of Stan Freberg.

Arch Oboler, a restlessly intelligent man who was also involved in the movies (*Five,* one of the first films to deal with the survival of mankind after World War III, was Oboler's brainchild) and the legitimate theater, utilized two of radio's great strengths: the first in the mind's innate obedience, its willingness to try to see whatever someone suggests it see, no matter how absurd; the second is the fact that fear and horror are blinding emotions that knock our adult pins from beneath us and leave us groping in the dark like children who cannot find the light switch. Radio is, of course, the "blind" medium, and only Oboler used it so well or so completely.

Of course, our modern ears pick up the necessary conventions of the medium that have been outgrown (mostly due to our growing dependence on the visual in our set of reality), but these were standard practices which audiences of the day had no trouble accepting (like Tourneur's papier-mâché rock wall in *Cat People*). If these conventions seem jarring to listeners of the eighties, as the asides in a Shakespearean play seem jarring to a novice playgoer, then that is our problem, to work out as best we can.

One of these conventions is the constant use of narration to move the story. A second is dialogue-as-description, a technique necessary to radio but one TV and the movies have rendered obsolete. Here, for instance, from "The Chicken Heart that Ate the World," is Dr. Alberts discussing the chicken heart itself with Louis—read the passage and then ask yourself how true this speech rings to your TV- and movie-trained ears:

"Look at it down there . . . a great blanket of evil covering everything. See how the roads are black with men and women and their children, fleeing for their lives. See how the protoplasmic gray reaches out and engulfs them."

On TV, this would be laughed out of court as total corn; it is not hip, as they say. But heard in the darkness, coupled with the drone of the light plane's engine in the background, it works very well indeed. Willingly or unwillingly, the mind conjures up the image Oboler wants: this great jellylike blob, beating rhythmically, swallowing up the refugees as they run. . . .

Ironically, television and the early talkies both depended on the largely auditory conventions of radio until these new mediums found their own voices—and their own conventions. Most of us can remember the narrative "bridges" used in the early TV dramas (there was, for instance, that peculiar-looking individual Truman Bradley, who gave us a mini-science lesson at the beginning of each week's episode of *Science Fiction Theater* and a mini-moral at the end of each episode; the last but perhaps the best example of the convention were the voice-overs done by the late Walter Winchell each week for *The Untouchables*). But if we look at those early talking pictures, we can also find these same dialogue-as-description and narration devices used. There is no real need for it, because we can see what's happening, but they remained for awhile just the same, a kind of useless appendix, present simply because evolution had not removed them. My favorite example of this comes from the otherwise innovative Max Fleischer Superman cartoons of the early forties. Each began with the narrator explaining solemnly to the audience that once there was a planet called Krypton "which glowed like a great green jewel in the heavens." And there it is, by George, glowing like a great green jewel in the heavens, right before our eyes. A moment later it blows to smithereens in a blinding flash of light. "Krypton exploded," the narrator informs us helpfully as the pieces fly away into space. Just in case we missed it.*

Oboler used a third mental trick in creating his radio dramas, and this goes back to Bill Nolan and his closed door. When it's thrown open, he says, we see a ten-foot bug, and the mind, whose capacity to visualize far outruns any state of the art, feels relief. The mind, although obedient (what is insanity conceived of by the sane, after all, if not a kind of mental disobedience?), is curiously pessimistic, and more often than not, downright morbid.

Because he rarely overdid the dialogue-as-description device (as did the creators of *The Shadow* and *Inner Sanctum*), Oboler was able to use this natural turn of the mind toward the morbid and the pessimistic to create some of the most outrageous effects ever paraded before the quaking ears of a mass audience. Today, violence on television has been roundly condemned (and largely exterminated, at least by the *Untouchables, Peter Gunn,* and *Thriller* standards of the bad old sixties) because so much of it is explicit—we *see* the blood flowing; that is the nature of the medium and part of the set of reality.

Oboler used gore and violence by the bucketload, but a good deal of it was implicit; the real horror didn't come alive

---

* "Staging" was another convention that both the early talkies and early TV leaned upon heavily until they found their own more fluid methods of storytelling. Check out some TV kinescopes from the fifties sometime, or an early talking film like *It Happened One Night, The Jazz Singer,* or *Frankenstein,* and notice how often the scenes are played out from one stationary camera location, as if the camera was in reality a representative playgoer with a front-row seat. Speaking of the pioneering director of silents, Georges Méliès, in his fine book *Caligari's Children,* S. S. Prawer makes the same observation: "The double exposures, jump-cuts, and other technical tricks which Méliès played with the shots he had taken from a fixed position corresponding to a fixed seat in the stalls of a theatre—these amused rather than frightened their audiences, and, in the end, wearied them sufficiently to ensure Méliès's bankruptcy."

In regard to the early talkies, which came nearly forty years after Méliès pioneered the fantasy film and the idea of "special effects," audio limitations dictated the stationary camera to some extent; the camera made a loud clacking noise as it operated, and the only way to beat it was to put it in a soundproof room with a glass window. Moving the camera meant moving the room, and that was expensive in terms of time as well as money. But it was more than camera noise, a factor Méliès certainly didn't have to contend with. A lot of it was simply that mental set thing again. Bound by stage conventions, many early directors simply found themselves creatively unable to innovate.

in front of a camera but on the screen of the mind. Perhaps the best example of this comes from an Oboler piece with the Don Martin–like title, "A Day at the Dentist's."

As the story opens, the play's "hero," a dentist, is just closing up shop for the day. His nurse says he has one more patient, a man named Fred Houseman.

"He says it's an emergency," she tells him.

"Houseman?" the dentist barks.

"Yes."

"Fred?"

"Yes . . . do you know him?"

"No . . . oh, no," the dentist says casually.

Houseman, it turns out, has come because Dr. Charles, the dentist who owned the practice previously, advertised himself as a "painless dentist"—and Houseman, although an ex-wrestler and footballer, is terrified of the dentist (as so many of us are . . . and Oboler damned well knows it).

Houseman's first uneasy moment comes when the doctor *straps* him into the dentist's chair. He protests. The dentist tells him in a low, perfectly reasonable voice (and oh, how we suspect the reason in that voice! After all, who sounds more sane than a dangerous lunatic?) that "In order to keep this painless, there must be absolutely no movement."

There is a pause, and then the sound of straps being buckled.

Tightly.

"There," the dentist says soothingly. "Snug as a bug in a rug . . . that's a curious thing to call you, isn't it? You're no bug, are you? You're more the lover-boy type . . . aren't you?"

Oh-oh, the morbid little guy inside speaks up. *This looks bad for old Fred Houseman. Yes indeedy.*

It is bad indeed. The dentist, still speaking in that low, pleasant, and oh-so-rational voice, continues to call Houseman "lover-boy." It turns out that Houseman ruined the girl who later became the dentist's wife; Houseman slandered her name from one end of town to the other. The dentist found out that

Houseman's regular dentist was Dr. Charles, and so he bought out Charles's practice, figuring that sooner or later Houseman would come back . . . come back to "the painless dentist."

And while he was waiting, the new dentist installed restraint straps on his chair.

Just for Fred Houseman.

All of this, of course, has parted company with any semblance of reality early on (but then, the same can be said of *The Tempest*—how's that for an impudent comparison?); yet the mind cares not a fig for that at this crucial juncture, and Oboler, of course, never cared at all; like the best writers of horror fiction, he is interested in effect above all else, preferably one that will wallop the listener like a twenty-pound chunk of slate. He achieves that quite nicely in "A Day at the Dentist's."

"W-What are you going to do?" Houseman asks fearfully, echoing the very question that has been troubling our own minds almost since the moment we were foolish enough to turn on this piece of cold-blooded grue.

The dentist's answer is simple and utterly terrifying—more terrifying because of the unpleasant seminar it convenes in our own minds, a seminar in which Oboler ultimately refuses to take part, thus leaving the question to hang for as long as we want to consider it. Under the circumstances, we may not want to consider it long at all.

"Nothing important," the dentist replies as he flicks a switch and the drill begins to whine. "Just going to drill a little hole . . . and let out some of lover-boy."

As Houseman gasps and slobbers with fear in the background, the sound of the drill comes up . . . and up . . . and up . . . and finally, out. The end.

The question, of course, is where exactly did the demon dentist drill the hole to "let out some of lover-boy"? It is a question that only radio, by the very nature of the medium, can pose really convincingly and leave unanswered so uneasily. We hate Oboler a little for not telling us, mostly because our minds are suggesting the most outrageously nasty possibilities.

My first thought was that the dentist had almost surely used the drill on one of Houseman's temples, murdering him with a little impromptu brain surgery.

But later, as I grew up and grew into a better comprehension of just what the nature of Houseman's crime had been, another possibility began to suggest itself. An even nastier one.

Even today, as I write this, I wonder: exactly where *did* that crazy man use his drill?

4

Well, enough is enough; it is time to move on from the ear to the eye. But before we go, I'd like to remind you of something that you probably already know. Many of the old radio programs, from *Inner Sanctum* to *Gangbusters* to the sudsy *Our Gal Sal* have been preserved on record and tape, and the quality of these recordings is actually better in most cases than the quality of the TV kinescopes that are broadcast on nostalgia programs from time to time. If you're interested in seeing how your own ability to suspend disbelief and to circumnavigate that visual set engendered by TV and the movies is holding up, you can get a start at almost any well-stocked record store. A *Schwann's Catalogue* of spoken-word records can be even more helpful; what your friendly neighborhood Record Mart doesn't have, they'll be glad to order. And if your interest in Arch Oboler has been at all piqued by the foregoing, let me whisper a little secret in your ear: *Drop Dead! An Exercise in Horror*— produced, written, and directed by Arch Oboler, available for your delectation on Capitol Records (Capitol: SM-1763). Probably more of a summer cooler than a tall glass of iced tea . . . if you can get rid of that visual set for forty minutes or so.

CHAPTER VI

The Modern American
Horror Movie—Text and Subtext

R ight now you could be thinking to yourself: this guy must have one hell of a nerve if he thinks he's gonna cover all the horror movies released between 1950 and 1980—everything from *The Exorcist* to the less-than-immortal *The Navy vs. the Night Monsters*—in a single chapter.

Well, actually it's going to be two chapters, and no, I don't expect to be able to cover them all, as much as I would like to; but yes, I must have some kind of nerve to be tackling the subject at all. Luckily for me, there are several fairly traditional ways of handling the subject so that at least an illusion of order and coherence emerges. The path I've chosen is that of the horror movie as text and subtext.

The place to start, I think, would be a swift recap of those points already made on the subject of the horror movie as art. If we say "art" is any piece of creative work from which an audience receives more than it gives (a liberal definition of art, sure, but in this field it doesn't pay to be too picky), then I believe that the artistic value the horror movie most frequently offers is its ability to form a liaison between our fantasy fears and our real fears. I've said and will reemphasize here that few horror movies are conceived with "art" in mind; most are conceived only with "profit" in mind. The art is not consciously created but rather thrown off, as an atomic pile throws off radiation.

I do not contend by saying the above that every exploitation horror flick is "art," however. You could walk down

Forty-second Street in Times Square on any given afternoon or evening and discover films with names like *The Bloody Mutilators, The Female Butcher,* or *The Ghastly Ones*—a 1972 film we are treated to the charming sight of a woman being cut open with a two-handed bucksaw; the camera lingers as her intestines spew out onto the floor. These are squalid little films with no whiff of art in them, and only the most decadent filmgoer would try to argue otherwise. They are the staged equivalent of those 8- and 16-millimeter "snuff" movies which have reputedly oozed out of South America from time to time.

Another point worth mentioning is the great risk a filmmaker takes when he/she decides to make a horror picture. In other creative fields, the only risk is failure—we can say, for instance, that the Mike Nichols film of *The Day of the Dolphin* "fails," but there is no public outcry, no mothers picketing the movie theaters. But when a horror movie fails, it often falls into painful absurdity or squalid porno-violence.

There are films which skate right up to the border where "art" ceases to exist in any form and exploitation begins, and these films are often the field's most striking successes. *The Texas Chainsaw Massacre* is one of these; in the hands of Tobe Hooper, the film satisfies that definition of art which I have offered, and I would happily testify to its redeeming social merit in any court in the country. I would not do so for *The Ghastly Ones.* The difference is more than the difference between a chainsaw and a bucksaw; the difference is something like seventy million light-years. Hooper works in *Chainsaw Massacre,* in his own queerly apt way, with taste and conscience. *The Ghastly Ones* is the work of morons with cameras.*

So, if I'm going to keep this discussion in order, I'll keep

---

* One success in skating over this thin ice does not necessarily guarantee that the filmmaker will be able to repeat such a success; while his innate talent saves Hooper's second film, *Eaten Alive,* from descending to *The Bloody Mutilators* category, it is still a disappointment. The only director I can think of who has explored this gray land between art and porno-exhibitionism successfully—even brilliantly—again and again with never a misstep is the Canadian filmmaker David Cronenberg.

coming back to the concept of value—of art, of social merit. If horror movies have redeeming social merit, it is because of that ability to form liaisons between the real and unreal—to provide subtexts. And because of their mass appeal, these subtexts are often culture-wide.

In many cases—particularly in the fifties and then again in the early seventies—the fears expressed are sociopolitical in nature, a fact that gives such disparate pictures as Don Siegel's *Invasion of the Body Snatchers* and William Friedkin's *The Exorcist* a crazily convincing documentary feel. When the horror movies wear their various sociopolitical hats—the B-picture as tabloid editorial—they often serve as an extraordinarily accurate barometer of those things which trouble the night-thoughts of a whole society.

But horror movies don't always wear a hat which identifies them as disguised comments on the social or political scene (as Cronenberg's *The Brood* comments on the disintegration of the generational family or as his *They Came from Within* treats of the more cannibalistic side-effects of Erica Jong's "zipless fuck"). More often the horror movie points even further inward, looking for those deep-seated personal fears—those pressure points—we all must cope with. This adds an element of universality to the proceedings, and may produce an even truer sort of art. It also explains, I think, why *The Exorcist* (a social horror film if there ever was one) did only so-so business when it was released in West Germany, a country which had an entirely different set of social fears at the time (they were a lot more worried about bomb-throwing radicals than about foul-talking young people), and why *Dawn of the Dead* went through the roof there.

This second sort of horror film has more in common with the Brothers Grimm than with the op-ed page in a tabloid paper. It is the B-picture as fairy tale. This sort of picture doesn't want to score political points but to scare the hell out of us by crossing certain taboo lines. So if my idea about art is correct (it giveth more than it receiveth), this sort of film is of value to the audience by helping it to better understand what those taboos and fears are, and why it feels so uneasy about them.

A good example of this second type of horror picture is RKO's *The Body Snatcher* (1945), liberally adapted—and that's putting it kindly—from a Robert Louis Stevenson story and starring Karloff and Lugosi. And by the way, the picture was produced by our friend Val Lewton.

As an example of the art, *The Body Snatcher* is one of the forties' best. And as an example of this second artistic "purpose"— that of breaking taboos—it positively shines.

I think we'd all agree that one of the great fears which all of us must deal with on a purely personal level is the fear of dying; without good old death to fall back on, the horror movies would be in bad shape. A corollary to this is that there are "good" deaths and "bad" deaths; most of us would like to die peacefully in our beds at age eighty (preferably after a good meal, a bottle of really fine *vino,* and a really super lay), but very few of us are interested in finding out how it might feel to get slowly crushed under an automobile lift while crankcase oil drips slowly onto our foreheads.

Lots of horror films derive their best effects from this fear of the bad death (as in *The Abominable Dr. Phibes,* where Phibes dispatches his victims one at a time using the Twelve Plagues of Egypt, slightly updated, a gimmick worthy of the Batman comics during their palmiest days). Who can forget the lethal binoculars in *Horrors of the Black Museum,* for instance? They came equipped with spring-loaded six-inch prongs, so that when the victim put them to her eyes and then attempted to adjust the field of focus . . .

Others derive their horror simply from the fact of death itself, and the decay which follows death. In a society where such a great store is placed in the fragile commodities of youth, health, and beauty (and the latter, it seems to me, is very often defined in terms of the former two), death and decay become inevitably horrible, and inevitably taboo. If you don't think so, ask yourself why the second grade doesn't get to tour the local mortuary along with the police department, the fire department, and the nearest McDonald's—one can imagine, or I can in my more morbid moments, the mortuary and McDonald's combined; the highlights of the tour, of course, would be a viewing of the McCorpse.

No, the funeral parlor is taboo. Morticians are modern priests, working their arcane magic of cosmetics and preservation in rooms that are clearly marked "off limits." Who washes the corpse's hair? Are the fingernails and toenails of the dear departed clipped one final time? Is it true that the dead are en-coffined *sans* shoes? Who dresses them for their final star turn in the mortuary viewing room? How is a bullet hole plugged and concealed? How are strangulation bruises hidden?

The answers to all these questions are available, but they are not common knowledge. And if you try to make the answers part of your store of knowledge, people are going to think you a bit peculiar. I know; in the process of researching a forthcoming novel about a father who tries to bring his son back from the dead, I collected a stack of funeral literature a foot high—and any number of peculiar glances from folks who wondered why I was reading *The Funeral: Vestige or Value?*

But this is not to say that people don't have a certain occasional interest in what lies behind the locked door in the basement of the mortuary, or what may transpire in the local graveyard after the mourners have left . . . or at the dark of the moon. *The Body Snatcher* is not really a tale of the supernatural, nor was it pitched that way to its audience; it was pitched as a film (as was that notorious sixties documentary *Mondo Cane*) that would take us "beyond the pale," over that line which marks the edge of taboo ground.

"Cemeteries raided, children slain for bodies to dissect!" the movie poster drooled. "Unthinkable realities and unbelievable FACTS of the dark days of early surgical research EXPOSED in THE MOST DARING SHRIEK-AND-SHUDDER SHOCK SENSATION EVER BROUGHT TO THE SCREEN!" (All of this printed on a leaning tombstone.)

But the poster does not stop there; it goes on very specifically to mark out the exact location of the taboo line and to suggest that not everyone may be adventurous enough to transgress this forbidden ground: "If You Can 'Take It' See GRAVES RAIDED! COFFINS ROBBED! CORPSES CARVED! MIDNIGHT MURDER! BODY BLACKMAIL! STALKING GHOULS! MAD REVENGE! MACABRE MYS-TERY! And Don't Say We Didn't Warn You!"

All of it has sort of a pleasant, alliterative ring, doesn't it?

2

These "areas of unease"—the political-social-cultural and those of the more mythic, fairy-tale variety—have a tendency to overlap, of course; a good horror picture will put the pressure on at as many points as it can. *They Came from Within,* for instance, is about sexual promiscuity on one level; on another level it's asking you how you'd like to have a leech jump out of a letter slot and fasten itself onto your face. These are not the same areas of unease at all.

But since we're on the subject of death and decay, we might look at a couple of films where this particular area of unease has been used well. The prime example, of course, is *Night of the Living Dead,* where our horror of these final states is exploited to a point where many audiences found the film well-nigh unbearable. Other taboos are also broken by the film: at one point a little girl kills her mother with a garden trowel . . . and then begins to eat her. How's that for taboo-breaking? Yet the film circles around to its starting point again and again, and the key word in the film's title is not *living* but *dead.*

At an early point, the film's female lead, who has barely escaped being killed by a zombie in a graveyard where she and her brother have come to put flowers on their dead mother's grave (the brother is not so lucky), stumbles into a lonely farmhouse. As she explores, she hears something dripping . . . dripping . . . dripping. She goes upstairs, sees something, screams . . . and the camera zooms in on the rotting, weeks-old head of a corpse. It is a shocking, memorable moment. Later, a government official tells the watching, beleaguered populace that, although they may not like it (i.e., they will have to cross that taboo line to do it), they must burn their dead; simply soak them with gasoline and light them up. Later still, a local sheriff expresses our own uneasy shock at having come so far over the taboo line. He answers a reporter's question by saying, "Ah, they're dead . . . they're all messed up."

The good horror director must have a clear sense of where the taboo line lies, if he is not to lapse into unconscious absurdity, and a gut understanding of what the countryside is like on the far side of it. In *Night of the Living Dead,* George Romero plays a number of instruments, and he plays them like a virtuoso. A lot has been made of this film's graphic violence, but one of the film's most frightening moments comes near the climax, when the heroine's brother makes his reappearance, still wearing his driving gloves and clutching for his sister with the idiotic, implacable single-mindedness of the hungry dead. The film is violent, as is its sequel, *Dawn of the Dead*—but the violence has its own logic, and I submit to you that in the horror genre, logic goes a long way toward proving morality.

The crowning horror in Hitchcock's *Psycho* comes when Vera Miles touches that chair in the cellar and it spins around to reveal Norman's mother at last—a wizened, shriveled corpse from which hollow eyesockets stare up blankly. She is not only dead; she has been stuffed like one of the birds which decorate Norman's office. Norman's subsequent entrance in dress and makeup is almost an anticlimax.

In AIP's *The Pit and the Pendulum* we see another facet of the bad death—perhaps the absolute worst. Vincent Price and his cohorts break into a tomb through its brickwork, using pick and shovel. They discover that the lady, his late wife, has indeed been buried alive; for just a moment the camera shows us her tortured face, frozen in a rictus of terror, her bulging eyes, her clawlike fingers, the skin stretched tight and gray. Following the Hammer films, this becomes, I think, the most important moment in the post-1960 horror film, signaling a return to an all-out effort to terrify the audience . . . and a willingness to use any means at hand to do it.

Other examples abound. No vampire movie can be complete without a midnight creep through the tombstones and the jimmying of a crypt door. The John Badham remake of *Dracula* has disappointingly few fine moments, but one rather good sequence occurs when Van Helsing (Laurence Olivier) discovers his daughter Mina's grave empty . . . and an opening at its bottom leading deeper into the earth.* This is English mining country, and we're told that the hillside where the cemetery has been laid out is honeycombed with old tunnels. Van Helsing nevertheless descends, and the movie's best passage follows— crawling, claustrophobic, and reminiscent of that classic Henry Kuttner story, "The Graveyard Rats." Van Helsing pauses at a pool for a moment, and his daughter's voice comes from behind him, begging for a kiss. Her eyes glitter unnaturally; she is still dressed in the cerements of the grave. Her flesh has decayed to a sick green color and she stands, swaying, in this passage under the earth like something from a painting of the Apocalypse. In this one moment Badham has not merely asked us to cross the taboo line with him; he has quite literally pushed us across it and into the arms of this rotting corpse—a corpse made more horrible because in life it conformed so perfectly to those conventional American standards of beauty: youth and health. It's only a moment, and the movie holds no other moment comparable to it, but it is a fine effect while it lasts.

3

"Thou shall not read the Bible for its prose," W. H. Auden says in one of his own finer moments, and I hope I can avoid a similar flaw in this informal little discussion of horror movies. For the next little while, I intend to discuss several groups

---

* Van Helsing's *daughter*? I hear you saying with justifiable dismay. Yes indeed. Readers familiar with Stoker's novel will see that Badham's film (and the stage play from which it was drawn) has rung any number of changes on the novel. In terms of the tale's interior logic, these changes of plot and relationship seem to work, but to what purpose? The changes don't cause Badham to say anything new about either the Count or the vampire myth in general, and to my mind there was no coherent reason for them at all. As we have too far too often, we can only shrug and say, "That's showbiz."

of films from the period 1950–1980, concentrating on some of those liaison points already discussed. We will discuss some of those movies which seem to speak in their subtexts to our more concrete fears (social, economic, cultural, political), and then some of those which seem to express universal fears which cut across all cultures, changing only slightly from place to place. Later we'll examine some books and stories in about the same way . . . but hopefully we can go on from there together and appreciate some of the books and movies in this wonderful genre just for themselves—for what they are rather than for what they do. We'll try not to cut the goose open to see how it laid the golden eggs (a surgical crime which you can lay at the door of every high school English teacher and college English prof that ever put you to sleep in class) or to read the Bible for its prose.

Analysis is a wonderful tool in matters of intellectual appreciation, but if I start talking about the cultural ethos of Roger Corman or the social implications of *The Day Mars Invaded the Earth,* you have my cheerful permission to pop this book into a mailer, return it to the publisher, and demand your money back. In other words, when the shit starts getting too deep, I intend to leave the area rather than perform in accepted English-teacher fashion and pull on a pair of hip-waders.

Onward.

4

There are any number of places where we could begin our discussion of "real" fears, but just for the fun of it, let's begin with something fairly off the wall: the horror movie as economic nightmare.

Fiction is full of economic horror stories, although very few of them are supernatural; *The Crash of '79* comes to mind, as well as *The Money Wolves, The Big Company Look,* and the wonderful Frank Norris novel, *McTeague.* I only want to discuss one movie in this context, *The Amityville Horror.* There may be others, but this one example will serve, I think, to illustrate another idea: that the horror genre is extremely limber, extremely adaptable, extremely *useful;* the author or filmmaker can use it as a crowbar to lever open locked doors or as a small, slim pick to tease the tumblers into giving. The genre can thus be used to open almost any lock on the fears which lie behind the door, and *The Amityville Horror* is a dollars-and-cents case in point.

There may be someone in some backwater of America who doesn't know that this film, starring James Brolin and Margot Kidder, is supposedly based on a true story (set down in a book of the same name by the late Jay Anson). I say "supposedly" because there have been several cries of "hoax!" in the news media since the book was published, and these cries have been renewed since the movie was released—and almost unanimously panned by the critics. Despite the critics, *The Amityville Horror* went serenely on to become one of 1979's top-grossing movies.

If it's all the same to you, I'd just as soon not go into the story's validity or nonvalidity here, although I hold definite views on the subject. Within the context of our discussion, whether the Lutzes' house was really haunted or whether the whole thing was a put-up job matters very little. All movies, after all, are pure fiction, even the true ones. The fine film version of Joseph Wambaugh's *The Onion Field* begins with a title card which reads simply *This is a True Story,* but it's not; the very medium fictionalizes, and there is no way to stop this from happening. We know that a police officer named Ian Campbell really was killed in that onion field, and we know that his partner, Karl Hettinger, escaped; if we have doubts, let us look it up in the library and stare at the cold print there on the screen of the microfilm reader. Let us look at the police photographs of Campbell's body; let us talk to the witnesses. And yet we know there were no cameras there, grinding away, when those two small-time hoods blew Ian Campbell away, nor was there a camera present when Hettinger began hooking things from department stores and removing them from the premises via armpit express. Movies produce fiction as a by-product the same way that boiling water produces steam . . . or as horror movies produce art.

If we were going to discuss the book version of *The Amityville Horror* (we're not, so relax) it would be important for us to first decide if we were talking about a fiction or a nonfiction work. But as far as the movie is concerned, it just doesn't matter, either way it's fiction.

So let us see *The Amityville Horror* only as a story, unmodified either by "true" or "make-believe." It is simple and straightforward, as most horror tales are. The Lutzes, a young married couple with two or three kids (Cathy Lutz's by a previous marriage), buy a house in Amityville. Previous to their tenancy, a young man has murdered his whole family at the direction of "voices." For this reason, the Lutzes get the house cheap. But it wouldn't have been cheap at half the price, they soon discover, because the house is haunted. Manifestations include black goop that comes bubbling out of the toilets (and before the festivities are over, it comes oozing out of the walls and the stairs as well), a roomful of flies, a rocking chair that rocks by itself, and something in the cellar that causes the dog to dig everlastingly at the wall. A window crashes on the little boy's fingers. The little girl develops an "invisible friend" who is apparently really there. Eyes glow outside the window at three in the morning. And so on.

Worst of all, from the audience's standpoint, Lutz himself (James Brolin) apparently falls out of love with his wife (Margot Kidder) and begins to develop a meaningful relationship with his ax. Before things are done, we are drawn to the inescapable conclusion that he is tuning up for something more than splitting wood.

It's probably bad form for a writer to recant something he's already written, but I'm going to nevertheless. I did an article on movies for *Rolling Stone* in late 1979, and I now think I was needlessly hard on *The Amityville Horror* in that piece. I called it a stupid sort of story, which it is; I called it simplistic and transparent, which it also is (David Chute, a film critic for *The Boston Phoenix,* quite rightly called it "The Amityville

Nonsense"), but these canards really miss the point, and as a lifelong horror fan, I should have known it. *Stupid, simplistic,* and *transparent* are also perfectly good words to describe the tale of The Hook, but that doesn't change the fact that the story is an enduring classic of its kind—in fact, those words probably go a long way toward explaining why it *is* a classic of its kind.

Stripped of its distracting elements (a puking nun, Rod Steiger shamelessly overacting as a priest who is just discovering the devil after forty years or so as a man of the cloth, and Margot Kidder—not too tacky!—doing calisthenics in a pair of bikini panties and one white stocking), *The Amityville Horror* is a perfect example of the Tale to be Told around the Campfire. All the teller really has to do is to keep the catalogue of inexplicable events in their correct order, so that unease escalates into outright fear. If this is done, the story will do its work . . . just as the bread will rise if the yeast is added at the right moment to ingredients which are at the correct temperature.

I don't think I realized how well the film was working on this level until I saw it for the second time at a small theater in western Maine. There was little laughter during the film, no hooting . . . and not much screaming, either. The audience did not seem to be just watching this film; it seemed to be *studying* it. The audience simply sat there in a kind of absorbed silence, taking it all in. When the lights went on at the end of the film, I saw that the audience was a much older one than I am accustomed to see at horror films; I'd put the average age between thirty-eight and forty-two. And there was a light on their faces—an excitement, a glow. Leaving, they discussed the film animatedly with one another. It was this reaction—which seemed to me markedly peculiar in terms of what the film had to offer—that started me thinking that a reevaluation of the film was in order.

Two things apply here: first, *The Amityville Horror* allows people to touch the unknown in a simple, uncomplicated way; it is as effective in this way as other "fads" have been before it, beginning, let us say, with the hypnosis/reincarnation vogue that followed *The Search for Bridey Murphy* and encompassing the flying-saucer flaps of the fities, sixties, and seventies; Raymond Moody's *Life After Life;* and a lively interest in such wild talents as telepathy, precognition, and the various colorful pronouncements of Castaneda's Don Juan. Simplicity may not always make great artistic sense, but it often makes the greatest impact on minds which have little imaginative capacity or upon minds in which the imaginative capability has been little exercised. *The Amityville Horror* is the primal haunted house story . . . and haunted houses are a concept which even the dullest mind has surely turned over at one time or another, if only around a childhood campfire or two.

Before going on to the second point (and I promise not to belabor you much more with *The Amityville Horror*), let's look at a section of a review of a 1974 horror film, *Phase IV. Phase IV* was a modest Paramount release starring Nigel Davenport and Michael Murphy. It dealt with ants taking over the world following a burst of solar radiation that made them smart—an idea perhaps inspired by science fiction writer Poul Anderson's short novel, *Brain Wave,* and then cross-pollinated with the 1954 picture *Them!* Both *Them!* and *Phase IV* share the same desert setting, although *Them!* shifts to the storm drains of Los Angeles for its slambang climax. It should be added that, similar settings or not, the two movies are a million miles away from each other in matters of tone and mood. The review of *Phase IV* I want to quote from was written by Paul Roen and published in *Castle of Frankenstein,* #24:

> It's heartening to learn that Saul Bass, the imaginative graphics artist who designed the opening titles for Hitchcock's three greatest thrillers, has himself now taken to directing suspense movies. His initial enterprise is *Phase IV,* a blend of '50s sci-fi and '70s eco-disaster survival. . . . The narrative isn't always developed with logic and coherence, but *Phase* is, nevertheless, a grueling suspense exercise. Davenport is a delight to watch; his cool detachment crumbles by degrees, while his mellifluous British accent

remains dignified throughout. . . . Bass's visuals are as sophisticated as one might expect, though often luridly colored; amber and green predominate [sic] the production.

This was the sort of fairly sophisticated reviewing one
learned to expect from *Castle of Frankenstein,* the best of the
"monster mags" and one that died much too soon. The point
the review makes is that here we have a horror movie which
stands in direct contrast to *The Amityville Horror.* Bass's ants
aren't even big. They're just little buggers who have all decided
to pull together. The movie did no great box-office business,
and I finally caught it at the drive-in back in 1976, filling out
the bottom half of a double bill with a picture that was much
inferior to it.

If you're a genuine horror fan, you develop the same sort
of sophistication that a follower of the ballet develops; you get
a feeling for the depth and texture of the genre. Your ear develops with your eye, and the sound of quality always comes
through to the keen ear. There is fine Waterford crystal, which
rings delicately when struck, no matter how thick and chunky
it may look; and then there are Flintstone jelly glasses. You can
drink your Dom Perignon out of either one, but friends, there
is a difference.

Anyway, *Phase IV* did poorly at the box office because for
all those people out there who are not fans, who find it hard
to suspend their disbelief, not much appears to be happening.
There are no "big moments," such as Linda Blair puking pea
soup on Max von Sydow in *The Exorcist . . .* or James Brolin
dreaming that he is axing his family to death in *The Amityville
Horror.* But as Roen points out, a person who loves the genre's
genuine Waterford (and there isn't enough of it . . . but then,
there never is enough of the good stuff in any field, is there?)
find a great deal happening in *Phase IV*—that delicate ring of
the real stuff is there, it can be perceived; it ranges from the
music to the silent and eerie desert vistas to Bass's fluid camera
and Michael Murphy's quiet, understated narration. The ear
detects that true ringing sound . . . and the heart responds.

I said all of that to say this: the opposite also applies. The ear which is constantly attuned to the "fine" sound—the decorous strains of chamber music, for instance—may hear nothing but horrid cacophony when exposed to bluegrass fiddle . . . but bluegrass music is mighty fine all the same. The point is that the fan of movies in general and horror movies in particular may find it easy—too easy—to overlook the crude charms of a film like *The Amityville Horror* after he or she has experienced films such as *Repulsion, The Haunting, Fahrenheit 451* (which may have seemed to be science fiction to some, but which is nevertheless a reader's nightmare), or *Phase IV.* In a real appreciation of horror films, a taste for junk food applies . . . an idea we'll take up more fully in the next chapter. For now, let it suffice to say that the fan loses his taste for junk food at his or her own peril, and when I hear by way of the grapevine that New York film audiences are laughing at a horror movie, I rush out to see it. In most cases I am disappointed, but every now and then I hear me some mighty good bluegrass fiddle, eat me some pretty good fried chicken, and get so excited that I mix me some metaphors, as I've done here.

All of which brings us around to the real watchspring of *The Amityville Horror,* and the reason it works as well as it does: the picture's subtext is one of economic unease, and this is a theme that director Stuart Rosenberg plays on constantly. In terms of the times—18 percent inflation, mortgage rates out of sight, gasoline selling at a cool dollar forty a gallon—*The Amityville Horror,* like *The Exorcist,* could not have come along at a more opportune moment.

This comes out most clearly in a scene which is the film's only moment of true and honest drama; a brief little vignette that breaks through the clouds of hokum like a sunray on a drizzly afternoon. The Lutz family is preparing to go to the wedding of Cathy Lutz's younger brother (who looks, in the film, as if he might be all of seventeen). They are, of course, in the Bad House when the scene takes place. The younger brother has lost the fifteen hundred dollars that is due the caterer, and he is in an understandable agony of panic and embarrassment.

Brolin says he'll write a covering check, which he does, and later he stands off the angry caterer, who has specified only cash, in a half-whispered washroom argument while the wedding party whoops it up outside. After the wedding, Lutz turns the living room of the Bad House upside down looking for the lost money, which has now become his money, and the only way of backing up the bank paper he has issued the caterer. Brolin's check may not have been 100 percent Goodyear rubber, but in his sunken, purple-pouched eyes we see a man who didn't really have the money any more than his hapless brother-in-law did, regardless. Here is a man tottering on the brink of his own financial crash. He finds the only trace under the couch: a bank money-band with the numerals $500 stamped on it. The band lies there on the rug, tauntingly empty. *"Where is it?"* Brolin screams, his voice vibrating with anger, frustration, and fear. At that one moment we hear the ring of Waterford, clear and true—or, if you like, we hear that one quiet phrase of pure music in a film that is otherwise all crash and bash.

Everything which *The Amityville Horror* does well is summed up in that scene. Its implications touch on everything about the Bad House's most obvious effect—and also the only one which seems empirically undeniable: little by little, it is ruining the Lutz family financially. The movie might as well have been subtitled *The Horror of the Shrinking Bank Account*. It's the more prosaic fallout of the place where so many haunted-house stories start. "It's on the market for a song," the realtor says with a big egg-sucking grin. "It's supposed to be haunted."

Well, the house that the Lutzes buy is indeed on the market for a song (and there's another good moment—all too short—when Cathy tells her husband that she will be the first person in her large Catholic family to actually own her own home; "We've always been renters," she says), but it ends up costing them dear. At the conclusion, the house seems to literally tear itself apart. Windows crash in, black goop comes dribbling out of the walls, the cellar stairs cave in . . . and I found myself wondering not if the Lutz clan would get out alive but if they had adequate homeowner's insurance.

Here is a movie for every woman who ever wept over a plugged-up toilet or a spreading water stain on the ceiling from the upstairs shower; for every man who ever did a slow burn when the weight of the snow caused his gutters to give way; for every child who ever jammed his fingers and felt that the door or window which did the jamming was out to get him. As horror goes, *Amityville* is pretty pedestrian. So's beer, but you can get drunk on it.

"Think of the bills," a woman sitting behind me in the theater moaned at one point . . . but I suspect it was her own bills she was thinking about. It was impossible to make a silk purse out of this particular sow's ear, but Rosenberg at least manages to give us Qiana, and the main reason that people went to see it, I think, is that *The Amityville Horror,* beneath its ghost-story exterior, is really a financial demolition derby.

Think of the bills, indeed.

5

The horror film as political polemic, then.

We've mentioned a couple of films of this stripe already— *Earth vs. the Flying Saucers* and the Siegel version of *Invasion of the Body Snatchers,* both from the fifties. All the best films of this political type seem to come from that period—although we may be coming full circle again; *The Changeling,* which at this writing seems on its way to become the big "sleeper" of the spring of 1980, is an odd combination of ghosts and Watergate.

If movies are the dreams of the mass culture—one film critic, in fact, has called watching a movie "dreaming with one's eyes open"—and if horror movies are the nightmares of the mass culture, then many of these fifties horrors express America's coming-to-terms with the possibility of nuclear annihilation over political differences.

We ought to eliminate the horror movies of that period that sprang from technological unease (the so-called "big bug" movies are among these) and also those "nuclear showdown" movies such as *Fail-Safe* and Ray Milland's intermittently interesting *Panic in the Year Zero*. These movies are not political in the sense that Siegel's *Invasion of the Body Snatchers* is political; that was a film where you could see the political enemy of your choice around every corner, symbolized in those ominous pods from space.

The political horror films of the period we're discussing here begin, I think, with *The Thing* (1951), directed by Christian Nyby and produced by Howard Hawks (who also had a hand in the direction, one suspects). It starred Margaret Sheridan, Kenneth Tobey, and James Arness as the blood-drinking human carrot from Planet X.

Briefly: A polar encampment of soldiers and scientists discovers a strong magnetic field emanating from an area where there has been a recent meteor fall; the field is strong enough to throw all their electronic gadgets and gizmos off whack. Further, a camera designed to start shooting pictures when and if the normal radiation background count suddenly goes up has taken photos of an object which dips, swoops, and turns at high speeds—strange behavior for a meteor.

An expedition is dispatched to the spot, and it discovers a flying saucer buried in the ice. The saucer, superhot on touchdown, melted its way into the ice, which then refroze, leaving only the tailfin sticking out (thus relieving the special-effects corps of a potentially big-budget item). The Army guys, who demonstrate frostbite of the brain throughout most of the film, promptly destroy the extraterrestrial ship while trying to burn it out of the ice with thermite.

The occupant (Arness) is saved, however, and carted back to the experimental station in a block of ice. He/it is placed in a storage shed, under guard. One of the guards is so freaked out by the Thing that he throws a blanket over it. Unlucky man! Quite obviously all his good stars are in retrograde, his biorhythms low, and his mental magnetic poles temporarily reversed. The blanket he's used is of the electric variety, and it miraculously melts the ice without shorting out. The Thing escapes, and the fun begins.

The fun ends about sixty minutes later with the creature being roasted medium-rare on an electric sidewalk sort of thing that the scientists have set up. A reporter on the scene reports the news of humankind's first victory over invaders from space to a presumably grateful world, and the film fades out, like *The Blob* seven years later, not with a THE END title card, but with a question mark.

The Thing is a small movie (in *An Illustrated History of the Horror Film,* Carlos Clarens quite rightly calls it "intimate") done on a low budget and as obviously done "on-set" as Lewton's *The Cat People.* Like *Alien,* which would come more than a quarter-century later, it achieves its best effects from feelings of claustrophobia and xenophobia, both of them feelings we're saving for those films with mythic, "fairy-tale" subtexts,* but as pointed out before, the best horror movies will try to get at you on many different levels, and *The Thing* is also operating on a political level. It has grim things to say about eggheads (and knee-jerk liberals; in the early fifties you could have put an equal sign between the two) who would indulge in the crime of appeasement.

The very presence of Kenneth Tobey and his squad of soldiers gives the film a militaristic, and thus political, patina. We're never under any illusions that this Arctic base has been set up just for the eggheads, who want to study such useless things as the aurora borealis and the formation of glaciers. No, this base is also spending the taxpayers' money in *important* ways: it is a part of the Distant Early Warning line, part of America's Vigilant and Unceasing Etc., Etc., Etc. In the chain of command, the scientists are very much under Tobey. After all, the film whispers to the audience, we know what these ivory-tower eggheads are like, don't we? Full of big ideas but not worth much in a situation calling for a practical man. Really, it says, when you get right down to it, those bigdome ideas

---

* Some would say that feelings of xenophobia are in themselves political, and there's an argument there to be made—but I would rather discuss it as a universal feeling, which I believe it to be, and exclude it (for now, at least) from the sort of subliminal propaganda we're discussing here.

make most scientists as responsible as a child with a box of matches. They may be great with their microscopes and telescopes, but it takes a man like Kenneth Tobey to understand about America's Vigilant and Unceasing Etc., Etc., Etc.

The Thing is the first movie of the fifties to offer us the scientist in the role of the Appeaser, that creature who for reasons either craven or misguided, would open the gates to the Garden of Eden and let all the evils fly in (as opposed, let us say, to those Mad Labs proprietors of the thirties, who were more than willing to open Pandora's Box and let all the evils fly out—a major distinction, although the end results are the same). That scientists should be so constantly vilified in the techno-horror films of the fifties—a decade that was apparently dedicated to the idea of turning out a whole marching corps of men and women in white lab coats—is perhaps not so surprising when we remember that it was science which opened those same gates so that the atomic bomb could be brought into Eden—first by itself and then trundled on missile carriers. The average Jane or Joe on the street during those spooky eight or nine years that followed the surrender of Japan had extremely schizoid feelings about science and scientists—recognizing the need for them and at the same time loathing the things they had let in forever. On the one hand, there was their pal, that neat little all-around guy, Reddy Kilowatt; on the other hand, before getting into the first reel of *The Thing* down at your local theater, you could watch newsreel footage as an Army mockup of a town *just like yours* was vaporized in a nuclear furnace.

Robert Cornthwaite plays the Appeasing Scientist in *The Thing,* and we hear from his lips the first verse of a psalm that any filmgoer who grew up in the fifties and sixties became familiar with very quickly: "We must preserve this creature for science." The second verse goes, "If it comes from a society more advanced than ours, it must come in peace. If we can only establish communications with it, and find out what it wants—"

Only scientists, Cornthwaite says, are capable of studying this creature from another world, and it must be studied; it must be debriefed; we gotta find out what heats up his rocket tubes. Never mind the fact that the creature has exhibited nothing but murderous tendencies, laying low a couple of huskies (it loses a hand in the process, but not to worry, it grows back) and living on blood instead of Green Thumb Plant Food.

Twice, near the film's conclusion, Cornthwaite is hauled away by soldiers; at the climax, he breaks free of his guards and faces the creature with his hands open and empty. He begs it to communicate with him and to see that he means it no harm. The creature stares at him for a long, pregnant moment . . . and then bats him casually aside, as you or I might swat a mosquito. The medium-rare roasting on the electric sidewalk follows.

Now I'm only a journeyman writer and I will not presume to teach history here (too much like trying to teach your grammy to suck eggs). I will point out that the Americans of that time were perhaps more paranoid about the idea of "appeasement" than at any other time before or since. The dreadful humiliation of Neville Chamberlain and England's resulting close squeak at the beginning of Hitler's war was still very much with those Americans, and why not? It had all happened only twelve years prior to *The Thing*'s release, and even Americans who were just turning twenty-one in 1951 could remember it all very clearly. The moral was simple—such appeasement doesn't work; you gotta cut 'em if they stand and shoot 'em if they run. Otherwise, they'll take you over a bite at a time (and in the case of *The Thing*, you could take that literally). The Chamberlain lesson to Americans of the early fifties was that there can be no peace at any price, and never appeasement. Although the Korean police action would mark the beginning of the end for the idea, in 1951 the idea of America as world policeman (a kind of international Clancy growling, "Whaddye think yer doin' there, boyo?" at such geopolitical burglars as North Korea) was still quite respectable, and many Americans undoubtedly saw the idea in even stronger terms: the United States not just as policeman, but as the gunslinger of the free world, the Texas Ranger who had pushed his way into the brawling saloon of

Asian/European politics in 1941 and who had cleaned house in a mere three and a half years.

So that moment comes in *The Thing* when Cornthwaite faces the creature—and is slammed roughly aside. It is a purely political moment, and audiences applauded the creature's destruction fervently when it came moments later. In the confrontation between Cornthwaite and the hulking Arness, there is a subtext which suggests Chamberlain and Hitler; in the destruction of the creature moments later by Tobey and his soldiers, audiences may have seen (and applauded) the quick, no-nonsense destruction of their favorite geopolitical villain— North Korea perhaps; more likely the dastardly Russians, who had so quickly replaced Hitler as the man in the black hat.

If all this seems much too heavy a cargo for a modest little fright flick like *The Thing* to bear, please remind yourself that a man's point of view is shaped by the events he experiences, and that a man's politics are shaped by his point of view. I am only suggesting that, given the political temper of the times and the cataclysmic world events which had occurred only a few years before, the viewpoint of this movie is almost preordained. What do you do with a blood-drinking carrot from outer space? Simple. Cut him if he stands and shoot him if he runs. And if you're an Appeasing Scientist like Robert Cornthwaite (with a yellow streak up your back as wide as the no-passing line on a highway, that subtext whispers), you simply get bulldozed under.

Carlos Clarens points out how remarkably the creature of this film resembles Universal's Frankenstein monster from twenty years before, but there is really nothing so remarkable about it, surely; this particular card from the Tarot should be familiar to us by now, and if it's not, the title helpfully informs us that we're again dealing with the Thing Without a Name. It perhaps strikes more modern viewers as strange that a creature intelligent enough to conquer space should be presented in the film as an out-and-out monster (as opposed, let us say, to the saucerians in *Earth vs. the Flying Saucers,* who speak English with a moderate warble but with the grammatical poise of an Oxford don; Hawks's Thing can only grunt like a pig getting its back scratched with a wire brush). One wonders why he came to Earth at all. My own suspicion is that he/it got off-course and that the original plan was for him to seed all of Nebraska or perhaps the Nile delta with little bits of himself. Just think—a home-grown invasion force (get in their way and they kill you, but smoke them and . . . *real* mellow, man—oooh, the *colors!*)

Yet even this is not much of an inconsistency when we put ourselves into the temper of the times again. The people of those times saw both Hitler and Stalin as creatures possessed of a certain low animal cunning—Hitler, after all, was first with the jet fighter and the offensive missile. But they were animals for all that, mouthing political ideas that were little more than grunts. Hitler grunted in German; Stalin in Russian, but a grunt is a grunt, for all that. And perhaps the creature in *The Thing* is saying something, after all, which is perfectly harmless—"The people of my star system wish to know if the Get Out of Jail Free card may be sold to another player," perhaps—but it sounds bad. Real bad.

By contrast, consider the other end of this telescope. The children of World War II produced *The Thing;* twenty-six years later a child of Vietnam and the self-proclaimed Love Generation, Steven Spielberg, gives us a fitting balance weight to *The Thing* in a film called *Close Encounters of the Third Kind.* In 1951, the soldier standing sentry duty (the one who has foolishly covered the block of ice in which the Thing has been entombed with an electric blanket, you will remember) empties his automatic into the alien when he hears it coming; in 1977, an old guy holds up a sign reading STOP AND BE FRIENDLY. Somewhere in between the two, John Foster Dulles evolved into Henry Kissinger, and the pugnacious politics of confrontation became détente.

In *The Thing,* Kenneth Tobey occupies himself with building an electric boardwalk to kill the creature; in *Close Encounters,* Richard Dreyfuss occupies himself with building a mockup of Devil's Tower, the creatures' landing place, in his living room. And he would be just as happy, we feel, to run around up there placing those landing lights. The Thing is a big, hulking brute; the creatures from the stars in Spielberg's film are small, delicate, childlike. They do not speak, but their mothership plays lovely harmonic tones—the music of the spheres, we assume. And Dreyfuss, far from wanting to murder these emissaries from space, goes with them.

I'm not saying that Spielberg is or would think of himself as a member of the Love Generation simply because he came to his majority while students were putting daisies in the muzzles of M-1's and while Hendrix and Joplin were playing the Fillmore West. Neither am I saying that Howard Hawks, Christian Nyby, Charles Lederer (who wrote the screenplay for *The Thing*), or John W. Campbell (whose novella formed the basis for the film) fought their way up the beaches of Anzio or helped to raise the Stars and Stripes on Iwo Jima. But events determine point of view and point of view determines politics, and *CE3K* seems to me every bit as preordained as *The Thing*. We can understand that the latter's "let the military handle this" thesis was a perfectly acceptable one in 1951, because the military had handled the Japs and the Nazis perfectly well in Duke Wayne's "Big One," and we can also understand that the former's attitude of "don't let the military handle this" was a perfectly acceptable one in 1977, following the military's less-than-startling record in Vietnam, or even in 1980 (when *CE3K* was rereleased with additional footage), the year when American military personnel lost the battle for our hostages to the Iranians following three hours of mechanical fuckups.

Political horror films are by no means common, but other examples come to mind. The hawkish ones, like *The Thing*, usually extol the virtues of preparedness and deplore the vices of laxness, and achieve a goodly amount of their horror by positing a society which is politically antithetical to ours and yet possesses a great deal of power—either technological or magical, it matters not which; as Arthur C. Clarke has pointed out, when you reach a certain point, there is absolutely no difference between the two. There is a wonderful moment near the beginning of George Pal's adaptation of *The War of the Worlds* when three men, one of whom is waving a white flag, approach the first of the alien spacecraft to land. Each of the three appears to come from a different class and a different race, but they are united, not just by their common humanity, but by a pervasive sense of *Americanness* which I don't believe was accidental. As they approach the smoking crater with their white flag, they evoke that Revolutionary War image we all grew up in school with: the drummer, the fifer, the flag-bearer. Thus their destruction by the Martians' heat ray becomes a symbolic act, calling up all the ideals Americans have ever fought for.

The film *1984* makes a similar statement, only here (the film being largely stripped of the rich resonance George Orwell brought to his novel) Big Brother has replaced the Martians.

In the Charlton Heston film *The Omega Man* (adapted from what David Chute calls "Richard Matheson's tough-minded, peculiarly *practical* vampire novel *I Am Legend*"), we see exactly the same sort of thing; the vampires become almost cartoon Gestapo agents in their black clothes and their sunglasses. Ironically, an earlier film version of that same novel (*The Last Man on Earth*, starring Vincent Price in a rare non-villain role as Matheson's Robert Neville) proposes a political idea which raises a different sort of horror. This film is more faithful to Matheson's novel, and as a result it offers a subtext which tells us that politics themselves are not immutable, that times change, and that Neville's very success as a vampire-hunter (his peculiarly *practical* success, to paraphrase Chute), has turned *him* into the monster, the outlaw, the Gestapo agent who strikes at the helpless as they sleep. For a nation whose political nightmares perhaps still include visions of Kent State and My Lai, this is a particularly apt idea. *The Last Man on Earth* is perhaps an example of the ultimate political horror film, because it offers us the Walt Kelly thesis: We have met the enemy and he is us.

All of which brings us to an interesting borderline that I want to point out but not step over—this is the point at which the country of the horror film touches the country of the black comedy. Stanley Kubrick has been a resident of this borderline area for quite some time. A perfectly good case could be made for classing Stanley Kubrick's *Dr. Strangelove, or How I Learned to Stop Worrying and Love the Bomb* as a political horror film without monsters (a guy needs a dime to phone Washington and stop World War III before it can get started; Keenan Wynn grudgingly obliges by blowing a Coke machine to smithereens with his burpgun so our hero can get at the change; but he tells this would-be savior of the human race that "you're going to have to answer to the Coca-Cola Company for this"); for *A Clockwork Orange* as a political horror film with human monsters (Malcolm McDowell stomping a hapless old man to the tune of "Singin' in the Rain"); and for *2001: A Space Odyssey* as a political horror film with an inhuman monster ("Please don't turn me off," the murderous computer HAL 9000 begs as the Jupiter probe's one remaining crewman pulls its memory modules one by one) that ends its cybernetic life by singing "A Bicycle Built for Two." Kubrick has consistently been the only American film director to understand that stepping over the borderline into taboo country is as often apt to cause wild laughter as it is horror, but any ten-year-old who ever laughed hysterically at a traveling-salesman joke would agree that it is so. Or it may simply be that only Kubrick has been smart enough (or brave enough) to go back to this country more than once.

6

"We have opened a door on an unimaginable power," the old scientist says gloomily at the conclusion of *Them!* "and there will be no closing it now."

At the end of D. F. Jones's novel *Colossus* (filmed as *Colossus: The Forbin Project*), the computer which has taken over everything tells Forbin, its creator, that people will do more than learn to accept its rule; they will come to accept it as a god. "Never!" Forbin responds in ringing tones that would do the hero of a Robert Heinlein space opera proud. But it is Jones himself who has the final word—and it's not a reassuring one. "Never?" reads the final paragraph of his cautionary tale.*

In the Richard Egan film *Gog* (directed by Herbert L. Strock), the equipment of an entire space-research station seems to go mad. A solar mirror twirls erratically, pursuing the heroine with what amounts to a lethal heat ray; a centrifuge designed to test would-be astronauts for their responses to heavy g-loads speeds up until the two test subjects are literally accelerated to death; and at the conclusion, the two BEM-like robots, Gog and Magog, go totally out of control, snapping their Waldo-like pincers and making weird Geiger-counter-like sounds as they roll forward on various errands of destruction ("I can control him," the cold-fish scientist says confidently only moments before Magog crushes his neck with one of those pincers).

"We grow them big out here," the old Indian in *Prophecy* says complacently to Robert Foxworth and Talia Shire as a tadpole as big as a salmon jumps out of a lake in northern Maine and flops around on the shore. Indeed they do; Foxworth also sees a salmon as big as a porpoise, and by the conclusion of the film, one is grateful that whales are not fresh-water mammals.

All the foregoing are examples of the horror film with a technological subtext . . . sometimes referred to as the "nature run amok" sort of horror picture (not that there's much natural about Gog and Magog, with their tractor treads and their forests of radio aerials). In all of them, it is mankind and mankind's technology which must bear the blame; "You brought it on yourselves," they all say; a fitting epitaph for the mass grave of mankind, I think, when the big balloon finally goes up and the ICBMs start to fly.

In *Them!* it is nuclear testing at White Sands that has

---

* D. F. Jones could hardly be classed as the Pollyanna of the science fiction world; in his follow-up to *Colossus,* a newly developed birth control pill that you only have to take once results in a worldwide sterility and the slow death of the human race. Cheery stuff, but Jones is not alone in his gloomy distrust of a technological world; there is J. G. Ballard, author of such grim tales as *Crash, Concrete Island,* and *High-Rise;* not to mention Kurt Vonnegut, Jr. (whom my wife fondly calls "Father Kurt"), who has given us such novels as *Cat's Cradle* and *Player Piano.*

produced the giant ants; the Cold War has spawned dat ole binary debbil Colossus; ditto the machines that have gone nuts in *Gog;* and it's mercury in the water, a side-effect of a paper-making process, that has produced the giant tadpoles and the mutant monstrosities in the John Frankenheimer film *Prophecy.*

It is here, in the techno-horror film, that we really strike the mother lode. No more panning for the occasional nugget, as in the case of the economic horror film or the political horror film; pard, we could dig the gold right out of the ground with our bare hands here, if we wanted to. Here is a corner of the old horror-film corral where even such an abysmal little wet fart of a picture as *The Horror of Party Beach* will yield a technological aspect upon analysis—you see, all those beach blanket boppers in their bikinis and ball-huggers are being menaced by monsters that were created when drums of radioactive waste leaked. But not to worry; although a few girls get carved up, all comes right in the end in time for one last wiener roast before school starts again.

Once more, these things happen only rarely because directors, writers, and producers want them to happen; they happen on their own. The producers of *The Horror of Party Beach,* for example, were two Connecticut drive-in owners who saw a chance to turn a quick buck in the low-budget horror-movie game (the reasoning seeming to be that if Nicholson and Arkoff of AIP could make X amount of dollars churning out B-pictures, then they might be able to make X^2 amount of dollars by turning out Z-pictures). The fact that they created a film which foresaw a problem that would become very real ten years down the road was only an accident . . . but an accident, like Three Mile Island, that perhaps had to happen, sooner or later. I find it quite amusing that this grainy, low-budget rock 'n' roll horror picture arrived at ground zero with its Geiger counters clicking long before *The China Syndrome* was even a twinkle in anyone's eye.

By now it must be obvious that all of these circles intersect, that sooner or later we always arrive back at the same terminus—the terminus which gives upon the land of the mass American nightmare. These are nightmares for profit, granted, but nightmares is nightmares, and in the last analysis it is the profit motive that becomes unimportant and the nightmare itself which remains of interest.

The producers of *The Horror of Party Beach* never sat down, I'm sure (just as I'm sure the producers of *The China Syndrome* did), and said to each other: "Look—we're going to warn the people of America about the dangers of nuclear reactors, and we will sugar-coat the pill of this vital message with an entertaining story line." No, the line of discussion would have been more apt to go like this: Because our target audience is young, we'll feature young people, and because our target audience is interested in sex, we'll site it on a sun-and-surf-type beach, which allows us to show all the flesh the censors will allow. And because our target audience likes grue, we'll give them these gross monsters. It must have looked like boffo box-office stuff: a hybrid of AIP's most consistently lucrative genre pictures—the monster movie and the beach-party movie.

But because any horror film (with the possible exception of the German expressionist films of the teens and twenties) has got to at least pay lip service to credibility, there had to be some *reason* for these monsters to suddenly come out of the ocean and start doing all these antisocial things (one of the film's highlights—maybe lowlights would be better—comes when the creatures invade a slumber party and kill ten or twenty nubile young things . . . talk about party-poopers!). What the producers decided upon was nuclear waste, leaking from those dumped canisters. I'm sure it was one of the least important points in their preproduction discussions, *and for that very reason* it becomes *very* important to our discussions here.

The reason for the monsters most likely came about in a kind of free-association process, the sort of test psychiatrists use to discover points of anxiety in their patients. And although *The Horror of Party Beach* has long since been consigned to oblivion, that image of the canisters marked with radiation symbols sinking slowly to the bottom of the ocean lingers in the memory. What in Christ's name are we *really* doing with all that nuclear sludge? the mind enquires uneasily—the burn-off, the dreck, the used plutonium slugs, and the worn-out parts that are as hot as a nickel-plated revolver and apt to stay that way for the next six hundred years or so? Does *anybody* know what in Christ's name we're doing with those things?

Any thoughtful consideration of techno-horror films—those films whose subtexts suggest that we have been betrayed by our own machines and processes of mass production—reveals very quickly another face in that dark Tarot hand we dealt out earlier: this time it's the face of the Werewolf. In talking about the Werewolf in *Dr. Jekyll and Mr. Hyde* I used the terms *Apollonian* (to suggest reason and the power of the mind) and *Dionysian* (to suggest emotion, sensuality, and chaotic action). Most films which express technological fears have a similar dual nature. Grasshoppers, *Beginning of the End* suggests, are Apollonian creatures, going about their business of hopping, eating, spitting tobacco juice, and making little grasshoppers. But following an infusion of nuclear wolfsbane, they grow to the size of Cadillacs, become Dionysian and disruptive, and attack Chicago. It is their very Dionysian tendencies—in this case, their sex drive—that spells the end for them. Peter Graves (as the Brave Young Scientist) rigs up a mating-call tape that is broadcast through loudspeakers from a number of boats circling on Lake Michigan, and the grasshoppers all rush to their deaths, believing themselves to be on their way to a really good fuck. A bit of a cautionary tale, you understand. I bet D. F. Jones loved it.

Even *Night of the Living Dead* has a techno-horror aspect, a fact that may be overlooked as the zombies move in on the lonely Pennsylvania farmhouse where the "good guys" are holed up. There is nothing really supernatural about all those dead folks getting up and walking; it happened because a space probe to Venus picked up some weird corpse-reviving radiation on its way back home. One suspects that chunks of such a satellite would be eagerly sought-after artifacts in Palm Springs and Fort Lauderdale.

The barometer effect of the subtexts of techno-horror films can be seen by comparing films of this type from the fifties, sixties, and seventies. In the fifties, the terror of the Bomb and of fallout was a real and terrifying thing, and it left a scar on those children who wanted to be good just as the depression of the thirties left a scar on their elders. A newer generation—now still teenagers, with no memory of either the Cuban missile crisis or of the Kennedy assassination in Dallas, raised on the milk of détente—may find it hard to comprehend the terror of these things, but they will undoubtedly have a chance to discover it in the years of tightening belts and heightening tensions which lie ahead . . . and the movies will be there to give their vague fears concrete focusing points in the horror movies yet to come.

It may be that nothing in the world is so hard to comprehend as a terror whose time has come and gone—which may be why parents can scold their children for their fear of the bogeyman, when as children themselves they had to cope with exactly the same fears (and the same sympathetic but uncomprehending parents). That may be why one generation's nightmare becomes the next generation's sociology, and even those who have walked through the fire have trouble remembering exactly what those burning coals felt like.

I can remember, for instance, that in 1968, when I was twenty-one, the issue of long hair was an extremely nasty, extremely explosive one. That seems as hard to believe now as the idea of people killing each other over whether the sun went around the earth or the earth went around the sun, but that happened, too.

I was thrown out of a bar called the Stardust in Brewer, Maine, by a construction worker back in that happy year of 1968. The guy had muscles on his muscles and told me I could come back and finish my beer "after you get a haircut, you faggot fairy." There were the standard catcalls thrown from passing cars (usually old cars with fins and cancer of the rocker panels): Are you a boy or are you a girl? Do you give head, honey? When was the last time you had a bath? And so on, as Father Kurt so rightly says.

I can remember such things in an intellectual, even analytical way, as I can remember having a dressing that had actually grown into the tissue yanked from the site of a cyst-removal operation that occurred when I was twelve. I screamed from the pain and then fainted dead away. I can remember the pulling sensation as the gauze tore free of the new, healthy tissue (the dressing removal was performed by a nurse's aide who apparently had no idea what she was doing), I can remember the scream, and I can remember the faint. What I can't remember is the pain itself. It's the same with the hair thing, and in a larger sense, all the other pains associated with coming of age in the decade of napalm and the Nehru jacket. I've purposely avoided writing a novel with a 1960s' time setting because all of that seems, like the pulling of that surgical dressing, very distant to me now—almost as if it had happened to another person. But those things did happen; the hate, paranoia, and fear on both sides were all too real. If we doubt it, we only need review that quintessential sixties counterculture horror film, *Easy Rider,* where Peter Fonda and Dennis Hopper end up being blown away by a couple of rednecks in a pickup truck as Roger McGuinn sings Bob Dylan's "It's All Right, Ma (I'm Only Bleeding)" on the soundtrack.

Similarly, it is difficult to remember in any gut way the fears that came with those boom years of atomic technology twenty-five years ago. The technology itself was strictly Apollonian; as Apollonian as nice-guy Larry Talbot, who "said his prayers at night." The atom was not split by a gibbering Colin Clive or Boris Karloff in some Eastern European Mad Lab; it was not done by alchemy and moonlight in the center of a rune-struck circle; it was done by a lot of little guys at Oak Ridge and White Sands who wore tweed jackets and smoked Luckies, guys who worried about dandruff and psoriasis and whether or not they could afford a new car and how to get rid of the goddam crabgrass on the lawn. Splitting the atom, producing fission, opening that door on a new world that the old scientist speaks of at the end of *Them!*—these things were accomplished on a business-as-usual basis.

People understood this and could live with it (fifties science books extolled the wonderful world the Friendly Atom would produce, a world refueled by nice safe nuclear reactors, and grammar school kids got free comic books produced by the power companies), but they suspected and feared the hairy, simian face on the other side of the coin as well: they feared that the atom might be, for a number of reasons both technological and political, essentially uncontrollable. These feelings of deep unease came out in movies such as *The Beginning of the End, Them!, Tarantula, The Incredible Shrinking Man* (where radiation combined with a pesticide causes a very personal horror for one man, Scott Carey), *The H-Man,* and *Four-D Man.* The entire cycle reaches its supreme pinnacle of absurdity in *Night of the Lepus,* where the world is menaced by sixty-foot bunnies.*

The concerns of the techno-horror films of the sixties and seventies change with the concerns of the people who lived through those times; the big bug movies give way to pictures such as *The Forbin Project* (The Software that Conquered the World) and *2001,* which both offer us the possibility of the computer as God, or the even nastier idea (ludicrously executed, I'll readily admit) of the computer as satyr, which is laboriously produced in *Demon Seed* and *Saturn 3.* In the sixties, horror proceeds from a vision of technology as an octopus—perhaps sentient—burying us alive in red tape and information-retrieval systems which are terrible when they work (*The Forbin Project*) and even more terrible when they don't: In *The Andromeda Strain,* for instance, a small scrap of paper gets caught in the striker of a teletype machine, keeps the bell from ringing, and

---

* And a host of others, many of them Japanese imports, all linked by either long-term radiation or nuclear blast as first cause: *Godzilla, Gorgo, Rodan, Mothra,* and *Ghidrah, the Three-Headed Monster.* The idea was even played for laughs once before Kubrick's *Dr. Strangelove,* in an odd little fifties picture called *The Atomic Kid,* starring Mickey Rooney.

thereby (in a fashion Rube Goldberg certainly would have approved of) nearly causes the end of the world.

Finally there are the seventies, culminating in Frankenheimer's not-very-good but certainly well-meant film *Prophecy*, which is so strikingly similar to those fifties big bug movies (only the first cause has changed), and *The China Syndrome*, a horror movie which synthesizes all three of these major technological fears: fears of radiation, fears for the ecology, fears of the machinery gone out of control, run wild.

Before leaving this all too brief look at pictures which depend on some mass unease over matters technological to provide the equivalent of The Hook (pictures which appeal to the Luddite hiding inside all of us), we should mention some of the films dealing with space travel which fall into this category . . . but we'll exclude such xenophobic pictures as *Earth vs. the Flying Saucers* and *The Mysterians* from our view. Pictures which focus on the possible Dionysian side of space exploration (such as *The Andromeda Strain* and *Night of the Living Dead*, where satellites bring back dangerous but non-sentient organisms from the void) ought to be differentiated from those purely xenophobic movies dealing with invasion from outer space— films where the human race is viewed in an essentially passive role, attacked by the equivalent of muggers from the stars. In pictures of this type, technology is often seen as the savior (as it is in *Earth vs. the Flying Saucers*, where Hugh Marlowe uses his sonic gun to interrupt the saucers' electromagnetic drive, or in *The Thing*, where Tobey and his men use electricity to barbecue the interstellar vegetable)—Apollonian science vanquishing the Dionysian bad guys from Planet X.

Although both *The Andromeda Strain* and *Night of the Living Dead* present space travel itself as an active danger, perhaps the best example of that idea combined with the brilliant mind dangerously hypnotized by the siren song of technology comes in *The Creeping Unknown*, a film that predates both of the former. In that film, the first of the critically acclaimed Quatermass series, the viewer is originally presented with one of the creepiest locked-room mysteries ever posited: three scientist-astronauts are sent into space, but only one returns . . . and he is catatonic. Telemetry and the presence of all three spacesuits seem to prove that the two missing spacemen never left the ship. So where did they go?

What happened, apparently, is that they picked up an interstellar hitchhiker, a plot device we see again in *It! The Terror from Beyond Space* and, of course, in *Alien*. This hitchhiker has consumed the survivor's two mates, leaving only a mass of sludgy gray stuff behind . . . and, of course, the hitchhiker (a kind of space spore) is now busily at work in the body of the survivor, Victor Carune, who is played with skull-like, spooky believability by Richard Wordsworth. Poor Carune ends up degenerating into a spongy, many-tentacled horror which is finally spotted clinging to a scaffolding in Westminster Abbey and dispatched (just in the nick of time; it is about to sporulate and create billions of these things) by a big jolt of electricity which sets it on fire.

All of this is fairly standard monster-movie fare. What elevates *The Creeping Unknown* to levels undreamed of in the philosophies of the creators of *The Horror of Party Beach* is Val Guest's somber, atmospheric direction, and the character of Quatermass himself, played by Brian Donlevy (other actors have since played Quatermass in other films, softening the interpretation a bit). Quatermass is a scientist who may or may not be mad, depending on your own views of technology. Certainly if he is nuts, there is enough Apollonian method in his madness to make him every bit as scary (and every bit as dangerous) as that blob of tentacle-waving goo that was once Victor Carune. "I'm a scientist, not a fortune-teller," Quatermass grunts contemptuously at a timid doctor who asks him what he thinks might happen next; when a fellow scientist tells him that if he tries to open the hatch of the crashed rocket he will roast the space travelers inside, Quatermass storms at him: "Don't tell me what I can and can't do!"

His attitude toward Canine himself is the cold-blooded attitude which a biologist might adopt toward a hamster or a Rhesus monkey. "He's coming along fine," Quatermass says of the catatonic Carune, who is sitting in something which vaguely resembles a dentist's chair and staring out at the world with eyes as black and dead as cinders coughed up from hell. "He knows we're trying to help him."

Yet in the end it is Quatermass triumphant—if only through blind luck. After the monster is destroyed, Quatermass brushes rudely by a police officer who is trying to tell him in a halting way that he prayed they would be successful. "One world at a time is enough for me," the policeman says; Quatermass ignores him.

At the door, his young assistant finds his way to him. "I only just heard, sir," he says. "Is there anything I can do?"

"Yes, Morris," Quatermass replies. "I'm going to need some help."

"Help, sir?"

"Going to start again," Quatermass amplifies—it is the film's last line of dialogue. It fades to a scene of yet another rocket blasting off into outer space.

Guest seems ambivalent about his ending and about the character of Quatermass, and it's that ambivalence which gives this early Hammer film its resonance and real power. Quatermass seems somehow closer to those very real Oak Ridge scientists of the postwar period than he does to the gibbering Mad Labs scientists of the thirties; his is no Dr. Cyclops in a white lab coat, chuckling evilly as he stares through his bottle-thick glasses at his creations. *Au contraire,* he is not only fairly good-looking and fearsomely intelligent, he is charismatic and impossible to turn from his purpose. If you are an optimist, you can see the coda of *The Creeping Unknown* as a testament to the glorious stubbornness of the human spirit, its determination to advance the store of knowledge at any cost. If, on the other hand, you are a pessimist, then Quatermass becomes the ultimate symbol of mankind's built-in limiting factor, and the high priest of the techno-horror film. The return of his first manned space probe has almost resulted in the end of the human race; Quatermass's response to this niggling little reversal is to launch another as quickly as he can. Foot-dragging politicians are apparently no match for the man's charisma, and as we see that rocket going up at the end of the picture, we're left with a question: *What will* this *one bring back?*

Even such a much-loved American institution as the motor vehicle has not entirely escaped the troubled dreams of Hollywood; a few years before being run out of his mortgaged house in Amityville, James Brolin had to face the terrors of *The Car* (1977), a customized something-or-other that looked like a squatty airport limo from one of hell's used-car lots. The movie degenerates into a ho-hum piece of hackwork before the end of the second reel (the sort of movie where you can safely go out for a popcorn refill at certain intervals because you know the car isn't going to strike again for ten minutes or so), but there is a marvelous opening sequence where the car chases two bicyclists through Utah's Zion National Park, its horn bleating arrhythmically as it gains on them and finally runs them down. There's something working in that opening sequence, something that calls up a deep, almost primitive unease about the cars we zip ourselves up in, thereby becoming anonymous . . . and perhaps homicidal.

A better film is the Steven Spielberg adaptation of Richard Matheson's short story *Duel,* a film which originally appeared as part of ABC's *Movie of the Week* series and went on to become something of a cult film. In this film, a psychotic trucker in a big ten-wheeler pursues Dennis Weaver over what seems to be at least a million miles of California highways. We never actually see the trucker (although we do see a beefy arm cocked out of the cab window once, and at another point we see a pair of pointy-toed cowboy boots on the far side of the truck), and ultimately it is the truck itself, with its huge wheels, its dirty windshield like an idiot's stare, and its somehow hungry bumpers, which becomes the monster—and when Weaver is finally able to lead it to an embankment and lure it over the edge, the noise of its "death" becomes a series of chilling Jurassic roars . . . the sound, we think, a tyrannosaurus rex would make going slowly down into a tar pit. And Weaver's response is that of any self-respecting caveman: he screams, shrieks, cuts capers, literally dances for joy. *Duel* is a gripping, almost painfully suspenseful rocket ride of a movie; perhaps not Spielberg's best work—that must almost certainly wait for the eighties and nineties—but surely one of the half-dozen best movies ever made for TV.

We could uncover other interesting tales of automotive horror, but they would be stories and novels, mostly; such turkeys as *Death Race 2000* and *Mad Max* hardly count. Modern Hollywood has apparently decided that, as the day of the privately owned gasoline vehicle enters its late afternoon, the automobile in most cases must be reserved for funny car chases (as in *Foul Play* and the cheerfully mind-croggling *Grand Theft Auto*) or a kind of sappy reverence (*The Driver*). The interested reader might enjoy an anthology (now available in paperback) edited by Bill Pronzini and titled *Car Sinister*. Fritz Leiber's contribution alone, a funny/sinister tale of Car Future titled "X Marks the Pedwalk," is worth the price of admission.

7

Social horror films.

We've already discussed a few films with social implications—pimples and the heartbreak of psoriasis in the fifties, not to mention Michael Landon drooling shaving cream all over his high school jacket. But there have been other films which tackle more serious social subjects. In some cases (*Rollerball, Wild in the Streets*), these films feature a logical or satirical extrapolation of current social trends and thus become science fiction. We'll restrict these, if you don't mind, on the grounds that they constitute another dance—a bit different from this dark cotillion we're currently engaged in.

There have been a few films which have tried to walk the borderline between horror and social satire; one of those which seems to me to tread this borderline most successfully is *The Stepford Wives*. The film is based on the novel by Ira Levin, and Levin has actually been able to pull this difficult trick off twice, the other case being that of *Rosemary's Baby*, which we'll talk about in some depth when we finally arrive at our discussion of the horror novel. For now we'll stick to *The Stepford Wives*, which has some witty things to say about Women's Liberation, and some disquieting things to say about the American male's response to it.

I spent some time trying to decide if the film, directed by Bryan Forbes and starring Katharine Ross and Paula Prentiss, really belonged in this book. It is as satiric as the best of Kubrick's work (although a good deal less elegant), and I defy an audience not to laugh when Ross and Prentiss step into the home of a neighbor (he's the local druggist, and a Walter Mitty type if ever there was one) and hear his wife moaning upstairs: "Oh, Frank, you're the greatest . . . Frank, you're the best . . . you're the champ . . ."*

The original Levin story avoided the label "horror novel" (something like the label "pariah dog" in the more exalted circles of literary criticism) because most critics saw it as Levin's sly poke at the Women's Movement. But the scarier implications of Levin's jape are not directed at women at all; they are aimed unerringly at those men who consider it only their due to leave for the golf course on Saturday morning after breakfast has been served them and to reappear (loaded, more likely than not) in time for their dinner to be served them.

I'm including it here—as social horror rather than social satire—because the film, after some uneasy backing and filling where it seems unsure of just what it *does* want to be—becomes just that: a social horror story.

Katharine Ross and her husband (played by Peter Masterson) move from New York City to Stepford, a Connecticut suburb, because they feel it will be better for the children, and themselves as well. Stepford is a perfect little village where kids wait good-humoredly for the school bus, where you can see

---

* But the credit for this particular scene belongs to neither Forbes nor Levin, but with the film's screenwriter, William Goldman, who is a very funny fellow. If you doubt, see his wonderful send-up of fantasy and fairy tales, *The Princess Bride*. I can think of no other satire, with the possible exception of *Alice in Wonderland*, which is so clearly an expression of love and humor and good temper.

two or three fellows washing their cars on any given day, where (you feel) the yearly United Fund quota is not only met but exceeded.

Yet there's a strangeness in Stepford. A lot of the wives seem a little . . . well, spacey. Pretty, always attired in flowing dresses that are almost gowns (a place where the movie slips, I think; as a labeling device, it's pretty crude. These women might as well be wearing stickers pasted to their foreheads which read I AM ONE OF THE *WEIRD* STEPFORD WIVES), they all drive station wagons, discuss housework with an inordinate degree of enthusiasm, and seem to spend any spare time at the supermarket.

One of the Stepford wives (one of the *weird* ones) cracks her head in a minor parking lot fender-bender; later we see her at a lawn party, repeating over and over again: "I simply *must* get that recipe . . . I simply *must* get that recipe . . . I simply *must* . . . " The secret of Stepford comes clear immediately. Freud, in a tone which sounds suspiciously like despair, asked: "Woman . . . what does she want?" Forbes and company ask the opposite question, and come up with a stinging answer. Men, the film says, do not want women; they want robots with sex organs.

There are several funny scenes in the movie (besides the aforementioned "Frank, you're the champ" sequence); my own favorite comes when, at a women's "bitch session" Ross and Prentiss have arranged, the *weird* Stepford wives begin discussing cleaning products and laundry soaps with a slow and yet earnest intensity; everyone seems to have walked right out of one of those commercials male Madison Avenue execs sometimes refer to as "Two C's in a K"—meaning two cunts in a kitchen.

But the movie waltzes slowly out of this brightly lit room of social satire and into a darker chamber by far. We feel the ring closing, first around Paula Prentiss, then around Katharine Ross. There is an uncomfortable passage when the artist who apparently creates the features for the robots sits sketching Ross, his eyes looking up from the sketch pad at her and then back down again; there is the smirking expression on the face of Tina Louise's husband as the bulldozer rips up the surface of her tennis court in preparation for the pool *he* always wanted; there is Ross discovering her husband sitting alone in the living room of their new house, a drink in his hand, weeping. She is deeply concerned, but we know that his shallow tears mean only that he has sold her out for a dummy with microchips in her head. Very soon she will lose all her interest in photography.

The movie reserves its ultimate horror and its most telling social shot for the closing moments of the film, when the "new" Katharine Ross walks in on the old one . . . perhaps, we think, to murder her. Under her flowing negligée which might have come from Frederick's of Hollywood, we see Ms. Ross's rather small breasts built up to the size of what men discussing women over beers sometimes refer to as "knockers." And of course, they are no longer the woman's breasts at all; they now belong solely to her husband. The dummy is not quite complete, however; there are two horrible black pools where the eyes should be. Bad enough, and more spectacular, probably, but it was the import of those silicone-swollen breasts that chilled me. The best social horror movies achieve their effect by implication, and *The Stepford Wives,* by showing us only the surface of things and never troubling to explain exactly how these things are done, implies plenty.

I'll not bore you by rehashing the plot of William Friedkin's *The Exorcist,* another film which relies on the unease generated by changing mores; I'll simply assume that if your interest in the genre has been sufficient to sustain you this far, then you've probably seen it.

If the late fifties and early sixties were the curtain-raiser on the generation gap ("Is it a boy or a girl?" etc., etc., etc.), then the seven years from 1966 to 1972 were the play itself. Little Richard, who had horrified parents in 1957 when he leaped atop his piano and began boogeying on it in his lizardskin loafers, looked tame next to John Lennon, who was proclaiming that the Beatles were more popular than Jesus—a statement that set off a rash of fundamentalist record-burnings. The

Brylcreem look was replaced by those long locks already discussed. Parents began to find strange herbs in their sons' and daughters' bureau drawers. The images in rock music had become increasingly distressing: *Mr. Tambourine Man* seemed to be about drugs; with the Byrds' *Eight Miles High* there could be no question. Radio stations continued to play discs by one group even after two male band members announced they were in love with each other. Elton John proclaimed his AC/DC sexual proclivities and continued successful; yet less than twenty years before, wildman Jerry Lee Lewis was blackballed from AM airplay when he married his fourteen-year-old cousin.

Then there was the war in Vietnam. Messrs. Johnson and Nixon spread it out like a great big rancid picnic lunch over there in Asia. Many of the young elected not to attend. "I got no quarrel with them Congs," Muhammed Ali announced, and was stripped of his boxing title for declining to take off his gloves and pick up an M-1. Kids began burning their draft cards, running away to Canada or Sweden, and marching with Viet Cong flags. In Bangor, where I hung out in my college days, a young man was arrested and incarcerated for replacing the seat of his Levis with an American flag. Some fun, huh, kid.

It was more than a generation gap. The two generations seemed, like the San Andreas fault, to be moving along opposing plates of social and cultural conscience, commitment, and definitions of civilized behavior itself. The result was not so much an earthquake as it was a timequake. And with all of this young vs. old nuttiness as a backdrop, Friedkin's film of *The Exorcist* appeared and became a social phenomenon in itself. Lines stretched around the block in every major city where it played, and even in towns which normally rolled up their sidewalks promptly at 7:30 P.M., midnight shows were scheduled. Church groups picketed; sociologists with pipes pontificated; newscasters did "back of the book" segments for their programs on slow nights. The country, in fact, went on a two-month possession jag.

The movie (and the novel) is nominally about the attempts

of two priests to cast a demon out of young Regan MacNeil, a pretty little subteen played by Linda Blair (who later went on to a High Noon showdown with a bathroom plunger in the infamous NBC movie *Born Innocent*). Substantatively, however, it is a film about explosive social change, a finely honed focusing point for that entire youth explosion that took place in the late sixties and early seventies. It was a movie for all those parents who felt, in a kind of agony and terror, that they were losing their children and could not understand why or how it was happening. It's the face of the Werewolf again, a Jekyll-and-Hyde tale in which sweet, lovely and loving Regan turns into a foul-talking monster strapped into her bed and croaking (in the voice of Mercedes McCambridge) such charming homilies as "You're going to let Jesus fuck you, fuck you, fuck you." Religious trappings aside, every adult in America understood what the film's powerful subtext was saying; they understood that the demon in Regan MacNeil would have responded enthusiastically to the Fish Cheer in Woodstock.

A Warner Brothers executive told me recently that movie surveys show the average filmgoer to be fifteen years of age, which may be the biggest reason why the movies so often seem afflicted with a terminal case of arrested development. For every film like *Julia* or *The Turning Point*, there are a dozen like *Roller Boogie* and *If You Don't Stop It, You'll Go Blind*. But it is worth noting that when the infrequent blockbusters which every film producer hopes for finally come along—pictures like *Star Wars, Jaws, American Graffiti, The Godfather, Gone With the Wind*, and of course *The Exorcist*—they always break the demographic hammerlock which is the enemy of intelligent filmmaking. It is comparatively rare for horror movies to do this, but *The Exorcist* is a case in point (and we have already spoken of *The Amityville Horror*, another film which has enjoyed a surprisingly old audience).

A film which appealed directly to the fifteen-year-olds that provide the spike point for movie-going audiences—and one with a subtext tailored to match—was the Brian De Palma adaptation of my novel *Carrie*. While I believe that both the book and the film depend on largely the same social situations to provide a text and subtext of horror, there's maybe enough difference to make a few interesting observations on De Palma's film version.

Both novel and movie have a pleasant *High School Confidential* feel, and while there are some superficial changes from the book in the film (Carrie's mother, for instance, seems to be presented in the film as a kind of weird renegade Roman Catholic), the basic story skeleton is pretty much the same. The story deals with a girl named Carrie White, the browbeaten daughter of a religious fanatic. Because of her strange clothes and shy mannerisms, Carrie is the butt of every class joke; the social outsider in every situation. She also has a mild telekinetic ability which intensifies after her first menstrual period, and she finally uses this power to "bring down the house" following a terrible social disaster at her high school prom.

De Palma's approach to the material was lighter and more deft than my own—and a good deal more artistic; the book tries to deal with the loneliness of one girl, her desperate effort to become a part of the peer society in which she must exist, and how her effort fails. If it had any thesis to offer, this deliberate updating of *High School Confidential*, it was that high school is a place of almost bottomless conservatism and bigotry, a place where the adolescents who attend are no more allowed to rise "above their station" than a Hindu would be allowed to rise above his or her caste.

But there's a little more subtext to the book than that, I think—at least, I hope so. If *The Stepford Wives* concerns itself with what men want from women, then *Carrie* is largely about how women find their own channels of power, and what men fear about women and women's sexuality . . . which is only to say that, writing the book in 1973 and only out of college three years, I was fully aware of what Women's Liberation implied for me and others of my sex. The book is, in its more adult implications, an uneasy masculine shrinking from a future of female equality. For me, Carrie White is a sadly misused teenager, an example of the sort of person whose spirit is so often broken for good in that pit of man- and woman-eaters that is your normal suburban high school. But she's also Woman, feeling her powers for the first time and, like Samson, pulling down the temple on everyone in sight at the end of the book.

Heavy, turgid stuff—but in the novel, it's only there if you want to take it. If you don't, that's okay with me. A subtext only works well if it's unobtrusive (in that I perhaps succeeded too well; in her review of De Palma's film, Pauline Kael dismissed my novel as "an unassuming potboiler"—as depressing a description as one could imagine, but not completely inaccurate).

De Palma's film is up to more ambitious things. As in *The Stepford Wives,* humor and horror exist side by side in *Carrie,* playing off one another, and it is only as the film nears its conclusion that horror takes over completely. We see Billy Nolan (well played by John Travolta) giving the cops a big aw-shucks grin as he hides a beer against his crotch early on; it is a moment reminiscent of *American Graffiti.* Not long after, however, we see him swinging a sledgehammer at the head of a pig in a stockyard—the aw-shucks grin has crossed the line into madness, somehow, and that line-crossing is what the film as a whole is about.

We see three boys (one of them the film's nominal hero, played by William Katt) trying on tuxedos for the Prom in a kind of Gas House Kids routine that includes Donald Duck talk and speeded-up action. We see the girls who have humiliated Carrie in the shower room by throwing tampons and sanitary napkins at her doing penance on the exercise field to tootling, lumbering music which is reminiscent of "Baby Elephant Walk." And yet beyond all these sophomoric and mildly amusing high school cut-ups, we sense a vacuous, almost unfocused hate, the almost unplanned revenge upon a girl who is trying to rise above her station. Much of De Palma's film is surprisingly jolly, but we sense his jocoseness is dangerous; behind it lurks the aw-shucks grin becoming a frozen rictus, and the girls laboring over their calisthenics were the same girls shouting, "Plug it up, plug it up, plug it up!" at Carrie not long before. Most of all, there is that bucket of pig's blood poised on the beam above the place where Carrie and Tommy (Katt) will eventually be crowned . . . only waiting its time.

De Palma is sly, and extremely adept at handling his mostly female cast. In writing the novel, I found myself slogging grimly toward the conclusion, trying to do the best job I could with what I knew about women (which was not a great deal). The strain shows in the finished book. It's a fast and entertaining read, I think, and (for me at least) quite gripping. But there's a certain heaviness there that a really good popular novel should not have, a feeling of *Sturm und Drang* that I could not get rid of no matter how hard I tried. The book seems clear enough and truthful enough in terms of the characters and their actions, but it lacks the style of De Palma's film.

The book attempts to look at the ant farm of high school society dead on; De Palma's examination of this *High School Confidential* world is more oblique . . . and more cutting. The film came along at a time when movie critics were bewailing the fact that there were no movies being made with good, meaty roles for women in them . . . but none of these critics seem to have noticed that in its film incarnation, *Carrie* belongs almost entirely to the ladies. Billy Nolan, a major—and frightening— character in the book, has been reduced to a semisupporting role in the movie. Tommy, the boy who takes Carrie to the Prom, is presented in the novel as a boy who is honestly trying to do something manly—in his own way he is trying to opt out of the caste system. In the film he becomes little more than his girlfriend's cat's-paw, her tool of atonement for her part in the shower room scene where Carrie is pelted with sanitary napkins.

"I don't go around with anyone I don't want to," Tommy said patiently. "I'm asking because I want to ask you." Ultimately, he knew this to be the truth.

In the film, however, when Carrie asks Tommy why he is favoring her with an invitation to the Prom, he offers her a dizzy sun 'n' surf grin and says, "Because you liked my poem." Which, by the way, his girlfriend wrote.

The novel views high school in a fairly common way: as that pit of man- and woman-eaters already mentioned. De Palma's social stance is more original; he sees this suburban white kids' high school as a kind of matriarchy. No matter where you look, there are girls behind the scenes, pulling invisible wires, rigging elections, using their boyfriends as stalking horses. Against such a backdrop, Carrie becomes doubly pitiful, because she is unable to do any of these things—she can only wait to be saved or damned by the actions of others. Her only power is her tele-kinetic ability, and both book and movie eventually arrive at the same point: Carrie uses her "wild talent" to pull down the whole rotten society. And one reason for the success of the story in both print and film, I think, lies in this: Carrie's revenge is something that any student who ever had his gym shorts pulled down in Phys Ed or his glasses thumb-rubbed in study hall could approve of. In Carrie's destruction of the gym (and her destructive walk back home in the book, a sequence left out of the movie because of tight budgeting) we see a dream revolution of the socially downtrodden.

8

Once upon a time there dwelt on the outskirts of a large forest a poor woodcutter with his wife and two children; the boy was called Hansel and the girl Gretel. He had al-ways had little enough to live on, and once, when there was a great famine in the land, he couldn't even provide them with daily bread. One night, as he was tossing about in his bed, full of cares and worry, he sighed and said to his wife: "What's to become of us? How are we to sup-port our poor children, now that we have nothing more for ourselves?" "I'll tell you what, husband," answered the woman, "early tomorrow morning we'll take the children into the thickest part of the wood; there we shall light a fire for them and give them each a piece of bread; then we'll go on to our work and leave them alone. They won't be able to find their way home and we shall thus be rid of them . . ."*

Previous to now, we have been discussing horror movies with subtexts which try to link real (if sometimes free-floating) anxieties to the nightmare fears of the horror film. But now, with this invocation from "Hansel and Gretel," that most cautionary of nursery tales, let us put out even this dim light of rationality and discuss a few of those films whose effects go considerably deeper, past the rational and into those fears which seem universal.

Here is where we cross into the taboo lands for sure, and it's best that I be frank with you up front. I think that we're all mentally ill; those of us outside the asylums only hide it a little better—and maybe not all that much better, after all. We've all known people who talk to themselves; people who sometimes squinch their faces into horrible grimaces when they believe no one is watching; people who have some hysterical fear—of snakes, the dark, the tight place, the long drop . . . and, of course, those final worms and grubs that are waiting so patiently underground to play their part in the great Thanksgiving table of life: what once ate must eventually be eaten.

When we pay our four or five bucks and seat ourselves at tenth-row center in a theater showing a horror movie, we are daring the nightmare.

Why? Some of the reasons are simple and obvious. To show that we can, that we are not afraid, that we can ride this roller coaster. Which is not to say that a really good horror movie may not surprise a scream out of us at some point, the way we may scream when the roller coaster twists through a complete three-sixty or ploughs through a lake at the bottom of the drop. And horror movies, like roller coasters, have always been the special province of the young; by the time one turns forty

---

* From *The Andrew Lang Fairy Tale Treasury*, edited by Cary Wilkens (New York: Avenel Books, 1979), p. 91.

or fifty, one's appetite for double-twists of 360° loops may be considerably depleted.

As pointed out, we also go to reestablish our feelings of essential normality; the horror movie is innately conservative, even reactionary. Freda Jackson as the horrible melting woman in *Die, Monster, Die!* confirms for us that, no matter how far we may be removed from the beauty of a Robert Redford or a Diana Ross, we are still light-years from true ugliness.

And we go to have fun.

Ah, but this is where the ground starts to slope away, isn't it? Because this is a very peculiar sort of fun indeed. The fun comes from seeing others menaced—sometimes killed. One critic has suggested that if pro football has become the voyeur's version of combat, then the horror film has become the modern version of the public lynching.

It is true that the mythic, "fairy-tale" horror film intends to take away the shades of gray (which is one reason why *When a Stranger Calls* doesn't work; the psycho, well and honestly played by Tony Beckley, is a poor shmuck beset by the miseries of his own psychoses; our unwilling sympathy for him dilutes the film's success as surely as water dilutes Scotch); it urges us to put away our more civilized and adult penchant for analysis and to become children again, seeing things in pure blacks and pure whites. It may be that horror movies provide psychic relief on this level because this invitation to lapse into simplicity, and even outright madness is extended so rarely. We are told we may allow our emotions a free rein . . . or no rein at all.

If we are all insane, then all insanity becomes a matter of degree. If your insanity leads you to carve up women like Jack the Ripper or the Cleveland Torso Murderer, we clap you away in the funny farm (except neither of those two amateur-night surgeons were ever caught, heh-heh-heh); if, on the other hand, your insanity leads you only to talk to yourself when you're under stress or to pick your nose on your morning bus, then you are left alone to go about your business . . . although it's doubtful that you will ever be invited to the best parties.

The potential lyncher is in almost all of us (I exclude saints, past and present, but then, most or all saints have been crazy in their own ways), and every now and then he has to be let loose to scream and roll around on the grass. . . . By God, I do believe I'm talking Werewolf again. Our emotions and our fears form their own body, and we recognize that it demands its own exercise to maintain proper muscle tone. Certain of these emotional "muscles" are accepted—even exalted—in civilized society; they are, of course, the emotions which tend to maintain the status quo of civilization itself. Love, friendship, loyalty, kindness—these are all the emotions which we applaud, emotions which have been immortalized in the bad couplets of Hallmark Cards and in the verses (I don't dare call it poetry) of Leonard Nimoy.

When we exhibit these emotions, society showers us with positive reinforcement; we learn this even before we get out of diapers. When, as children, we hug our rotten little puke of a sister and give her a kiss, all the aunts and uncles smile and twit and cry, "Isn't he the *sweetest* little thing?" Such coveted treats as chocolate-covered graham crackers often follow. But if we deliberately slam the rotten little puke of a sister's fingers in the door, sanctions follow—angry remonstrance from parents, aunts, and uncles; instead of a chocolate-covered graham cracker, a spanking.

But anticivilization emotions don't go away, and they demand periodic exercise. We have such "sick" jokes as, "What's the difference between a truckload of bowling balls and a truckload of dead babies?" (You can't unload a truckload of bowling balls with a pitchfork . . . a joke, by the way, which I heard originally from a ten-year-old.) Such a joke may surprise a laugh or a grin out of us even as we recoil, a possibility which confirms the thesis: if we share a Brotherhood of Man, then we also share an Insanity of Man. None of which is intended as a defense of either the sick joke or insanity, but merely as an explanation of why the best horror films, like the best fairy tales, manage to be reactionary, anarchistic, and revolutionary all at the same time.

My agent, Kirby McCauley, likes to relate a scene from Andy Warhol's film *Bad*—and he relates it in the fond tones of the confirmed horror-movie buff. A mother throws her baby from the window of a skyscraper; we cut away to the crowd below and hear a loud splat. Another mother leads her son through the crowd and up to the mess (which is obviously a watermelon with seeds removed), points to it, and says, to the effect, "That's what will happen to you if you're bad!" It's a sick joke, like the one about the truckload of dead babies—or the one about the babes in the woods, which we call "Hansel and Gretel."

The mythic horror movie, like the sick joke, has a dirty job to do. It deliberately appeals to all that is worst in us. It is morbidity unchained, our most base instincts let free, our nastiest fantasies realized . . . and it all happens, fittingly enough, in the dark. For these reasons, good liberals often shy away from horror films. For myself, I like to see the most aggressive of them—*Dawn of the Dead*, for instance—as lifting a trapdoor in the civilized forebrain and throwing a basket of raw meat to the hungry alligators swimming around in that subterranean river beneath.

Why bother? Because it keeps them from getting out, man. It keeps them down there and me up here. It was Lennon and McCartney who said that all you need is love, and I would agree with that. As long as you keep the gators fed.

9

And now this word from the poet Kenneth Patchen. It comes from his small, clever book *But Even So*:

> *Come now,*
> *my child,*
> *if we were planning*
> *to harm you, do you think*
> *we'd be lurking here*
> *beside the path*

> *in the very dark-*
> *est part of*
> *the forest?*

This is the mood which the best films of mythic "fairy-tale horror" summon up in us, and it also suggests that, below the level
of simple aggression and simple morbidity, there is a final level
where the horror movie does its most powerful work. And that
is well for us, because without more, the human imagination
would be a poor, degraded thing, in need of no more in the way
of horror than such things as *Last House on the Left* and *Friday
the 13th*. The horror movie is planning to harm us, all right,
and that is exactly why it is lurking here in the very darkest
part of the forest. At this most basic level, the horror film isn't
fooling around: it wants to get you. Once it has reduced you to
a level of childlike expectation and point of view, it will begin
playing one or more of a very few simple harmonic melodies—
the greatest limitation (and therefore the greatest challenge)
of the horror form is its very strictness. The things that really scare people on a gut level can be reduced like fractions to
an irreducible handful. And when that has finally happened,
analyses such as those I've given in the foregoing pages become
impossible . . . and even if analysis were possible, it would be
irrelevant. One can point out effect, and that must be the end
of the matter. To try and go any further is as useless as trying to divide a prime number by two and come out even. But
effect may be enough; there are films, like Browning's *Freaks,*
that have the power to reduce us to jelly, to make us mutter (or
whimper) to ourselves, "Please let it stop"; they are those films
which hold their spell over us in spite of all we can do, even
including the recitation of that most magic spell-breaking in-
cantation: "It's only a movie." And they can all be invoked with
that wonderful fairy-tale door-opener, "Once upon a time."

So, before we proceed any further, here's a little quiz for you.
Get a scrap of paper and something to write with and jot down
your answers. Twenty questions; give yourself five points per
question. And if you score below 70, you need to go back and

do some postgraduate work in the *real* fright films . . . the ones that scare us just because they scare us.

Ready? Okay. Name these films:

1. Once upon a time, the husband of the world's champion blind lady had to go away for awhile (to slay a dragon, or something of that sort) and a wicked man named Harry Roat, who came from Scarsdale, came by to see her while her husband was gone.

2. Once upon a time, three babysitters went out on Halloween night, and only one of them was still alive come All Saints Day.

3. Once upon a time a lady who stole some money spent a not-so-enchanted evening at an out-of-the-way motel. Everything seemed pretty much okay until the motel owner's mother came by; mother did something very naughty.

4. Once upon a time some bad people tampered with the oxygen line in one operating room of a major hospital and a lot of people went to sleep for a long, long time—just like Snow White. Only these people never woke up.

5. Once upon a time there was a sad girl who picked up men in bars, because when the men came home with her, she didn't feel so sad. Except one night she picked up a man who was wearing a mask. Underneath the mask he was the bogeyman.

6. Once upon a time some brave explorers landed on another planet to see if someone needed help. Nobody did, but by the time they got going again, they discovered that *they* had picked up the bogeyman.

7. Once upon a time a sad lady named Eleanor went on an adventure in an enchanted castle. In the enchanted castle, Lady Eleanor was not so sad, because she found some new friends. Except that the friends left, and she stayed . . . forever.

8. Once upon a time a young man tried to bring a

magic potion from another country to his own aboard a magic flying carpet. But he was caught before he could get on his magic carpet, and the bad people took away his magic potion and locked him in an evil dungeon.

9. Once upon a time there was a little girl who looked sweet, but she was really very wicked. She locked the janitor up in his room and set his highly flammable bed of wood-chips and excelsior on fire because he was mean to her.

10. Once upon a time there were two little children, very much like Hansel and Gretel, in fact, and when their father died, their mommy married a wicked man who pretended to be very good. This wicked man had LOVE tattooed on the fingers of one hand and HATE tattooed on the fingers of the other.

11. Once upon a time there was an American lady living in London whose sanity was under some question. She thought she saw a murder in the old boarded-up house next door.

12. Once upon a time a lady and her brother went to put flowers on their mother's grave and the brother, who liked to play mean tricks, scared her by saying, "They're coming to get you, Barbara." Except that it turned out they really *were* coming to get her . . . but they got him, first.

13. Once upon a time all the birds in the world got mad at the people and started to kill the people because the birds were under an evil spell.

14. Once upon a time a crazyman with an ax started to chop up his family, one by one, in an old Irish house. When he chopped off the groundskeeper's head, it rolled right down into the family pool— wasn't that funny?

15. Once upon a time two sisters grew old together in an enchanted castle in the Kingdom of Hollywood. Once one of them had been famous in the Kingdom

of Hollywood, but that was long, long ago. The other one was stuck in a wheelchair. And do you know what happened? The sister who could walk served her paralyzed sister a dead rat for dinner! Wasn't that funny?

16. Once upon a time there was a cemetery caretaker who discovered that if he put black pins into the vacant plots on his cemetery map, the people who owned those plots would die. But when he took out the black pins and put in white pins, do you know what happened? The movie turned into a big pile of shit! Wasn't that funny?

17. Once upon a time a bad man stole the little princess and buried her alive . . . or at least, he said he did.

18. Once upon a time there was a man who invented some magic eyedrops, and he could use them to see through people's cards in Las Vegas and make lots of money. He could also see through girls' clothes at cocktail parties, which was maybe not such a nice thing to do, but wait a minute. This man kept seeing more . . . and more . . . *and more* . . .

19. Once upon a time there was a lady who was saddled with Satan's child, and he knocked her over a gallery railing with his trike. What a mean thing to do! But lucky mommy! Because she died soon after, she didn't have to do the sequel!

20. Once upon a time some friends went on a canoe trip down a magic river, and some bad men saw that they were having fun and decided to fix them for it. That was because the bad men didn't want those other fellows, who came from the city, to have a good time in their woods.

Okay, did you write down all of your answers? If you find you have four or more blanks—not even an educated guess to plug in there—you have been spending far too much time seeing "quality" films like *Julia, Manhattan,* and *Breaking Away.*

And while you've been watching Woody Allen give his imitation of an ingrown hair (a *liberal* ingrown hair, of course), you missed some of the scariest films ever made. For the record, the answers are:

1. WAIT UNTIL DARK
2. HALLOWEEN
3. PSYCHO
4. COMA
5. LOOKING FOR MR. GOODBAR
6. ALIEN
7. THE HAUNTING
8. MIDNIGHT EXPRESS
9. THE BAD SEED
10. THE NIGHT OF THE HUNTER
11. NIGHT WATCH
12. NIGHT OF THE LIVING DEAD
13. THE BIRDS
14. DEMENTIA-13
15. WHAT EVER HAPPENED TO BABY JANE?
16. I BURY THE LIVING
17. MACABRE*
18. X—THE MAN WITH THE X-RAY EYES
19. THE OMEN
20. DELIVERANCE

The first thing we can note about this list of films is that, of the twenty (which I would call the basic coursework in films of gut-level horror in the period we're discussing here), fully fourteen have nothing supernatural going on in them . . . fifteen if you count *Alien*, which is at least nominally science fiction

---

* This William Castle feature—his first, but unfortunately not his last—was perhaps the biggest "gotta-see" picture of my grammar school days. Its title was pronounced by my friends in Stratford, Connecticut as *McBare*. "Gottasee" or not, very few of our parents would let us go because of the grisly ad campaign. I, however, exercised the inventiveness of the true aficionado and got to see it by telling my mother I was going to *Davy Crockett*, a Disney film which I felt I could summarize safely because I had most of the bubble-gum cards.

(I do count it as a supernatural tale, however; I think of it as Lovecraft in outer space, mankind finally going to the Elder Gods rather than they coming to us). So we might be able to say, paradox or not, that movies of fairy-tale horror demand a heavy dose of reality to get them rolling. Such reality frees the imagination of excess baggage and makes the weight of unbelief easier to lift. The audience is propelled into the movie by the feeling that, under the right set of circumstances, this could happen.

The second thing we could note is that a quarter of them bear a reference either to "night" or "the dark" in their titles. The dark, it goes almost without saying, provides the basis for our most primordial fears. As spiritual as we may believe our natures to be, our physiology is similar to that of all the rest of the mammals that creep, crawl, trot, or walk; we must make do with the same five senses. There are many mammals whose eyesight is keen, but we are not among them. There are mammals—dogs, for instance—which have even lousier eyesight than we do, but their lack of brainpower has forced them to develop other senses to a keenness we cannot even imagine (although we may think we can). With dogs, the overdeveloped senses are those of hearing and smell.

So-called psychics like to prate of a "sixth sense," a vague term which sometimes means telepathy, sometimes precognition, sometimes God knows what, but we have a sixth sense, it is probably just (some just!) the keenness of our reasoning facilities. Fido may be able to follow a hundred scents of which we are completely unaware, but the little bugger is never going to be any good at checkers, or even Go Fish. This reasoning power has made it unnecessary for us to breed keener senses into the gene pool; in fact, a large part of the population has sensory equipment which is actually substandard even by human standards—hence eyeglasses and hearing aids. But we are able to make do because of our Boeing-747 brains.

All of which is very fine when you're doing a deal in a well-lit executive boardroom or ironing the laundry in the living room on a sunny afternoon; but when the lights fail during a thunderstorm and we're left to creep around from place to place, trying to remember where we left the goddamn candles, the situation changes. Even a 747, sophisticated on-board radar and all, can't land in a heavy fog bank. When the lights go out and we find ourselves stranded in a shoal of darkness, reality itself has an unpleasant way of fogging in.

When we cut off one avenue of sensory input, that sense simply shuts down (although it never shuts down 100 percent, of course; even in a dark room, we will see a trace pattern in front of our eyes, and in the most perfect silence we will hear a faint hum . . . such "phantom input" only means that the circuits are open and standing by). The same does not happen with our brains—fortunately or unfortunately, depending on the situation. It's fortunate if you happen to be stuck in a boring situation; you can use your sixth sense to plan the next day's work, to wonder what life might be like if you won the grand prize in the state lottery or the Reader's Digest Sweepstakes, or to speculate on what that sexy Miss Hepplewaite does—or doesn't—wear under those tight dresses of hers. On the other hand, the brain's constant function can be a mixed blessing. Ask anyone who is a victim of chronic insomnia.

I tell people who say that horror movies don't scare them to make this simple experiment. Go see a film like *Night of the Living Dead* all alone (have you ever noticed how many people go to horror movies, not just in pairs or groups, but in actual *packs?*). Afterwards, get in your car, drive to an old, deserted, crumbling house—every town has at least one (except Stepford, Connecticut, but they have their own problems there). Let yourself in. Mount to the attic. Sit down up there. Listen to the house groan and creak around you. Notice how much those creaks sound like someone—or some*thing*—mounting the stairs. Smell the must. The rot. The decay. Think about the film you have just seen. Consider it as you sit there in the dark, unable to see what might be creeping up . . . what might be just about to place its dirty, twisted claw on your shoulder . . . or around your neck . . .

This sort of thing can prove, by its very darkness, to be an enlightening experience.

Fear of the dark is the most childlike fear. Tales of terror are customarily told "around the campfire" or at least after sundown, because what is laughable in the sunshine is often tougher to smile at by starlight. This is a fact that every maker of horror films and writer of horror tales recognizes and uses— it is one of those unfailing pressure points where the grip of horror fiction is surest.* This is particularly true of the filmmakers, of course, and of all the tools that the filmmaker can bring to bear, it is perhaps this fear of the dark that seems the most natural, since movies must, by their very nature, be viewed in the dark.

It was Michael Cantalupo, an assistant editor at Everest House, who reminded me of a gimmick used in the first-run engagements of *Wait Until Dark,* and in this context it bears an affectionate mention. The last fifteen or twenty minutes of that film are utterly terrifying, partially due to virtuoso performances turned in by Audrey Hepburn and Alan Arkin (and in my view, Arkin's performance as Harry Roat, Jr., from Scarsdale may be the greatest evocation of screen villainy ever, rivalling and perhaps surpassing Peter Lorre's in *M*), partially due to the brilliant gimmick on which Frederick Knott's story turns.

Hepburn, in a final desperate effort to save her life, breaks every damned lightbulb in the apartment and hallway, so that she and the sighted Arkin will be on even terms. Trouble is, she forgets one light . . . but you and I probably would have forgotten it, too. It's the bulb inside the refrigerator.

Anyway, the in-theater gimmick was to turn out every damn light in the auditorium except for the EXIT lights over the doors. I never realized until the last ten minutes of *Wait Until Dark* how much light there is in most theaters, even when the movie's playing. There are those tiny "dim-bulbs" set into the ceiling if

---

* Now and then someone will run brilliantly counter to the tradition and produce a piece of what is sometimes called "sunlit horror." Ramsey Campbell does this particularly well; see his aptly named collection of short stories *Demons by Daylight*, for instance.

the theater is one of the new breed, those gauche but somehow lovely electric *flambeaux* glowing along the walls in the older ones. In a pinch, you can always find your way back to your seat after using the bathroom by the light being thrown from the screen itself. Except that the climactic few minutes of *Wait Until Dark* are set entirely in that black apartment. You have only your ears, and what they hear—Miss Hepburn screaming, Arkin's tortured breathing (he's been stabbed a bit earlier on, and we're allowed to relax a little, to think he might even be dead, when he pops out again like a malefic jack-in-the-box)— isn't very comforting. So there you sit. Your big old Boeing-747 brain is cranked up like a kid's jalopy with the pedal to the metal, and it has very little concrete input to work on. So you sit there, sweating it out, hoping the lights will eventually come on again . . . sooner or later, they do. Mike Cantalupo told me he saw *Wait Until Dark* in a theater so sleazy that even the EXIT lights were broken.

Man, that must have been bad.

Mike's recollection of that took me fondly back to another film—William Castle's *The Tingler,* which had a similar (if, in the Castle style, infinitely more crass) gimmick. Castle, whom I've already mentioned in connection with *Macabre*—known to all us WASPy little kids as *McBare,* you'll remember—was the king of the gimmicks; he originated the $100,000 "fright insurance" policy, for instance; if you dropped dead during the film, your heirs got the money. Then there was the great "Nurse on Duty at All Performances" gimmick; there was the "You *Must* Have Your Blood Pressure Taken in the Lobby Before Viewing This Horrifying Film" gimmick (that one was used as part of *The House on Haunted Hill* promo), and all sorts of other gimmicks.

The exact plot specifics of *The Tingler,* a film so exquisitely low budget that it probably made back its production costs after a thousand people had seen it, now escape me, but there was this monster (the Tingler, natch) that lived on fear. When its victims were so scared they couldn't even scream, it attached itself to their spines and sorta . . . well . . . *tingled* them to death.

I know that must sound pretty fucking stupid, but in the film, it worked (although it probably helped to be eleven years old when you saw it). As I remember, one sexy miss got it in the bathtub. Bad news.

But never mind the plot; let's get on to the gimmick. At one point the Tingler got into a movie theater, killed the projectionist, and somehow shorted out the electricity. At that moment in the theater where you were watching the movie, all the lights went out and the screen went dark. Now as it happened, the only thing that could get the Tingler to let go of your spine once it had attached itself was a good loud scream, which changed the quality of the adrenaline it fed on. And at this point, a narrator on the soundtrack cried out, "The Tingler is now in this theater! It may be under *your* seat! So scream! Scream! *Scream for your lives!!*" The audience was of course happy to oblige, and in the next scene we see the Tingler fleeing for *its* life, vanquished for the time being by all those screaming people. Nor was that all; according to Dennis Etchison, there was yet *another* gimmick used by Castle during *The Tingler*'s first run (in showcase theaters only). Certain rows of these theaters, Dennis says, "were wired with buzzing devices attached to the backs or bottoms of the seats, so at the appropriate moment you could hear—and *feel*—the Tingler in your row!"*

Besides the movies which raise the scary concept of the dark in their titles, almost every other film listed in the little quiz I gave you uses that fear of the dark heavily. All but approximately eighteen minutes of John Carpenter's *Halloween* are set after nightfall. In *Looking for Mr. Goodbar,* the final horrible sequence (my wife ran for the women's room, believing she was going to toss her cookies), where Tom Berenger stabs Diane

---

* God, it's fun to think about some of the desperate gimmicks that have been used to sell bad horror movies—like those Dish Nights and Bank Nights used to lure people into the movie houses during the thirties, they linger pleasantly in the memory. During one imported Italian turkey, *The Night Evelyn Came Out of the Grave* (nifty title!), the theaters advertised "bloodcorn," which was ordinary popcorn with a red food dye added. During *Jack the Ripper,* a 1960 example of "Hammer-style horror" written by Jimmy Sangster, the black-and-white film turned to gruesome color during the last five minutes, when the Ripper, who has unwisely chosen to hide in an elevator shaft, is squished under a descending car.

Keaton to death, is shot in her dark apartment, with only a flickering strobe-light for illumination. In *Alien,* that constant motif of the dark barely needs mentioning. "In space, no one can hear you scream," the ad copy read; it also could have said, "In space, it is always one minute after midnight." Dawn never comes in that Lovecraftian gulf between the stars.

Hill House is always spooky, but it saves its really big effects— the face in the wall, the bulging doors, the booming noises, the thing that held Eleanor's hand (she thought it was Theo, but—gulp!—it wasn't)—for well past sunset. It was another Everest House editor, Bill Thompson (who has been my editor for about a thousand years; perhaps in a previous life I was *his* editor and now he's having his revenge), who reminded me of *The Night of the Hunter*—and *mea culpa* that I should have needed reminding—and told me that one of the scenes of horror which has remained with him over the years was the sight of Shelley Winters's hair floating in the water after the homicidal preacher has disposed of her in the river. It happens, naturally, after dark.*

There is an interesting similarity between the scene in which the little girl kills her mother with a garden trowel in *Night of the Living Dead* and the climactic scene in *The Birds,* where Tippi Hedren is trapped in the attic and attacked by crows, sparrows, and gulls. Both of these scenes are classic examples of how dark and light can be used selectively. We will remember, most of us, from our own childhoods that a lot of light had the power to vanquish imagined evils and fears, but sometimes a little light only made them worse. It was the streetlight outside that made the branches of a nearby tree look like witch fingers, or it was the moonlight streaming in the window that made the jumble of toys pushed away in the closet take on the aspect of a crouching Thing ready to shamble in and attack at any moment.

---

* Dennis Etchison (see the Forenote to the 1983 Edition) disputes Bill Thompson's memory— he says it happens in daytime, else Shelley Winters would not have been visible—or photographable—at the bottom of that river. (This raises the interesting idea that we *make* the dark in our memories . . .)

During the matricide scene in *Night of the Living Dead* (which, like the shower scene in *Psycho,* seems almost endless to our shocked eyes the first time we see it), the little girl's arm strikes a hanging lightbulb, and the cellar becomes a nightmare dreamscape of shifting, swinging shadows—revealing, concealing, revealing again. During the attack of the birds in the attic, it is the big flashlight Ms. Hedren carries which provides this strobe effect (also mentioned in connection with *Looking for Mr. Goodbar* and used again—more irritatingly and pointlessly—during Marlon Brando's incoherent monologue near the end of *Apocalypse Now*) and also provides the scene with a pulse, a beat—at first the flashlight beam moves rapidly as Ms. Hedren uses the light to ward off the birds . . . but as she is gradually sapped of strength and lapses first into shock and then into unconsciousness, the light moves more and more slowly, sinking to the floor. Until there is only dark . . . and in that dark, the tenebrous, whirring flutter of many wings.

I'll not belabor the point by analyzing the "darkness quotient" in all these films, but will close this aspect of the discussion by pointing out that even in those few movies that achieve that feeling of "sunlit horror," there are often feary moments in the dark—Genevieve Bujold's climb up the service ladder and over the operating room in *Coma* takes place in the dark, as does Ed's (Jon Voight) climb up the bluff near the end of *Deliverance* . . . not to mention digging up the grave containing the jackal bones in *The Omen,* and Luana Anders's creepy discovery of the underwater "memorial" to the long-dead little sister in Francis Coppola's first feature film (made for AIP), *Dementia-13.*

Still, before leaving the subject entirely, here's a further sampling: *Night Must Fall, Night of the Lepus, Dracula, Prince of Darkness, The Black Pit of Dr. M., The Black Sleep, Black Sunday, The Black Room, Black Sabbath, Dark Eyes of London, The Dark, Dead of Night, Night of Terror, Night of the Demon, Nightwing, Night of the Eagle* . . .

Well, you get it. If there had been no such thing as darkness, the makers of horror movies would have needed to invent it.

10

I have held out mention of one of the films from the quiz, partially because it's the antithesis of many of those we've already discussed—it depends for its horror not upon darkness but upon light—and also because it leads naturally into a brief discussion of something else that the mythic, or "fairy-tale" horror movie will do to us if it can. We all understand about the "gross-out," which is fairly easy to achieve,* but it is only in the horror movies that the gross-out—that most childish of emotional impulses—sometimes achieves the level of art. Now, I can hear some of you say that there is nothing artistic about grossing somebody out—all you really have to do is chew your food and then hang your open mouth in your table-mate's face—but what about the works of Goya? Or Andy Warhol's Brillo boxes and soup cans, for that matter?

Even the very worst horror movies sometimes achieve a moment or two of success on this level. Dennis Etchison reminisced fondly with me on the phone one day not too long ago about a brief sequence in *The Giant Spider Invasion* where a lady drinks her morning high-potency vitamin cocktail, all unknowing that a rather plump spider fell into the blender just before she turned it on. Yum yum. In the eminently forgettable film *Squirm,* there is that one forgettable moment (for all two hundred of us who saw the picture) when the lady taking a shower looks up to see why the water stopped coming and sees a showerhead clogged with dangling nightcrawlers. In Dario Argento's *Suspiria,* a bunch of schoolgirls are subjected to a rain of maggots . . . while getting ready for bed, no less. All of it has nothing to do with the film's plot, but it is vaguely interesting, in a repulsive sort of way. In *Maniac,* directed by former softcore filmmaker William Lustig, there is the incredible moment when the homicidal ding-dong (Joe Spinell) carefully scalps one of his victims; the camera does not even leer at this—it

---

* I can remember, as a kid, one of my fellow kids asking me to imagine sliding down a long, polished bannister which suddenly and without warning turns into a razor blade. Man, I was *days* getting over that.

merely stares at it with a kind of dead, contemplative eye that makes the scene well-nigh impossible to watch.

As noted previously, good horror movies often operate most powerfully on this "wanna-look-at-my-chewed-up-food?" level—a primitive, childish level. I would call it the "YUCH factor" . . . sometimes also known as the "Oh my God, was that *gross!*" factor. This is the point at which most good liberal film critics and most good reactionary film critics part company on the subject of the horror film (see, for instance, the difference between Lynn Minton's review of *Dawn of the Dead* in *McCall's*—she left after two reels or so—and the cover story in the Arts section of *The Boston Phoenix* on the same film). Like punk rock music, the horror movie capable of delivering the good gross-out wallop finds its art in childish acts of anarchy— the moment in *The Omen* where the photographer is decapitated by a pane of glass is art of the most peculiar sort, and one cannot blame critics who find it easier to respond to Jane Fonda as a wholly unbelievable screen incarnation of Lillian Hellman in *Julia* than to stuff like this.

But the gross-out *is* art, and it is important that we have an understanding of this. Blood can fly everywhere and the audience will remain largely unimpressed. If on the other hand, the audience has come to like and understand—or even just to appreciate—the characters they are watching as real people, if some artistic link has been formed there, blood can fly everywhere and the audience *cannot* remain unimpressed. I can't remember, for instance, anyone who walked out of Arthur Penn's *Bonnie and Clyde* or Peckinpah's *The Wild Bunch* who didn't look as if he or she had been hit on the head with a very large board. Yet people walk out of other Peckinpah films—*Bring Me the Head of Alfredo Garcia, Cross of Iron*—yawning. That vital linkage just never happens.

That's all fine, and there is little argument about the virtues of *Bonnie and Clyde* as art, but let us return momentarily to the pureed arachnid in *The Giant Spider Invasion*. This doesn't qualify as art in respect to that idea of linkage between audience and character at all. Believe me, we don't care very much about the lady who drinks the spider (or anyone else in this movie, for that matter), but all the same there is that moment of *frisson,* that one moment when the groping fingers of the filmmaker find a chink in our defenses, shoot through it, and squeeze down on one of those psychic pressure points. We identify with the woman who is unknowingly drinking the spider on a level that has nothing to do with her character; we identify with her solely as a human being in a situation which has suddenly turned rotten—in other words, the gross-out serves as the means of a last-ditch sort of identification when the more conventional and noble means of characterization have failed. When she drinks the drink, we shudder—and reaffirm our own humanity.*

Having said all that, let's turn to *X—The Man with the X-Ray Eyes,* one of the most interesting and offbeat little horror movies ever made, and one that ends with one of the most shuddery gross-out scenes ever filmed.

This 1963 movie was produced and directed by Roger Corman, who at that time was in the process of metamorphosing from the dull caterpillar who had produced such meatloaf movies as *Attack of the Crab Monsters* and *The Little Shop of Horrors* (not even notable for what was one of Jack Nicholson's earliest films) and into the butterfly who was responsible for such interesting and rather beautiful horror films as *The Masque of the Red Death* and *The Terror. The Man with the X-Ray Eyes* marks the point where this strange two-step creature came out of its cocoon, I think. The screenplay was written by Ray Russell, the author of *Sardonicus* and a number of other stories and novels—among them the rather overripe *Incubus* and the much more successful *Princess Pamela.*

In *The Man with the X-Ray Eyes,* Ray Milland plays a scientist

---

* This might lead to the accusation that my definition of the horror movie as art is much too wide—that I just let in everything. That is not true at all—movies like *Massacre at Central High* and *Bloody Mutilators* work on no level. And if my ideas concerning the boundaries of art seem rather lenient, that's too bad. I'm no snob, and if you are, that's your problem. In my business, if you lose your taste for good baloney, it's time you got into some other line of work.

who develops eyedrops which enable him to see through walls, clothing, playing cards, you name it; a kind of super-Murine, if you will. But once the process begins, there is no slowing it down. Milland's eyes begin to undergo a physical change, first becoming thickly bloodshot and then taking on a queer yellow cast. It is at this point that we begin to feel rather nervous—perhaps we sense the gross-out coming, and in a very real sense it's already arrived. Our eyes are one of those vulnerable chinks in the armor, one of those places where we can be had. Imagine, for instance, jamming your thumb into someone's wide-open eye, feeling the squish, seeing it sorta squirt out at you. Nasty, right? Immoral to even consider such a thing. But surely you remember that time-honored Halloween party game Dead Man, where peeled grapes are passed from hand to hand to hand in the dark, to the solemn intonation of "These are the dead man's eyes"? Ulp, right? Yuck, right? Or as my kids say, *Guh-ROSS!*

Like our other facial equipment, eyes are something we all have in common—even that old poop the Ayatollah Khomeini had a pair. But to the best of my knowledge, no horror movie has ever been made about a nose out of control, and while there has never been a film called *The Crawling Ear,* there *was* one called *The Crawling Eye.* We all understand that eyes are the most vulnerable of our sensory organs, the most vulnerable of our facial accessories, and they are (ick!) *soft.* Maybe that's the worst . . .

So when Milland dons shades for the second half of the movie, we become increasingly nervous about what might be going on behind those shades. In addition, something else is happening—something that elevates *The Man with the X-Ray Eyes* to a rather higher plateau of art. It becomes a kind of Lovecraftian horror movie, but in a sense that is different—and somehow purer—than the sort of Lovecraftiness used in *Alien.*

The Elder Gods, Lovecraft told us, are out there, and their one desire is to somehow get back in—and there are lines of power accessible to them, Lovecraft intimates, which are so powerful that one look at the sources of these lines of power would drive mortal men to madness; forces so powerful that a whole galaxy aflame could not equal its thousandth part.

It is one of these power sources, I think, that Ray Milland begins to glimpse as his sight continues to improve at a steady, inexorable pace. He sees it first as a prismatic, shifting light somewhere out in the darkness—the trippy sort of thing you might see at the top of an LSD high. Corman, you'll remember, also gave us Peter Fonda in *The Trip* (co-written by Jack Nicholson), not to mention *The Wild Angels,* which contains that wonderful moment when a dying Bruce Dern croaks out, "Somebody gimme a straight cigarette." Anyway, this bright core of light Milland sometimes sees gradually grows larger and clearer. Worse still, it may be alive . . . and aware it's being watched. Milland has seen through everything to the very edges of the universe and beyond, and what he has found there is driving him crazy.

This force eventually becomes so clear to him that it fills the whole screen during the point-of-view shots: a bright, shifting, monstrous thing that won't quite come into focus. At last Milland can stand it no longer. He drives his car to a deserted spot (that bright Presence hanging before his eyes all the time) and whips off his shades to reveal eyes which have gone an utter, glistening black. He pauses for a moment . . . and then rips his own eyes out. Corman freezes the frame on those staring, bloody sockets. But I have heard rumors—they may or may not be true—that the final line of dialogue was cut from the film as *too* horrifying. If true, it was the only possible capper for what has already happened. According to the rumor, Milland screams: *I can still see!*

11

This is only to dip our fingers in that deep, deep pool of common human experience and fears which form the myth-pool. It would be possible to go on with dozens of other specifics; with phobias such as the fear of heights (*Vertigo*), fear of snakes

(*Sssssss*), of cats (*Eye of the Cat*), of rats (*Willard, Ben*)—and all those movies which depend on the gross-out for their ultimate effect. Beyond these there are even wider vistas of myth . . . but we have to save something for later, right?

And no matter how many specifics we cover, we'll always find ourselves returning to that idea of phobic pressure points . . . just as the most lovely waltz relies, at bottom, on the simplicity of the box-step. The horror movie is a closed box with a crank on the side, and in the last analysis it all comes back to turning that crank until Jack jumps out into our faces, holding his ax and grinning his murderous grin. Like sex, the experience is infinitely desirable, but a discussion of specific effect takes on a certain sameness.

Rather than going on and on over what is essentially the same plot of ground, let's close our brief discussion of the horror movie as myth and fairy tale with what is, after all, the Big Cassino: death itself. Here is the trump card which all horror movies hold. But they do not hold this card as a veteran bridge-player would hold it, understanding all its implications and possibilities for gain; they hold it, rather, as a child would hold the card which will make the winning pair in a game of Old Maid. In that fact lies both the limiting factor of the horror movie as art and its endless, morbidly captivating charm.

"Death," the boy Mark Petrie thinks at one point in *'Salem's Lot*, "is when the monsters get you." And if I had to restrict everything I have ever said or written about the horror genre to one statement (and many critics will say I should have done, ha-ha), it would be that one. It is not the way adults look at death; it is a crude metaphor which leaves little room for the possibility of heaven, hell, Nirvana, or that old wheeze about how the great wheel of Karma turns and we'll get 'em next life, gang. It is a view which—like most horror movies—addresses itself not to any philosophical speculation about "the afterlife" but which speaks only of the moment when we finally have to shuffle off this mortal coil. That instant of death is the only truly universal rite of passage, and the only one for which we have no psychological or sociological input to explain what changes we may expect as a result of having passed through. All we know is that we go; and while we have some rules of—etiquette, would it be called?—which bear on the subject, that actual moment has a way of catching folks unprepared. People pass away while making love, while standing in elevators, while putting dimes in parking meters. Some go in midsneeze. Some die in restaurants, some in cheap one-night hotels, and a few while sitting on the john. We cannot count on dying in bed or with our boots on. So it would be remarkable indeed if we did not fear death a little. It's just sort of there, isn't it, the great irreducible x-factor of our lives, faceless father of a hundred religions, so seamless and ungraspable that it usually isn't even discussed at cocktail parties. Death becomes myth in the horror movies, but let's be clear on the fact that horror movies mythicize death on the simplest level: death in the horror movies is when the monsters get you.

We fans of the horror movies have seen people clubbed, burned at the stake (Vincent Price, as the Witchfinder General in AIP's *The Conqueror Worm,* surely one of the most revolting horror pictures to be released by a major studio in the sixties, had a regular cookout at the climax of this one), shot, crucified, stabbed through the eyes with needles, eaten alive by grasshoppers, by ants, by dinosaurs, and even by cockroaches; we have seen people beheaded (*The Omen, Friday the 13th, Maniac*), sucked dry of their blood, gobbled up by sharks (who could forget the little kid's torn and bloodstained rubber float nudging gently against the shoreline in *Jaws?*) and piranha fish; we have seen bad guys go down screaming in pools of quicksand and pools of acid; we have seen our fellow humans squashed, stretched, and bloated to death; at the end of Brian De Palma's *The Fury,* John Cassavetes literally explodes.

Again, liberal critics, whose concepts of civilization, life, and death are usually more complex, are apt to frown on this sort of gratuitous slaughter, to see it (at best) as the moral equivalent of pulling wings off flies, and, at worst, as that symbolic lynch mob in action. But there is something in that wing-pulling simile that bears examination. There are few children who have not pulled the wings off a few flies at some point in their development, or squatted patiently on the sidewalk to see how a bug dies. In the opening scene of *The Wild Bunch* a group of happy, giggling children burn a scorpion to death—a scene indicative of what people who care little (or know little) about children often erroneously call "the cruelty of childhood." Children are rarely cruel on purpose, and they even more rarely torture, as they understand the concept;* they may, however, kill in the spirit of experimentation, watching the death struggles of the bug on the sidewalk in the same clinical way that a biologist would watch a guinea pig die after inhaling a whiff of nerve gas. Tom Sawyer, we'll remember, just about broke his neck in his hurry to get a look at Huck's dead cat, and one of the payments he accepts for the "privilege" of whitewashing his fence is a dead rat "and a string to swing it on."

Or consider this:

> Bing Crosby is said to have told a story about one
> of his sons at the age of six or so who was inconsolable
> when his pet turtle died. To distract the boy, Bing sug-
> gested that they have a funeral, and his son, seeming only
> slightly consoled, agreed. The two took a cigar box, lined
> it carefully with silk, painted the outside black, and then
> dug a hole in the back yard. Bing carefully lowered the
> "coffin" into the grave, said a long, heartfelt prayer, and
> sang a hymn. At the end of the service, the boy's eyes were
> shining with sorrow and excitement. Then Bing asked if
> he would like to have one last look at his pet before they
> covered the coffin with earth. The boy said he would, and
> Bing raised the cigar-box lid. The two gazed down rever-
> ently, and suddenly the turtle moved. The boy stared at

---

* From *Kids: Day in and Day Out*, edited by Elisabeth Scharlatt (New York: Simon and Schuster, 1979); this particular story related by Walter Jerrold.

it for a long time, then looked up at his father and said, "Let's kill it."*

Kids are endlessly, voraciously curious, not only about death but about everything—and why not? They are like people who just came in and sat down during a good movie that's been on for thousands of years. They want to know what the story is, who the characters are, and most of all, what the interior logic of the play may be—is it a drama? a tragedy? a comedy? perhaps an out-and-out farce? They don't know because they have not (as yet) had Socrates, Plato, Kant, or Erich Segal to instruct them. When you're five, your big gurus are Santa Claus and Ronald McDonald; life's burning questions include whether or not you can eat crackers upside down and if that stuff in the middle of the golfball really is a deadly poison. When you're five, you seek knowledge down those avenues that are open to you.

Pursuant to this, I'll tell you my own dead cat story. When I was nine and living in Stratford, Connecticut, two friends of mine—brothers—from down the street discovered the stiffening body of a dead cat in the gutter near Burrets' Building Materials, which was across the street from the vacant lot where we played baseball. I was called into consultation to add my thoughts to the problem of the dead cat. The very *interesting* problem of the dead cat.

It was a gray cat, quite obviously mashed by a passing car. Its eyes were half-open, and we all noticed that there seemed to be dust and road grit gathering on them. First deduction: You don't care if dust gets in your eyes when you're dead (all our deductions assumed that if it was true for cats, then it must be true for kids).

---

* Now, don't get me wrong or misinterpret what I'm saying. Kids can be mean and unlovely, and when you see them at their worst, they can make you think black thoughts about the future of the human race. But meanness and cruelty, although related, are not the same thing at all. A cruel action is a studied action; it requires a bit of thought. Meanness, on the other hand, is unpremeditated and unthinking. The results may be similar for the person—usually another child—who gets the butt end, but it seems to me that in a moral society, intent or lack of it is pretty important.

We examined it for maggots.

No maggots.

"Maybe there's maggots inside it," Charlie said hopefully (Charlie was one of the fellows who referred to the William Castle film as *McBare,* and on rainy days he was apt to call me up and ask me if I wanted to come down the street to his house and read "comet bwoots").

We examined the dead cat for maggots, turning it from one side to the other—using a stick, of course; no telling what germs you might get from a dead cat. There were no maggots that we could see.

"Maybe there's maggots in its *brain,*" Charlie's brother Nicky said, his eyes glowing. "Maybe there's maggots inside it, eating up its *braiiiin.*"

"That's impossible," I said. "Your brains are, like, airtight. Nothin' can get inside there."

They absorbed this.

We stood around the dead cat in a circle.

Then Nicky said suddenly: "If we drop a brick on its heinie, will it shit?"

This question of postmortem biology was absorbed and discussed. It was finally agreed that the test should be made. A brick was found. There was a discussion of who should get to bombs-away the brick on the dead cat. The problem was solved in time-honored fashion: we put our feet in. The rites of eenie-meenie-miney-moe were invoked. Foot after foot left the circle until only Nicky's was left.

The brick was dropped.

The dead cat did not shit.

Deduction number two: After you're dead, you won't shit if someone drops a brick on your ass.

Soon after, a baseball game started up, and the dead cat was left.

As the days passed, an ongoing investigation of the cat continued, and it is always the dead cat in the gutter out in front of Burrets' Building Materials that I think of when I read Richard Wilbur's fine poem "The Groundhog." The maggots put in their appearance a couple of days later, and we watched their fever-boil with horrified, revolted interest. "They're eatin' his eyes," Tommy Erbter from up the street pointed out hoarsely. "Look at that, you guys, they're even eatin' his *eyes*."

Eventually the maggots moved out, leaving the dead cat looking considerably thinner, its fur now faded to a dull, uninteresting color, sparse and knotted. We came less frequently. The cat's decay had entered a less gaudy stage. Still, it was my habit to check the cat on my mile's walk to school each morning; it was just another stop on the way, part of the morning's ritual—like running a stick over the picket fence in front of the empty house or skipping a couple of stones across the pond in the park.

In late September the tag-end of a hurricane hit Stratford. There was a minor flood, and when the waters went down a couple of days later, the dead cat was gone—it had been washed away. I remember it well now, and I suppose I will all my life, as my first intimate experience with death. That cat may be gone from the charts, but not from my heart.

Sophisticated movies demand sophisticated reactions from their audiences—that is, they demand that we react to them as adults. Horror movies are not sophisticated, and because they are not, they allow us to regain our childish perspective on death—perhaps not such a bad thing. I'll not descend to the romantic oversimplification that suggests we see things more clearly as children, but I will suggest that children see more intensely. The greens of lawns are, to the child's eye, the color of lost emeralds in H. Rider Haggard's conception of King Solomon's Mines, the blue of the winter sky is as sharp as an icepick, the white of new snow is a dream-blast of energy. And black . . . is blacker. Much blacker indeed.

Here is the final truth of horror movies: They do not love death, as some have suggested; they love life. They do not celebrate deformity but by dwelling on deformity, they sing of health and energy. By showing us the miseries of the damned, they help us to rediscover the smaller (but never petty) joys of our own lives. They are the barber's leeches of the psyche, drawing not bad blood but anxiety . . . for a little while, anyway.

The horror movie asks you if you want to take a good close look at the dead cat (or the shape under the sheet, to use a metaphor from the introduction to my short story collection) . . . but not as an adult would look at it. Never mind the philosophical implications of death or the religious possibilities inherent in the idea of survival; the horror film suggests we just have a good close look at the physical artifact of death. Let us be children masquerading as pathologists. We will, perhaps, link hands like children in a circle, and sing the song we all know in our hearts: time is short, no one is really okay, life is quick and dead is dead.

Omega, the horror film sings in those children's voices. Here is the end. Yet the ultimate subtext that underlies all good horror films is, *But not yet. Not this time.* Because in the final sense, the horror movie is the celebration of those who feel they can examine death because it does not yet live in their own hearts.

CHAPTER VII

The Horror Movie as Junk Food

B y now, serious horror fans may be wondering uneasily if I have lost my wits—always assuming I had any to begin with. I've found a few (very few, it's true, but still a few) good things to say about *The Amityville Horror*, and have even mentioned *Prophecy*, generally agreed to be a terrible horror movie, in a light not exactly unfavorable. If you are one of these uneasy ones, I must add to your feelings by telling you that I intend to say a great many good things about the Englishman James Herbert, author of *The Rat*, *The Fog*, and *The Survivor* in a later chapter—but that is a different case, because Herbert is not a bad novelist; he is simply regarded as one by fantasy fans who've not read his work.

I am no apologist for bad filmmaking, but once you've spent twenty years or so going to horror movies, searching for diamonds (or diamond-chips) in the dreck of the B-pics, you realize that if you don't keep your sense of humor, you're done for. You also begin to seek the patterns and appreciate them when you find them.

There's something else that needs saying here, too, and I might as well give it to you straight from the shoulder: once you've seen enough horror films, you begin to get a taste for really shitty movies. Films that are just bad (like *The Comeback*, Jack Jones's ill-advised foray into the field of the horror film) can be dismissed impatiently, with never a backward glance. But real fans of the genre look back on a film like *The Brain from Planet Arous* (It Came From Another World WITH AN

INSATIABLE LUST FOR EARTH WOMEN!) with something like real love. It is the love one spares for an idiot child, true, but love is love, right? Right.

In this spirit, let me quote—in its marvelous entirety— a review from *The Castle of Frankenstein*'s TV Movieguide. The Movieguide was published in the magazine at irregular intervals right up until the day when Calvin Beck's remarkable journal ceased publication. This review is, in fact, from the Movieguide which appeared in the last issue of *CofF*, #24. Here is what an uncredited reviewer (Beck himself, perhaps) had to say about the 1953 movie *Robot Monster*:

> It is a handful of flicks like this that makes all these listing chores [i.e., The Movieguide feature] something to look forward to. Certainly among the finest terrible movies ever made, this ridiculous gem presents as economical a space invasion as ever committed to film: one (1) Ro-Man invader consisting of (a) a gorilla suit, (b) a diving helmet with a set of antennae. Hiding out in one of the more familiar Hollywood caves with his extraterrestrial bubble machine (no, we're not being facetious: it actually is a 2-way "alien" radio-TV thing, consisting of an old war-surplus short-wave set resting on a small kitchen table, that emits Lawrence Welk-like bubbles), Ro-Man's trying to wipe out the last six humans left on earth and thus make the planet safe for colonization by Ro-Men (from the planet Ro-Man, where else?). This early 3-D effort has attained legendary (and richly deserved) status as one of the most laughable of all poverty row quickies, although the pic does make some scatterbrained sense when viewed as a child's eye monster fantasy (it's all a dream experienced by a sci-fi-crazed '50s tyke). Rousing musical score by Elmer Bernstein is great and keeps it all moving. Directed in three frenzied days by Phil Tucker, who also did the little-known and equally hysterical Lenny Bruce vehicle, DANCE HALL RACKET.

Stars George Nader, Claudia Barrett, John Mylong, Selena Royle.

Ah, Selena, where are you now?

I have seen the film discussed in this review, and will personally testify that every word is true. A bit further on in this chapter we will listen to what *CofF* had to say about two other legendary bad movies, *The Blob* and *Invasion of the Saucer Men*, but I don't believe my heart can stand it right now. Let me just add that I made a grave mistake concerning *Robot Monster* (and Ro-Man can be seen, in a mad sort of way, as the forerunner of the evil Cylons in *Battlestar Galactica*) about ten years ago. It came on the Saturday night Creature Feature, and I prepared for the occasion by smoking some pretty good reefer. I don't smoke dope often, because when stoned *everything* strikes me funny. That night I almost laughed myself into a hernia. Tears were rolling down my cheeks and I was literally on the floor for most of the movie. Luckily, the movie only runs sixty-three minutes; another twenty minutes of watching Ro-Man tune his war-surplus shortwave/bubble machine in "one of the more familiar Hollywood caves" and I think I would have laughed myself to death.

Since any affectionate discussion of really horrible movies (as opposed to horror movies) is in the nature of a breast baring, I must admit here that I not only liked John Frankenheimer's *Prophecy*, I actually saw it three times. The only bad movie to equal this score in my personal pantheon is the William Friedkin movie *Sorcerer*. I liked that one because there were a lot of close-ups in it of sweaty people working hard and laboring machines; truck engines and huge wheels spinning in soupy mud and frayed fanbelts on the giant screen. Great stuff. I thought *Sorcerer* was marvelous fun.*

But never mind Friedkin; onward into the Maine woods with John Frankenheimer. Except that the film was really shot

---

* I wasn't able to have any fun with Friedkin's more recent film, *Cruising*, although it fascinated me because I suspect it indicates the wave of the future for the bad film which has a big budget; it has a sparkly look that is still somehow cheesy—it's like a dead rat in a Lucite block.

on location in Washington State . . . and looks it. This film concerns a public health officer (Robert Foxworth) and his wife (Talia Shire) who come to Maine to investigate possible water pollution infractions on the part of a paper mill. The movie is apparently supposed to be set somewhere in northern Maine— perhaps in the Allagash—but David Seltzer's screenplay has somehow transferred an entire southern Maine county a hundred and fifty miles north. Just another example of the magic of Hollywood, I guess. In the TV version of 'Salem's Lot, Paul Monash's screenplay has the little town of Salem's Lot located on the outskirts of Portland . . . but the young lovers, Ben and Susan, blithely go off to the movies in Bangor at one point—a three-hour drive. Hi-ho.

Foxworth is a figure that any dedicated horror-movie buff has seen a hundred times before: the Dedicated Young Scientist with Just a Touch of Gray in His Hair. His wife wants a baby, but Foxworth refuses to bring a kid into a world where rats sometimes eat babies and the technological society keeps dumping radioactive waste into the oceans. He jumps at the trip to Maine to get away from patching up ratbites for awhile. His wife jumps at it because she's pregnant and wants to break it to him gently. As dedicated to the idea of zero population growth as he may be, Foxworth has apparently left all the responsibility for actually preventing the baby to his wife, who, played by Ms. Shire, succeeds in looking extremely tired throughout the film. We can readily believe she may be whoopsing her cookies every morning.

But once in Maine, this slightly odd couple finds a lot of other stuff going on as well. The Indians and the paper company are at swords' points over the alleged pollution issue; early on, one of the company men nearly opens up the leader of the Indian protestors with a Steihl chainsaw. Nasty. Nastier still are the evidences of pollution. Foxworth notices that the old Indian wallah (one dares not call him Chief) is regularly burning his hands with his cigarettes because he feels no pain—a classic sign of mercury poisoning, Foxworth tells Shire gravely. A tadpole the size of a salmon jumps up on the bank of the lake, and while fishing Foxworth sees a salmon roughly the size of Flipper.

Unfortunately for his pregnant wife, Foxworth catches some fish and they eat them. Very bad for the baby, as it turns out . . . although the question of exactly what Ms. Shire may deliver a few months down the road is left to our imaginations. By the time we finish the movie, the question seems less than burning.

Mutated babies are discovered in a net placed in a stream—horrible, rugose things with black eyes and malformed bodies, things that mewl and cry in almost human voices. These "children" are the movie's one startling effect.

Mother is out there someplace . . . and she makes her appearance soon enough, looking sort of like a skinned pig and sort of like a bear turned inside-out. It pursues Foxworth, Shire, and the motley band they are a part of. A helicopter pilot has his head crunched off (but it is a discreet crunch; this is a PG movie) and the Bad Old Executive Who Has Told Lies at Every Turn is similarly gobbled up. At one point the monster-mother wades across a lake that looks like it might be a child's wading pool shot from table-top level (bringing back fond memories of such Japanese triumphs of special-effects technology as *Ghidrah, the Three-Headed Monster* and *Godzilla vs. the Smog Monster*) and crashes its way into a cabin where the dwindling band of refugees has taken refuge. Although he is presented to us as a city boy from the word go, Foxworth manages to dispatch the monster with a bow and arrow. And as Foxworth and Shire fly out of the wilderness, another monster rears its shaggy head to stare after their departing light plane.

George Romero's film *Dawn of the Dead* came out at about the same time as *Prophecy* (June–July 1979) and I found it remarkable (and amusing) that Romero had made a horror film for about two million dollars that managed to look like six million, while Frankenheimer made a twelve-million-dollar movie that managed to look like about two.

Lots of stuff is wrong with the Frankenheimer film. None of the major Indian parts are played by real Indians; the old

Indian wallah has a teepee in a northern New England area which was populated by lodge-building Indians; the science, while not completely wrong, is used in an opportunistic way that is not really fair considering the fact that the movie's makers purported to have made a movie of "social conscience"; the characters are stock; the special effects (with the exception of those weird baby mutants) are bad.

All of that I will cheerfully agree to. But I come stubbornly, helplessly back to the fact that I liked *Prophecy*, and just writing about it has made me long to rush out and see it a fourth (and maybe a fifth) time. I mentioned that you begin to see and appreciate patterns in horror movies, and to love them. These patterns are sometimes as stylized as the movements in a Japanese *noh* play or the passages in a John Ford western. And *Prophecy* is a throwback to the fifties horror films as surely as the Sex Pistols and the Ramones are throwbacks to the "dirty white boys" of the rockabilly explosion in 1956–1959.

For me, settling into *Prophecy* is as comfortable as settling into an old easy chair and visiting with good friends. All the components are there; Robert Foxworth could as easily be Hugh Marlowe from *Earth vs. the Flying Saucers* or Richard Carlson in *It Came from Outer Space* or Richard Denning in *The Black Scorpion*. Talia Shire could as easily be Barbara Rush or Mara Corday or one of half a dozen other monster-movie heroines from that same Big Bug era (although I would be lying if I didn't admit to some disappointment in Ms. Shire, who was brilliant as Rocky Balboa's shy and hesitant *amour* Adrian; she's not as pretty as I remember Mara Corday being, and she never appears in a white one-piece swimsuit, when everyone knows that this particular type of horror movie demands that at one point the heroine must appear—and be menaced—while wearing a white one-piece swimsuit).

The monster is pretty hokey-looking, too. But I loved that old monster, spiritual sister to Godzilla, Mighty Joe Young, Gorgo, and all the dinosaurs that were ever embedded in ice floes and managed to get out so they could go thundering slowly down Fifth Avenue, squashing electronics shops and eating policemen; the monster in *Prophecy* gave me back a splendid part of my misspent youth, a part which included such irascible friends as the Venusian Ymir and the Deadly Mantis (who knocks over a city bus on which, for one splendid moment, the word TONKA can be clearly read). She's a pretty fine monster all the same.

The mercury pollution causing all those monsters is pretty good, too—an updating of the old radiation-caused-these-Big-Bugs plot device. Then there's the fact that the monster gets all the bad guys. At one point she kills a little kid, but the kid, who is on a hiking trip with his parents, really deserves to go. He has brought along his suitcase radio and is Defiling the Wilderness with Rock 'N Roll. All that is missing from *Prophecy* (and its omission may have only been an oversight) is a sequence where the monster stomps the rotten old paper mill flat.

The Giant Spider Invasion also comes equipped with a plot straight out of the fifties, and there were even a lot of fifties actors and actresses on view in it, including Barbara Hale and Steve Brodie . . . halfway through it, I had the feeling that what I had really stumbled on was a crazed episode of the old *Perry Mason* series.

In spite of the title, there is really only one giant spider, but we don't feel cheated because it's a dilly. It appears to be a Volkswagen covered with half a dozen bearskin rugs. Four spider legs, operated by people crammed inside this VW spider, one assumes, have been attached to each side. The taillights double neatly as blinking red spider eyes. It is impossible to see such a budget-conscious special effect without feeling a wave of admiration.

Other bad movies abound; each fan has his or her favorite. Who could forget the large canvas bag that was supposed to be *Caltiki, the Immortal Monster* in the 1959 Italian movie? Or the Japanese version of *Dr. Jekyll and Mr. Hyde—The Monster*? Other favorites of mine include the flaming Winston cigarette filter that was supposed to be a crash-landing alien spaceship in *Teenage Monster* and Allison Hayes as a refugee from a pro basketball team in *The Attack of the Fifty-Foot Woman*. (If only she could have wandered across into Bert I. Gordon's *The Amazing Colossal Man*. . . . Think of the children if they had clicked!) Then there was the wonderful moment in the 1978 film *Ruby*, a routine terror job about a haunted drive-in, when one of the characters punches a button on the Coke machine and gets a cup of blood. Inside the machine, you see, all of the tubes have been hooked up to a still-warm human corpse.

In *Children of Cain*, a Western horror picture (almost, but not quite, up to the level of *Billy the Kid Meets Dracula*), John Carradine goes West with barrels of salt water instead of fresh strapped to the sides of his Conestoga wagon. All the better to preserve his collection of severed heads (maybe because the historical period would have made the Coke machine an anachronism). In one of those lost-continent-type pictures—this one starring Cesar Romero—all the dinosaurs were cartoons. Nor should we forget Irwin Allen's *The Swarm*, with its unbelievable matte jobs and its cast of Familiar Faces. Here is a picture that manages to even better *Prophecy*'s time; it is a twelve-million-dollar picture that manages to look like a buck-ninety-eight.

2

From *Castle of Frankenstein*:

> **The Blob**
> This sf-horror comes out as a slightly flat imitation of both "Rebel Without a Cause" and "The Creeping Unknown." Oozing out-of-space horror consumes humans until destroyed in ridiculous ending.

This uncharacteristically out-of-patience review of a film which was the first starring vehicle for an actor who then billed himself as "Steven McQueen" ignores several fine touches: the theme song, for instance, by a group that sounds suspiciously like the Chords doing outtakes from "Sh-Boom," is played over a happy little cartoon of expanding blobs. The tune, if you care, was written by a kid named Burt Bacharach. The *real* blob, which arrives on earth inside a hollow meteor, looks at first like a melted blueberry Popsicle and later quite a bit like a giant Jujube. In spite of this unpromising start, the film has its genuine moments of unease and horror. The blob smoothly engulfs the arm of a farmer who has been unwise enough to touch it, and then turns a sinister red as the farmer screams in agony. Later, after McQueen and his girlfriend discover the farmer and take him to the local doctor, the blob devours first the nurse and then the doctor himself in the shadowy office. Michael J. Rodi, who brought the exact sequence to my attention in a letter following the hardcover edition of this book (which means, dear friends, that I got it wrong the first time), adds that "McQueen and his girlfriend return . . . just in time to witness the doctor clawing at his venetian blinds before being consumed."

Also, the *CofF* review is uncharacteristically wrong about the film's conclusion: the blob proved immortal. It was frozen and flown up to the Arctic to await the sequel, *Beware the Blob* (also released as *Son of the Blob*). Perhaps the film's finest moment for those of us who consider ourselves connoisseurs of bad special effects comes when the blob swallows a small diner whole. We see the blob oozing slowly across a color photograph of the diner's interior. Admirable. Must have made Bert I. Gordon envious.

Concerning *Invasion of the Saucer-Men,* a 1957 American-International picture, *CofF* regained some of its more customary *savoir faire:*

> Ludicrous sf quickie, on lowest teenage level. Space invaders are cute little saucermen who inject alcohol into victims' veins. The ending is quite funny (hic!).

Invasion of the Saucer-Men comes from AIP's Brass Age (it really can't be called AIP's Golden Age; that came later, during the spate of films loosely based on the works of Edgar Allen Poe—most of those were pretty stupid, wandering far afield from the source material, but at least they were pretty to look at). The picture was shot in seven days, and in the conclusion, the Heroic Teenagers use their hot-red headlights to "light" the monsters to death. Wasn't Elisha Cook, Jr., killed in the first reel, as he was so often? And Nick Adams can be seen in the background wearing his hat backwards—what a crazy kid, right? The monsters are like, all wasted, so let's go down to the malt shop, daddy-O!

In a later example of AIP low-budget mania, *Invasion of the Star Creatures* (1962), a group of Army men stranded in the trackless desert encounter a group of female invaders from space. All of these female invaders have beehive hairdos and look like Jacqueline Kennedy. Much is made of the fact that these fellows are totally cut off from the outside world and must deal with the problem themselves, but there are jeep tracks all over the place (not to mention a lot of foam rocks and, in several scenes, the shadow of the boom mike used to record the sound). One suspects that the film's utterly sleazy look may have come about because the producers overspent on star power; the cast list included such well-loved lights of the American cinema as Bob Ball, Frankie Ray, and Gloria Victor.

CofF had this to say about *I Married a Monster from Outer Space*, a 1958 Paramount release which formed the lower half of "summer shocker" double bills along with either *The Blob* or the hilarious Pat Boone film *Journey to the Center of the Earth:*

> Kiddy-oriented sf programmer. Gloria Talbot marries a monster from outer space which is disguised to look like Tom Tryon. Good argument against hasty marriages, but not much of a movie.

Still, this one was a lot of fun, if only for the once-in-a-life-time chance it offered to see Tom Tryon with a snout. And before leaving this one and proceeding on to what (sadly) may be the worst of the Grade-Z movies, I'd like to say something a little more serious about the peculiar relationship which obtains between terrible horror movies (of which there are a dozen for each good one, as this chapter testifies) and the genuine fan of the genre.

The relationship is not entirely masochistic, as the foregoing may make it seem. A film like *Alien* or *Jaws* is, for either the true fan or simply the ordinary moviegoer who has a sometime interest in the macabre, like a wide, deep vein of gold that doesn't even have to be mined; it can simply be dug out of the hillside. But that isn't mining, remember; it's just digging. The true horror film aficionado is more like a prospector with his panning equipment or his wash-wheel, spending long periods going patiently through common dirt, looking for the bright blink of gold dust or possibly even a small nugget or two. Such a working miner is not looking for the big strike, which may come tomorrow or the day after or never; he has put those illusions behind him. He's only looking for a livin' wage, something to keep him going yet awhile longer.

As a result, horror-movie fans communicate their likes to each other by a kind of grapevine which is part word of mouth, part fanzine reviews, part convention-hall chatter at such meetings as the World Fantasy Convention, the Kubla Khan Ate, or the IguanaCon. Word gets around. Long before David Cronenberg made something of a splash with *Rabid*, fans were muttering that he was someone to watch on the basis of an earlier film—an extremely low-budget flick called *They Came from Within*, starring X-rated queen Marilyn (*Behind the Green Door*) Chambers—and Cronenberg got a bravura performance out of her, by the way. My agent, Kirby McCauley, raves about a small picture called *Ritual*, filmed in Canada and starring Hal Holbrook. These films don't get wide American release, but if you watch the papers faithfully, you may see one of them playing at the drive-in as a pick-up second feature below some overrated major studio flick. Similarly, I heard about a little-known early John Carpenter film called *Assault on Precinct 13* from Peter Straub, the author of *Ghost Story* and *If You Could See Me Now*. Done on a shoestring (and Carpenter's first feature, *Dark Star*, is reputed to have cost somewhere in the neighborhood of $60,000, a sum that makes even George Romero look like Dino De Laurentiis), Carpenter's talent as a director nonetheless shines through, and Carpenter went on to do *Halloween* and *The Fog*.

These are the nuggets, the horror-film fan's reward for sifting through films like *Planet of the Vampires* and *The Monster from Green Hell*. My own "discovery" (if you don't object to the word) is a little film called *Tourist Trap*, starring Chuck Connors. Connors himself isn't very good in the film—he tries gamely, but he's simply miscast. Yet the film wields an eerie, spooky power. Wax figures begin to move and come to life in a ruined, out-of-the-way tourist resort; there are a number of effective, atmospheric shots of the dummies' blank eyes and reaching hands, and the special effects are effective. As a film that deals with the queer power that inanimate dummies, mannequins, and human replicas can sometimes cast over us, it is a more effective film than the expensive and ill-advised film made from William Goldman's bestseller, *Magic*.*

But to get back to *I Married a Monster from Outer Space:* bad as it is, there is one absolutely chilling moment in the movie. I won't say that it's worth the price of admission, but it works . . . boy, does it work! Tryon has married his girlfriend (Gloria Talbot) and they are on their honeymoon. While she stretches out on the bed, dressed in the obligatory filmy white nightgown and waiting for the consummation of all those steamy clinches on the beach, Tryon, who is still a good-looking man and who was even better looking twenty years ago, goes out on the balcony of their hotel room for a cigarette. A thunderstorm is brewing, and a sharp stroke of lightning abruptly renders that handsome face transparent for a moment. We see the horrible alien face beneath—runnelled and knotted

---

* Home Box Office, in its endless quest for prime-time filler, is now making many of these "little" films available in a way that such spotty distributors as New World Pictures have never been able to do. Of course, there's no shortage of dreck on HBO either, as any subscriber will tell you; still, there is an occasional prize in the pay-TV box, which is usually full of such mouldy cinematic Cracker Jacks as *Guyana: Cult of the Damned* and *Moment by Moment*. In the last year or so HBO has offered Cronenberg's *The Brood* and an interesting AIP picture called *The Evictors* (starring Vic Morrow and Michael Parks), which got no American theatrical distribution . . . and *Tourist Trap*.

and warty. It is a "seat-jumper" for sure, and during the fade-out we perhaps have time to think about the consummation to follow . . . and gulp.

If movies such as *Tourist Trap* and *Rituals* are the nuggets fans sometimes find by sticking around for the B picture (and no one is so optimistic as the dyed-in-the-wool fan), a moment such as this one is the equivalent of the gold dust that can sometimes be panned out by the faithful toiler. Or to put it another way, there is that marvelous Sherlock Holmes story, "The Adventure of the Blue Carbuncle," where the Christmas goose, when slit open, yields up the beautiful and priceless stone that has been lodged in its gullet. You sit through a lot of shlock, and maybe—just maybe—there is that *frisson* that makes it at least partially worthwhile.

There is no such *frisson* in *Plan 9 from Outer Space*, unfortunately, to which I reluctantly award the booby-prize as the worst horror film ever made. Yet there is nothing funny about this one, no matter how many times it has been laughed at in those mostly witless compendiums which celebrate the worst of everything. There's nothing funny about watching a Bela Lugosi (actually, a stand-in was used for most shots) wracked with pain, a morphine monkey on his back, creeping around a southern California development with his Dracula cape pulled up over his nose.

Lugosi died shortly after this abysmal, exploitative, misbegotten piece of trash was released, and I've always wondered in my heart if maybe poor old Bela didn't die as much of shame as of the many illnesses that were overwhelming him. It was a sad and squalid coda to a great career. Lugosi was buried (at his own request) in his Dracula cape, and one likes to think—or hope—that it served him better in death than it did in the miserable waste of celluloid that marked his last screen appearance.

3

Before we move on to horror on TV, where failures in the genre have been every bit as common (but somehow less spectacular), it seems appropriate to finish here by asking a question: Why have there been so many bad horror movies?

Before trying to answer that, let's be honest and say that a great many movies are very bad—not all the turkeys are gobbling in the horror pen, if you take my meaning. Consider *Myra Breckinridge*, *Valley of the Dolls*, *The Adventurers*, and *Bloodline* . . . to mention just a few. Even Alfred Hitchcock produced one of those Thanksgiving birds, and unfortunately, it was his last picture: *Family Plot*, with Bruce Dern and Karen Black. And these pictures only scratch the surface of a list that could continue on for a hundred pages or more. Probably more.

There's an impulse to say something's wrong here. There may well be. If another business—United Airlines, let us say, or IBM—ran their affairs the way 20th Century-Fox ran the making of *Cleopatra*, their boards of directors would soon be down at the local 7-11 store, buying pizza mix with foodstamps— or maybe the stockholders would just break down the door and wheel in the guillotine. It seems almost incredible to believe that any major studio could even approach the brink of bankruptcy in a country that loves the movies as much as this one does; one might as well try to imagine, you might think, Caesar's Palace or the Dunes wiped out by a single crapshooter. But in fact there is *not one* major American film studio which has not at least once during the thirty-year period under discussion here tottered on the brink. MGM is perhaps the most infamous case, and for a period of seven years the MGM lion ceased to roar almost entirely. Perhaps significantly, during this period when MGM was leaving the unreal world of the movies and pinning its hopes for corporate survival upon the unreal gambling world (the MGM Grand in Vegas, surely one of the world's more vulgar pleasure domes), their one major success was a horror movie—Michael Crichton's *Westworld*, in which a disintegrating Yul Brynner, dressed in black and looking like a nightmare revenant from *The Magnificent Seven,* intones again and again: "Draw. Draw. Draw." They draw . . . and lose. Yul is pretty fast, even with his circuits showing.

Is this, you ask me, any way to run a railroad?

My own answer is no . . . but the failure of so many films released by "the majors" seems more explicable to me than the failure of so many of the horror films released by what *Variety* calls "the indies." At this writing, three of my novels have been released as films: *Carrie* (United Artists/theatrical/1976) *'Salem's Lot* (Warners/television/1979), and *The Shining* (Warners/theatrical/1980), and in all three cases I feel that I have been fairly treated . . . and yet the clearest emotion in my mind is not pleasure but a mental sigh of relief. When dealing with the American cinema, you feel like you won if you just broke even.

Once you've seen the film industry's workings from the inside, you realize that it is a creative nightmare. It becomes difficult to understand how anything of quality—an *Alien,* a *Place in the Sun,* a *Breaking Away*—can be made. As in the Army, the first rule of studio filmmaking is CYA: Cover Your Ass. On any critical decision, it is well to consult at least half a dozen people, so that someone else's butt will go up in that fabled sling if the film drops dead and twenty million dollars goes swirling down the toilet. And if your butt must go up, it then becomes possible to make sure it doesn't go up alone.

There are, of course, filmmakers who either don't know this kind of fear or whose particular visions are so clear and fierce that such fear of failure never becomes a factor in the equation. Brian De Palma comes to mind, and Francis Coppola (who teetered on the edge of being fired from *The Godfather* shoot for months, and yet persisted in his own particular vision of the film), Sam Peckinpah, Don Siegel, Steven Spielberg.* This factor of vision is so real and apparent that even when a direc-

---

* Compare, for instance, the single and unified vision which powers Spielberg's *Jaws* to the sequel, which was produced by committee and directed by the unfortunate Jeannot Szwarc, who was brought in from the bullpen in the late innings to mop up, and who deserved better.

tor such as Stanley Kubrick makes such a maddening, perverse, and disappointing film as *The Shining*, it somehow retains a brilliance that is inarguable; it is simply there.

The real danger inherent in studio films is mediocrity. A clinker like *Myra Breckinridge* has its own horrid fascination—it is like watching slow-motion footage of a head-on collision between a Cadillac and a Lincoln Continental. But what are we to make of films like *Nightwing, Capricorn One, Players*, or *The Cassandra Crossing*? These are not bad films—not the way that *Robot Monster* or *Teenage Monster* are bad, certainly—but they are mediocre. They're blah. You leave the theater after one of these films with no taste in your mouth but the popcorn you ate. They are films where, halfway through the second reel, you begin wishing for a cigarette.

As the cost of production balloons up and up, the risks of going for all of it become greater and greater, and even a Roger Maris looked pretty stupid when he was badly fooled, totally overswung the ball, and fell on his ass. The same obtains in films, and I would predict—with some hesitation, because the film industry is such a crazy place—that we will never again see such a colossal risk as the one Coppola took with *Apocalypse Now* or the one Cimino was allowed to take with *Heaven's Gate*. If anyone tries, that dry, dusty snapping sound you'll hear coming from the West Coast will be the accountants of every major studio out there snapping the corporate checkbooks closed.

But the indies . . . what about the indies? There is less to lose here, certainly; in fact Chris Steinbrunner, an amusing guy and an astute follower of the films, likes to call many of these flicks "backyard movies." By his definition, *The Horror of Party Beach* was a backyard film; so were *The Flesh Eaters* and Tobe Hooper's *The Texas Chainsaw Massacre*. (*Night of the Living Dead*, which was made by an existing film company with access to TV studio facilities in Pittsburgh, doesn't qualify as "backyard.") It's a good term for those films made by amateurs, gifted or otherwise, on a shoestring budget with no major distribution guaranteed—these films are the much more expensive equivalent of the unsolicited manuscript. These are guys who are shooting with nothing to lose, shooting for the moon. And yet most of these films are just awful.

Why?

Exploitation, that's why.

It was exploitation that caused Lugosi to put finish to his career by creeping around a suburban tract development in his Dracula cape; it was exploitation that prompted the making of *Invasion of the Star Creatures* and *Don't Look in the Basement* (and believe me, I didn't have to keep telling myself it was only a movie; I knew what it was—in a word, wretched). After sex, low-budget moviemakers are attracted to horror because it seems to be a genre which is easily exploited—an easy lay, like the sort of girl every guy wanted to date (at least once) in high school. Even good horror can sometimes have a tawdry carnival freak-show feel . . . but it's a feel that can be deceptive.

And if it is courtesy of the indies that we have seen the greatest failures (the Ro-Man's war-surplus shortwave/bubble machine), then it is also courtesy of them that we have seen some of the most unlikely triumphs. *The Horror of Party Beach* and *Night of the Living Dead* were made on similar budgets; the difference is George Romero and his vision of what the horror movie is and what the horror movie is supposed to do. In the former we have the monsters attacking a slumber party in a scene which becomes hilarious; in the latter we have an old woman peering nearsightedly at a bug on a tree and then munching it up. You hear your mouth trying to laugh and scream at the same time, and that is Romero's remarkable achievement.

Werewolf in a Girls' Dormitory and *Dementia-13* were made on similar nothing budgets; here the difference is Francis Coppola, who created an almost unbearable atmosphere of mounting menace in the latter, a black-and-white, rapidly shot suspense movie (which was made on location in Ireland, for tax purposes).

It is, perhaps, too easy to become enamored of bad films as "camp"; the great success of *The Rocky Horror Picture Show* may point to nothing so much as the degeneration of the average moviegoer's critical capacity. It might be well to go back to the basics and remember that the difference between bad movies and good (or between bad art—or nonart—and good or great art) is talent, and the inventive utilization of that talent. The worst movie sends its own message, which is simply to stay away from other movies done by these people; if you have seen one film by Wes Craven, for instance, it is safe enough, I think, to skip the others. The genre labors under enough critical disapproval and outright dislike; one need not make a bad situation worse by underwriting films of porno-violence and those which want to plunder our pocketbooks and no more. And there is no need to do it, because even in the movies there is no real pricetag on quality . . . not when Brian De Palma found it possible to make a fine, scary film like *Sisters* for something like $800,000.

The reason for seeing bad movies, I suppose, is that you don't know it's going to be bad until you've seen it for yourself—as previously pointed out, most movie critics cannot be trusted here. Pauline Kael writes well, and Gene Shalit demonstrates a certain rather tiresome surface wit, but when these two—and other critics—go to see a horror movie, they don't know what they are seeing.* The true fan does; he or she has developed his or her basis for comparison over a long and sometimes painful span of time. The real movie freak is as much an appreciator as the regular visitor to art galleries or museums, and this basis for comparison is the bedrock upon whatever theses or point(s) of view he or she may develop must stand. For the horror fan, films such as *Exorcist II* form the setting for the occasional bright gemstone that is discovered in the darkness of a sleazy second-run moviehouse: Kirby McCauley's *Rituals* or my own low-budget favorite, *Tourist Trap*.

You don't appreciate cream unless you've drunk a lot of milk, and maybe you don't even appreciate milk unless you've drunk

---

* The one exception is Judith Crist, who seems to genuinely like horror movies and who is often able to look past a poverty-row budget to whatever is working there—I've always wondered what she made of *Night of the Living Dead*.

some that's gone sour. Bad films may sometimes be amusing, sometimes even successful, but their only real usefulness is to form that basis of comparison: to define positive values in terms of their own negative charm. They show us what to look for because it is missing in themselves. After that has been determined, it becomes, I think, actively dangerous to hold on to these bad films . . . and they must be discarded.*

---

* If you are interested in my own determination of the best horror movies of the last thirty years, see Appendix I.

CHAPTER VIII

The Glass Teat, or,
This Monster Was Brought to You
by Gainesburgers

All those of you out there among the great un-
washed who ever believed that TV sucks were dead
wrong, you see; as Harlan Ellison pointed out in
his sometimes amusing, sometimes scathing essays
on television, TV does *not* suck; it is sucked. Ellison called his
two-volume diatribe on the subject *The Glass Teat,* and if you've
not read it, be aware that it comes recommended as a kind of
compass with this particular stretch of the territory. I read the
book with amazed absorption three years ago, the fact that Ellison had devoted valuable time and space to such forgettable
series of yesteryear as *Alias Smith and Jones* barely obtruding on
a total volcanic effect that made me suspect I was experiencing
something roughly similar to a six-hour rant delivered by Fidel
Castro. Always assuming that Fidel was really on that day.

Ellison circles back and back to television in his work, like a
man held in thrall by a snake he knows to be ultimately deadly.
For no apparent reason, the longish introduction to *Strange
Wine* (a book we'll discuss at some length next chapter), El-
lison's 1978 collection of short stories, is a diatribe on TV titled
"Revealed at Last! What Killed the Dinosaurs! And You Don't
Look So Terrific Yourself."

When you strip Ellison's TV-rap to its core, it is simple
enough and not blazingly original (for blazing originality, you
have to read how he says it): TV is a spoiler, Ellison says. It

spoils story; it spoils those who make the stories; eventually it spoils those who watch the stories; the milk from this particular teat is poisoned. This is a thesis I would agree with completely, but let me point out two facts.

Harlan has a TV. A big one.

I have a TV which is even bigger than Harlan's. It is, in fact, a Panasonic CinemaVision which dominates one whole corner of my living room.

Mea culpa, all right.

I can rationalize Harlan's TV and my own monster, although I cannot completely excuse either of us—and I should add that Ellison is a bachelor, and he can watch the thing twenty hours a day if he wants and hurt nobody but himself. I, on the other hand, have three young children in the house—ten, eight, and four—who are exposed to this gadget; to its possible radiation, its untrue colors, and its magic window on a vulgar, tawdry world where cameras ogle the butts of Playboy bunnies and linger over endless visions of an upper-upper-upper-middle-class materialism that, for most Americans, has never existed and never will. Mass starvation is a way of life in Biafra; in Cambodia, dying children are shitting out their own collapsed intestines; in the Middle East a kind of messianic madness is in danger of swallowing up all rationality; and here at home we sit mesmerized by Richard Dawson on *Family Feud* and watch Buddy Ebsen as Barnaby Jones. I think my own three kids have a better fix on the reality of Gilligan, the Skipper, and Mr. Howell than they do on the reality of what happened at Three Mile Island in March of 1979. In fact, I know they do.

Horror has not fared particularly well on TV, if you except something like the six o'clock news, where footage of black GIs with their legs blown off, villages and kids on fire, bodies in trenches, and whole swatches of jungle being coated with good old Agent Orange sent kids into the streets, where they would march and light candles and say dopey, talismanic "in" things to each other until we withdrew, the North Vietnamese took over, and more starvation on mass levels resulted—not to mention opening the way for such really upstanding, humanitarian personages as Cambodia's Pol Pot. The whole sour stew sure wasn't much like a TV show, was it? Just ask yourself if any chain of events so ridiculous could ever have happened on *Hawaii Five-O*. The answer is of course not. If Steve McGarrett had been President from 1968 to 1976, the whole abortion could have been avoided. Steve, Danny, and Chin Ho would have cleared the mess up.

The sort of horrors we have been discussing in this book labor under the very fact of their unreality (a fact which Harlan Ellison himself recognizes well; he refuses to allow the word *fantasy* to be printed on book covers as a description term for the stories inside). We have treated the question "Why do you want to write horror stories in a world that is so full of real horrors?"; I am now suggesting that the reason horror has done so poorly, by and large, on TV, is a statement which is closely related to that question, to wit: "It is very difficult to write a successful horror story in a world which is so full of real horrors." A ghost in the turret room of a Scottish castle just cannot compete with thousand-megaton warheads, CBW bugs, or nuclear power plants that have apparently been put together from Aurora model kits by ten-year-olds with poor eye-hand coordination. Even Old Leatherface in *The Texas Chainsaw Massacre* pales beside those dead sheep in Utah, killed by one of Our Finer Nerve Gases. If the wind had been blowing the other way when that happened, Salt Lake City might have gotten a really good dose of what killed the sheep. And, my good friends, someday the wind is not going to be blowing the right way. You may count on it; tell your Congressman I said so. Sooner or later the wind always changes.

Well, horror can be done. That emotion can still be triggered by people who are dedicated to doing it, and there's something optimistic in the fact that people can still, in spite of all the world's real horrors, be brought to the point of the scream by something that is patently impossible. It can be done by the writer or the director . . . *if their hands are untied.*

For the writer, the most galling thing about TV must be that he or she is forbidden from bringing all of his or her powers to bear, the predicament of the TV writer is strikingly similar to the predicament of the human race as envisioned in Kurt Vonnegut's short story "Harrison Bergeron," where bright people are fitted with electro-shock caps to disrupt their thinking periodically, agile people are fitted with weights, and people with great artistic talent are forced to wear heavy, distorting glasses to destroy their clearer perception of the world around them. As a result, a perfect state of equality has been achieved . . . but at what a price.

The ideal writer for the TV medium is a fella or a gal with a smidgen of talent, a lot of gall, and the soul of a drone. In Hollywood's current and exquisitely vulgar parlance, he or she must "give good meeting." Let any of these qualifications be tampered with, and the writer is apt to start feeling like poor old Harrison Bergeron. It has made Ellison, who wrote for *Star Trek, The Outer Limits*, and *The Young Lawyers*, to name just a few, a little bit crazy, I think. But if he weren't, it would be impossible to respect him. His craziness is a kind of Purple Heart, like Joseph (*Police Story*) Wambaugh's ulcers. There is no reason why a writer cannot make a living doing TV on a constant week-in-week-out basis; all that writer really needs is a low Alpha-wave pattern and a perception of writing as the mental equivalent of bucking crates of soda up onto a Coca-Cola truck.

Part of this is the result of federal regulation and part of it is proof of the maxim which states that power corrupts and absolute power corrupts absolutely. TV is in almost every American home, and the financial stakes are enormous. As a result, television has become more and more cautious over the years. It has become like a fat old spayed tomcat dedicated to the preservation of the status quo and to the concept of LOP—Least Objectionable Programming. Television is, in fact, like that fat, wimpy kid who most of us can remember from our childhood neighborhoods, the big, slack kid who would cry if you gave him two-for-flinching, the kid who always looked guilty when the teacher asked who put the mouse in her drawer, the kid who was always picked on because he was always afraid of being picked on.

Now the simple fact of horror fiction in whatever medium you choose . . . the *bedrock* of horror fiction, we might say, is simply this: you gotta scare the audience. Sooner or later you gotta put on the gruesome mask and go booga-booga. I can remember an official in the fledgling New York Mets organization worrying about the improbable crowds that gang of happy-go-lucky schmucks was drawing. "Sooner or later we're going to have to sell these people some steak along with the sizzle," was how this fellow expressed it. The same is true with horror. The reader will not feed forever on innuendo and vapors; sooner or later even the great H. P. Lovecraft had to produce whatever was lurking in the crypt or in the steeple.

Most of the great film directors in the field have chosen to get the horror up front; to cram a large block of it down the viewer's throat until he almost chokes on it and then lead the viewer on, teasing him, drawing every cent of the psychological interest due on that original scare.

The primer that every would-be horror director studies in this matter is, of course, the definitive horror film of the period we're discussing—Alfred Hitchcock's *Psycho*. Here is a movie where blood was kept to a minimum and terror was kept to a maximum. In the famous shower scene we see Janet Leigh; we see the knife; but we never see the knife in Janet Leigh. You may think you saw it, but you did not. Your *imagination* saw it, and that is Hitchcock's great triumph. All the blood we see in the shower is swirling down the drain.*

Psycho has never been shown during prime time at a network movie, but once that forty-five seconds in the shower has been removed, the film could almost be a made-for-TV movie (in content, anyway; in terms of style, it is light-years from the run-of-the-tube TV flick). In effect, what Hitchcock does is

---

* I would date the more overtly violent horror movies not from *Psycho* but from two nonhorror movies, shot in living, bloody color: Sam Peckinpah's *The Wild Bunch* and Arthur Penn's *Bonnie and Clyde*.

serve us a big raw steak of terror not even halfway through his film. The rest, even the climax, is really only sizzle. And without that forty-five seconds, the film becomes nearly humdrum. In spite of its reputation, *Psycho* is an admirably restrained horror movie; Hitchcock even elected to shoot in black and white so that the blood in the shower scene would not look like blood at all, and one oft-told tale—almost surely apocryphal—is that Hitch toyed with shooting the movie in color—except for the shower scene, which would be in black and white.

As we enter upon our discussion of horror on television, always keep this fact somewhere near to hand: television has really asked the impossible of its handful of horror programs—to terrify without really terrifying, to horrify without really horrifying, to sell audiences a lot of sizzle and no steak.

Earlier on I said I could rationalize if not excuse the fact of Ellison's TV and my own, and the rationalization goes back to what I've already said about really awful movies. Of course, TV is far too homogenized to cough up anything as charmingly awful as *The Giant Spider Invasion* with its fur-covered Volkswagen, but every now and then talent shines through and something good turns up . . . and even if the something is not out-and-out good, like Spielberg's *Duel* or John Carpenter's *Someone's Watching Me*, the viewer may find at least some cause for hope. More Child than adult in pursuit of his particular taste, hope springs eternal in the breast of the fantasy-horror fan. You tune in, knowing almost certainly that it's going to be bad yet hoping against hope—irrationally—that it is going to be good. Excellence occurs surely, but every now and then a program will come along which at least bucks the odds enough to produce something interesting, such as the late-1979 NBC-TV movie *The Aliens Are Coming*. Every now and then we are given some cause for hope.

And with that hope to guard us against the dreck like a magic talisman, let us go and make our visit. Just close your eyes while we dance through the cathode tube here; it has a bad habit of first hypnotizing and then anesthetizing.

Just ask Harlan.

2

Probably the best horror series ever put on TV was *Thriller*, which ran on NBC from September of 1960 until the summer of 1962—really only two seasons plus reruns. It was a period before television began to face up to an increasing barrage of criticism about its depiction of violence, a barrage that really began with the JFK assassination, grew heavier following the assassinations of RFK and Martin Luther King, and finally caused the medium to dissolve into a sticky syrup of situation comedies—history may record that dramatic television finally gave up the ghost and slid down the tubes with a hearty cry of "Na-noo, na-noo!"

The contemporaries of *Thriller* were also weekly blood-baths; it was the time of *The Untouchables*, starring Robert Stack as the unflappable Eliot Ness and featuring the grue-some deaths of hoodlums without number (1959–1963); *Peter Gunn* (1958–1961); and *Cain's Hundred* (1961–1962), to name just a few. It was TV's violent era. As a result, after a slow first thirteen weeks, *Thriller* was able to become something more than the stock imitation of *Alfred Hitchcock Presents* that it was apparently meant to be (early episodes dealt with cheat-ing husbands trying to hypnotize their wives into walking over high cliffs, poisoning Aunt Martha to inherit her fortune so that the gambling debts could be paid off, and all that tiresome sort of thing) and took on a tenebrous life of its own. For the brief period of its run between January of 1961 and April of 1962—perhaps fifty-six of its seventy-eight total episodes—it really was one of a kind, and its like was never seen on TV again.

Thriller was an anthology-format show (as all of the super-natural-terror TV programs which have enjoyed even a modi-cum of success have been) hosted by Boris Karloff. Karloff had appeared on TV before quite often, beginning after the Universal horror wave of the early to mid-thirties finally ran weakly out in that series of comedies in the late forties. One earlier program, telecast on the fledgling ABC-TV network, had a brief run in the autumn of 1949. It was originally titled *Starring Boris Karloff,* fared no better following a title change to *Mystery Playhouse Starring Boris Karloff,* and was canceled. In feeling and tone, however, it was startlingly similar to *Thriller,* which came along eleven years later. Here is the summary of one plot from *Starring Boris Karloff;* it might as well be a *Thriller* episode:

> An English hangman unduly enjoys his work, which brings him payment of five guineas per hanging. He revels in the snap of the victim's neck, and the dangling arms. When his pregnant wife discovers his true occupation she leaves him. Twenty years later the hangman is called upon to execute a young man, which he does with pleasure, despite the fact that he has secret evidence (of the youth's innocence). . . . Only then is he confronted by his ex-wife, who tells him he has just hung his own son. Enraged, he strangles his wife and is subsequently sent to the gallows himself. Another hangman collects five golden guineas.*

The plot is kissing cousin to an episode from *Thriller*'s second season. In that one, the executioner was French, in charge of the guillotine instead of the gallows, and was presented as a sympathetic character (although his work has apparently not affected his appetite; he's a mountain of a man). He is due to execute a particularly foul murderer the next day at dawn. The killer has not given up hope, however; his girlfriend has wormed her way into the lonely herdsman's affections, and the two of them hope to take advantage of an old loophole in the law (and I should say here that I have no idea if the loophole is a genuine one, like the American concept of double jeopardy, or simply the plot device of Cornell Woolrich, who wrote the story) which holds that if the executioner croaks on the day he is to do business, that day's condemned prisoner walks free.

---

* From *The Complete Directory to Prime Time Network TV Shows, 1946–Present,* edited by Tim Brooks and Earle Marsh (New York: Ballantine Books, 1979), p. 586.

The lady serves the executioner a huge breakfast laced with strong poison. He eats heartily, as usual, and then sets off for the prison. He's halfway there when the first agonizing pains strike. The rest of the episode is a chilly exercise in suspense as the camera cuts back and forth between the cell of the condemned man and the executioner's agonized walk through the streets of Paris. The executioner, obviously a type-A personality, is determined to do his duty.

He reaches the prison, collapses halfway across the courtyard . . . and then begins to crawl toward the guillotine. The prisoner is brought out, dressed in the proper open-collared white shirt (the screenwriter had obviously read his *Tale of Two Cities*) and the two of them converge at the guillotine. Now at the end of his rope (ha-ha), the executioner nevertheless manages to get the screaming prisoner's head in the stock and positioned over the basket before collapsing, stone dead.

The condemned prisoner, on his knees with his butt poking up—looking a bit like a turkey caught in a shakepole fence—begins screaming that he's free! Free, do you bear? Ah-hah-hah-hah! The doctor who was to pronounce the condemned dead now finds himself called upon to perform that duty upon the erstwhile executioner. He tries for a pulse and finds none—but when he drops the executioner's wrist, it falls on the guillotine's lever. The blade swishes down—*thud!* We fade out, knowing that rough justice has been done.

Karloff was seventy-four at the beginning of *Thriller*'s two-year run, and not in the best of health; he suffered from a chronically bad back and had to wear weights to stand upright. Some of these infirmities dated back to his original film appearance as Frankenstein's monster in 1931. He no longer starred in all the programs—many of the guest stars on the *Thriller* program were nonentities who went on to become full-fledged nobodies (one of those guest stars, Reggie Nalder, went on to play the vampire Barlow in the CBS-TV film version of *'Salem's Lot*)—but fans will remember a few memorable occasions when he did ("The Strange Door," for instance). The old magic was still there, still intact. Lugosi might have finished his career in misery and poverty, but Karloff, despite a few embarrassments like *The Snake People*, went out as he came in: as a gentleman.

Produced by William Frye, *Thriller* was the first television program to discover the goldmine in those back issues of *Weird Tales*, the memory of which had been kept alive up until then mostly in the hearts of fans, a few quickie paperback anthologies, and, of course, in those limited-edition Arkham House anthologies. One of the most significant things about the *Thriller* series from the standpoint of the horror fan was that it began to depend more and more upon the work of writers who had published in those "shudder pulps" . . . the writers who, in the period of the twenties, thirties, and forties, had begun to guide horror out of the Victorian-Edwardian ghost-story channel it had been in for so long, and toward our modern perception of what the horror story is and what it should do. Robert Bloch was represented by "The Hungry Glass," a story in which the mirrors of an old house harbor a grisly secret; Robert E. Howard's "Pigeons from Hell," one of the finest horror stories of our century, was adapted, and remains the favorite of many who remember *Thriller* with fondness.* Other episodes include "A Wig for Miss DeVore," in which a red wig keeps an actress magically young . . . until the final five minutes of the program, when she loses it—and everything else. Miss DeVore's lined, sunken face; the young man staggering blindly down the stairs of the decaying bayou mansion with a hatchet buried in his head ("Pigeons from Hell"); the fellow who sees the faces of his fellow men and women turned into hideous monstrosities when he puts on a special pair of glasses ("The Cheaters," from another Bloch story)—these may not have constituted fine art,

---

* And some say it was the single most frightening story ever done on TV. I would disagree with that. My own nominee for that honor would be the final episode of a little-remembered program called *Bus Stop* (adapted from the William Inge play and film). The series, a straight drama show, was canceled following the furor over an episode starring then rock star Fabian Forte as a psychopathic rapist—the episode was based on a Tom Wicker novel. The final episode, however, deviated wildly into the supernatural, and for me, Robert Bloch's adaptation of his own short story "I Kiss Your Shadow" has never been beaten on TV—and rarely anywhere else—for eerie, mounting horror.

but in *Thriller's* run, we find those qualities appreciated above all others by fans of the genre: a literate story coupled with the genuine desire to frighten the viewer into spasms.

Years after *Thriller*, a production company associated with NBC—the network upon which *Thriller* was telecast—optioned three stories from my 1978 collection, *Night Shift*, and invited me to do the screenplay. One of these stories was a piece called "Strawberry Spring," about a psychopathic Jack-the-Ripper-type killer who is roaming a fogbound college campus. About a month after turning the script in, I got a call from an NBC munchkin at Standards and Practices (read: The Department of Censorship). The knife my killer used to commit his murders had to go, the munchkin said. The killer could stay, but the knife had to go. Knives were too phallic. I suggested we turn the killer into a strangler. The munchkin evinced great enthusiasm. I hung up, feeling like a very brilliant fellow, and turned the stabber into a strangler. The script was finally coughed out of the network's large and voracious gullet by Standards and Practices, however, strangler and all. Too gruesome and intense was the final verdict.

I guess none of them remembered Patricia Barry in "A Wig for Miss DeVore."

3

Blackness on the TV screen.

Then there's a picture there—some kind of picture—but it's rolling helplessly at first, then losing horizontal resolution.

Black again, broken by a single wavy white line, oscillating hypnotically.

The voice accompanying all this is quiet, reasonable.

"There is nothing wrong with your TV set. We are controlling transmission. We can control the vertical. We can control the horizontal. For the next hour we will control all that you see and hear. You are about to experience the awe and mystery which reaches from the inner mind to . . . the Outer Limits."

Nominally science fiction, more actually a horror program,

The Outer Limits was, perhaps, after *Thriller*, the best program of its type ever to run on network TV. Purists will scream nonsense and blasphemy; that not even *Thriller* could compete with the immortal *Twilight Zone*. That *The Twilight Zone* is damn near immortal is something I will not argue with; in big city markets like New York, Chicago, Los Angeles, and San Francisco it seems to run eternally, hallelujah, world without end, sandwiched into its own twilight zone just after the late evening news and just before the PTL Club. Perhaps only such ancient sitcoms as *I Love Lucy* and *My Little Margie* can compete with *The Twilight Zone* for that sort of fuzzy, black-and-white, vampiristic life which syndication allows.

But, with a dozen or so notable exceptions, *The Twilight Zone* had very little to do with the sort of horror fiction we're dealing with here. It was a program which specialized in moral tales, many of them smarmy (such as the one where Barry Morse buys a player piano which causes his guests to reveal their true selves; the piano ends up causing him to admit that he is a selfish little sonofabitch); many others well meant but simplistic and almost painfully corny (as in the one where the sun does not rise because the atmosphere of human injustice has just gotten too black, folks, too black—the radio announcer gravely reports that things are particularly black over Dallas and Selma, Alabama. . . . Get it, guys? Get it?). Other episodes of *The Twilight Zone* were really little more than sentimental riffs on old supernatural themes: Art Carney discovers he really is Santa Claus after all; the tired commuter (James Daly) finds peace in an idyllic, bucolic little town called Willoughby.

The Twilight Zone did occasionally strike notes of horror— the best of these vibrate in the back teeth years later—and we will discuss some of these before we finish with the Magic Box. But for sheer hard-edged clarity of concept, *The Twilight Zone* really could not match *The Outer Limits,* which ran from September of 1963 until January of 1965. The program's executive producer was Leslie Stevens; its line-producer was Joseph Stefano, who wrote the screenplay for Hitchcock's *Psycho* and an eerie little exercise in terror called *Eye of the Cat* a year or two later. Stefano's vision of what the program was about was an extraordinarily clear one. Each episode, he insisted, had to have a "bear"—some sort of monstrous creature that would make an appearance before the station break at the half hour. In some cases the bear was not harmful in and of itself, but you could bet that before the end of the show, some outside force— usually a villainous mad scientist—would cause it to go on a rampage. My favorite *Outer Limits* "bear" literally came out of the woodwork (in an episode titled, surprisingly enough, "It Came Out of the Woodwork") and was sucked into a cleaning woman's vacuum cleaner, where it began to grow . . . and grow . . . and grow.

Other "bears" included a Welsh coal miner (played by David McCallum) who is given an evolutionary "trip" forward in time some two million years. He comes back with a huge bald head which dwarfs his pallid, sickly looking face, and Lays Waste to the Neighborhood. Harry Guardino was menaced by a huge "ice creature"; the first astronauts on Mars, in an episode written by Jerry Sohl (a science fiction novelist perhaps best known for *Costigan's Needle*), were menaced by a gigantic sand snake. In the pilot episode, "The Galaxy Being," a creature of pure energy is accidentally absorbed through a radio antenna on earth and is finally dispatched by overfeeding itself (shades of that old Richard Carlson meller, *The Magnetic Monster!*). Harlan Ellison wrote two episodes, "Soldier" and "Demon with a Glass Hand," the latter considered by the editors of *The Science Fiction Encyclopedia* and others to be perhaps the finest episode of the series, which also included many scripts by Stefano and one by a young man named Robert Towne, who would go on to write *Chinatown.**

The cancellation of *The Outer Limits* was more due to stupid

---

* For much of this material I am indebted to the entry on *The Outer Limits* in *The Science Fiction Handbook*, published by Doubleday (New York: 1979). The entry (p. 441 of this huge volume) was written by John Brosnan and Peter Nicholls.

In addition, there is a magazine-type publication devoted to reviewing *The Outer Limits*. Each issue is $2.50, and it is available from Ted Rypel, 11100 Governor Ave., Cleveland, Ohio 44111.

programming on the part of its parent network, ABC, than to any real lack of interest, even though the show had become slightly flabby in the second season following Stefano's departure. To some extent it could be said that when Stefano left, he took all the good bears with him. The series was never quite the same. Still, a good many programs have been able to endure a flabby stretch without cancelation (TV is, after all, a pretty flabby medium). But when ABC switched *The Outer Limits* from its Monday-night time slot, where it was up against two fading game shows, to Saturday night—a night when the younger audience *The Outer Limits* was aimed at was either at the movies or just out cruising—it faded quietly from the scene.

We have mentioned syndication briefly, but the only fantasy program which can be seen regularly on the independent TV stations is *The Twilight Zone*, which was, by and large, nonviolent. *Thriller* can be seen late at night in certain big-city markets that have one or more of those independent stations, but a run of *The Outer Limits* is a much rarer catch. Although it was presented, during its first run, in what is now considered "the family hour," a change in mores has made it one of those "iffy" programs for the independents, who feel safer running sitcoms, game shows, and movies (not to mention the old put-your-hands-on-your-TV-set-brother-and-you-will-be-*healed!* bit).

And by the way, if you get it in your area, warm up the old Betamax and send me the complete catalogue by way of the publisher. On second thought, you better not. It's probably illegal. But treasure the run while you've got it; like *Thriller*, the like of *The Outer Limits* will not be seen again. Even *The Wonderful World of Disney* is going off the air after a twenty-six-year run.

4

We'll not say from the sublime to the ridiculous, because TV rarely produces the sublime, and series TV has never produced it; let us instead say from the workmanlike to the atrocious.

The Night Stalker.

Earlier on in this chapter I said that television was too homogenized to cough up anything that was really charmingly
awful; ABC-TV's *The Night Stalker* series is the exception that
proves the rule.

It's not the movie that I'm talking about, remember. The
film of *The Night Stalker* was one of the best movies ever made
for TV. It was based on an abysmal horror novel, *The Kolchak
Tapes*, by Jeff Rice—the novel was issued as a paperback after
the unpublished manuscript landed on producer Dan Curtis's
desk and became the basis of the film.

A short side trip here, if you don't mind too much. Dan
Curtis became associated with the horror field as producer of
what must have been the strangest soap opera ever to run on
the tube; it was called *Dark Shadows*. *Shadows* became something of a nine-days' wonder during the last two years of its
run. Originally conceived as a soft-focus ladies' gothic of the
type then so popular in paperback (they have now been largely
replaced by those sweet/savage love stories à la Rosemary
Rogers, Katherine Woodiwiss, and Laurie McBain), it eventually mutated—like *Thriller*—into something quite different
from what had first been intended. *Dark Shadows*, under Curtis's
inspired hand, became a kind of supernatural mad hatters' tea
party (it even came on the air at the traditional hour for tea,
four in the afternoon), and hypnotized viewers were treated to
a seriocomic panorama of hell—a weirdly evocative combination of Dante's ninth circle and Spike Jones. One member of
the put-upon Collins family, Barnabas Collins, was a vampire.
He was played by Jonathan Frid, who became an overnight
celebrity. His celebrity, unfortunately, was every bit as lasting
as Vaughan Meader's (and if you don't remember Vaughan
Meader, send me a stamped, self-addressed postcard and I will
enlighten you).

One tuned in to *Dark Shadows* every day, convinced that
things could become no more lunatic . . . and yet somehow they
did. At one point the entire cast of characters was transported
back into the seventeenth century for a six-week turn in fancy

dress. Barnabas had a cousin who was a werewolf. Another cousin was a combination witch-succubus. Other soap operas have always, of course, practiced their own bemusing forms of madness; my own favorite has always been the Kid Trick. The way the Kid Trick works is this: one of the characters on a soap opera will have a baby in March. By July it will be two; in November it will be six; the following February it will be lying in the hospital, comatose, after being hit by a car while returning home from the sixth grade; and by the March following its birth, the child will be eighteen and ready to begin *really* joining in the fun by getting the girl next door pregnant, or turning suicidal, or possibly by announcing to his horrified parents that he's a homosexual. The Kid Trick is worthy of a Robert Sheckley alternate-world story, but at least the characters on most soap operas stay dead once their life-support machinery is turned off (following which there will be a four-month trial with the turner-offer in the dock for mercy killing). The actors and actresses who "died" picked up their final checks and went job hunting again. Not so on *Dark Shadows*. The dead simply came back as ghosts. It was *better* than the Kid Trick.

Dan Curtis went on to make two theatrical films based on the *Dark Shadows* plot and using its cast of undead characters—such a jump from TV to the movies is not unheard of (*The Lone Ranger* is a case where it also happened), but it's rare, and the films, while not great, were certainly viewable. They were done with style, wit, and all those buckets of gore Curtis couldn't use on TV. They were also made with tremendous energy . . . a trait which helped to make *The Night Stalker* film the highest-rated made-for-TV movie ever telecast up until that time. (It has since been surpassed in the ratings eight or nine times, and one of the films that has outpointed it was the pilot film for—choke!—*The Love Boat*.)

Curtis himself is a remarkable, almost hypnotic man, friendly in a brusque, almost abrasive way, apt to hog the credit for his enterprises, but in such an engaging way that nobody really seems to mind. A throwback to an older and perhaps tougher breed of Hollywood filmmakers, Curtis has never had any noticeable problems in deciding where to plant his feet. If he likes you, he stands up for you. If he doesn't, you're a "no-talent sonofabitch" (a phrase that has always pleased me a great deal, and after reading this passage, Curtis may well call me up and use it on me). He would be notable if for no other reason than he may be the only producer in Hollywood effectively able to make a picture as frankly scary as *The Night Stalker*. The film was scripted by Richard Matheson, who has written for TV with better pace and more dramatic flair than anyone since Reginald Rose, perhaps. Curtis went on to make another picture with Matheson and William F. Nolan which fans still talk about—*Trilogy of Terror*, with Karen Black. The segment of this trio of stories most frequently mentioned was the final one, based on Matheson's short story "Prey." In it, Ms. Black gives a tour-de-force solo performance as a woman pursued by a tiny devil-doll with a spear. It is a bloody, gripping, scary fifteen minutes, and it perhaps most clearly sums up what I'm trying to say about Dan Curtis: he has an unerring, crude talent for finding the terror place inside you and squeezing it with a cold hand.

The Night Stalker dealt with a pragmatic reporter named Carl Kolchak who works the Las Vegas beat. Played by Darren McGavin, his face somehow simultaneously tired, awed, cynical, and wiseacre beneath his battered straw fedora, Kolchak is a believable enough character, more Lew Archer than Clark Kent, dedicated above all else to make a buck in Casino City.

He stumbles upon a string of murders that have apparently been committed by a vampire, and follows a series of leads deeper and deeper into the supernatural, engaging at the same time in a war of words with the Powers That Be in Vegas. In the end he tracks the vampire to the old house which has become its abode and drives a stake through its heart. The final twist is predictable but nonetheless satisfying: Kolchak is discredited and fired, cut loose from an establishment that has no room for vampires in either its philosophy or its public relations; he is able to dispatch the bloodsucker (Barry Atwater), but the final victor is Las Vegas boosterism. McGavin, a talented actor, has rarely been as good—as *believable*—as he was in *The Night Stalker* movie.* It is his very pragmatism that enables us to believe in the vampire; if a hardnose like Carl Kolchak can believe it, the film suggests convincingly, then it must be so.

The success of *The Night Stalker* did not go unnoticed at ABC, which was perennially hit-hungry in those days before Mork, the Fonz, and all those other great characters made their way into the lineup. So a sequel, *The Night Strangler*, quickly followed. This time the murders were being committed by a doctor who had discovered the secret of eternal life—always provided he could slay five victims every five years or so to make up a new batch of elixir. In this one (set in Seattle), pathologists were covering up the fact that bits of decayed human flesh had been found on the necks of the strangulation victims—the doctor, you see, always began to get a little ripe as his five-year cycle neared its end. Kolchak uncovered the cover-up and tracked the monster to its lair in Seattle's so-called "secret city," an underground section of old Seattle which Matheson visited on a vacation trip in 1970.† And, needless to say, Kolchak managed to dispatch the zombie medico.

ABC decided it wanted to make a series out of Kolchak's continuing adventures, and such a series, predictably titled *Kolchak: The Night Stalker*, premiered on Friday, September 13th, 1974. The series limped through one season, and it was an abysmal flop. There were production problems from the beginning; Dan Curtis, who had been the guiding force behind the two successful TV movies, had nothing to do with the series (no one I queried seems to really know why). Matheson, who had written the two original movies, never turned in a single

---

* The part is really only a refinement of the part of David Ross, a private eye McGavin played in a wonderful (if short-lived) NBC series called *The Outsider*. Probably only the late David Janssen as Harry Orwell and Brian Keith as Lew Archer (in a series that only lasted three weeks—if you blinked, you missed it) can compare with McGavin's performance as a private eye.

† For much of the material on *The Night Stalker*, I am indebted to Berthe Roeger's comprehensive analysis of both the two movies and the series, published in *Fangoria* magazine (issue #3, December 1979). The same issue contains an invaluable episode-by-episode chronology of the series' run.

script for the series. Paul Playden, the original producer, re-signed his post before the series began its run and was replaced by Cy Chermak. Most of the directors were forgettable; special effects were done on a shoestring. One of my favorite effects, which at least comes close to the fur-covered VW in *The Giant Spider Invasion*, was on view in an episode entitled "The Spanish Moss Murders." In this one, Richard Kiel—who would become famous as Jaws in the last two James Bond pictures— cavorted through a number of Chicago back alleys with a not-very-well-concealed zipper running up the back of his Swamp Monster suit.

But the basic problem with the *Night Stalker* series was the problem which dogs any nonanthology series dealing with the supernatural or the occult: a complete breakdown in the ability to suspend disbelief. We could believe Kolchak once, as he tracked the vampire down in Vegas; with some added effort we could even believe in him twice, tracking down the undead doc in Seattle. Once the series got going, it was harder. Kolchak goes out to cover the last cruise of a fine old luxury liner and discovers that one of his fellow passengers is a werewolf. He sets out to cover an up-and-coming politician's campaign for the Senate and discovers the candidate has sold his soul to the devil (and considering Watergate and Abscam, I hardly find this supernatural or unusual). Kolchak also stumbles across a prehistoric reptile in Chicago's sewer system ("The Sentry"); a succubus ("Legacy of Terror"); a coven of witches ("The Trevi Collection"); and in one of the most tasteless programs ever done for network TV, a headless motorcyclist ("Chopper"). Eventually, suspension of disbelief becomes utterly impossible—even, one suspects, for the production staff, which began to play poor Kolchak more and more for laughs. In a sense, what we saw in this series was a speeded-up version of the Universal Syndrome: from horror to humor. But it took the Universal Pictures monsters some eighteen years to get from one state to the other; it only took *The Night Stalker* twenty episodes.

As Berthe Roeger points out, *Kolchak: The Night Stalker* enjoyed a brief and quite successful revival when the series was rerun as part of CBS's late-night program of oldies. Roeger's conclusion, however, that its success was due to any merit in the series itself seems off the mark to me. If the tune-in was large, I suspect it was for the same reason that the theater always fills up at midnight for *Reefer Madness*. I've mentioned the siren song of crap before, and here it is again. I suspect that people tuned in once, couldn't believe how bad this thing was, and kept tuning in on successive nights to make sure that their eyes had not deceived them.

They hadn't; perhaps only *Voyage to the Bottom of the Sea*, the launching pad for that apostle of disaster, Irwin Allen, can compete with *Kolchak* for total collapse. Yet we should remember that not even Seabury Quinn, with his Jules de Grandin series in *Weird Tales*, was able to keep the continuing-character format rolling very successfully, and Quinn was one of the most talented writers of the pulp era. *Kolchak: The Night Stalker* (which became known during its run to some pundits as *Kolchak's Monster of the Week*) nonetheless holds a certain warm spot in my heart—a *small* warm spot, it is true—and in the hearts of a great many fans. There is something childlike and unsophisticated in its very awfulness.

5

"*There is a fifth dimension beyond that which is known to man. It is a dimension as vast as space and as timeless as infinity. It is the middle ground between light and shadow, between science and superstition, between the pit of man's fears and the summit of his knowledge. It is the dimension of the imagination. It is an area we call . . . The Twilight Zone.*"

With this rather purple invocation—which did not sound purple at all in Rod Serling's measured and almost matter-of-fact delivery—viewers were invited to enter a queerly boundless other world . . . and enter they did. *The Twilight Zone* ran on CBS from October of 1959 through the summer of 1965—from the torpor of the Eisenhower administration to LBJ's escalation of American involvement in Vietnam, the first of the long hot summers in American cities, and the advent of the Beatles.

Of all the dramatic programs which have ever run on American TV, it is the one which comes closest to defying any over-all analysis. It was not a western or a cop show (although some of the stories had western formats or featured cops 'n' robbers); it was not really a science fiction show (although *The Complete Directory to Prime Time Network TV Shows* categorizes it as such); not a sitcom (although some of the episodes were funny); not really occult (although it did occult stories frequently— in its own peculiar fashion), not really supernatural. It was its own thing, and in a large part that fact alone seems to account for the fact that a whole generation is able to associate the Ser-ling program with the budding of the sixties . . . at least, as the sixties are remembered.

Rod Serling, the program's creator, came to prominence in what has been referred to as television's "golden age"— although those who have termed it so because they remember fondly such anthology programs as *Studio One, Playhouse 90,* and *Climax* have somehow managed to forget such chestnuts as *Mr. Arsenic, Hands of Mystery, Doorway to Danger,* and *Doodles Weaver*—programs which ran during the same period, and which by comparison make such current TV programs as *Vegas* and *That's Incredible!* look like great American theater. Televi-sion never really has had a golden age; only successive seasons of sounding brass which vary slightly as to the trueness of the tone.

Nevertheless, television has produced isolated spasms of quality, and three of Serling's early teleplays—*Patterns, The Comedian,* and *Requiem for a Heavyweight*—form a large part of what television viewers mean when they speak of a "golden age" . . . although Serling was by no means alone. There were others, including Paddy Chayefsky (*Marty*) and Reginald Rose (*Twelve Angry Men*) who contributed to that illusion of gold.

Serling was the son of a Binghamton, New York, butcher, a Golden Gloves champ (at approximately five feet four, Serling's class was fly-weight), and a paratrooper during World War II.

He began to write (unsuccessfully) in college and went on to write (unsuccessfully) for a radio station in Cincinnati. "That experience proved frustrating," Ed Naha related in his fond reprise of Serling's career. "His introspective characters came under attack by . . . executives who wanted their 'people to get their teeth into the soil'! Serling recalled the period years later: 'What those guys wanted wasn't a writer, but a plow.' "*

Serling quit radio and began to freelance. His first success came in 1955 (*Patterns*, starring Richard Kiley and Everett Sloane—and later, in the film version, Van Heflin and Everett Sloane, the story of a dirty corporate power play and the resulting moral squeeze on one executive—the teleplay won Serling his first Emmy), and he never looked back . . . but he somehow never really moved on, either. He wrote a number of feature films—*Assault on a Queen* was maybe the worst of them; *Planet of the Apes* and *Seven Days in May* were two of the good ones—but television was his home, and Serling never really outgrew it, as did Chayefsky (*Hospital, Network*). Television was his home, where he lived most comfortably, and after a five-year hiatus following the cancelation of *The Twilight Zone*, he turned up on the tube again, this time as the host of *Night Gallery*. Serling himself expressed feelings of doubt and depression about his deep involvement in this mediocre medium. "But God knows," he said in his last interview, "when I look back over thirty years of professional writing, I'm hard-pressed to come up with anything that's important. Some things are literate, some things are interesting, some things are classy, but very damn little is important."†

Serling apparently saw *The Twilight Zone* as a way of going underground and keeping his ideals alive in television following the cancelation of the prestige drama programs in the late

---

* For this and much of the material on Serling and *The Twilight Zone*, I'm indebted to "Rod Serling's Dream," by Ed Naha, published in *Starlog #15* (August 1978), and to Gary Gerani, who compiled the complete episode guide in the same issue.

† Quoted in an interview conducted by Linda Brevelle shortly before Serling's death and published under the title, "Rod Serling's Last Interview" (a rather ghoulish title, I think, but then, what do I know?), in the 1976 *Writer's Yearbook*.

fifties and early sixties. And to an extent, I suppose he succeeded. Under the comforting guise of "it's only make-believe," *The Twilight Zone* was able to deal with questions of fascism ("He Lives," starring Dennis Hopper as a young neo-Nazi guided by the shadowy figure of Adolf Hitler), ugly mass hysteria ("The Monsters Are Due on Maple Street"), and even Joseph Conrad's heart of darkness—rarely has any television program dared to present human nature in such an ugly, revealing light as that used in "The Shelter," in which a number of suburban neighbors along Your Street, U.S.A., are reduced to animals squabbling over a fallout shelter during a nuclear crisis.

Other episodes generated a kind of existential weirdness that no other series has been able to match. There was, for instance, "Time Enough at Last," starring Burgess Meredith* as a myopic bank clerk who can never find time enough to read. He survives an H-bomb attack, in fact, because he is reading in the vault when the bombs fall. Meredith is delighted with the holocaust; he finally has all the time to read that a man could want. Unfortunately, he breaks his glasses shortly after reaching the library. One of the guiding moral precepts of *The Twilight Zone* seems to have been that a little irony is good for your blood.

If *The Twilight Zone* had bowed on TV as we have found it in the period 1976–1980, it would have undoubtedly disappeared after an initial run of six to nine episodes. Its ratings were low to begin with . . . like in the cellar. It was up against a fairly popular Robert Taylor cops 'n' robbers meller, *The Detectives*, on ABC, and the immensely popular *Gillette Cavalcade of Sports* on NBC—this was the show that invited you to put your feet up and watch such fighters as Carmen Basilio and Sugar Ray Robinson get their faces changed.

But television moved more slowly in those days, and scheduling was less anarchistic. *The Twilight Zone*'s first season

---

* Meredith became perhaps the most familiar face of all to *Twilight Zone* fans, save for Serling's own. Probably his best-remembered role came in "Printer's Devil," where he plays a newspaper owner who is really Satan . . . complete with a jutting, crooked cigar that was somehow diabolical.

consisted of thirty-six half-hour episodes, and by the season's midpoint the ratings had begun to pick up, helped by good word-of-mouth and glowing reviews. The reviews played their part by helping CBS decide that they had that potentially valuable commodity, a "prestige program."* Nevertheless, problems continued. The program had problems finding a steady sponsor (this was back in the days, you must remember, when dinosaurs walked the earth and TV time was cheap enough to allow a single sponsor to pay for an entire program—hence *GE Theater, Alcoa Playhouse, The Voice of Firestone, The Lux Show, Coke Time,* and a host of others; to this writer's knowledge, the last program to be wholly sponsored by one company was *Bonanza,* sponsored by GM), and CBS began to wake up to the fact that Serling had put none of his cudgels away but was now wielding them in the name of fantasy.

During that first season, *The Twilight Zone* presented "Perchance to Dream," the late Charles Beaumont's first contribution to the series, and "Third from the Sun," by Richard Matheson. The gimmick of the latter—that the group of protagonists is fleeing not from Earth but *to* it—is one that has been utterly beaten to death by now (most notably by that deepspace turkey *Battlestar Galactica*), but most viewers can remember the snap of that ending to this day. It was the episode which marks the point at which many occasional tuners-in became addicts. Here, for once, was something Completely New and Different.

During its third season, *The Twilight Zone* was either canceled (Serling's version) or squeezed out by insoluble scheduling problems (the CBS version). In either case, it returned the following year as an hour-long program. In his article "Rod Serling's Dream," Ed Naha says: "The 'something different' the

---

* In 1972 CBS discovered another "prestige program"—*The Waltons,* created by Earl Hamner, Jr., who wrote a good many *Twilight Zones* . . . including, coincidentally, "The Bewitchin' Pool," the last original *Twilight Zone* episode to be telecast on the network. Placed against brutal competition—NBC's *The Flip Wilson Show* and ABC's own version of The Church of What's Happening Now, *The Mod Squad*—CBS stuck with Hamner's creation in spite of the low ratings because of the prestige factor. *The Waltons* went on to outlive its competition and at this writing has run seven seasons.

elongated (*Twilight Zone*) came up with turned out to be boredom. After thirteen publicly shunned episodes, the 60-minute *Twilight Zone* was canceled."

It was indeed canceled—only to return for a final, mostly dull, season as a half-hour show again—but because of boredom? In my own view, the hour-long episodes of *The Twilight Zone* included some of the best of the entire run. There was "The Thirty-Fathom Grave," in which the crew of a Navy destroyer hears ghosts tapping inside a sunken submarine; "Printer's Devil"; "The New Exhibit" (one of *The Twilight Zone's* few excursions into outright horror, this dealt with a wax museum janitor played by Martin Balsam who discovers that the Murderers' Row exhibit has come to life); and "Miniature," which starred Robert Duvall in a Charles Beaumont script about a man who escapes back into the gay nineties.

As Naha points out, by its final season "no one at CBS really cared about the series." He goes on to say that ABC, which had had some success with *The Outer Limits,* extended feelers to Serling about doing a sixth season with them. Serling refused. "I think ABC wanted to make a trip to the graveyard every week," he said.

For Serling, life was never quite the same. The angry young man who had written *Patterns* began doing television commercials—that unmistakable voice could be heard huckstering tires and cold remedies in a bizarre turn that recalls the broken fighter in *Requiem for a Heavyweight* who ends up performing in fixed wrestling matches. And in 1970 he began making that "trip to the graveyard every week," not on ABC but on NBC, as host and sometime writer of *Night Gallery.* The series was inevitably compared to *The Twilight Zone* in spite of the fact that *Gallery* was really a watered-down *Thriller* with Serling doing the Boris Karloff hosting job.

Serling had none of the creative control he had enjoyed while doing *The Twilight Zone.* (He complained at one point that the studio was trying to turn *Night Gallery* "into *Mannix* with a shroud.") Nonetheless, *Night Gallery* produced a number of interesting episodes, including adaptations of H. P. Lovecraft's

"Cool Air" and "Pickman's Model." It also presented an episode which must rate as one of the most frightening ever telecast on TV. "Boomerang," based on a story by Oscar Cook, dealt with a little bug called an earwig. The earwig is placed in the villain's ear and began to—ulp!—chew its way through his brain, leaving the man in an excruciating, sweaty state of agony (the physiological reason for this, since the brain has no pain receptors, is never explained). He is told there's only one chance in a billion that the pesky little beast will actually chew on a straight course across to his other ear and thus find the exit; much more likely is the possibility that it will just continue chewing its way around in there until the fellow goes mad . . . or commits suicide. The viewer is immensely relieved when the near-impossible happens and the earwig actually does come out the other side . . . and then, the kicker comes: the earwig was female. And it laid eggs in there. Millions of them.

Most *Night Gallery* episodes were nowhere near as chilling, and the series was canceled after limping along in one form or another for three labored years. It was Serling's last star turn.

"On his fortieth birthday," Naha says, "Serling made his first parachute jump since World War II." Serling's reason? "I did it," he said, "to prove that I wasn't old." But he looked old; a comparison of his early *Twilight Zone* publicity photos and those taken on the *Night Gallery* set before those mostly idiotic paintings shows a change which is nearly shocking. Serling's face had become lined, his neck wattled; it is the face of a man who has been partially dissolved in television's vitriol. In 1972 he received an interviewer in his study, which was lined with framed reviews of *Requiem, Patterns*, and other teleplays from the early days.

"Sometimes I come in here just to look," he said. "I haven't had reviews like that in years. Now I know why people keep scrapbooks—just to prove to themselves it really happened." The man who jumped from a plane on his fortieth birthday to prove to himself that he wasn't old refers to himself constantly as old in the Linda Brevelle interview some nine years later; she characterizes him as "vibrant and alive" during their meeting at

La Taverna, Serling's favorite L.A. watering hole, but again and again those disquieting phrases crop up; at one point he says, "I'm not an old man yet, but I'm not a young man, either"; at another he says he *is* an old man. Why didn't he get out of the creative demo derby? At the end of *Requiem for a Heavyweight*, Jack Palance says he must go back into the ring—even though the whole thing is fixed—because the ring is all he knows. It's as good an answer as any.

Serling, a fierce workaholic who sometimes smoked four packs of cigarettes a day, suffered a crippling heart attack in 1975 and died following open-heart surgery. His legacy consisted of a few fine early plays and *The Twilight Zone*, a series which has become one of those peculiar TV legends, like *The Fugitive* and *Wanted: Dead or Alive*. What are we to make of this program which is so revered (by people who were mostly children when they originally viewed it)? "I guess a third of the shows were pretty damned good," Serling told an interviewer. "Another third would have been passable. Another third are dogs."

The fact is that Serling himself wrote sixty-two of the first ninety-two *Twilight Zone*s typing them, dictating them to a secretary, talking them into a dictaphone—and, of course, smoking nonstop. Fantasy fans will recognize the names of almost all the other writers, those who contributed the other thirty episodes: Charles Beaumont, Richard Matheson, George Clayton Johnson, Earl Hamner, Jr., Robert Presnell, E. Jack Neuman, Montgomery Pittman, and Ray Bradbury. The simple fact is that most of the bow-wows which escaped the kennel had Serling's name on them. They include "Mr. Denton on Doomsday," "The Sixteen-Millimeter Shrine," "Judgment Night," "The Big Tall Wish" (a shameless tear-jerker about a kid who helps a broken-down pug win his last match), and too many others for me to want to mention.

Even the recollection most people seem to have of *The Twilight Zone* has always bothered me; it is the concluding "twists" that most people seem to remember, but the show's actual success seemed to be based on more solid concepts, concepts which form a vital link between the old pulp fiction predating the fifties (or those *Thriller* programs which used the pulps as the basis of their best stories) and the "new" literature of horror and fantasy. Week after week, *The Twilight Zone* presented ordinary people in extraordinary situations, people who had somehow turned sideways and slipped through a crack in reality . . . and thus into Serling's "zone." It is a powerful concept, and surely the clearest road into the land of fantasy for viewers and readers who do not ordinarily care to visit that land. But the concept was by no means original with Serling; Ray Bradbury had begun putting the ordinary and the horrible cheek-by-jowl in the forties, and when he began to move on into more arcane lands and to use the language in more and more novel ways, Jack Finney came upon the scene and began refining the same extraordinary-in-the-ordinary themes. In a benchmark collection of short stories called *The Third Level*, the literary equivalent of those startling Magritte paintings where railroad trains are roaring out of fireplaces or those Dali paintings where clocks are lying limply over the branches of trees, Finney actually defined the boundaries of Serling's *Twilight Zone*. In the lead story, Finney tells of a man who finds a mythical third level to Grand Central Station (which only has two concourse levels, for those of you who aren't familiar with that neat old building). The third level is a kind of way station in time, giving egress on a happier, simpler time (those same late 1800s which so many put-upon *Twilight Zone* heroes escaped into, and essentially the same period Finney himself returns to in his celebrated novel, *Time and Again*). In many ways, Finney's third level satisfies all the definitions of Serling's *Twilight Zone*, and in many ways it was Finney's concept that made Serling's concept possible. One of Finney's great abilities as a writer has been his talent for allowing his stories to slip unobtrusively, almost casually, across the line and into another world . . . as when a character, picking through his change, happens upon a dime which bears not the likeness of FDR but of Woodrow Wilson, or when another Finney character begins on a journey to the idyllic planet Verna as a passenger aboard a rickety old charter bus that is eventually parked in a tumble-down country barn ("Of Missing Persons"). Finney's most important accomplishment, which the best episodes of *The Twilight Zone* echo (and which the best of the post-*Zone* writers of fantasy have also echoed), is that Daliesque ability to create the fantasy . . . *and then not apologize for it or explain it.* It simply hangs there, fascinating and a little sickening, a mirage too real to dismiss: a brick floating over a refrigerator, a man eating a TV dinner full of eyeballs, kids on a toy-littered floor playing with their pet dinosaur. If the fantasy seems real enough, Finney insisted, and Serling after him, we don't need any wires or mirrors. It was, in a large part, Finney and Serling who finally answered H. P. Lovecraft, who showed a new direction. For me and those of my generation, the answer was like a thunderclap of revelation, opening a million entrancing possibilities.

And yet Finney, who perhaps understood Serling's concept of "that middle ground between light and shadow" better than anyone else, was never represented on *The Twilight Zone*—not as a scriptwriter, not as a source. Serling later adapted *Assault on a Queen* (1966), a work which can most humanely be characterized as unfortunate. It contains all the preachy, talking-heads stuff that brought so many of his *Twilight Zone* scripts low. It's one of the minor tragedies of the field that what might have been an inspired meeting of two like minds should have turned out so poorly. But if you feel disappointed by my analysis of *The Twilight Zone* (and some, I suspect, may feel that I have spat on an icon), I urge you to find a copy of Finney's *The Third Level*, which will show you what *The Twilight Zone* could have been.

And still, the program left us with a number of powerful memories, and Serling's analysis that a third of the shows were pretty damn good may not have been far from the mark. Anyone who watched the show regularly can remember William Shatner, held in thrall by a penny fortune-telling machine in a cheesy restaurant located in a one-stoplight town ("Nick of Time"); Everett Sloane succumbing to gambling mania in "The Fever," and the hoarse, metallic cry of the coins

(*"Fraa-aaa-nklin!"*) calling him back to do battle with the diabolical slot-machine; the beautiful woman who is reviled for her ugliness in a world of piglike humanoids (Donna Douglas of *The Beverly Hillbillies* in "Eye of the Beholder"). And, of course, those two classics by Richard Matheson, "The Invaders" (starring a grimly brilliant Agnes Moorhead as a country woman fighting off tiny invaders from space, a story which foreshadows Matheson's later treatment of a similar subject in "Prey") and "Nightmare at 20,000 Feet," in which William Shatner plays a newly recovered mental patient who sees an evil-looking gremlin pulling at the housing of an airliner's motor.

The Twilight Zone also showcased a wide range of performers (Ed Wynn, Kenan Wynn, Buster Keaton, Jack Klugman, Franchot Tone, Art Carney, Pippa Scott, Robert Redford, and Cloris Leachman, among others), writers, and directors (Buzz Kulik, Stuart Rosenberg, and Ted Post, to name a few). It frequently featured startling and exciting music by the late Bernard Herrmann; the best special effects were done by William Tuttle, probably only second to Dick Smith (or the new makeup genius, Tom Savini) in wizardry.

It was a pretty good show, the way the most fondly remembered TV series are pretty good shows . . . but ultimately, no better. TV is the endless gobbler of talent, something new and poisonous under the sun, and if *Zone* is ultimately weaker than our fond memories of it would like to allow, the fault lies not with Serling but with TV itself—the hungry maw, the bottomless pit of shit. Serling wrote a total of eighty-four episodes, something like 2,200 pages of script according to the screenwriter's rule of thumb that one page of script equals one minute of video. This is a staggering pile of work, and it really isn't surprising that the all-too-occasional clunker like "I Am the Night—Color Me Black" got through. Rod Serling was only able to do so much in the name of Kimberly-Clark and Chesterfield Kings. Then television ate him up.

6

And as far as TV is concerned, I guess it's time for everybody to get out of the pool. I don't have enough John Simon in me to really enjoy shooting TV's creative cripples as they crawl and squirm around in the great TV Cancelation Corral. I've even tried to treat *Kolchak: The Night Stalker* with affection, because I certainly feel a degree of affection for it. Bad as it was, it wasn't any worse than some of the Saturday matinee creature features that enlivened my life as a kid—*The Black Scorpion* or *The Beast of Hollow Mountain,* for instance.

Individual TV programs have produced brilliant or near-brilliant excursions into the supernatural—*Alfred Hitchcock Presents*, for instance, gave us adaptations of several Ray Bradbury stories (the best of them was probably "The Jar"), one terrifying William Hope Hodgson story, "The Thing in the Weeds," a nonsupernatural bone-freezer from the pen of John D. Mac-Donald ("The Morning After"), and fans of the bizarre will remember the episode where the cops ate the murder weapon—a leg of lamb. . . . that one based on a story by Roald Dahl.

There was "They're Coming," the original hour-long pilot for *The Twilight Zone*, and the short French film "An Occurrence at Owl Creek Bridge," which appeared on American television for the first time as a *Twilight Zone* episode (this adaptation of the Bierce story cannot be seen during syndication runs of *The Twilight Zone*). Another Bierce story, "One of the Missing," ran on PBS in the winter of 1979. And speaking of PBS, there was also an interesting adaptation of *Dracula* done there. Originally telecast in 1977, it featured Louis Jourdan as the legendary Count. This videotaped drama is both moody and romantic; Jourdan gives a more effective performance than Frank Langella in the John Badham film, and the scenes of Dracula crawling down the wall of his castle are marvelous. The Jourdan version also comes closer to the heart of the vampire's sexuality, presenting to us in Lucy, the three weird sisters, and in Dracula himself creatures who possess a loveless sexuality—one which kills. It is more powerful than the ho-hum romance of the Badham version, in spite of Langella's energetic job in the title role. Jack Palance has also played Dracula on television (in another Matheson screenplay and another Dan Curtis production) and did quite well by the Count . . . although I prefer Jourdan's performance.

Other one-shot TV movies and specials run from the merely forgettable (NBC's ill-advised adaptation of Thomas Tryon's *Harvest Home,* for instance) to some really hideous pieces of work: Cornell Wilde in *Gargoyles* (Bernie Casey plays the head gargoyle as a kind of five-thousand-year-old Ayatollah Khomeini) and Michael Sarrazin is the mistitled—and misbegotten—*Frankenstein: The True Story.* The risk rate is so high that when my own novel *'Salem's Lot* was adapted for television after Warners had tried fruitlessly to get it off the ground as a theatrical film for three years, my feeling at its generally favorable reception was mostly relief. For awhile it seemed that NBC might turn it into a weekly series, and when that rather numbing prospect passed by the boards, I felt relief again.

Most television series have ranged from the ludicrous (*Land of the Giants*) to the utterly inane (*The Monsters, Struck by Lightning*). The anthology series of the last ten years have meant well, by and large, but have been emasculated by pressure groups both without and within; they have been sacrificed on the altar of television's apparent belief that both drama and melodrama are best appreciated while in a semidoze. There was *Journey to the Unknown,* a British import (from the Hammer studios). Some of the stories were engrossing, but ABC made it clear rather quickly that it had no real interest in frightening anyone, and the series died quickly. *Tales of the Unexpected,* produced by Quinn Martin (*The FBI, The Fugitive, The Invaders, The New Breed,* and God knows how many others), was more interesting, concentrating on psychological horrors (in one episode, reminiscent of Anne Rivers Siddons's *The House Next Door,* a murderer sees his victim rise from the dead on his television set), but low ratings killed the program after a short run . . . a fate that might have been *The Twilight Zone's,* had not the network stuck by it.

In fine, the history of horror and fantasy on television is a short and tacky one. Let's turn the magic eye off and turn to the bookshelf; I want us to talk about some stories where all the artificial boundaries are removed—both those of visual set and of network restriction—and the author is free to "get you" in any way he can. An uneasy concept, and some of these books scared the hell out of me even as they were delighting me. Maybe you've had the same experience . . . or maybe you will.

Just take my arm and step this way.

CHAPTER IX

Horror Fiction

It might not be impossible to present an overview of American horror and fantasy fiction during the last thirty years, but it wouldn't be just a chapter in this book; it would be a book in itself, and probably a dull one (maybe even a text, that apotheosis of the Dull Book species).

For our purposes, I can't imagine why we would want to deal with all the books published in the genre anyway; most of them are just downright bad, and as with TV, I have no taste for the job of beating the field's most spectacular violators with their shortcomings. If you want to read John Saul and Frank de Felitta, go right ahead. It's your three-fifty. But I'm not going to discuss them here.

My plan is to discuss ten books that seem representative of everything in the genre that is fine: the horror story as both literature and entertainment, a living part of twentieth-century literature, and worthy successors to such books as *Frankenstein, Dr. Jekyll and Mr. Hyde, Dracula,* and Chambers's *The King in Yellow.* They are books and stories which seem to me to fulfill the primary duty of literature—to tell us the truth about ourselves by telling us lies about people who never existed.

Some of the books discussed here have been "best sellers"; some have been written by members of the so-called "fantasy community"; some have been written by people with no interest in fantasy or the supernatural for its own sake, but who have seen it as a particularly useful tool to be used once and then perhaps put aside forever (although many have also found that the use of this tool is apt to become habit-forming). Most of them—even those which cannot be neatly pigeonholed as "best sellers"—have been steady sellers across the years, probably because the horror tale, which is regarded by most serious critics in about the same light that Dr. Johnson regarded women preachers and dancing dogs, manages to consistently satisfy as entertainment even when it's only good. When it's great, it can deliver a megaton wallop (as it does in *Lord of the Flies*) that other forms of literature can rarely equal. Story has always been the abiding virtue of the horror tale, from "The Monkey's Paw" to T. E. D. Klein's utterly flabbergasting novella of monsters (from Costa Rica, yet!) under the streets of New York, "Children of the Kingdom." That being so, one only wishes that those great writers among us who have also succeeded in becoming our greatest bores in recent years would attempt something in the genre and stop poking around in their navels for intellectual fluff.

I hope that by discussing these ten books, I can dilate upon those virtues of story and entertainment and perhaps even indicate some of the themes which seem to run through most good horror stories. I *should* be able to do this if I'm doing my job, because there just aren't that many thematic trails to go down. For all of their mythic hold over us, the field of the supernatural is a narrow one in the greater spread of general literature. We can depend on the reappearance of the Vampire, and our furry friend (who sometimes wears its fur on the inside) the Werewolf, and the Thing Without a Name. But the time has also come to bring on that fourth archetype: the Ghost.

We may also find ourselves returning to the tension between Apollonian and Dionysian, since this tension exists in all horror fiction, the bad as well as the good, leading back to that endlessly fascinating question of who's okay and who isn't. That's really the taproot, isn't it? And we may also find that narcissism is the major difference between the old horror fiction and the new; that the monsters are no longer just due on Maple Street, but may pop up in our own mirrors—at any time.

2

Probably *Ghost Story* by Peter Straub is the best of the supernatural novels to be published in the wake of the three books that kicked off a new horror "wave" in the seventies—those three, of course, being *Rosemary's Baby, The Exorcist,* and *The Other.* The fact that these three books, all published within five years of each other, enjoyed such wide popularity, helped to convince (or reconvince) publishers that horror fiction had a commercial potential much wider than the readership of such defunct magazines as *Weird Tales* and *Unknown* or the paperback reissues of Arkham House books.[*]

The resulting scrambling to get the next "big" shiver-and-shake novel produced some really terrible books. As a further result, the wave had begun to withdraw by the mid-seventies, and more traditional best-sellers began to reappear: stories of sex, big business, sex, spies, gay sex, doctors in trouble, kinky sex, historical romances, sexy celebrities, war stories, and sex. That isn't to say that publishers stopped looking for occult/horror novels or stopped publishing them; the mills of the publishing world grind slowly but exceedingly fine (which is one reason that such an amazing river of gruel streams forth every spring and fall from the larger New York publishing houses), and the so-called "mainstream horror novel" will probably be with us yet awhile. But that first heady rush is over, and editors in New York no longer automatically scramble for the Standard Contract Form and fill in a meaty advance as soon as something in the story comes out of the woodwork. . . . Aspiring writers please take note.

---

[*] A word about Arkham House. There is probably no dedicated fantasy fan in America who doesn't have at least one of those distinctive black-bound volumes upon his or her shelf . . . and probably in a high place of honor. August Derleth, the founder of this small Wisconsin-based publishing house, was a rather uninspired novelist of the Sinclair Lewis school and an editor of pure genius: Arkham was first to publish H. P. Lovecraft, Ray Bradbury, Ramsey Campbell, and Robert Bloch in book form . . . and these are only a few of Derleth's legion. He published his books in limited editions ranging from five hundred to four thousand copies, and some of them—Lovecraft's *Beyond the Wall of Sleep* and Bradbury's *Dark Carnival,* for instance—are now highly sought-after collectors' items.

Against this background, Coward, McCann, and Geoghegan published Peter Straub's *Julia* in 1975. It was not his first novel; he had published a novel called *Marriages*—a nonsupernatural "this-is-the-way-we-live-now" sort of story—two years previous. Although Straub is an American, he and his wife lived in England and Ireland for ten years, and in both execution and intent, *Julia* is an English ghost story. The setting is English, most of the characters are English, and most importantly, the novel's diction is English—cool, rational, almost disconnected from any kind of emotional base. There is no sense of the Grand Guignol in the book, although the book's most vital situation certainly suggests it: Kate, the daughter of Julia and Magnus, has choked on a piece of meat and Julia kills her daughter while trying to perform a tracheotomy with a kitchen knife. The girl, it would appear, then returns as a malevolent spirit.

We aren't given the tracheotomy in any detail—the blood splashing the walls and the mother's hand, the terror and the cries. This is the past; we see it in reflected light. Much later, Julia sees the girl who may or may not be Kate's ghost burying something in the sand. When the girl leaves, Julia digs up the hole, discovering first a knife and then the mutilated corpse of a turtle. This reflection back upon the botched tracheotomy is elegant, but it has little heat.

Two years later Straub published a second supernatural novel, *If You Could See Me Now*. Like *Julia*, *If You Could See Me Now* is a novel occupied with the idea of the revenant, that vengeful spirit from an undead past. All of Straub's supernatural novels work effectively when dealing with these old ghosts; they are stories of the past continuing to work on the present in a malevolent way. It has been suggested that Ross McDonald is writing gothics rather than private eye novels; it could be said that Peter Straub is writing gothics rather than horror novels. What distinguishes his work in *Julia*, *If You Could See Me Now*, and, most splendidly, in *Ghost Story* is his refusal to view the gothic conventions as static ones. All three of these books have much in common with the classic gothics of the genre—*The Castle of Otranto*, *The Monk*, *Melmoth the Wanderer*, even

Frankenstein (although in terms of its telling, *Frankenstein* is actually less a gothic and more a modern novel than *Ghost Story*)—they are all books where the past eventually becomes more important than the present.

This would seem a valid enough course for the novel to follow to any people who see uses in the study of history, you would think, but the gothic novel has always been considered something of a curiosity, a widget on the great machine of English-speaking fiction. Straub's first two novels seem to me to be mostly unconscious attempts to do something with this widget; what distinguishes *Ghost Story* and makes it such a success is that with this book, Straub seems to have grasped exactly—consciously—what the gothic romance is about, and how it relates to the rest of literature. Put another way, he has discovered what the widget was supposed to do, and *Ghost Story* is a vastly entertaining manual of operation.

"[*Ghost Story*] started as a result of my having just read all the American supernatural fiction I could find," Straub says. "I reread Hawthorne and James, and went out and got all of Lovecraft and a lot of books by his 'set'—this was because I wanted to find out what my tradition was, since I was by then pretty firmly in the field—I also read Bierce, Edith Wharton's ghost stories, and a lot of Europeans. . . . The first thing I thought of was having a bunch of old men tell stories to each other—and then I hoped I could think of some device that would link all the stories. I very much like the idea of stories set down in novels—a lot of my life seems to have been spent listening to older people tell me stories about their families, their youth, all the rest. And it seemed like a formal challenge. After that I thought of cannibalizing certain old classic stories, and plugging them into the Chowder Society. This idea excited me. It seemed very audacious, and I thought that was very good. So I went ahead, after I got to that point in the book, and wrote junked-up versions of "My Kinsman, Major Molyneux," *The Turn of the Screw,* and started on "The Fall of the House of Usher." But by then the lead-in threatened to become the whole book. So I dropped the Poe story (the Hawthorne story came out when I edited the first draft). I was thinking at the time that the Chowder Society would follow these with their own stories—Lewis's monologue about the death of his wife, Sears and Ricky splitting a monologue (trading fours, in a way) about the death of Eva Galli.

The first striking thing about *Ghost Story* is its resemblance to *Julia*. That book begins with a woman who has lost a child; *Ghost Story* begins with a man who has found one. But these two children are eerily similar and there is an atmosphere of evil about both of them.

From *Julia:*

> Almost immediately, she saw the blonde girl again. The child was sitting on the ground at some distance from a group of other children, boys and girls who were carefully watching her. . . . The blonde girl was working intently at something with her hands, wholly concentrated on it. Her face was sweetly serious. . . . This was what gave the scene the aspect of a performance. . . . The girl was seated, her legs straight out before her, in the sandy overspill from one of the sandboxes. . . . She was speaking softly now to her audience, ranged on the scrubby grass before her in groups of three and four. . . . They were certainly unnaturally quiet, completely taken up by the girl's theatrics.

Is it this little girl, who is holding her audience spellbound by cutting up a turtle before their eyes, the same little girl who accompanied Don Wanderley on his strange trip south from Milburn, New York, to Panama City, Florida? This is the little girl as Don first sees her. You decide.

> And that was how he found her. At first, he was doubtful, watching the girl who had appeared in the playground one afternoon. She was not beautiful, not even attractive— she was dark and intense, and her clothes never seemed to be clean. The other children avoided her . . . perhaps children were quicker at seeing real differences than

adults. . . . Don had only one real clue that she was not the ordinary child she appeared to be, and he clung to it with a fanatic's desperation. The first time he had seen her, he had gone cold.

Julia, in the book of the same name, speaks to a small black child about the unnamed girl who has mutilated the turtle. The black girl wanders over to Julia and begins the conversation by asking:

> "What's your name?"
> "Julia."
> The girl's mouth opened a fraction wider.
> "Doolya?"
> Julia raised her hand for a moment to the child's springy ruff of hair. "What's your name?"
> "Mona."
> "Do you know the girl who was just playing in here? The girl with the blonde hair who was sitting and talking?"
> Mona nodded.
> "Do you know her name?"
> Mona nodded again. "Doolya."
> "Julia?"
> "Mona. Take me with you."
> "Mona, what was that girl doing? Was she telling a story?"
> "She does. Things." The girl blinked.

In *Ghost Story*, Don Wanderley similarly speaks with another child about the child who so disturbs him:

> "What's the name of that girl?" He asked, pointing.
> The boy shuffled his feet, blinked and said "Angie."
> "Angie what?"
> "Don't know."
> "Why doesn't anybody ever play with her?"

The boy squinted at him, cocking his head; then, deciding he could be trusted, leaned forward charmingly, cupped his hands beside his mouth to tell a dark secret. "Because she's *awful.*"

Another theme which runs through both novels—a very Henry Jamesian theme—is the idea that ghosts, in the end, adopt the motivations and perhaps the very souls of those who behold them. If they are malevolent, their malevolence comes from us. Even in their terror, Straub's characters recognize the kinship. In their appearance, his ghosts, like the ghosts James, Wharton, and M. R. James conjure up, are Freudian. Only in their final exorcism do Straub's ghosts become truly inhuman—emissaries from the world of "outside evil." When Julia asks Mona the name of the turtle-killing little girl, Mona gives back her own name ("Doolya," she says). And when, in *Ghost Story,* Don Wanderley tries to ascertain who this eerie little girl is, this disquieting exchange follows:

> "Okay, let's try again," he said. "What are you?"
>
> For the first time since he had taken her into the car, she really smiled. It was a transformation, but not of a kind to make him feel easier; she did not look any less adult. "You know," she said.
>
> He insisted. "What are you?"
>
> She smiled all through her amazing response. "I am you."
>
> "No. I am me. You are you."
>
> "I am you."

Ghost Story is at first glance an extravagant mishmash of every horror and gothic convention ever yarned in all those B-pictures we've just finished talking about. There are animal mutilations. There's demon possession (Gregory Bate, a secondary villain, battens upon his younger sister, who escapes, and his younger brother . . . who doesn't. There's vampirism, ghoulishness (in the literal sense of the word; Gregory dines on his victims after they're dead), and werewolvery of a most singular and frightening sort. Yet all of these fearsome legends are really only the outer shell of the novel's real heart, where there stands a woman who may be Eva Galli . . . or Alma Mobley . . . or Anna Mostyn . . . or possibly a little girl in a dirty pink dress whose name, supposedly, is Angie Maule. What are you? Don asks. I am you, she responds. And that is where the heartbeat of this extraordinary book seems the strongest. What is the ghost, after all, that it should frighten us so, but our own face? When we observe it we become like Narcissus, who was so struck by the beauty of his own reflection that he lost his life. We fear the Ghost for much the same reason we fear the Werewolf: it is the deep part of us that need not be bound by piffling Apollonian restrictions. It can walk through walls, disappear, speak in the voices of strangers. It is the Dionysian part of us . . . but it is still us.

Straub seems aware that he is carrying a basket dangerously overloaded with horrors, and turns the fact splendidly to his own advantage. The characters themselves feel that they have entered a horror story; the protagonist, Don Wanderley, is a writer of horror stories, and within the town of Milburn, New York, which becomes the world of this novel, there is the smaller world of Clark Mulligan's Rialto Theater, which is showing a horror-movie festival during the book's progress: a microcosm within the macrocosm. In one of the book's key scenes Gregory Bate throws one of the book's good guys, young Peter Barnes, through the movie screen while *Night of the Living Dead* is showing in the empty theater. The town of Milburn has become snowed in and overrun with the living dead, and at this point Barnes is literally thrown into the movie. It shouldn't work; it should be overt and cute. But Straub's firm prose *makes* it work. It preserves Straub's hall-of-mirrors approach (three of the book's epigrams are Straub's own free rendering of the Narcissus story), which keeps us constantly aware that the face looking out of all those mirrors is also the face looking in; the book suggests we need ghost stories because we, in fact, are the ghosts.* Is this really such a difficult or paradoxical idea when you consider how short our lives are in a wider life-scheme where redwoods live two thousand years and the Galapagos sea turtles may live for a thousand?

Most of *Ghost Story*'s power comes from the fact that of the four archetypes we have discussed, the Ghost is the most potent. The concept of the Ghost is to the good novel of the supernatural what the concept of the Mississippi is to Twain's *Huckleberry Finn*—really more than symbol or archetype, it is a major part of that myth-pool in which we all must bathe. "Don't you want to hear about the manifestations of the different spirits in her?" the younger priest asks the older before they go up to Regan MacNeil before the final confrontation in *The Exorcist*. He begins to enumerate them, and Father Merrin cuts him off curtly: "There is only one."

And although *Ghost Story* clanks and roars with the trappings of vampirism and werewolvery and flesh-eating ghouls, there is really only Alma/Anna/Ann-Veronica . . . and little Angie Maule. She is described by Don Wanderley as a shape-changer (what the Indians called a manitou), but even this is a branch rather than the taproot; all of these manifestations are like the up cards in a hand of stud poker. When we turn over the hole card, the one that makes the hand, we find the central card of our Tarot hand: the Ghost.

We know that ghosts aren't inherently evil—in fact, most of us have heard or read of a case or cases where ghosts have been rather helpful; the shade who told Auntie Clarissa not to take that plane or who warned Grampy Vic to go home fast because the house was catching on fire. My mother told me that after suffering a near-fatal heart attack, a close friend of hers had a visit from Jesus Christ in his hospital room. Jesus just opened

---

* At one point, while under strain, Don gives a long, rambling lecture to an undergraduate class on the subject of Stephen Crane. In the course of his talk he describes *The Red Badge of Courage* as "a great ghost story in which the ghost never appears." Considering the book's moody approach to the subjects of cowardice and bravery, it is an oddly apt description of that novel.

the door of Emil's I.C. room and asked him how he was doing. Emil allowed as how he was afraid he was a goner, and asked Jesus if He had come to take him. "Not yet," Jesus said, leaning casually against the door. "You've got another six years in you. Relax." He then left. Emil recovered. That was in 1953; I heard the story from my mother around 1957. Emil died in 1959—six years after his heart attack.

I have even had some truckle with "good ghosts" in my own work; near the end of *The Stand*, Nick Andros, a character who has been killed earlier in an explosion, returns to tell half-witted but good-hearted Tom Cullen bow to care for the novel's hero, Stu Redman, after Stu has fallen gravely ill with pneumonia. But for the purposes of the horror novel the ghosts must be evil, and as a result we find ourselves back in a familiar place: examining the Apollonian/Dionysian conflict and watching for the mutant.

In *Ghost Story*, Don Wanderley is summoned by four old men who call themselves the Chowder Society. Don's uncle, the fifth member, died of an apparent heart attack the year before while attending a party thrown for the mysterious actress Ann-Veronica Moore. As with all good gothics, a summary of the plot beyond this basic situation would be unfair—not because the veteran reader of this material will find much that is new in the plot (it would be surprising if he, she, or we did, in light of Straub's intention to fuse as many of the classic ghost story elements as possible), but because a bare summary of any gothic makes the book look absurdly complex and labored. Most gothics are overplotted novels whose success or failure hinges on the author's ability to make you believe in the characters and partake of the mood. Straub succeeds winningly at this, and the novel's machinery runs well (although it is extremely loud machinery; as already pointed out, that is also one of the great attractions of the gothic—it's *PRETTY GODDAM LOUD!*). The writing itself is beautifully tuned and balanced.

The bare situation is enough to delineate the conflict in *Ghost Story;* in its way it is as clearly a conflict between the Apollonian and Dionysian as Stevenson's *Dr. Jekyll and Mr.*

Hyde, and its moral stance, like that of most horror fiction, is firmly reactionary. Its politics are the politics of the four old men who make up the Chowder Society—Sears James and John Jaffrey are staunch Republicans, Lewis Benedikt owns what amounts to a medieval fiefdom in the woods, and while we are told that Ricky Hawthorne was at one time a socialist, he may be the only socialist in history who is so entranced by new ties that he feels an urge, we are told, to wear them to bed. All of these men—as well as Don Wanderley and young Peter Barnes—are perceived by Straub as beings of courage and love and generosity (and as Straub himself has pointed out in a later letter to me, none of these qualities run counter to the idea of reactionism; in fact, they may well define it). In contrast, the female revenant (all of Straub's evil ghosts are female) is cold and destructive, living only for revenge. When Don makes love to this creature in its Alma Mobley incarnation, he touches her in the night and feels "a shock of concentrated feeling, a shock of revulsion—as though I had touched a slug." And during a weekend spent with her, Don wakes up and sees Alma standing at the window and looking blankly out at the fog. He asks her if anything is wrong, and she replies. At first he persuades himself that her reply has been "I saw a ghost." A later truth forces him to admit she may have said "I am a ghost." A final act of memory retrieval convinces him that she has said something far more telling: "You are a ghost."

The battle for Milburn, New York—and for the lives of the last three members of the Chowder Society—commences. The lines are clearly and simply drawn for all the complexities of plot and the novel's shifting voices. We have three old men, one young man, and one teenage boy watching for the mutant. The mutant arrives. In the end, a victor emerges. This is standard enough stuff. What distinguishes it—what "brings it up"— is Straub's mirroring effect. Which Alma is the real Alma? Which evil is the real evil? As previously noted, it is usually easy to divide horror novels in another way—those that deal with "inside evil" (as in *Dr. Jekyll and Mr. Hyde*) and those that deal with "outside" or predestinate evil (as in *Dracula*).

But occasionally a book comes along where it is impossible to discover exactly where that line is. *The Haunting of Hill House* is such a book; *Ghost Story* is another. A great many writers who have attempted the horror story have also realized that it is exactly this blurring about where the evil is coming from that differentiates the good or the merely effective from the great, but realization and execution are two different things, and in attempting to produce the paradox, most succeed only in producing a muddle. . . . *Lovers Living, Lovers Dead* by Richard Lutz is one example. This is a case where you either hit the target dead-bang or miss it altogether. Straub hits it.

"I really wanted to expand things much more than I ever had before," Straub says. "I wanted to work on a large canvas. *'Salem's Lot* showed me how to do this without getting lost among a lot of minor characters. Besides the large canvas, I also wanted a certain largeness of effect. . . . I had been imbued with the notion that horror stories are best when they are ambiguous and low key and restrained. Reading [*'Salem's Lot*], I realized that idea was self-defeating. Horror stories were best when they were big and gaudy, when the natural operative quality in them was let loose. So part of the 'expansion' was an expansion of effect—I wanted to work up to big climaxes, create more tension than I ever had, build in big big scares. What all this means is that my ambition was geared up very high. Very much on my mind was doing something which would be *very* literary, and at the same time take on every kind of ghost situation I could think of. Also I wanted to play around with reality, to make the characters confused about what was actually real. So: I built in situations in which they feel they are 1.) acting out roles in a book; 2.) watching a film; 3.) hallucinating; 4.) dreaming; 5.) transported into a private fantasy.* This kind of thing, I think, is what our kind of book can do very well, what it is naturally suited to do. The material is sort of naturally absurd

---

* The best of these occurs when Lewis Benedikt goes to his death. He sees a bedroom door formed by an interlocking spray of pine needles while hunting in the woods. He goes through the door and into a deadly fantasyland.

and unbelievable, and therefore suits a narrative in which the characters are bounced around a whole set of situations, some of which they know rationally to be false. And it seemed fitting to me that this kind of plot would emerge from a group of men telling stories—it was self-referring, which always pleases me very deeply in novels. If the structure had a relationship to the events, the book has more resonance."

He offers a final anecdote about writing the book: "There was one very happy accident. . . . Just when I was going to start the second part, two Jehovah's Witnesses showed up on the doorstep, and I bought three or four pamphlets from them. One . . . had a headline about Dr. Rabbitfoot—this was for a story written by a trombonist named Trummy Young, who once played with Louis Armstrong. Dr. Rabbitfoot was a minstrel trombonist he saw as a child. So I immediately fastened on the name, and started Book Two with the character."

In the course of the novel, young Peter Barnes is picked up either by Alma Mobley or another so-called "nightwatcher" while hitching a ride. In this shape, the supernatural creature is a small, tubby man in a blue car—a Jehovah's Witness. He gives Peter a copy of *The Watchtower*, which is forgotten by the reader in the explosive course of events over the next forty pages or so. Straub has not forgotten, though. Later, after telling his story to Don Wanderley, Peter is able to produce the pamphlet the Jehovah's Witness has given him. The headline reads: DR. RABBITFOOT LED ME TO SIN.

One wonders if this was the headline of the actual copy of *The Watchtower* which the Jehovah's Witness sold to Straub in his London home as he worked out the first draft of *Ghost Story*.

3

Let us move now from ghosts to the natural (or unnatural, if you prefer) habitat of ghosts: the haunted house. There are haunted-house stories beyond numbering, most of them not very good (*The Cellar,* by Richard Laymon, is one example of the less successful breed). But this little subgenre has also produced a number of excellent books.

I'll not credit the haunted house as a genuine card in the Tarot hand of the supernatural myth, but I will suggest that we might widen our field of enquiry a bit and find that we *have* discovered another of those springs which feed the myth-pool. For want of a better name, we might call this particular archetype the Bad Place, a term which encompasses much more than the fallen-down house at the end of Maple Street with the weedy lawn, the broken windows, and the moldering FOR SALE sign.

It is neither my purpose nor my place here to discuss my own work, but readers of it will know that I've dealt with the archetype of the Bad Place at least twice, once obliquely (in *'Salem's Lot*) and once directly (in *The Shining*). My interest in the subject began when a friend and I took it into our heads to explore the local "haunted house"—a decrepit manse on the Deep Cut Road in my hometown of Durham, Maine. This place, in the manner of deserted dwellings, was called after the name of the last residents. So in town it was just the Marsten House.

This ramshackle abode stood on a hill high enough to overlook a good part of our section of town—a section known as Methodist Corners. It was full of fascinating junk—medicine bottles with no labels which still had odd and vile-smelling liquids in them, stacks of moldy magazines (JAPS COME OUT OF THEIR RAT-HOLES ON IWO! proclaimed the blurb on one yellowed issue of *Argosy*), a piano with at least twenty-five dead keys, paintings of long-dead people whose eyes seemed to follow you, rusty silverware, a few pieces of furniture.

The door was locked and there was a NO TRESPASSING sign nailed to it (so old and faded it was barely legible), but this did not stop us; such signs rarely stop self-respecting ten-year-olds. We simply went in through an unlocked window.

After having explored the downstairs thoroughly (and ascertained to our satisfaction that the old-fashioned sulphur matches we had found in the kitchen would no longer light but only produce a foul smell), we went upstairs. Unknown to us, my brother and cousin, two and four years older than my friend and I, had crept in after us. As the two of us poked through the upstairs bedrooms, they began to play horrible, jagged chords on the piano down in the living room.

My buddy and I screamed and clutched each other—for a moment the terror was complete. Then we heard those two dorks laughing downstairs and we grinned at each other shamefacedly. Nothing really of which to be afraid; just a couple of older boys scaring the old Irish bejaysus out of a couple of younger ones. No, nothing really of which to be afraid, but I don't recall that we ever returned there. Certainly not after dark. There might have been . . . things. And that was not even a really Bad Place.

Years later I read a speculative article which suggested that so-called "haunted houses" might actually be psychic batteries, absorbing the emotions that had been spent there, absorbing them much as a car battery will store an electric charge. Thus, the article went on, the psychic phenomena we call "hauntings" might really be a kind of paranormal movie show—the broadcasting back of old voices and images which might be parts of old events. And the fact that many haunted houses are shunned and get the reputation of being Bad Places might be due to the fact that the strongest emotions are the primitive ones—rage and hate and fear.

I did not accept the ideas in this article as gospel truth—it seems to me that the writer who deals with psychic phenomena in his or her fiction has a responsibility to deal with such phenomena respectfully but not in a state of utter, worshipful belief—but I did find the idea interesting, both for the idea itself and because it suggested a vague but intriguing referent in my own experience: that the past *is* a ghost which haunts our present lives constantly. And with my rigorous Methodist upbringing, I began to wonder if the haunted house could not be turned into a kind of symbol of unexpiated sin . . . an idea which turned out to be pivotal in the novel *The Shining*.

I guess I liked the idea itself—as divorced from any symbolism or moral reference—because it's always been difficult for me to understand why the dead would want to hang around old deserted houses, clanking chains and groaning spectrally to frighten the passersby . . . if they could go elsewhere. It sounds like a drag to me. The theory suggested that the inhabitants might indeed have gone on, leaving only a psychic residue behind. But even so (as Kenneth Patchen says), that did not rule out the possibility that the residue might be extremely harmful, as lead-based paint can be harmful to children who eat flakes of it years after it has been applied.

My experience in the Marsten House with my friend crosspatched with this article and with a third element—teaching Stoker's *Dracula*—to create the fictional Marsten House, which stands overlooking the little town of Jerusalem's Lot from its eminence not far from the Harmony Hill Cemetery. But *'Salem's Lot* is a book about vampires, not hauntings; the Marsten House is really only a curlicue, the gothic equivalent of an appendix. It was there, but it wasn't doing much except lending atmosphere (it becomes a little more important in Tobe Hooper's TV-film version, but its major function still seems to be to stand up there on that hill and look broody). So I went back to the house-as-psychic-battery idea and tried to write a story in which that concept would take center stage. *The Shining* is set in the apotheosis of the Bad Place: not a haunted house but a haunted hotel, with a different "real" horror movie playing in almost every one of its guest rooms and suites.

I needn't point out that the list of possible Bad Places does not begin with haunted houses and end with haunted hotels; there have been horror stories written about haunted railroad stations, automobiles, meadows, office buildings. The list is endless, and probably all of it goes back to the caveman who had to move out of his hole in the rock because he heard what sounded like voices back there in the shadows. Whether they were actual voices or the voices of the wind is a question we still ask ourselves on dark nights.

I want to talk here about two stories dealing with the archetype of the Bad Place, one good, one great. As it happens, both deal with haunted houses. Fair enough, I think; haunted cars and railway stations are nasty, but your house is the place where you're supposed to be able to unbutton your armor and put your shield away. Our homes are the places where we allow ourselves the ultimate vulnerability: they are the places where we take off our clothes and go to sleep with no guard on watch (except perhaps for those ever more popular drones of modern society, the smoke-detector and the burglar alarm). Robert Frost said home is the place that, when you go there, they have to take you in. The old aphorisms say that home is where the heart is, there's no place like home, that a heap of lovin' can make a house a home. We are abjured to keep the home fires burning, and when fighter pilots finish their missions they radio that they are "coming home." And even if you are a stranger in a strange land, you can usually find a restaurant that will temporarily assuage your homesickness as well as your hunger with a big plate of home-cooked home fries.

It doesn't hurt to emphasize again that horror fiction is a cold touch in the midst of the familiar, and good horror fiction applies this cold touch with sudden, unexpected pressure. When we go home and shoot the bolt on the door, we like to think we're locking trouble out. The good horror story about the Bad Place whispers that we are not locking the world out; we are locking ourselves in . . . with *them*.

Both of these tales adhere quite stringently to the conventional haunted-house formula; we are allowed to see a chain of hauntings, working together to reinforce the concept of the house as a Bad Place. One might even say that the truest definition of the haunted house would be "a house with an unsavory history." The author must do more than simply bring on a repertory company of ghosts, complete with clanking chains, doors that bang open or shut in the middle of the night, and strange noises in the attic or the cellar (the attic's especially good for a bit of low, throbbing terror—when was the last time you explored yours with a candle during a power failure while a strong autumn wind blew outside?); the haunted-house tale demands a historical context.

Both *The House Next Door,* by Anne Rivers Siddons (1978), and *The Haunting of Hill House,* by Shirley Jackson (1959), provide this historical context. Jackson establishes it immediately in the first paragraph of her novel, stating her tale's argument in lovely, dreamlike prose:

> No live organism can continue for long to exist sanely under conditions of absolute reality; even larks and katydids are supposed, by some, to dream. Hill House, not sane, stood by itself against its hills, holding darkness within; it had stood so for eighty years and might stand for eighty more. Within, walls continued upright, bricks met neatly, floors were firm, and doors were sensibly shut; silence lay steadily against the wood and stone of Hill House, and whatever walked there, walked alone.

I think there are few if any descriptive passages in the English language that are any finer than this; it is the sort of quiet epiphany every writer hopes for: words that somehow transcend words, words which add up to a total greater than the sum of the parts. Analysis of such a paragraph is a mean and shoddy trick, and should almost always be left to college and university professors, those lepidopterists of literature who, when they see a lovely butterfly, feel that they should immediately run into the field with a net, catch it, kill it with a drop of chloroform, and mount it on a white board and put it in a glass case, where it will still be beautiful . . . and just as dead as horseshit.

Having said that, let us analyze this paragraph a bit. I promise not to kill it or mount it, however; I have neither the skill nor the inclination (but show me any graduate thesis in the field of English/American lit, and I will show you a mess of dead butterflies, most of them killed messily and mounted inexpertly). We'll just stun it for a moment or two and then let it fly on.

All I really want to do is point out how *many* things this single paragraph does. It begins by suggesting that Hill House is a living organism; tells us that this live organism does not exist under conditions of absolute reality; that because (although here I should add that I may be making an induction Mrs. Jackson did not intend) it does not dream, it is not sane. The paragraph tells us how long its history has been, immediately establishing that historical context that is so important to the haunted-house story, and it concludes by telling us that *something* walks in the rooms and halls of Hill House. All of this in two sentences.

Jackson introduces an even more unsettling idea by implication. She suggests that Hill House *looks* all right on the surface. It is not the creepy old Marsten place from *'Salem's Lot* with its boarded-up windows, mangy roof, and peeling walls. It's not the tumble-down brooding place at the ends of all those dead-end streets, those places where children throw rocks by daylight and fear to venture after dark. Hill House is looking pretty good. But then, Norman Bates was looking pretty good, too, at least on the surface. There are no drafts in Hill House, but it (and those foolish enough to go there, we presume) does not exist under conditions of absolute reality; therefore, it does not dream; therefore, it is not sane. And, apparently, it kills.

If Shirley Jackson presents us with a history—a sort of supernatural provenance—as a starting point, then Anne Rivers Siddons gives us the provenance itself.

The House Next Door is a novel only in terms of its first-person narrator, Colquitt Kennedy, who lives with her husband, Walter, next to the haunted house. We see their lives and their way of thinking change as a result of their proximity to the house, and the novel establishes itself, finally, when Colquitt and Walter feel impelled to "step into the story." This happens quite satisfyingly in the book's closing fifty pages, but during much of the book Colquitt and Walter are very much sideline characters. The book is compartmentalized into three longish sections, and each is really a story in itself. We are given the story of the Harralsons, the Sheehans, and the Greenes, and we see the house next door mainly through their experiences. In other words, while *The Haunting of Hill House* provides us with a supernatural provenance—the bride whose carriage overturned, killing her seconds before she was to get her first glimpse of Hill House, for example—merely as background stuff, *The House Next Door* could have been subtitled "The Making of a Haunted House."

This approach works well for Ms. Siddons, who does not write prose with the beautiful simplicity of Mrs. Jackson, but who nevertheless acquits herself well and honorably here. The book is well planned and brilliantly cast ("People like us don't appear in *People* magazine," the first sentence of the book reads, and Colquitt goes on to tell us just how she and her husband, two private people, ended up not only in *People* magazine, but ostracized by their neighbors, hated by city realtors, and ready to burn the house next door to the ground). This is no gothic manse covered with drifting tatters of fog off the moor; there are no battlements, no moats, not even a widow's walk. . . . Whoever heard of such things in suburban Atlanta, anyway? When the story opens, the haunted house hasn't even been built.

Colquitt and Walter live in a rich and comfortable section of suburban Atlanta. The machinery of social intercourse in this suburb—a suburb of a New South city where many of the Old South virtues still hold, Colquitt tells us—is smoothly running and almost silent, well oiled with u.m.c. money. Next to their home is a wooded lot which has never been developed because of the difficult topography. Enter Kim Dougherty, young hotshot architect; he builds a contemporary home on the lot that fits the land like a glove. In fact . . . it looks almost alive. Colquitt writes of her first look at the house plans:

> I drew my breath at it. It was magnificent. I do not
> as a rule care for contemporary architecture, [but] . . .
> This house was different. It commanded you, somehow,
> yet soothed you. It grew out of the penciled earth like an
> elemental spirit that had lain, locked and yearning for

the light, through endless deeps of time, waiting to be released. . . . I could hardly imagine the hands and machinery that would form it. I thought of something that had started with a seed, put down deep roots, grown in the sun and rains of many years into the upper air. In the sketches, at least, the woods pressed untouched around it like companions. The creek enfolded its mass and seemed to nourish its roots. It looked—inevitable.

Events follow in ordained fashion. Dionysian change is coming to this Apollonian suburb where hitherto there has been a place for everything and everything is in its place. That night, when Colquitt hears an owl hooting in the woodlot where Dougherty's house will soon go up, she finds herself tying a knot in the corner of her bedsheet to ward off bad luck, as her grandmother did.

Dougherty is building the house for a young couple, the Harralsons (but he would have been just as happy building it for Adolf Hitler and Eva Braun, he tells the Kennedys over drinks; it's the house that interests him, not the owners). Buddy Harralson is an up-and-coming young lawyer. His little-girl-Chi-Omega-Junior-Leaguer wife, hideo-comically known as Pie (as in Punkin Pie, her daddy's nickname), loses first her baby to the house in a miscarriage which occurs there when she's four months pregnant, then her dog, and finally, on the evening of her housewarming, everything else.

Exit Harralsons, enter Sheehans. Buck and his wife, Anita, are trying to recover from the loss of their only child, who went down in a flaming helicopter while serving in Vietnam. Anita, who is recovering from a mental breakdown as a result of the loss (which dovetails a little too neatly with the loss of her father and brother years before in a similar accident), begins to see movies of her son's horrible death on the television in the house. A neighbor who is helping out also catches part of this lethal film. Other stuff happens . . . there is a climax . . . and exit Sheehans. Then, last but hardly least in terms of the grand guignol, comes the Greenes.

If all this sounds familiar, it comes as no surprise to either of us. *The House Next Door* is a frame story, the sort of thing one likes to speculate, that Chaucer might have done if he had written for *Weird Tales*. It is a form of horror tale that the movies have tried more often than novelists or short-story writers. In fact, the moviemakers seem to have tried a good many times to put a dictum that critics of the genre have handed down for years into actual practice: that the horror tale works best when it is brief and comes directly to the point (most people associate that dictum with Poe, but Coleridge stated it before him, and in fact Poe was offering a guideline for the writer of all short stories, not just those dealing with the supernatural and the occult). Interestingly enough, the dictum seems to fail in actual practice. Most horror movies employing the frame-story device to tell three or four short tales work unevenly or not at all.*

Does *The House Next Door* work? I think it does. It doesn't work as well as it *could* work, and the reader is left with what may be the wrong set of ambiguities about Walter and Colquitt Kennedy, but still, it works.

"[*The House Next Door*] came about, I suspect," Ms. Siddons writes, "because I have always been fond of the horror or occult genre, or whatever you may call it. It seemed to me that most of my favorite writers had tackled the ghost story at one time or another. Henry James, Edith Wharton, Nathaniel Hawthorne, Dickens, et al., and I have enjoyed the more contemporary writers in the genre as much as I have the old classicists. Shirley Jackson's *Hill House* is as nearly perfect a haunted-house tale as I have ever read . . . and [my favorite of all time, I think is] M. F. K. Fisher's enchanting little *The Lost, Strayed, Stolen.*

"The point would seem to be that, as every foreword to every anthology of horror stories you ever read assures you, the ghost

---

* But there are exceptions to every rule, obviously. While two adaptations of old EC-comics horror yarns, *Tales from the Crypt* and *Vault of Horror*, are miserable failures, Robert Bloch did two "frame-story" films for the British Amicus production company, *The House That Dripped Blood* and *Asylum.* The stories in both of these were adapted from Bloch's own short stories, and both are good fun. Of course, the champ is still *Dead of Night*, the 1946 British film starring Michael Redgrave and directed by Robert Hamer, Cavalcanti, Charles Crichton, and Basil Dearden.

story *is* timeless; it cuts across all lines of culture and class and all levels of sophistication; it communicates immediately somewhere in the vicinity of the base of your spine, and touches that crouching thing in all of us that still peers in abject terror past the fire into the dark beyond the cave door. If all cats are gray in the dark, so, basically, are all people afraid of it.

"The haunted house has always spoken specially and directly to me as the emblem of particular horror. Maybe it's because, to a woman, her house is so much more than that: it is kingdom, responsibility, comfort, total world to her . . . to most of us, anyway, whether or not we are aware of it. It is an extension of ourselves; it tolls in answer to one of the most basic chords mankind will ever hear. My shelter. My earth. My second skin. Mine. So basic is it that the desecration of it, the corruption, as it were, by something alien takes on a peculiar and bone-deep horror and disgust. It is both frightening and . . . violating, like a sly, terrible burglar. A house askew is one of the not-rightest things in the world, and is terrible out of all proportion to its actual visitant. . . .

"I came to write of a new house that was . . . let's say malignant . . . for the very simple reason that I wanted to see if I could write a good ghost story. . . . I was tired and rather simple-minded from a two-year stint of heavy, serious, 'writery' writing, yet I wanted to be at work, and thought the ghost story would be fun . . . and as I was casting about in my mind for a good hook, or handle, a young architect bought the lovely, wooded lot next to our house and began to build a contemporary house on it. My writing room, upstairs under the eaves of our old house, looks right into the lot next door, and I would sit and stare dreamily out my window and watch the wild woods and hills go down and the house go up, and one day the inevitable 'What if' that starts all writers writing bloomed in my mind, and we were off. 'What if,' I thought, 'instead of an ancient haunted priory on the coast of Cornwall or a pre-Revolutionary farmhouse in Bucks County with a visitant or two, or even the ruins of an antebellum plantation house with a hoop-skirted spectre wailing around the desecrated chimney for her lost world, you had a brand-new contemporary going up in an affluent suburb of a large city? You'd expect the priory and the farmhouse and the plantation to be haunted. But the contemporary? Wouldn't that give it an even meaner, nastier, little fillip? Serve to emphasize by contrast and horror? I thought it would. . . .

"I'm still not sure how I arrived at the idea that the house would use its sheer loveliness to attract people, and then begin to turn their own deepest weaknesses, their soft spots, against them. It seems to me that in this day of pragmatists and materialists, a conventional spectre would be almost laughable; in the suburb that I envisioned, the people do not believe in that sort of thing; it is almost improper. A traditional ghoulie would be laughed out of the neighborhood. So what *would* get to my quasi-sophisticated suburbanite? What would break relationships and crumble defenses and penetrate suburban armors? It would have to be different in each case. Each person has his own built-in horror button. Let's have a house that can isolate and push it, and then you've really got a case of the suburban willies.

"The plot of the book emerged in one typewriter sitting almost whole and in infinite detail, as though it had been there all along just waiting to be uncovered. . . . *The House Next Door* was plotted and whole in a day. From there it looked to be great fun, and I set off on it with a light heart, because I thought it would be an easy book to write. And in a sense, it was: these are my people. I am of this world. I know them from the skin out. They were of course, caricatures in most cases; most of the people I know are, thankfully, far more eccentric and not so determinedly suburban as this set of folks. But I needed them to be the way they were to make a point. And I found the limning of them went like greased lightning.

"Because the whole point of this book, of course, is not so much the house and its peculiar, terrible power, but what effect it has on the neighborhood, and on the relationships between neighbors and friends, and between families, when they are forced to confront and believe the unbelievable. This has always been the power of the supernatural to me . . . that it blasts and breaks relationships between people and other people and between people and their world and, in a way, between people and the very essences of themselves. And the blasting and breaking leaves them defenseless and alone, howling in terror before the thing that they have been forced to believe. For belief is everything; belief is all. Without belief, there is no terror. And I think it is even more terrible when a modern man or woman, girded round with privilege and education and all the trappings of the so-called good life and all the freight of the clever, pragmatic, vision-hungry modern mind, is forced to confront utter, alien, and elemental evil and terror. What does he know of this, what has it to do with him? What has the unspeakable and the unbelievable got to do with second homes and tax shelters and private schools for the kids and a pâté in every terrine and a BMW in every garage? Primitive man might howl before his returning dead and point; his neighbor would see, and howl along with him. . . . The resident of Fox Run Chase who meets a ghoulie out by the hot tub is going to be frozen dead in his or her Nikes on the tennis courts the next day if he or she persists in gabbling about it. And there he is, alone with the horror and ostracized on all sides. It's a double turn of the screw, and I thought it would make a good story.

"I still think it did . . . I think it holds up well. . . . But it is only now that I am able to read the book with any equanimity. About a third of the way through it, the writing ceased to be fun and became something as oppressive to me as it was obsessive; I realized I was into something vast and terrible and not at all funny; I was hurting and destroying people or allowing them to be hurt and destroyed, which amounts to the same thing. There is in me . . . some leftover streak of Puritan ethic, or squinty-eyed Calvinistic morality, that insists that THINGS MUST HAVE A POINT. I dislike anything gratuitous. Evil must not be allowed to get away unpunished, even though I know that it does, every day. Ultimately . . . there must be a day of reckoning for the Bad Thing, and I still have no idea if this is a strength or weakness. . . . It certainly does not lend itself to subtleties, but I do not see myself as a 'clever' writer. And so *The House Next Door* became very serious business indeed to me; I knew that Colquitt and Walter Kennedy, whom I really liked very much indeed, would be destroyed by the house they in turn destroyed at the end of the book, but to me there was very real gallantry in the fact that they knew this themselves, and went ahead anyway . . . I was glad they did not run away . . . I would hope that, faced with something as overwhelmingly vast and terrible and left with so few options, I would have the grace and courage to do as they did. I speak of them as though they were outside my control because I feel as if they are, and most of the way through the book I felt this. . . . There is an inevitability about the outcome . . . that, to me, was inherent even on the first page of the book. It happened this way because this is the way it would have happened in this time and this place to these people. That is a satisfying feeling to me, and it is not one that I have had about all my books. And so in that sense, I feel that it succeeds. . . .

"On its simplest level, I think it works well as a piece of horror fiction that depends on the juxtaposition of the unimaginably terrible with the utterly ordinary . . . the wonderful Henry James 'terror in sunlight' syndrome. *Rosemary's Baby* is the absolute master of this particular device, and it was that quality, in part, that I strove for. I also feel good about the fact that, to me, all the characters are still extremely sympathetic people, even this long after writing and after this many rereadings. I cared very much what happened to them as I unveiled them on the pages, and I still care about them.

"Maybe it succeeds, too, in being an utterly contemporary horror tale. Maybe this is the wave of the future. It isn't the thing that goes bump in your house in the night that is going to do you in in this brave new world; it's your house itself. In a world where the very furniture of your life, the basic bones of your existence, turn terrible and strange, perhaps the only thing we're going to have to fall back on is whatever innate decency we can find deep within ourselves. In a way, I do not think this is a bad thing."

A phrase that stands out in Siddons's analysis of her own work—at least it stands out to me—is this one: "... to me there was very real gallantry," she says, "in the fact that they knew this themselves, and went ahead anyway ..." We might think of this as a uniquely Southern sentiment, and as ladylike as she is, Anne Rivers Siddons is squarely in a Southern tradition of gothic writers.

She tells us she has jettisoned the ruins of the antebellum plantation, and so she has, but in a wider sense, *The House Next Door* is very much the same spooky, tumble-down plantation home where writers as seemingly disparate but as essentially similar as William Faulkner, Harry Crews, and Flannery O'Connor—probably the greatest American short-story writer of the postwar era—have lived before her. It is a home where even such a really gruesomely bad writer as William Bradford Huie has rented space from time to time.

If the Southern experience were to be viewed as unfilled soil, then we would have to say that almost any writer, no matter how good or bad, who deeply feels that Southern experience could plant a seed and have it grow—as an example I recommend Thomas Cullinan's novel *The Beguiled* (made into a good Clint Eastwood film, directed by Don Siegel). Here is a novel which is "written pretty good," as a friend of mine likes to put it—meaning, of course, nuthin' special. No Saul Bellow, no Bernard Malamud, but at least not down there in steerage with people like Harold Robbins and Sidney Sheldon, who apparently wouldn't know the difference between a balanced line of prose and a shit-and-anchovy pizza. If Cullinan had elected to write a more conventional novel, it would stick out in no one's mind. Instead, he came up with this mad gothic tale about a Union soldier who loses his legs and then his life to the deadly angels of mercy who dwell in a ruined girls' school that has been left behind in Sherman's march to the sea. This is Cullinan's little acre of that patch of unfilled soil, soil which has always been amazingly rich. One is tempted to believe that outside of the South, such an idea wouldn't raise much more than ragweed. But in this soil, it grows a vine of potent, crazed beauty—the reader is mesmerized with horror by what goes on in that forgotten school for young ladies.

On the other hand, William Faulkner did more than drop a few seeds; he planted the whole damn garden . . . and everything he turned his hand to after 1930, when he really discovered the gothic form for fair, seemed to come up. The essence of the Southern gothic in Faulkner's work comes, for me, in *Sanctuary*, when Popeye stands on the scaffold, about to be hanged. He has combed his hair neatly for the occasion, but now, with the rope around his neck and his hands tied behind his back, his hair has fallen lankly across his forehead. He begins to jerk his head, trying to flip his hair back into place. "I'll fix that for you," the executioner tells him, and pulls the trigger on the scaffold's trapdoor. Exit Popeye, with hair in his face. I believe with all my heart that no one brought up north of the Mason-Dixon Line could have thought of that scene, or written it right if he or she had done. Ditto the long, lurid, and excruciating scene in the doctor's waiting room which opens Flannery O'Connor's novella "Revelation." There are no doctor's waiting rooms like that outside the Southern imagination; holy Jesus, what a crew.

My point is that there is something frighteningly lush and fertile in the Southern imagination, and this seems particularly so when it turns into the gothic channel.

The case of the Harralsons, the first family to inhabit the Bad Place in Siddons's novel shows quite clearly how the author has put her own Southern gothic imagination to work. Pie Harralson, the girl-wife-Chi-Omega-Junior-Leaguer, wields an unhealthy sort of attraction over her father, a beefy, choleric man from the "wire grass south." Pie seems quite aware that her husband, Buddy, makes a triangle with her at the apex and daddy at one of the lower corners. She plays the two of them off one another. The house itself is only another pawn in the love-hate-love affairs she seems to be having with her father ("That weird thing she has with him," one character says dismissively). Near the end of her first conversation with Colquitt and Walter, Pie says gleefully: "Oh, Daddy's just going to *hate* this house! Oh, he's going to be fit to be tied!"

Buddy, meanwhile, has been taken under the wing of Lucas Abbott, a new arrival at the law office where Buddy works. Abbott is a Northerner, and we hear passingly that Abbott left New York as the result of a scandal: ". . . something about a law clerk."

The house next door, which turns people's own deepest weaknesses against them, as Siddons says, fuses these elements neatly and horribly. Near the end of the housewarming party, Pie begins to scream. The guests rush to see what has happened to her. They find Buddy Harralson and Lucas Abbott embracing, naked, in the bedroom where the coats have been left. Pie's Daddy has found them first, and he is in the process of expiring of a stroke on the floor while his Punkin Pie screams on . . . and on . . . and on.

Now if that isn't Southern gothic, what is?

The essence of the horror in this scene (which for some reason reminds me strongly of that heart-stopping moment in *Rebecca* where the nameless narrator stops the party cold by floating down the stairs in the costume also worn by Maxim's dreadful first wife) lies in the fact that social codes have not merely been breached; they have been exploded in our shocked faces. Siddons pulls this particular dynamite blast off perfectly. It is a case of everything going just about as totally wrong as things can go; lives and careers are ruined irrevocably in a passage of seconds.

We need not analyze the psyche of the horror writer; nothing is so boring or so annoying as people who ask things like, "Why are you so weird?" or "Was your mother scared by a two-headed dog while you were *in utero*?" Nor am I going to do that here, but I'll point out that much of the walloping effect of *The House Next Door* comes from its author's nice grasp of social boundaries. Any writer of the horror tale has a clear—perhaps even a morbidly overdeveloped—conception of where the country of the socially (or morally, or psychologically) acceptable ends and that great white space of Taboo begins. Siddons is better at marking the edges of the socially acceptable from the socially nightmarish than most (although Daphne Du Maurier comes to mind again), and I'll bet that she was taught young that you don't eat with your elbows on the table . . . or make abnormal love in the coatroom.

She returns to the breach of social codes again and again (as she does in an earlier, nonsupernatural novel about the south, *Heartbreak Hotel*), and on its most rational, symbolic level, *The House Next Door* can be read as a funny-horrible sociological treatise on the mores and folkways of the Modestly Suburban Rich. But beneath this, the heart of the Southern gothic beats strongly. Colquitt tells us she could not bear to tell her closest friend what she saw on the day when Anita Sheehan finally and irrevocably lost her mind, but she is able to tell us in vivid, shocking detail. Horrified or not, Colquitt saw it all. She herself makes a "New South/Old South" comparison near the beginning of the novel, and the novel taken as a whole is another. On the surface we see "the obligatory tobacco-brown Mercedeses," vacations at Ocho Rios, Bloody Marys sprinkled thickly with fresh dill at Rinaldi's. But the stuff underneath, the stuff which makes the heart of this novel pulse with such a tremendous crude strength, is the Old South—the Southern gothic stuff. Underneath, *The House Next Door* is not situated in a tony Atlanta suburb at all; it is located in that grimly grotty country of the heart that Flannery O'Connor mapped so well. Scratch Colquitt Kennedy deeply enough and we find O'Connor's Mrs. Turpin, standing in her pigpen and waiting for a revelation.

If the book has a serious problem, it lies in our perception of Walter, Colquitt, and the third major character, Virginia Guthrie. Our feelings about these characters are not particularly sympathetic, and while it is not a rule that they should be, the reader may find it hard to understand why Siddons likes them, as she says she does. Through most of the book, Colquitt herself is particularly unappetizing: vain, class-conscious, money-conscious, sexually priggish, and vaguely exhibitionistic at the same time. "We like our lives and our possessions to run smoothly," she tells the reader with a maddening complacency early on. "Chaos, violence, disorder, mindlessness all upset us. They do not frighten us, precisely, because we are aware of them. We watch the news, we are active in our own brand of rather liberal politics. We know we have built a shell for ourselves, but we have worked hard for the means to do it; we have chosen it. Surely we have the right to do that."

In all fairness, part of this is meant to set us up for the changes that Colquitt and Walter undergo as a result of the supernatural didoes next door—that damned house is doing what Bob Dylan called bringing it all back home. Siddons undoubtedly means to tell us that the Kennedys eventually arrive at a new plateau of social consciousness; after the episode with the Sheehans, Colquitt tells her husband: "You know, Walter, we've never stuck our necks out. We've never put ourselves or anything we really value on the line. We've taken the best life has to give . . . and we really haven't given anything back." If this is so, then Siddons succeeds. The Kennedys pay with their lives. The novel's problem may be that the reader is apt to feel that the dues paid were fair ones.

Siddons's own view on just what the Kennedys' rising social consciousness means is also muddier than I would like. If it is a victory, it seems to be of the Pyrrhic variety; their world has been destroyed by their conviction that they must warn the world against the house next door, but their conviction seems to have given them remarkably little inner peace in return—and the book's kicker seems to indicate that their victory has a decidedly hollow ring.

Colquitt does not just put on her sun hat when she goes to do the garden; she puts on her *Mexican* sun hat. She is justly proud of her job, but the reader may feel a bit more uneasy about her serene confidence in her own looks: "I have what I want and do not need the adulation of very young men, even though, I modestly admit, there have been some around my agency who have offered it." We know that she looks good in tight jeans; Colquitt herself helpfully points this out. We have the feeling that if the book had been written a year or two later,

Colquitt would be pointing out that she looks good in her Calvin Klein jeans. The point of all this is that she's not a character most people will be able to hope for easily, and whether or not her personal tics help or hinder in the book's steady, downturning funnel toward disaster is something that the reader will have to decide for herself or himself.

Equally problematic is the book's dialogue. At one point Colquitt hugs the newly arrived Anita Sheehan and tells her, "Welcome to the neighborhood once again, Anita Sheehan. Because you're a whole new lady and one I like immensely, and I hope you're going to be very, very happy here." I don't quibble with the sentiment; I just wonder if people, even in the South, really talk like this.

Let's say this: the major problem with *The House Next Door* is the muddiness of character development. A lesser problem is one of actual execution—a problem that crops up mostly in the dialogue, as the narration is adequate and the imagery often oddly beautiful. But as a gothic, the book succeeds admirably.

Now let me suggest that, in addition to being a Southern gothic novel, Anne Rivers Siddons's *The House Next Door,* whatever its shortcomings in terms of characterization or execution, succeeds on far more important ground; it is a prime example of what Irving Malin calls "the new American gothic"—so is Straub's *Ghost Story,* for that matter, although Straub seems much more clearly aware of the species of fish he has netted (the clearest indication of this is his use of the Narcissus myth and the spooky use of the lethal mirror).

John G. Park employed Malin's idea of the new American gothic in an article for *Critique: Studies in Modern Fiction.** Park's article is on Shirley Jackson's novel *The Sundial,* but what he says about that book is equally applicable to a whole slew of American ghost and horror stories, including several of my own. Here is Malin's "list of ingredients" for the modern gothic, as explained by Park in his article.

---

* The article "Waiting for the End: Shirley Jackson's *The Sundial*" by John G. Park, *Critique,* Vol. XIX, No. 3, 1978.

First, a microcosm serves as the arena where universal forces collide. In the case of the Siddons book, the house next door serves as this microcosm.

Second, the gothic house functions as an image of authoritarianism, of imprisonment, or of "confining narcissism." By narcissism, Park and Malin seem to mean a growing obsession with one's own problems; a turning inward instead of a growing outward. The new American gothic provides a closed loop of character, and in what might be termed a psychological pathetic fallacy, the physical surroundings often mimic the inward-turning of the characters themselves—as they do in *The Sundial.*

This is an exciting, even fundamental change in the intent of the gothic. Once upon a time the Bad Place was seen by critics as symbolic of the womb—a primarily sexual symbol which perhaps allowed the gothic to become a safe way of talking about sexual fears. Park and Malin are suggesting that the new American gothic, created primarily in the twenty or so years since Shirley Jackson published *The Haunting of Hill House,* uses the Bad Place not to symbolize sexual interests and fear of sex but interest in the self and fear of the self . . . and if anyone should ever ask you why there has been such a bulge in the popularity of horror fiction and horror films over the last five years or so, you might point out to your questioner that the rise of the horror film in the seventies and early eighties and the rise of such things as Rolfing, primal screaming, and hot-tubbing run pretty much in tandem, and that most of the really popular examples of the horror genre, from *The Exorcist* to Cronenberg's *They Came from Within,* are fine examples of the new American gothic, where we have, instead of a symbolic womb, a symbolic mirror.

---

* Or in *The Shining,* which was written with *The Sundial* very much in mind. In *The Shining,* the characters are snowbound and isolated in an old hotel miles from any help. Their world has shrunk and turned inward; the Overlook Hotel becomes the microcosm where universal forces collide, and the inner weather mimics the outer weather. Critics of Stanley Kubrick's film version would do well to remember that it was these elements, consciously or unconsciously, which Kubrick chose to accentuate.

This may sound like a lot of academic bullshit, but it's really not. The purpose of horror fiction is not only to explore taboo lands but to confirm our own good feelings about the status quo by showing us extravagant visions of what the alternative might be. Like the scariest bad dreams, the good creepshow often does its work by turning the status quo inside out—what scares us the most about Mr. Hyde, perhaps, is the fact that he was a part of Dr. Jekyll all along. And in an American society that has become more and more entranced by the cult of me-ism, it should not be surprising that the horror genre has turned more and more to trying to show us a reflection we won't like—our own.

While looking at *The House Next Door,* we find we can lay the Tarot card of the Ghost aside—there are no ghosts *per se* in the house which is owned by the Harralsons, the Sheehans, and the Greenes. The card which seems to fit better here is the card that always seems to come up when we deal with narcissism: the card of the Werewolf. More traditional werewolf stories almost always—knowingly or unknowingly—mimic the classic story of Narcissus; in the Lon Chaney, Jr., version, we observe Chaney observing himself in the Ever-Popular Pool of Water as he undergoes the transformation back from monster to Larry Talbot. We see the exact same scene occur in the original TV film of *The Incredible Hulk* as the Hulk returns to his David Banner form. In Hammer's *Curse of the Werewolf,* the scene is repeated yet again, only this time it's Oliver Reed who's watching himself undergo the change. The real *problem* with the house next door, we see, is that it changes people into the very things they most abhor. The real *secret* of the house next door is that it is a dressing-room for werewolves.

"Nearly all the characters of the new American gothic are narcissistic," Park sums up, "in one form or another, weaklings who try to read their own preoccupations into reality." This sums up Colquitt Kennedy, I think; and it also sums up Eleanor, the protagonist of Shirley Jackson's *The Haunting of Hill House;* and Eleanor Vance is surely the finest character to come out of this new American gothic tradition.

"The inspiration to write a ghost story," Lenemaja Friedman writes in her study of Jackson's work, "came to Miss Jackson . . . as she was reading a book about a group of nineteenth-century psychic researchers who rented a haunted house in order to study it and record their impressions of what they had seen and heard for the purpose of presenting a treatise to the Society for Psychic Research. As she recalls: 'They thought they were being terribly scientific and proving all kinds of things, and yet the story that kept coming through their dry reports was not at all the story of a haunted house, it was the story of several earnest, I believe misguided, certainly determined people, with their differing motivations and backgrounds.' The story so excited her that she could hardly wait to create her own haunted house and her own people to study it.

"Shortly thereafter, she states, on a trip to New York, she saw at the 125th Street station, a grotesque house—one so evil-looking, one that made such a somber impression, that she had nightmares about it long afterward. In response to her curiosity, a New York friend investigated and found that the house, intact from the front, was merely a shell since a fire had gutted the structure. . . . In the meantime, she was searching newspapers, magazines, and books for pictures of suitably haunted-looking houses; and at last she discovered a magazine picture of a house that seemed just right. It looked very muck like the hideous building she had seen in New York: '. . . it had the same air of disease and decay, and if ever a house looked like a candidate for a ghost, it was this one.' The picture identified the house as being in a California town; consequently, hoping her mother in California might be able to acquire some information about the house, she wrote asking for help. As it happened, her mother was not only familiar with the house but provided the startling information that Miss Jackson's great-grandfather had built it."*

Heh-heh-heh, as the Crypt-Keeper used to say.

---

* From *Shirley Jackson*, by Lenemaja Friedman (Boston: Twayne Publishers, 1975), p. 121. Ms. Friedman quotes directly from Shirley Jackson's account of how the book came to be; Miss Jackson's account was published in an article entitled "Experience and Fiction."

On its simplest level, *Hill House* follows the plan of those Psychic Society investigators of whom Miss Jackson had read: it is a tale of four ghost-busters who gather in a house of ill repute. It recounts their adventures there, and culminates with a scary, mystifying climax. The ghost-busters—Eleanor, Theo, and Luke—have come together under the auspices of one Dr. Montague, an anthropologist whose hobby is investigating psychic phenomena. Luke, a young wise-guy type of fellow (memorably played by Russ Tamblyn in Robert Wise's sensitive film version of the book), is there as a representative of the owner, his aunt; he regards the whole thing as a lark . . . at least at first.

Eleanor and Theo have been invited for different reasons. Montague has combed the back files of several psychic societies, and has sent invitations to a fairly large number of people who have been involved with "abnormal" events in the past—the invitations, of course, suggest that these "special" people might enjoy summering with Montague at Hill House. Eleanor and Theo are the only two to respond, each for her own reasons. Theo, who has demonstrated a fairly convincing ability with the Rhine cards, is on the outs with her current lover (in the film, Theo—played by Claire Bloom—is presented as a lesbian with a letch for Eleanor; in Jackson's novel there is the barest whiff that Theo's sexual preferences may not be 100 percent AC).

But it is Eleanor, on whose house stones fell when she was a little girl, that the novel is vitally concerned with, and it is the character of Eleanor and Shirley Jackson's depiction of it that elevates *The Haunting of Hill House* into the ranks of the great supernatural novels—indeed, it seems to me that it and James's *The Turn of the Screw* are the only two great novels of the supernatural in the last hundred years (although we might add two long novellas: Machen's "The Great God Pan" and Lovecraft's "At the Mountains of Madness").

"Nearly all the characters of the new American gothic are narcissistic . . . weaklings who try to read their own preoccupations into reality."

Try this shoe on Eleanor, and we find it fits perfectly. She is obsessively concerned with herself, and in Hill House she finds a huge and monstrous mirror reflecting back her own distorted face. She is a woman who has been profoundly stunted by her upbringing and her family life. When we are inside her mind (which is almost constantly, with the exception of the first chapter and the last), we may find ourselves thinking of that old Oriental custom of foot binding—only it is not Eleanor's feet that have been bound; it is that part of her mind where the ability to live any sort of independent life must begin.

"It is true that Eleanor's characterization is one of the finest in Miss Jackson's works," Lenemaja Friedman writes. "It is second only to that of Merricat in the later novel *We Have Always Lived in the Castle*. There are many facets to Eleanor's personality: she can be gay, charming, and witty when she feels wanted; she is generous and willing to give of herself. At the same time, she resents Theo's selfishness and is ready to accuse Theo of trickery when they discover the sign on the wall. For many years, Eleanor has been filled with frustration and hate: she has come to hate her mother and then finally her sister and brother-in-law for taking advantage of her more submissive and passive nature. She struggles to overcome the guilt she feels for the death of her mother.

"Although one comes to know her quite well, she remains mysterious. The mystery is a product of Eleanor's uncertainty and her mental and emotional changes, which are difficult to fathom. She is insecure and, therefore, unstable in her relationships with others and her relationship to the house. She feels the irresistible force of the spirits and longs, finally, to submit to them. When she does decide not to leave Hill House, one must assume she is slipping into madness.'"[*]

Hill House, then, is the microcosm where universal forces collide, and in his piece on *The Sundial* (published in 1958, a year before *The Haunting of Hill House*), John G. Park goes on

---

[*] Friedman, *Shirley Jackson*, p. 133.

to speak of "the voyage . . . [the] attempt to flee . . . an attempt to escape . . . cloying authoritarianism . . ."

This is, in fact, the place where Eleanor's own voyage begins, and also the motive for that voyage. She is shy, withdrawn, and submissive. The mother has died, and Eleanor has judged and found herself guilty of negligence—perhaps even murder. She has remained firmly under the thumb of her married sister following her mother's death, and early on there's a bitter argument over whether Eleanor will be allowed to go to Hill House at all. And Eleanor, who is thirty-two, habitually claims to be two years older.

She does manage to get out, practically stealing the car which she has helped to purchase. The jailbreak is on, Eleanor's attempt to escape what Park calls "cloying authoritarianism." The journey will lead her to Hill House, and as Eleanor herself thinks—with a growing, feverish intensity as the story progresses—"journeys end in lovers meeting."

Her narcissism is perhaps most strikingly established by a fantasy she indulges in while still on the way to Hill House. She stops the car, full of "disbelief and wonder" at the sight of a gate flanked by ruined stone pillars in the middle of a long line of oleanders. Eleanor recalls that oleanders are poisonous . . . and then:

> Will I, she thought, will I get out of my car and go between the ruined gates and then, once I am in the magic oleander square, find that I have wandered into a fairyland, protected poisonously from the eyes of people passing? Once I have stepped between the magic gateposts, will I find myself through the protective barrier, the spell broken? I will go into a sweet garden, with fountains and low benches and roses trained over arbors, and find one path—jeweled, perhaps, with rubies and emeralds, soft enough for a king's daughter to walk upon with her little sandaled feet—and it will lead me directly to the palace which lies under a spell. I will walk up low stone steps past stone lions guarding and into a courtyard where a

fountain plays and the queen waits, weeping, for the princess to return. . . . And we shall live happily ever after.

The depth of this sudden fantasy is meant to startle us, and it does. It suggests a personality to which fantasizing has become a way of life . . . and what happens to Eleanor at Hill House comes uncomfortably close to fulfilling this strange fantasy-dream. Perhaps even the happily-ever-after part, although I suspect Shirley Jackson would doubt that.

More than anything, the passage indicates the unsettling, perhaps mad depths of Eleanor's narcissism—weird home movies play constantly inside her head, movies of which she is the star and the sole moving force—movies which are the exact opposite of her real life, in fact. Her imagination is restless, fertile . . . and perhaps dangerous. Later, the stone lions she has imagined in the passage quoted turn up as ornamental bookends in the totally fictional apartment she has imagined for Theo's benefit.

In Eleanor's life, that turning-inward which Park and Malin associate with the new American gothic is a constant thing. Shortly after the enchanted castle fantasy, Eleanor stops for lunch and overhears a mother explaining to a waitress why her little girl will not drink her milk. "She wants her cup of stars," the mother says. "It has stars in the bottom, and she always drinks her milk from it at home. She calls it her cup of stars because she can see the stars while she drinks her milk."

Eleanor immediately turns this into herself: "Indeed yes, Eleanor thought; indeed, so do I; a cup of stars, of course." Like Narcissus himself, she is quite unable to deal with the outside world in any other way than as a reflection of her inner world. The weather in both places is always the same.

But leave Eleanor for the time being, making her way toward Hill House "which always waits at the end of the day." We'll beat her there, if that's okay with you.

I said that *The House Next Door* forms a provenance in its entirety; the provenance of Hill House is established in classic ghost-story fashion by Dr. Montague in just eleven pages.

The story is told (of course!) by the fire with drinks in hand. The salient points: Hill House was built by an unreconstructed Puritan named Hugh Crain. His young wife died moments before she would have seen Hill House for the first time. His second wife died of a fall—cause unknown. His two little girls remained in Hill House until the death of Crain's third wife (nothing there—that wife died in Europe), and were then sent to a cousin. They spent the rest of their lives quarreling over ownership of the mansion. Later, the older sister returns to Hill House with a companion, a young girl from the village.

The companion becomes particularly important because it is in her that Hill House seems most specifically to mirror Eleanor's own life. Eleanor too was a companion, during her mother's long terminal illness. Following the death of old Miss Crain, there are stories of neglect; "of a doctor called too late," Montague says, "of the old lady lying neglected upstairs while the younger woman dallied in the garden with some village lout . . ."

More bitter feeling followed the death of the old Miss Crain. There was a court case over ownership between the companion and the young Miss Crain. The companion finally wins . . . and shortly after commits suicide by hanging herself in the turret. Later tenants have been . . . well, uncomfortable in Hill House. We have hints that some have been more than uncomfortable; that some of them may actually have fled from Hill House, screaming in terror.

"Essentially," Montague says, "the evil is in the house itself, I think. It has enchained and destroyed its people and their lives, and it is a place of contained ill will." And the central question that *The Haunting of Hill House* poses for the reader is whether or not Montague is right. He prefaces his story with several classical references to what we've been calling the Bad Place—the Hebraic for haunted, as in haunted house, *tsaraas*, meaning "leprous"; Homer's phrase for it, *aidao domos*, meaning a house of Hades. "I need not remind you," Montague says, ". . . that the concept of certain houses as unclean or forbidden—perhaps sacred—is as old as the mind of man."

As in *The House Next Door,* the one thing we can be sure of is that there are no actual ghosts in Hill House. None of the four characters come upon the shade of the companion flapping up the hall with a rope burn around her ectoplasmic neck. This is well enough, however—Montague himself says that in all the records of psychic phenomena, one cannot find any case where a ghost actually hurt a person. What they do if they are malign, he suggests, is work on the mind.

One thing we do know about Hill House is that it is *all wrong.* It is no one thing we can put our finger on; it's everything. Stepping into Hill House is like stepping into the mind of a madman; it isn't long before you weird out yourself.

> No human eye can isolate the unhappy coincidence of line and place which suggests evil in the face of a house, and yet somehow a maniac juxtaposition, a badly turned angle, some chance meeting of roof and sky, turned Hill House into a place of despair. . . . The face of Hill House seemed awake, with a watchfulness from the blank windows and a touch of glee in the eyebrow of a cornice.

And even more chilling, more to the point:

> Eleanor shook herself, turning to see the room complete. It had an unbelievably faulty design which left it chillingly wrong in all its dimensions, so that the walls seemed always in one direction a fraction longer than the eye could endure, and in another direction a fraction less than the barest tolerable length; this is where they want me to *sleep,* Eleanor thought incredulously; what nightmares are waiting, shadowed, in those high corners—what breath of mindless fear will drift across my mouth . . . and shook herself again. *Really,* she told herself, *really,* Eleanor.

We see a horror story developing here that Lovecraft would have embraced enthusiastically, had he lived long enough to read it. It might even have taught the Old Providence Spook a thing or two. H.P.L. was struck by the horror of wrong geometry; he wrote frequently of non-Euclidian angles that tortured the eye and hurt the mind, and suggested other dimensions where the sum of a triangle's three corners might equal more or less than 180°. Contemplating such things, he suggested, might be enough in itself to drive a man crazy. Nor was he far wrong; we know from various psychological experiments that when you tamper with a man or woman's perspective on their physical world, you tamper with what may actually be the fulcrum of the human mind.

Other writers have dealt with this fascinating idea of perspective gone haywire; my own favorite is Joseph Payne Brennan's short story "Canavan's Back Yard," where an antiquarian bookdealer discovers that his weedy, ordinary backyard is much longer than it seems—it runs, in fact, all the way to the portholes of hell. In Charles L. Grant's *The Hour of the Oxrun Dead*, one of the main characters discovers he can no longer find the borders of the town where he has lived all his life. We see him crawling along the verge of the highway, looking for the way back in. Unsettling stuff.

But Jackson handled the concept better than anyone, I think—certainly better than Lovecraft, who understood it but apparently couldn't show it. Theo enters the bedroom she will share with Eleanor looking incredulously at a stained-glass window, a decorative urn, the pattern in the carpet. There is nothing wrong with these things taken one by one; it is just that when we add up the perceptual equivalent of their angles, we come out with a triangle where the sum of the corners equals a bit more (or a bit less) than 180°.

As Anne Rivers Siddons points out, everything in Hill House is skewed. There is nothing which is perfectly straight or perfectly level—which may be why doors keep swinging open or shut. And this idea of skew is important to Jackson's concept of the Bad Place because it heightens those feelings of altered perception. Being in Hill House is like tripping on a low-watt dosage of LSD, where everything seems strange and you feel you will begin to hallucinate at any time. But you never quite do. You just look incredulously at a stained-glass window . . . or a decorative urn . . . or the pattern on the carpet. Being in Hill House is like looking into one of those trick rooms where folks look big at one end and small at the other. Being in Hill House is like lying in bed in the dark on the night you went three drinks beyond your capacity . . . and feeling the bed begin to spin slowly around and around. . . .

Jackson suggests (always in her low, insinuating voice—this, along with *The Turn of the Screw*, may very well be where Peter Straub got the idea that the horror story works best when it is "ambiguous and low-key and restrained") these things quietly and rationally; she is never strident. It is just, she says, that being in Hill House does something fundamental and unpleasant to the screen of perception. This is what, she suggests, being in telepathic contact with a lunatic would be like.

Hill House is evil; we'll accept Montague's postulate. But how responsible is Hill House for the phenomena that follow? There are knockings in the night—huge thunderings, rather, which terrify both Theo and Eleanor. Luke and Professor Montague attempt to track down a barking dog and get lost within a stone's throw of the house—shades of Canavan the book-dealer (Brennan's story predates *The Haunting of Hill House)* and Charles Grant's strange little town of Oxrun, Connecticut. Theo's clothes are splattered with some foul red substance ("red paint," Eleanor says . . . but her terror suggests a more sinister substance) that later disappears. And written in the same red substance, first in the hall and then over the wardrobe where the ruined clothes have been hung are these words: COME HOME, ELEANOR . . . HELP ELEANOR COME HOME ELEANOR.

Here, in this writing, is where the lives of Eleanor and of this evil house, this Bad Place, become inextricably entwined. The house has singled her out. The house has chosen her . . . or is it the other way around? Either way, Eleanor's idea that "journeys end in lovers meeting" becomes ever more ominous.

Theo, who has some telepathic ability, begins to suspect

more and more that Eleanor herself is responsible for most of the manifestations. A land of low-key tension has built up between the two women, ostensibly over Luke, with whom Eleanor has begun to fall in love, but it probably springs more deeply from Theo's intuition that not everything which is happening in Hill House is *of* Hill House.

We know there has been an incident of telekinesis in Eleanor's past; at the age of twelve, stones fell from the ceilings "and pattered madly on the roof." She denies—hysterically denies—that she had anything at all to do with the incident of the stones, focusing instead on the embarrassment it caused her, the unwanted (she *says* it was unwanted, anyway) attention that it brought upon her. Her denials have an odd effect upon the reader, one of increasing weight in light of the fact that most of the afferent phenomena which the four of them experience in Hill House could be ascribed either to poltergeists or to telekinetic phenomena.

"They never even told me what was going on," Eleanor says urgently even after the conversation has moved on from the episode of the stones—no one is even really listening to her, but in the closed circle of her own narcissistic world, it seems to her that this strange, long-ago phenomenon must be all they can think of (as it is all she can think of—the outer weather must reflect the inner weather). "My mother said it was the neighbors, they were always against us because she wouldn't mix with them. My mother—"

Luke interrupts her to say, "I think all we want here is the facts." But for Eleanor, the facts of her own life are all she can cope with.

How responsible is Eleanor for the tragedy which ensues? Let's look again at the peculiar words the ghost-busters find written in the hall: HELP ELEANOR COME HOME ELEANOR. *The Haunting of Hill House*, submerged as it is in the twin ambiguities of Eleanor's personality and those of Hill House itself, becomes a novel that can be read in many different ways, a novel which suggests almost endless paths and a wide range of conclusions, HELP ELEANOR, for instance. If Eleanor herself is responsible for the writing, is she asking for help? If the house is responsible, is it asking her for help? Is Eleanor creating the ghost of her own mother? Is it mother who is calling for help? Or has Hill House probed Eleanor's mind and written something which will play on her gnawing sense of guilt? That long-ago companion whom Eleanor so resembles hanged herself after the house became hers, and guilt may well have been her motive. Is the house trying to do the same to Eleanor? In *The House Next Door*, this is exactly how the contemporary Kim Dougherty has built works on the minds of its tenants—probing for the weak points and preying on them. Hill House may be doing this alone . . . it may be doing it with Eleanor's help . . . or Eleanor may be doing it alone. The book is subtle, and the reader is left in large part to work these questions out to his or her own satisfaction.

What about the rest of the phrase—COME HOME ELEANOR? Again we may hear the voice of Eleanor's dead mother in this imperative, or the voice of her own central self, crying out against this new independence, this attempt to escape Park's "cloying authoritarianism" and into an exhilarating but existentially scary state of personal freedom. I see this as the most logical possibility. As Metrical tells us in Jackson's final novel that "we have always lived in the castle," so Eleanor Vance has always lived in her own closed and suffocating world. It is not Hill House which frightens her, we feel; Hill House is another closed and suffocating world, walled in, cupped by hills, secure behind locked gates when the dark of night has fallen. The real threat she seems to feel comes from Montague, even more from Luke, and most of all from Theo. "You've got foolishness and wickedness all mixed up," Theo tells Eleanor after Eleanor has voiced her unease at painting her toenails red like Theo's. She simply tosses the line off, but such an idea strikes very close to the basis of Eleanor's most closely held life concepts. These people pose to Eleanor the possibility of another way of life, one which is largely antiauthoritarian and antinarcissistic. Eleanor is attracted and yet repelled by the prospect—this is a woman who, at thirty-two, feels daring when buying two pairs of slacks, after all. And it is not very daring of me to suggest that COME HOME ELEANOR is an imperative Eleanor has delivered to herself; that she is Narcissus unable to leave the pool.

There is a third implication here, however, one which I find almost too horrifying to contemplate, and it is central to my own belief that this is one of the finest books ever to come out of the genre. Quite simply stated, COME HOME ELEANOR may be Hill House's invitation for Eleanor to join it. Journeys end in lovers meeting is Eleanor's phrase for it, and as her end approaches, this old children's rhyme occurs to her:

> Go in and out the windows,
> Go in and out the windows,
> Go in and out the windows,
> As we have done before.
>
> Go forth and face your lover,
> Go forth and face your lover,
> Go forth and face your lover,
> As we have done before.

Either way—Hill House or Eleanor as the central cause of the haunting—the ideas Park and Malin set forth hold up. Either Eleanor has succeeded, through her telekinetic ability, in turning Hill House into a giant mirror reflecting her own subconscious, or Hill House is a chameleon, able to convince her that she has finally found her place, her own cup of stars caught in these brooding hills.

I believe that Shirley Jackson would like us to come away from her novel with the ultimate belief that it was Hill House all along. That first paragraph suggests "outside evil" very strongly—a primitive force like that which inhabits Anne River Siddons's house next door, a force which is divorced from humankind. In Eleanor's end we may feel that there are three layers of "truth" here: Eleanor's belief that the house is haunted; Eleanor's belief that the house is her place, that it has just been waiting for someone like her, Eleanor's final realization that she has been used by a monstrous organism—that she has, in fact, been manipulated on the subconscious level into believing that she has been pulling the strings. But it has all been done with mirrors, as the magicians say, and poor Eleanor is murdered by the ultimate falsehood of her own reflection in the brick and stone and glass of Hill House:

> I am really doing it, she thought, turning the wheel to send the car directly at the great tree at the curve of the driveway. I am really doing it, I am doing this all by my-self, now, at last: this is me. I am really really really doing it by myself.
>
> In the unending, crashing second before the car hurled into the tree, she thought clearly, *Why* am I doing this? Why am I doing this? Why don't they stop me?

"I am doing this all by myself now, at last: this is me," Eleanor thinks—but of course it is impossible for her to believe otherwise in the context of the new American gothic. Her last thought before her death is not of Hill House, but of herself.

The novel ends with a reprise of the first paragraph, closing the loop and completing the circuit . . . and leaving us with an unpleasant surmise: if Hill House was not haunted before, it certainly is now. Jackson finishes by telling us that whatever walked in Hill House walked alone.

For Eleanor Vance, that would be business as usual.

4

A novel that makes a neat bridge away from the Bad Place (and perhaps it's time we got away from these haunted houses before we come down with a terminal case of the creeps) is Ira Levin's *Rosemary's Baby* (1967). I used to be fond of telling people, at the time Roman Polanski's film version came out, that it was one of those rare cases where if you had read the book you didn't have to see the movie, and if you had seen the movie, you didn't have to read the book.

That is not really the truth (it never is), but Polanski's film version is remarkably true to Levin's novel, and both seem to share an ironic turn of humor. I don't believe anyone else could have made Levin's remarkable little novel quite so well . . . and by the way, while it is remarkable for Hollywood to remain so faithful to a novel (one sometimes thinks that major movie companies pay staggering sums for books just so they can tell their authors all the parts of them that don't work—surely some of the most expensive ego-tripping in the history of American arts and letters), it is not remarkable in Levin's case. Every novel he has ever written* has been a marvel of plotting. He is the Swiss watchmaker of the suspense novel; in terms of plot, he makes what the rest of us do look like those five-dollar watches you can buy in the discount drugstores. This fact alone has made Levin almost invulnerable to the depredations of the story-changers, those subvertors who are more concerned with visual effect than with a coherent storyline. Levin's books are constructed as neatly as an elegant house of cards; pull one plot twist, and everything comes tumbling down. As a result, moviemakers have been pretty much forced to show us what Levin built.

About the film Levin himself says, "I've always felt that the film of *Rosemary's Baby* is the single most faithful adaptation of a novel ever to come out of Hollywood. Not only does it incorporate whole chunks of the book's dialogue, it even follows the colors of clothing (where I mentioned them) and the layout of the apartment. And perhaps more importantly, Polanski's directorial style of not aiming the camera squarely at the horror but rather letting the audience spot it for themselves off at the side of the screen coincides happily, I think, with my own writing style.

"There was a reason for his fidelity to the book, inciden-

---

* In case you're one of the five or six readers of popular fiction in America who has missed them, they are *A Kiss Before Dying, Rosemary's Baby, This Perfect Day, The Stepford Wives,* and *The Boys from Brazil.* He has written two Broadway plays, *Veronica's Room* and the immensely successful *Deathtrap.* Less known is a modest but chillingly effective made-for-TV movie called *Dr. Cook's Garden,* starring Bing Crosby in a wonderfully adroit performance.

tally. . . . His screenplay was the first adaptation he had written of someone else's material; his earlier films had all been originals. I think he didn't know it was permitted—nay, almost mandatory!—to make changes. I remember him calling me from Hollywood to ask in which issue of the *New Yorker* Guy had seen the shirt advertised. To my chagrin I had to admit I'd faked it; I had assumed any issue of the *New Yorker* would have a handsome shirt advertised in it. But the correct issue for the time of the scene didn't."

Levin has written two horror novels—*Rosemary's Baby* and *The Stepford Wives*—and while both shine with the exquisite plotting that is Levin's trademark, probably neither is quite as effective as his first book, which is unfortunately not much read these days. *A Kiss Before Dying* is a gritty suspense story told with great élan—rarity enough, but what is even more rare is that the book (written while Levin was in his early twenties) contains surprises which really surprise . . . and it is relatively impervious to that awful, dreadful goblin of a reader, he or she WHO TURNS TO THE LAST THREE PAGES TO SEE HOW IT CAME OUT.

Do you do this nasty, unworthy trick? Yes, you! I'm talking to you! Don't slink away and grin into your hand! Own up to it! Have you ever stood in a bookshop, glanced furtively around, and turned to the end of an Agatha Christie to see who did it, and how? Have you ever turned to the end of a horror novel to see if the hero made it out of the darkness and into the light? If you have ever done this, I have three simple words which I feel it is my duty to convey: SHAME ON YOU! It is low to mark your place in a book by folding down the corner of the page where you left off; TURNING TO THE END TO SEE HOW IT CAME OUT is even lower. If you have this habit, I urge you to break it . . . break it at once!*

Well, enough of this digression. All I intended to say about

---

* I have always wanted to publish a novel with the last thirty pages simply left out. The reader would be mailed these final pages by the publisher upon receipt of a satisfactory summary of everything that had happened in the story up to that point. That would certainly put a spoke in the wheels of those people who TURN TO THE END TO SEE HOW IT CAME OUT.

A Kiss Before Dying is that the book's biggest surprise—the real screeching bombshell—is neatly tucked away about one hundred pages into the story. If you should happen upon this moment while thumbing randomly through the book, it means nothing to you. If you have read everything faithfully up to that point, it means . . . everything. The only other writer I can think of offhand who had that wonderful ability to totally ambush the reader was the late Cornell Woolrich (who also wrote under the name of William Irish), but Woolrich did not have Levin's dry wit. Levin speaks affectionately of Woolrich as an influence on his own career, mentioning *Phantom Lady* and *The Bride Wore Black* as particular favorites.

Levin's wit is probably a better place to start with *Rosemary's Baby* than his ability to plot a story. His output of novels has been relatively small—it averages out to one every five years or so—but it's interesting to note that one of the five, *The Stepford Wives,* works best as outright satire (William Goldman, the novelist-screenwriter who adapted that book for the screen, knew it; you will remember that earlier on we mentioned "Oh Frank, you're the best, you're the champ"), almost as farce, and *Rosemary's Baby* is a kind of socioreligious satire. We might also mention *The Boys from Brazil,* Levin's most recent novel, when we speak of his wit. The title itself is a pun, and although the book deals (even if only peripherally) with subjects such as the German death camps and the so-called "scientific experiments" that were carried out there (some of the "scientific experiments," we will recall, included trying to impregnate women with the sperm of dogs and administering lethal doses of poison to identical twins in order to see if they would expire in a similar span of time), it vibrates with its own nervous wit and seems to parody those Martin-Bormann-is-alive-and-well-and-living-in-Paraguay books that are apparently going to be with us even unto the end of the world.

I am not suggesting that Ira Levin is either Jackie Vernon or George Orwell masquerading in a fright wig—nothing so simple or simplistic. I am suggesting that the books he has written achieve suspense without turning into humorless thudding tracts (two novels of the Humorless, Thudding Tract School of horror writing are *Damon,* by C. Terry Cline, and *The Exorcist,* by William Peter Blatty—Cline has since improved as a writer, and Blatty has fallen silent . . . forever, if we are lucky).

Levin is one of the few writers who has returned more than once to the field of horror and the supernatural and who seems unafraid of the fact that much of the material the genre deals with is utterly foolish—and at that, he has done better than many critics, who visit the genre the way rich white ladies once visited the children of New England factory slaves on Thanksgiving with food baskets and on Easter with chocolate eggs and bunnies. These slumming critics, unaware both of their own infuriating elitism and their total ignorance of what popular fiction does and what it is about, are able to see the foolishness spawned as a by-product of the bubbling potions, the pointy black hats, and all the other clanking huggermugger trappings of the supernatural tale, but are unable to see—or refuse to see—the strong and universal archetypes that underlie the best of them.

The foolishness is there, all right; this is Rosemary's first look at the child she has given birth to:

> His eyes were golden-yellow, all golden-yellow, with neither whites nor irises; all golden-yellow, with vertical black-slit pupils.
> She looked at him.
> He looked at her, golden-yellowly, and then at the swaying upside-down crucifix.
> She looked at them watching her and knife-in-hand screamed at them, *"What have you done to his eyes?"*
> They stirred and looked to Roman.
> "He has His Father's eyes," he said.

We have lived and suffered with Rosemary Woodhouse for two hundred and nine pages up to this point, and Roman Castevet's response to her question seems almost like the punchline of a long, involved shaggy-dog story—one of the ones that ends with something like, "My, that's a long way to tip a Rari," or "Rudolph the Red knows rain, dear." Besides yellow eyes, Rosemary's baby turns out to have claws ("They're very nice," Roman tells Rosemary, ". . . very tiny and pearly. The mitts are only so He doesn't scratch Himself . . ."), and a tail, and the buds of horns. While I was teaching the book at the University of Maine to an undergraduate class entitled Themes in Horror and the Supernatural, one of my students mused that ten years later Rosemary's baby would be the only kid on his Little League team who needed a custom-tailored baseball cap.

Basically, Rosemary has given birth to the comic-book version of Satan, the L'il Imp we were all familiar with as children and who sometimes put in an appearance in the motion picture cartoons, arguing with a L'il Angel over the main character's head. Levin broadens the satire by giving us a Satanist coven comprised almost entirely of old people; they argue constantly in their waspy voices about how the baby should be cared for. The fact that Laura-Louise and Minnie Castevet are much too old to care for a baby somehow adds the final macabre touch, and Rosemary's first tentative bonding to her baby comes when she tells Laura-Louise that she is rocking "Andy" much too fast, and that the wheels of his bassinette need to be oiled.

Levin's accomplishment is that such satire does not deflate the horror of his story but actually enhances it. *Rosemary's Baby* is a splendid confirmation of the idea that humor and horror lie side by side, and that to deny one is to deny the other. It is a fact Joseph Heller makes splendid use of in *Catch-22* and which Stanley Elkin used in *The Living End* (which might have been subtitled "Job in the Afterlife").

Besides satire, Levin laces his novel with veins of irony ("It's good for your blood, dearie," the Old Witch in the E. C. comics used to say). Early on, the Castevets invite Guy and Rosemary over for dinner; Rosemary accepts, on the condition that it won't be too much trouble.

"Honey, if it was trouble I wouldn't ask you," Mrs. Castevet said. "Believe me, I'm as selfish as the day is long."

Rosemary smiled. "That isn't what Terry told me," she said.

"Well," Mrs. Castevet said with a pleased smile, "Terry didn't know what she was talking about."

The irony is that everything Minnie Castevet says here is the literal truth; she really is as selfish as the day is long, and Terry—who ends up either being murdered or committing suicide when she discovers that she is to be or has been used as an incubator for Satan's child—really didn't know what she was talking about. But she found out. Oh yes. Heh-heh-heh.

My wife, raised in the Catholic church, claims that the book is also a religious comedy with its own shaggy-dog punchline. *Rosemary's Baby*, she claims, only proves what the Catholic church has said about mixed marriages all along—they just don't work. This particular bit of comedy grows richer, perhaps, when we add the fact of Levin's own Jewishness against the Christian backdrop of custom used by the Satanist coven. Seen in this light, the book becomes a kind of you-don't-have-to-be-Jewish-to-love-Levy's view of the battle of good and evil.

Before leaving the idea of religion and talking a bit about the feelings of paranoia which really seem to lie central to the book, let me suggest that while Levin's tongue is in his cheek part of the time, that is no reason for us to expect it to be there all of the time. *Rosemary's Baby* was written and published at the time the God-is-dead tempest was whirling around in the teapot of the sixties, and the book deals with questions of faith in an unpretentious but thoughtful and intriguing way.

We might say that the major theme of *Rosemary's Baby* deals with urban paranoia (as opposed to the small-town or rural paranoia we will see in Jack Finney's *The Body Snatchers*), but that an important minor theme could be stated along these lines: The weakening of religious conviction is an opening wedge for the devil, both in the macrocosm (questions of world faith) and in the microcosm (the cycle of Rosemary's faith as she goes from belief as Rosemary Reilly, to unbelief as Rosemary Woodhouse, to belief again as the mother of her infernal Child). I'm not suggesting that Ira Levin believes this Puritanical thesis—although he may, for all I know. I am suggesting, however, that it makes a nice fulcrum on which to turn his plot, and that he plays fair with the idea and explores most of its implications. In the religious pilgrim's progress that Rosemary goes through, Levin gives us a seriocomic allegory of faith.

Rosemary and Guy begin as typical young marrieds; Rosemary is practicing birth control as a matter of course in spite of her rigid Catholic upbringing, and both of them have decided they will have children only when they—not God—decide they are ready. After Terry's suicide (or was it murder?), Rosemary has a dream in which she is being scolded by an old parochial school teacher, Sister Agnes, for bricking up the school windows and getting them disqualified from a beautiful-school contest. But mingling with the dream are real voices from the Castevet apartment next door, and it is Minnie Castevet, speaking through the mouth of Sister Agnes in Rosemary's dream, that we are listening to:

> "Anybody! Anybody!" Sister Agnes said. "All she has to
> be is young, healthy, and not a virgin. She doesn't have to
> be a no-good drug-addict whore out of the gutter. Didn't I
> say that in the beginning? Anybody. As long as she's young
> and healthy and not a virgin."

This dream sequence does several useful things. It amuses us in a nervous, edgy sort of way; it lets us in on the fact that the Castevets were in some way involved in the death of Terry; it allows us to see shoaling waters ahead for Rosemary. Perhaps this is stuff that only interests another writer—it's more like two mechanics inspecting a nifty four-barrel carburetor than it is like classical analysis—but Levin does his job so unobtrusively that maybe it doesn't hurt for me to take the pointer and say, "Here! This is where he's starting to get close to you; this is the point of entry, and now he will begin working inward toward your heart."

Yet the most significant thing about the passage is that Rosemary has woven a dream of Catholic intent around the words her lightly sleeping mind has overheard. She casts Minnie Castevet as a nun . . . and so she is, although she is a nun of a rather blacker persuasion than that long-ago Sister Agnes. My wife also says that one of the basic tenets of the Catholic church she grew up with was, "Give us your children and they will be ours forever." The shoe fits here, and Rosemary wears it. And ironically enough, it is the superficial weakening of her faith which allows the devil a doorway into her life . . . but it is the immutable bedrock of that same faith that allows her to accept "Andy," horns and all.

This is Levin's handling of religious views in the microcosm—on the surface, Rosemary is a typical young modern who could have stepped whole and breathing from Wallace Stevens's poem "Sunday Morning"—the church bells mean nothing to her as she sits peeling her oranges. But beneath, that parochial schoolgirl Rosemary Reilly is very much there.

His handling of the macrocosm is similar—just bigger.

At the dinner party the Castevets have for the Woodhouses, conversation turns to the impending visit of the Pope to New York. "I tried to keep the book's unbelievabilities believable," Levin remarks, "by incorporating bits of 'real life' happenings along the way. I kept stacks of newspapers, and writing about a month or two after the fact, worked in events such as the transit strike and Lindsay's election as mayor. When, having decided for obvious reasons that the baby should be born on June 25th, I checked back to see what had been happening on the night Rosemary would have to conceive, you know what I found: the Pope's visit, and the Mass on television. Talk about serendipity! From then on I felt the book was Meant To Be."

The conversation between Guy Woodhouse and the Castevets concerning the Pope seems predictable, even banal, but it expresses the very view which Levin gently suggests is responsible for the whole thing:

> "I heard on TV that he's going to postpone and wait until (the newspaper strike) is over," Mrs. Castevet said.
>
> Guy smiled. "Well," he said, "that's show biz."
>
> Mr. and Mrs. Castevet laughed, and Guy along with them. Rosemary smiled and cut her steak. . . .
>
> Still laughing, Mr. Castevet said, "It *is*, you know: That's *just* what it is: show biz!"
>
> "You can say *that* again," Guy said.
>
> "The costumes, the rituals," Mr. Castevet said; "every religion, not only Catholicism. Pageants for the ignorant."
>
> Mrs. Castevet said, "I think we're offending Rosemary."
>
> "No, not at all," Rosemary said.
>
> "You aren't religious, my dear, are you?" Mr. Castevet asked.
>
> "I was brought up to be," Rosemary said, "but now I'm an agnostic. I wasn't offended. Really I wasn't."

We don't doubt the truth of Rosemary Woodhouse's statement, but underneath that surface there is a little parochial schoolgirl named Rosemary Reilly who is *very* offended, and who probably regards such talk as blasphemy.

The Castevets are conducting a bizarre sort of job interview here, testing Rosemary and Guy for the depth and direction of their commitments and beliefs; they are revealing their own contempt for the church and things sacred; but, Levin suggests, they are also expressing views which are commonly held . . . and not just by Satanists.

Yet faith must exist beneath, he suggests; it is the surface weakening that allows the devil in, but beneath, even the Castevets are in vital need of Christianity, because without the sacred there is no profane. The Castevets seem to sense Rosemary Reilly existing beneath Rosemary Woodhouse, and it is her husband, Guy, an authentic pagan, that they use as a go-between. And Guy lowers himself admirably to the occasion.

We are not allowed to doubt that it is the softening of Rosemary's faith that has given the devil a door into her life. Her sister Margaret, a good Catholic, calls Rosemary long distance not long after the Castevets' plot has begun to move. "I've had the funniest feeling all day long, Rosemary. That something happened to you. Like an accident or something."

Rosemary isn't favored with such a premonition (the closest she gets is her dream of Sister Agnes speaking in Minnie Castevet's voice) because she isn't worthy of it. Good Catholics, Levin says—and we may not sense his tongue creeping back into his cheek—get the good premonitions.

The religious motif stretches through the book, and Levin does some clever things with it, but perhaps we could close off our discussion of it with some thoughts about Rosemary's remarkable "conception dream." First, it is significant that the time chosen for the devil to impregnate Rosemary coincides with the Pope's visit. Rosemary's mousse is drugged, but she eats only a little of it. As a result, she has a dreamlike memory of her sexual encounter with the devil, but it is one her subconscious couches in symbolic terms. Reality flickers in and out as Guy prepares her for her confrontation with Satan.

In her dream, Rosemary finds herself on a yacht with the assassinated President Kennedy. Jackie Kennedy, Pat Lawford, and Sarah Churchill are also in attendance. Rosemary asks JFK if her good friend Hutch (who becomes Rosemary's protector until he is struck down by the coven; he is the one who warns Rosemary and Guy early on that the Bramford is a Bad Place) is coming; Kennedy smiles and tells her the cruise is "for Catholics only." This is one qualification Minnie has not mentioned earlier, but it helps confirm the idea that the person the coven is really interested in is Rosemary Reilly. Again, it seems to be the blasphemy that they are mostly concerned with; the spiritual lineage of Christ must be perverted to allow them to accomplish a successful birth.

Guy removes Rosemary's wedding ring, symbolically ending

their marriage, but also becoming a kind of best-man-in-reverse; Rosemary's friend Hutch comes with weather warnings (and what is a hutch anyway but a safe place for rabbits?). During intercourse, Guy actually becomes the devil, and closing the dream out we see Terry again, this time not as a failed bride of Satan but as a sacrificial opener of the way.

In less expert hands such a dream scene might have become tiresome and didactic, but Levin carries it off lightly and quickly, compressing the entire sequence into just five pages.

But the strongest watchspring of *Rosemary's Baby* isn't the religious subtheme but the book's use of urban paranoia. The conflict between Rosemary Reilly and Rosemary Woodhouse enriches the story, but if the book achieves horror—and I think it does—it does so because Levin is able to play upon these innate feelings of paranoia so skillfully.

Horror is a groping for pressure points, and where are we any more vulnerable than in our feelings of paranoia? In many ways, *Rosemary's Baby* is like a sinister Woody Allen film, and the Woodhouse/Reilly dichotomy is useful here, too. Besides being a Catholic forever beneath her agnostic veneer, Rosemary is, beneath her carefully acquired cosmopolitan varnish, a small-town girl . . . and you can take the girl out of the country, but et cetera, et cetera.

There is a saying—and I would be happy to attribute it if I could remember who to attribute it to—that perfect paranoia is perfect awareness. In a crazy sort of way, Rosemary's story is of a coming to that sort of awareness. We become paranoid before she does (Minnie, for instance, being purposely slow with the dishes so Roman can talk to Guy—or make him a pitch—in the other room), but following her dreamlike encounter with the devil and her subsequent pregnancy, her own paranoia follows along. When she wakes up the next morning, she finds scratches—as if from claws—all over her body. "Don't yell," Guy says, showing her his fingernails; "I already filed them down."

Before long, Minnie and Roman have begun a campaign to get Rosemary to use their obstetrician—the famous Abe

Sapirstein—instead of the young guy she had been going to. *Don't do that, Rosemary,* we want to tell her; *he's one of* them.

Modern psychiatry teaches that there is no difference between us and the paranoid-schizophrenic in Bedlam except that we somehow manage to keep our crazier suspicions under control while theirs have slipped their tethers; a story like *Rosemary's Baby* or Finney's *The Body Snatchers* seems to confirm the idea. We have discussed the horror story as a tale which derives its effect from our terror of things which depart the norm; we have looked at it as a taboo land which we enter with fear and trembling, and also as a Dionysian force which may invade our comfy Apollonian status quo without warning. Maybe all horror stories are really about disorder and the fear of change, and in *Rosemary's Baby* we have the feeling that everything is beginning to bulge at once—we can't see all the changes, but we sense them. Our dread for Rosemary springs from the fact that she seems the only normal person in a whole city of dangerous maniacs.

Before we have reached the midpoint of Levin's tale, we suspect *everybody*—and in nine cases out of ten we have been right to do so. We are allowed to indulge our paranoia on Rosemary's behalf to the utmost, and all our nightmares come true. On my first reading of the book, I remember even suspecting Dr. Hill, the nice young obstetrician Rosemary has given up in favor of Dr. Sapirstein. Of course, Hill is not a Satanist . . . he just gives Rosemary back to them when she comes to him for protection.

If horror novels do serve as catharsis for more mundane fears, then Levin's *Rosemary's Baby* seems to reflect back and effectively use the city dweller's very real feelings of urban paranoia. In this book there really are no nice people next door, and the worst things you ever imagined about that dotty old lady down in 9-B turn out to be true. The real victory of the book is that it allows us to be crazy for a while.

5

From urban paranoia to small-town paranoia: Jack Finney's *The Body Snatchers*.* Finney himself has the following things to say about his book, which was orginally published as a Dell paperback original in 1955:

"The book . . . was written in the early 1950s, and I don't really remember a lot about it. I do recall that I simply felt in the mood to write something about a strange event or a series of them in a small town; something inexplicable. And that my first thought was that a dog would be injured or killed by a car, and it would be discovered that a part of the animal's skeleton was of stainless steel; bone and steel intermingled, that is, a thread of steel running into bone and bone into steel so that it was clear the two had grown together. But this idea led to nothing in my mind. . . . I remember that I wrote the first chapter—pretty much as it appeared, if I am recalling correctly—in which people complained that someone close to them was in actuality an imposter. But I didn't know where this was to lead, either. However, during the course of fooling around with this, trying to make it work out, I came across a reputable scientific theory that objects might in fact be pushed through space by the pressure of light, and that dormant life of some sort might conceivably drift through space . . . and [this] eventually worked the book out.

"I was never satisfied with my own explanation of how these dry leaflike objects came to resemble the people they imitated; it seemed, and seems, weak, but it was the best I could do.

"I have read explanations of the 'meaning' of this story, which amuse me, because there is no meaning at all; it was just a story meant to entertain, and with no more meaning than that. The first movie version of the book followed the book

---

* As previously noted, the late-seventies remake of the Finney novel resets the story in San Francisco, opting for an urban paranoia which results in a number of sequences strikingly like those which open Polanski's film version of *Rosemary's Baby*. But Philip Kaufman lost more than he gained, I think, by taking Finney's story out of its natural small-town-with-a-bandstand-in-the-park setting.

with great faithfulness, except for the foolish ending; and I've always been amused by the contentions of people connected with the picture that they had a message of some sort in mind. If so, it's a lot more than I ever did, and since they followed my story very closely, it's hard to see how this message crept in. And when the message has been defined, it has always sounded a little simple-minded to me. The idea of writing a whole book in order to say that it's not really a good thing for us all to be alike, and that individuality is a good thing, makes me laugh."

Nevertheless, Jack Finney has written a great deal of fiction about the idea that individuality is a good thing and that conformity can start to get pretty scary after it passes a certain point.

His comments (in a letter to me dated December 24, 1979) about the first film version of *The Body Snatchers* raised a grin on my own face as well. As Pauline Kael, Penelope Gillian, and all of those sober-sided film critics so often prove, no one is so humorless as a big-time film critic or so apt to read deep meanings into simple doings ("In *The Fury*," Pauline Kael intoned, apparently in all seriousness, "Brian De Palma has found the junk heart of America.")—it is as if these critics feel it necessary to prove and re-prove their own literacy; they are like teenage boys who feel obliged to demonstrate and redemonstrate their macho . . . perhaps most of all to themselves. This may be because they are working on the fringes of a field which deals entirely with pictures and the spoken word; they must surely be aware that while it requires at least a high school education to understand and appreciate all the facets of even such an accessible book as *The Body Snatchers,* any illiterate with four dollars in his or her pocket can go to a movie and find the junk heart of America. Movies are merely picture books that talk, and this seems to have left many literate movie critics with acute feelings of inferiority. Filmmakers themselves are often happy to participate in this grotesque critical overkill, and I applauded Sam Peckinpah in my heart when he made this laconic reply to a critic who asked him why he had *really* made such a violent picture as *The Wild Bunch:* "I like shoot-em-ups." Or so he was reputed to have said, and if it ain't true, gang, it oughtta be.

The Don Siegel version of *The Body Snatchers* is an amusing case where the film critics tried to have it both ways. They began by saying that both Finney's novel and Siegel's film were allegories about the witch-hunt atmosphere that accompanied the McCarthy hearings. Then Siegel himself spoke up and said that this film was really about the Red Menace. He did not go so far as to say that there was a Commie under every American's bed, but there can be little doubt that Siegel at least believed he was making a movie about a creeping fifth column. It is the ultimate in paranoia, we might say: they're there *and they look just like us!*

In the end it's Finney who comes away sounding the most right; *The Body Snatchers* is just a good story, one to be read and savored for its own unique satisfactions. In the quarter-century since its original publication as a humble paperback original (a shorter version appeared in *Collier's,* one of those good old magazines that fell by the wayside in order to make space on the newsstands of America for such intellectual publications as *Hustler, Screw,* and *Big Butts*), the book has been rarely out of print. It reached its nadir as a Fotonovel in the wake of the Philip Kaufman remake; if there is a lower, slimier, more antibook concept than the Fotonovel, I don't know what it would be. I think I'd rather see my kids reading a stack of Beeline Books than one of those photo-comics.

It reached its zenith as a Gregg Press hardcover in 1976. Gregg Press is a small company which has re-issued some fifty or sixty science fiction and fantasy books—novels, collections, and anthologies—originally published as paperbacks, in hardcover. The editors of the Gregg series (David Hartwell and L. W. Currey) have chosen wisely and well, and in the library of any reader who cares honestly about science fiction—and about books themselves as lovely artifacts—you're apt to find one or more of these distinctive green volumes with the red-gold stamping on the spines.

Oh dear God, we're off on another tangent. Well, never

mind; I believe that what I started to say was simply that I think Finney's contention that *The Body Snatchers* is just a story is both right and wrong. My own belief about fiction, long and deeply held, is that story *must* be paramount over all other considerations in fiction; that story *defines* fiction, and that all other considerations—theme, mood, tone, symbol, style, even characterization—are expendable. There are critics who take the strongest possible exception to this view of fiction, and I really believe that they are the critics who would feel vastly more comfortable if *Moby Dick* were a doctoral thesis on cetology rather than an account of what happened on the *Pequod's* final voyage. A doctoral thesis is what a million student papers have reduced this tale to, but the story still remains—"This is what happened to Ishmael." As story still remains in *Macbeth, The Faerie Queen, Pride and Prejudice, Jude the Obscure, The Great Gatsby* . . . and Jack Finney's *The Body Snatchers*. And story, thank God, after a certain point becomes irreducible, mysterious, impervious to analysis. You will find no English master's thesis in any college library titled "The Story-Elements of Melville's *Moby Dick*." And if you do find such a thesis, send it to me. I'll eat it. With A-l Steak Sauce.

All very fine. And yet I don't think Finney would argue with the idea that story values are determined by the mind through which they are filtered, and that the mind of any writer is a product of his outer world and inner temper. It is just the fact of this filter that has set the table for all those would-be English M.A.'s, and I certainly would not want you to think that I begrudge them their degrees—God knows that as an English major I slung enough bullshit to fertilize most of east Texas—but a great number of the people who are sitting at the long and groaning table of Graduate Studies in English are cutting a lot of invisible steaks and roasts . . . not to mention trading the Emperor's new clothes briskly back and forth in what may be the largest academic yard sale the world has ever seen.

Still, what we have here is a Jack Finney novel, and we can say certain things about it simply because it is a Jack Finney novel. First, we can say that it will be grounded in absolute reality—a prosy reality that is almost humdrum, at least to begin with. When we first meet the book's hero (and here I think Finney probably would object if I used the more formal word *protagonist* . . . so I won't), Dr. Miles Bennell, he is letting his last patient of the day out; a sprained thumb. Becky Driscoll enters—and how is that for the perfect all-American name?—with the first off-key note: her cousin Wilma has somehow gotten the idea that her Uncle Ira really isn't her uncle anymore. But this note is faint and barely audible under the simple melodies of small-town life that Finney plays so well in the book's opening chapters . . . and Finney's rendering of the small-town archetype in this book may be the best to come out of the 1950s.

The keynote that Finney sounds again and again in these first few chapters is so low-key pleasant that in less sure hands it would become insipid: nice. Again and again Finney returns to that word; things in Santa Mira, he tells us, are not great, not wild and crazy, not terrible, not boring. Things in Santa Mira are nice. No one here is laboring under that old Chinese curse "May you live in interesting times."

"For the first time I really saw her face again. I saw it was the same nice face . . ." This from page nine. A few pages later: "It was nice out, temperature around sixty-five, and the light was good; . . . still plenty of sun."

Cousin Wilma is also nice, if rather plain. Miles thinks she would have made a good wife and mother, but she just never married. "That's how it goes," Miles philosophizes, innocently unaware of any banality. He tells us he wouldn't have believed her the type of woman to have mental problems, "but still, you never know."

This stuff shouldn't work, and yet somehow it does; we feel that Miles has somehow stepped through the first-person convention and is actually talking to us, just as it seems that Tom Sawyer is actually talking to us in the Twain novel . . . and Santa Mira, California, as Finney presents it to us, is exactly the sort of town where we would almost expect to see

Tom whitewashing a fence (there would be no Huck around, sleeping in a hogshead, though; not in Santa Mira).

The Body Snatchers is the only Finney book which can rightly be called a horror novel, but Santa Mira—which is a typical "nice" Finney setting—is the perfect locale for such a tale. Perhaps one horror novel is all that Finney had to write; certainly it was enough to set the mold for what we now call "the modern horror novel." If there is such a thing, there can be no doubt at all that Finney had a large hand in inventing it. I have used the phrase "off-key note" earlier on, and that is Finney's actual method in *The Body Snatchers*, I think; one off-key note, then two, then a ripple, then a run of them. Finally the jagged, discordant music of horror overwhelms the melody entirely. But Finney understands that there is no horror without beauty; no discord without a prior sense of melody; no nasty without nice.

There are no Plains of Leng here; no Cyclopean ruins under the earth; no shambling monsters in the subway tunnels under New York. At about the same time Jack Finney was writing *The Body Snatchers*, Richard Matheson was writing his classic short story "Born of Man and Woman," the story that begins: "today my mother called me retch, you retch she said." Between the two of them, they made the break from the Lovecraftian fantasy that had held sway over serious American writers of horror for two decades or more. Matheson's short story was published well before *Weird Tales* went broke; Finney's novel was published by Dell a year after. Although Matheson published two early short stories in *Weird Tales*, neither writer is associated with this icon of American fantasy-horror magazines; they represent the birth of an almost entirely new breed of American fantasist, just as, in the years 1977–1980, the emergence of Ramsey Campbell and Robert Aickman in England may represent another significant turn of the wheel.*

---

* At the same time Finney and Matheson began administering their own particular brands of shock treatment to the American imagination, Ray Bradbury began to be noticed in the fantasy community, and during the fifties and sixties, Bradbury's name would become the one most readily identified with the genre in the mind of the general reading public. But for

I have mentioned that Finney's short story "The Third Level" predates Rod Selling's *The Twilight Zone* series; in exactly the same fashion, Finney's little town of Santa Mira predates and points the way toward Peter Straub's fictional town of Milburn, New York; Thomas Tryon's Cornwall Coombe, Connecticut; and my own little town of 'Salem's Lot, Maine. It is even possible to see Finney's influence in Blatty's *The Exorcist,* where foul doings become fouler when set against the backdrop of Georgetown, a suburb which is quiet, graciously rich . . . and nice.

Finney concentrates on sewing a seam between the prosaic reality of his little you-can-see-it-before-your-eyes town and the outright fantasy of the pods which will follow. He sews the seam with such fine stitchwork that when we cross over from the world that really is and into a world of utter make-believe, we are hardly aware of any change. This is a major feat, and like the magician who can make the cards walk effortlessly over the tips of his fingers in apparent defiance of gravity, it looks so easy that you'd be tempted to believe anyone could do it. You see the trick, but not the long hours of practice that went into creating the effect.

We have spoken briefly of paranoia in *Rosemary's Baby;* in *The Body Snatchers,* the paranoia becomes full, rounded, and complete. If we are all incipient paranoids—if we all take a quick glance down at ourselves when laughter erupts at the cocktail party, just to make sure we're zipped up and it isn't us they're laughing at—then I'd suggest that Finney uses this incipient paranoia quite deliberately to manipulate our emotions in favor of Miles, Becky, and Miles's friends, the Belicecs.

Wilma, for instance, can present no proof that her Uncle Ira is no longer her Uncle Ira, but she impresses us with her strong conviction and with a deep, free-floating anxiety as pervasive as a migraine headache. Here is a kind of paranoid dream, as

---

me, Bradbury lives and works alone in his own country, and his remarkable, iconoclastic style has never been successfully imitated. Vulgarly put, when God made Ray Bradbury He broke the mold.

seamless and as perfect as anything out of a Paul Bowles novel
or a Joyce Carol Oates tale of the uncanny:

> Wilma sat staring at me, eyes intense. "I've been wait-
> ing for today," she whispered. "Waiting till he'd get a hair-
> cut, and he finally did." Again she leaned toward me, eyes
> big, her voice a hissing whisper. "There's a little scar on
> the back of Ira's neck; he had a boil there once, and your
> father lanced it. You can't see the scar," she whispered,
> "when he needs a haircut. But when his neck is shaved,
> you can. Well, today—I've been waiting for this!—today
> he got a haircut—"
> I sat forward, suddenly excited. "And the scar's *gone?*
> You mean—"
> "No!" she said, almost indignantly, eyes flashing. "It's
> *there*—the scar—exactly like Uncle Ira's!"

So Finney serves notice that we are working here in a world
of utter subjectivity . . . and utter paranoia. Of course *we* believe Wilma at once, even though we have no real proof; if for
no other reason, we know from the title of the book that the
"body snatchers" are out there somewhere.

By putting us on Wilma's side from the start, Finney has
turned us into equivalents of John the Baptist, crying in the
wilderness. It is easy enough to see why the book was eagerly
seized upon by those who felt, in the early fifties, that there was
either a Communist conspiracy afoot, or perhaps a fascist conspiracy that was operating in the name of anti-Communism.
Because, either way or neither way, this is a book about conspiracy with strong paranoid overtones . . . in other words, exactly
the sort of story to be claimed as political allegory by political
loonies of every stripe.

Earlier on, I mentioned the idea that perfect paranoia is perfect awareness. To that we could add that paranoia may be the
last defense of the overstrained mind. Much of the literature
of the twentieth century, from such diverse sources as Bertolt
Brecht, Jean-Paul Sartre, Edward Albee, Thomas Hardy, even

F. Scott Fitzgerald, has suggested that we live in an existential sort of world, a planless insane asylum where things just happen. IS GOD DEAD? asks the *Time* magazine cover in the waiting room of Rosemary Woodhouse's Satanic obstetrician. In such a world it is perfectly credible that a mental defective should sit on the upper floor of a little-used building, wearing a Hanes T-shirt, eating take-out chicken, and waiting to use his mail-order rifle to blow out the brains of an American president; perfectly possible that another mental defective should be able to stand around in a hotel kitchen a few years later waiting to do exactly the same thing to that defunct president's younger brother; perfectly understandable that nice American boys from Iowa and California and Delaware should have spent their tours in Vietnam collecting ears, many of them extremely tiny; that the world should begin to move once more toward the brink of an apocalyptic war because of the preachings of an eighty-year-old Moslem holy man who is probably foggy on what he had for breakfast by the time sunset rolls around.

All of these things are mentally acceptable if we accept the idea that God has abdicated for a long vacation, or has perchance really expired. They are mentally acceptable, but our emotions, our spirits, and most of all our passion for order—these powerful elements of our human makeup—all rebel. If we suggest that there was no reason for the deaths of six million Jews in the camps during World War II, no reason for poets bludgeoned, old women raped, children turned into soap, that it just happened and nobody was really responsible—things just got a little out of control here, ha-ha, so sorry—then the mind begins to totter.

I saw this happen at first-hand in the sixties, at the height of the generational shudder that began with our involvement in Vietnam and went on to encompass everything from parietal hours on college campuses and the voting franchise at eighteen to corporate responsibility for environmental pollution.

I was in college at the time, attending the University of Maine, and while I began college with political leanings too far to the right to actually become radicalized, by 1968 my mind had been changed forever about a number of fundamental questions. The hero of Jack Finney's later novel, *Time and Again,* says it better than I could:

> I was ... an ordinary person who long after he was grown retained the childhood assumption that the people who largely control our lives are somehow better informed than, and have judgment superior to, the rest of us; that they are more intelligent. Not until Vietnam did I finally realize that some of the most important decisions of all time can be made by men knowing really no more than most of the rest of us."

For me, it was a nearly overwhelming discovery—one that really began to happen, perhaps, on that day in the Stratford Theater when the announcement that the Russians had orbited a space satellite was made to me and my contemporaries by a theater manager who looked like he had been gutshot at close range.

But for all of that, I found it impossible to embrace the mushrooming paranoia of the last four years of the sixties completely. In 1968, during my junior year at college, three Black Panthers from Boston came to my school and talked (under the auspices of the Public Lecture Series) about how the American business establishment, mostly under the guidance of the Rockefellers and AT&T, was responsible for creating the neofascist political state of Amerika, encouraging the war in Vietnam because it was good for business, and also encouraging an ever more virulent climate of racism, stateism, and sexism. Johnson was their puppet; Humphrey and Nixon were also their puppets; it was a case of "meet the new boss, same as the old boss," as the Who would say a year or two later; the only solution was to take it into the streets. They finished with the Panther slogan, "all power comes out of the barrel of a gun," and adjured us to remember Fred Hampton.

Now, I did not and do not believe that the hands of the Rockefellers were utterly clean during that period, nor those of AT&T; I did and do believe that companies like Sikorsky and Douglas Aircraft and Dow Chemical and even the Bank of America subscribed more or less to the idea that war is good business (but never invest your son as long as you can slug the draft board in favor of the right kind of people; when at all possible, feed the war machine the spies and the niggers and the poor white trash from Appalachia, but not our boys, oh no, never *our* boys!); I did and do believe that the death of Fred Hampton was a case of police manslaughter at the very least. But these Black Panthers were suggesting a huge umbrella of conscious conspiracy that was laughable ... except the audience wasn't laughing. During the Q-and-A period, they were asking sober, concerned questions about just how the conspiracy was working, who was in charge, how they got their orders out, et cetera.

Finally I got up and said something like, "Are you really suggesting that there is an actual Board of Fascist Conspiracy in this country? That the conspirators—the presidents of GM and Esso, plus David and Nelson Rockefeller—are maybe meeting in a big underground chamber beneath the Bonneville Salt Flats with agendas containing items on how more blacks can be drafted and the war in Southeast Asia prolonged?" I was finishing with the suggestion that perhaps these executives were arriving at their underground fortress in flying saucers—thus handily accounting for the upswing in UFO sightings as well as for the war in Vietnam—when the audience began to shout angrily for me to sit down and shut up. Which I did posthaste, blushing furiously, knowing how those eccentrics who mount their soapboxes in Hyde Park on Sunday afternoons must feel. I did not much relish the feeling.

The Panther who spoke did not respond to my question (which, to be fair, wasn't a question at all, really); he merely said softly, "*You* got a surprise, didn't you, man?" This was greeted with a burst of applause and laughter from the audience.

I *did* get a surprise—and a pretty unpleasant one, at that. But some thought has convinced me that it was impossible for those of my generation, propelled harum-scarum through the sixties, hair flying back from our foreheads, eyes bugging out with a mixture of delight and terror, from the Kingsmen doing "Louie Louie" to the blasting fuzztones of the Jefferson Airplane, to get from point A to point Z without a belief that someone—even Nelson Rockefeller—was pulling the strings.

In various ways throughout this book I've tried to suggest that the horror story is in many ways an optimistic, upbeat experience; that it is often the tough mind's way of coping with terrible problems which may not be supernatural at all but perfectly real. Paranoia may be the last and strongest bastion of such an optimistic view—it is the mind crying out, "*Something rational and understandable is going on here! These things do not just happen!*"

So we look at a shadow and say there was a man on the grassy knoll at Dallas; we say that James Earl Ray was in the pay of certain big Southern business interests, or maybe the CIA; we ignore the fact that American business interests exist in complex circles of power, often revolving in direct opposition to one another, and suggest that our stupid but mostly well-meant involvement in Vietnam was a conspiracy hatched by the military-industrial complex; or that, as a recent rash of badly spelled and printed posters in New York suggested, that the Ayatollah Khomeini is a puppet of—yeah, you guessed it—David Rockefeller. We suggest, in our endless inventiveness, that Captain Mantell did not die of oxygen starvation back there in 1947 while chasing that odd daytime reflection of Venus which veteran pilots call a sundog; no, he was chasing a ship from another world which exploded his plane with a death ray when he got too close.

It would be wrong of me to leave you with any impression that I am inviting the two of us to have a good laugh at these things together; I am not. These things are not the beliefs of madmen but the beliefs of sane men and women trying desperately, not to preserve the status quo, but just to find the fucking thing. Add when Becky Driscoll's cousin Wilma says her Uncle Ira isn't her Uncle Ira, we believe her instinctively and immediately. If we don't believe her, all we've got is a spinster going quietly dotty in a small California town. The idea does not appeal; in a sane world, nice middle-aged ladies like Wilma aren't s'posed to go bonkers. It isn't right. There's a whisper of chaos in it that's somehow more scary than believing she might be right about Uncle Ira. We believe because belief affirms the lady's sanity. We believe her because . . . because . . . *because something is going on*! All those paranoid fantasies are really not fantasies at all. We—and Cousin Wilma—are right; it's the *world* that's gone haywire. The idea that the world has gone haywire is pretty bad, but as we can cope with Bill Nolan's fifty-foot bug once we see what it really is, so we can cope with a haywire world if we just know where our feet are planted. Bob Dylan speaks to the existentialist in us when he tells us that "Something is going on here/But you don't know what it is/Do you, Mr. Jones?" Finney—in the guise of Miles Bennell—takes us firmly by the arm and tells us that he knows exactly what's going on here: it's those goddamn pods from space! *They're* responsible!

It's fun to trace the classic threads of paranoia Finney weaves into his story. While Miles and Becky are at a movie, Miles's writer friend Jack Belicec asks Miles to come and take a look at something he's found in his basement. The something turns out to be the body of a naked man on a pool table, a body which seems to Miles, Becky, Jack, and Jack's wife, Theodora, somehow unformed—not yet quite shaped. It's a pod, of course, and the shape it is taking is Jack's own. Shortly we have concrete proof that something is terribly wrong:

> Becky actually moaned when we saw the [finger] prints, and I think we all felt sick. Because it's one thing to speculate about a body that's never been alive, a blank. But it's something very different, something that touches whatever is primitive deep in your brain, to have that

speculation proved. There were no prints; there were five absolutely smooth, solidly black circles.

These four—now aware of the pod conspiracy—agree not to call the police immediately but to see how the pods develop. Miles takes Becky home and then goes home himself, leaving the Belicecs to stand watch over the thing on the pool table. But in the middle of the night Theodora Belicec freaks out and the two of them show up on Miles's doorstep. Miles calls a psychiatrist friend, Mannie Kaufman (a shrink? we are immediately suspicious; we don't need a shrink here, we want to shout at Miles; call out the Army!), to come and sit with the Belicecs white he goes after Becky . . . who earlier has confessed to feeling that her father is no longer her father.

On the bottom shelf of a cupboard in the Driscoll basement, Miles finds a blank which is developing into a pseudo-Becky. Finney does a brilliant job of describing what this coming-to-being would look like. He compares it to fine-stamping medallions; to developing a photograph; and later to those eerie, lifelike South American dolls. But in our current state of high nervousness, what really impresses us is how neatly the thing has been tucked away, hidden behind a closed door in a dusty basement, biding its time.

Becky has been drugged by her "father," and in a scene simply charged with romance, Miles spirits her out of the house and carries her through the sleeping streets of Santa Mira in his arms; it is no trick to imagine the gauzy stuff of her nightgown nearly glowing in the moonlight.

And the fallout of all this? When Mannie Kaufman arrives, the men return to the Belicec house to investigate the basement:

> There was no body on the table. Under the bright, shadowless light from the overhead lay the brilliant green felt, and on the felt, except at the corners and along the sides, lay a sort of thick gray fluff that might have fallen, or been jarred loose, I supposed, from the open rafters.

For an instant, his mouth hanging open, Jack stared at the table. Then he swung to Mannie, and his voice protesting, asking for belief, he said, "It was there on the table! Mannie, it *was!*"

Mannie smiled, nodding quickly. "I believe you, Jack . . ."

But we know that's what all of these shrinks say . . . just before they call for the men in the white coats. *We* know that fluff isn't just fluff from the overhead rafters; the damned thing has gone to seed. But nobody else knows it, and Jack is quickly reduced to the final plea of the helpless paranoiac: You gotta believe me, doc!

Mannie Kaufman's rationalization for the increasing number of people in Santa Mira who no longer believe their relatives are their relatives is that Santa-Mirans are undergoing a case of low-key mass hysteria, the sort of thing that may have been behind the Salem witch trials, the mass suicides in Guyana, even the dancing sickness of the Middle Ages. But below this rationalistic approach, existentialism lurks unpleasantly. These things happen, he seems to suggest, just because they happen. Sooner or later they will work themselves out.

They do, too. Mrs. Seeley, who believed her husband wasn't her husband, comes in to tell Miles that everything is fine now. Ditto the girls who were scared of their English instructor for awhile. And ditto Cousin Wilma, who calls up Miles to tell him how embarrassed she is at having caused such a fuss; of *course* Uncle Ira is Uncle Ira. And in every case, one other fact—a name—stands out: Mannie Kaufman was there, helping them all. Something is wrong here, all right, but we know very well what it is, thank you, Mr. Jones. We have noticed the way Kaufman's name keeps cropping up. We're not stupid, right? Damn right we're not! And it's pretty obvious that Mannie Kaufman is now playing for the visiting team.

And one more thing. At Jack Belicec's insistence, Miles finally decides to call a friend in the Pentagon and spill the whole incredible story. About his long distance call to Washington, miles tells us:

> It isn't easy explaining a long, complicated story over the telephone. . . . And we had bad luck with the connection. At first I heard Ben and he heard me, as clearly as though we were next door to each other. But when I began telling him what had been happening here, the connection faded. Ben had to keep asking me to repeat, and I almost had to shout to make him understand me. You can't talk well, you can't even think properly, when you have to repeat every other phrase, and I signaled the operator and asked for a better connection . . . I'd hardly resumed when a sort of buzzing sound started in the receiver in my ear, and then I had to try to talk over that . . .

"They," of course, are now in charge of communications coming into and going out of Santa Mira ("We are controlling transmission," that somehow frightening voice which introduced *The Outer Limits* each week used to say; "*We* will control the horizontal . . . *we* will control the vertical . . . we can roll the image, make it flutter . . . we can change the focus . . ."). Such a passage will also strike a responsive chord in any old antiwar protester, SDS member, or activist who ever believed his or her home phone was tapped or that the guy with the Nikon on the edge of the demonstration was taking his or her picture for a dossier someplace. *They* are everywhere; *they* are watching; *they* are listening. Surely it is no wonder that Siegel believed that Finney's novel was about a-Red-under-every-bed or that others believed it was about the creeping fascist menace. As we descend deeper and deeper into the whirlpool of this nightmare it might even become possible to believe it was the pod people who were on the grassy knoll in Dallas, or that it was the pod people who obediently swallowed their poisoned Kool-Aid at Jonestown and then spritzed it down the throats of their squalling infants. It would be such a relief to be able to believe that.

Miles's conversation with his Army friend is the book's clearest delineation of the paranoid mind at work. Even when you know the whole story, you aren't allowed to communicate it to those in authority . . . and it's hard to think with that buzzing in your head!

Linked to this is the strong sense of xenophobia Finney's major characters feel. The pods really are "a threat to our way of life," as Joe McCarthy used to say. "They'll have to declare martial law," Jack tells Miles, "a state of siege, or something—anything! And then do whatever has to be done. Root this thing out, smash it, crush it, kill it."

Later, during their brief flight from Santa Mira, Miles and Jack discover two pods in the trunk of the car. This is how Miles describes what happens next:

> And there they lay, in the advancing, retreating waves of flickering red light: two enormous pods already burst open in one or two places, and I reached in with both hands, and tumbled them out onto the dirt. They were weightless as children's balloons, harsh and dry on my palms and fingers. At the feel of them on my skin, I lost my mind completely, and then I was trampling them, smashing and crushing them under my plunging feet and legs, not even knowing that I was uttering a sort of hoarse, meaningless cry—"Unhh! Unhh! Unhh!"—of fright and animal disgust.

No friendly old men holding up signs reading STOP AND BE FRIENDLY here; here we have Miles and Jack, mostly out of their minds, doing the funky chicken over these weird and insensate invaders from space. There is no discussion (vis-à-vis *The Thing*) of what we could learn from these things to the benefit of modern science. There is no white flag here, no parley; Finney's aliens are as strange and as ugly as those bloated leeches you sometimes find clinging to your skin after swimming in still ponds. There is no reasoning here, nor any effort to reason; only Mile's blind and primitive reaction to the alien outsider.

The book which most closely resembles Finney's is Robert A. Heinlein's *The Puppet Masters;* like Finney's novel, it is perhaps nominally sf but is in fact a horror novel. In this one invaders from Saturn's largest moon, Titan, arrive on Earth, ready, willing, and able to do business. Heinlein's creatures are not pods; they are the leeches in actuality. They are sluglike creatures that ride on the backs of their hosts' necks the way that you or I might ride a horse. The two books are similar—strikingly so—in many ways. Heinlein's narrator begins by wondering aloud if "they" were truly intelligent. He ends after the menace has been defeated. The narrator is one of those building and manning rocketships aimed at Titan; now that the tree has been chopped down, they will burn the roots. "Death and destruction!" the narrator exults, thus ending the book.

But what exactly is the threat which the pods in Finney's novel pose? For Finney, the fact that they will mean the end of the human race seems almost secondary (pod people have no interest in what an old acquaintance of mine likes to refer to as "doing the trick"). The real horror, for Jack Finney, seems to be that they threaten all that "nice"—and I think this is where we came in. On his way to his office not too long after the pod invasion is well launched, Miles describes the scenery this way:

> . . . the look of Throckmorton Street depressed me. It seemed littered and shabby in the morning sun, a city trash basket stood heaped and unemptied from the day before, the globe of an overhead streetlight was broken, and a few doors down . . . a shop stood empty. The windows were whitened, and a clumsily painted *For Rent* sign stood leaning against the glass. It didn't say where to apply, though, and I had a feeling no one cared whether the store was ever rented again. A smashed wine bottle lay in the entranceway of my building, and the brass nameplate set in the gray stone of the building was mottled and unpolished.

From Jack Finney's fiercely individualistic point of view, the worst thing about the Body Snatchers is that they will allow the nice little town of Santa Mira to turn into something resembling a subway station on Forty-second Street in New York. Humans, Finney asserts, have a natural drive to create order out of chaos (which fits well enough with the book's paranoid themes). Humans want to improve the universe. These are old-fashioned ideas, perhaps, but Finney is a traditionalist, as Richard Gid Powers points out in his introduction to the Gregg Press edition of the novel. From where Finney stands, the scariest thing about the pod people is that chaos doesn't bother them a bit and they have absolutely no sense of aesthetics: this is not an invasion of roses from outer space but rather an infestation of ragweed. The pod people are going to mow their lawns for awhile and then give it up. They don't give a shit about the crabgrass. They aren't going to be making any trips down to the Santa Mire True Value Hardware so they can turn that musty old basement annex into a rec room in the best do-it-yourself tradition. A salesman who blows into town complains about the state of the roads. If they aren't patched soon, he says, Santa Mira will be cut off from the world. But do you think the pod people are going to lose any sleep over a little thing like that? Here's what Richard Gid Powers says in his introduction about Finney's outlook:

> With the hindsight afforded by Finney's later books, it is easy to see what the critics overlooked [when they] interpreted both the book and the movie . . . simply as products of the anti-Communist hysteria of the McCarthyite fifties, a know-nothing outburst against "alien ways of life" . . . that threatened the American way. Miles Bennell is a precursor of all the other traditionalist heroes of Jack Finney's later books, but in *The Body Snatchers*, Miles's town of Santa Mira, Marin County, California still is the unspoiled mythical *gemeinschaft* community that later heroes have had to travel through time to recapture. When Miles begins to suspect that his neighbors are no longer

real human beings and are no longer capable of sincere human feelings, he is encountering the beginning of the insidious modernization and dehumanization that faces later Finney heroes as an accomplished fact.

Miles Bennell's victory over the pods is fully consistent with the adventures of subsequent Finney characters: his resistance to depersonalization is so fierce that the pods finally give up on their plans for planetary colonization and mosey off to another planet where the inhabitants' hold on their self-integrity is not so strong.

Further on, Powers has this to say about the archetypical Finney hero in general and the purposes of this book in particular.

> Finney's heroes, particularly Miles Bennell, are all inner-directed individualists in an increasingly other-directed world. Their adventures could be used as classroom illustrations of Tocqueville's theory about the plight of a free individual in a mass democracy.... *The Body Snatchers* is a raw and direct mass-market version of the despair over cultural dehumanization that fills T.S. Eliot's "Wasteland" and William Faulkner's *The Sound and the Fury*. Finney adroitly uses the classic science fiction situation of an invasion from outer space to symbolize the annihilation of the free personality in contemporary society ... he succeeded in creating the most memorable of all pop cultural images of what Jean Sheperd was describing on late-night radio as "creeping meatballism": fields of pods that hatch into identical, spiritless, emotional vacuous zombies—who look so damned much just like you and me!

Finally, when we examine *The Body Snatchers* in light of the Tarot hand we have dealt ourselves, we find in Finney's novel almost every damned card. There is the Vampire, for surely those whom the pods have attacked and drained of life have become a modern, cultural version of the undead, as Richard

Gid Powers points out; there is the Werewolf, for certainly these people are not really people at all, and have undergone a terrible sea change; the pods from space, a totally alien invasion of creatures who need no spaceships, can certainly also fit under the heading of the Thing Without a Name . . . and you might even say (if you wanted to stretch a point, and why the hell not?) that citizens of Santa Mira are no more than Ghosts of their former selves these days.

Not bad legs for a book which is "just a story."

6

Ray Bradbury's *Something Wicked This Way Comes* defies any neat and easy categorization of analysis . . . and so far, at least, it has also defied the moviemakers, in spite of any number of options and scenarios, including Bradbury's own. This novel, originally published in 1962 and promptly given a critical pasting by critics in both the science fiction and fantasy genres,* has gone on through two dozen printings since its original publication. For all of that, it has not been Bradbury's most successful book, or his best-known one; *The Martian Chronicles, Fahrenheit 451*, and *Dandelion Wine* have probably all outsold it, and are certainly better known to the general reading public. But I believe that *Something Wicked This Way Comes,* a darkly poetic tall tale set in the half-real, half-mythical community of Green Town, Illinois, is probably Bradbury's best work—a shadowy descendant from that tradition that has brought us stories about Paul Bunyan and his blue ox, Babe, Pecos Bill, and Davy Crockett. It is not a perfect book; at times Bradbury lapses into the purple overwriting that has characterized too much of his work in the seventies. Some passages are self-

---

* Not much new in this. Writers in the fantasy and science fiction genres moan about the critical coverage they get from mainstream critics—sometimes with justification, sometimes without—but the fact is most critics inside the genre are intellectual dorks. The genre magazines have a long and ignoble history of roasting novels which are too large for the genres from which they've come; Robert Heinlein's *Stranger in a Strange Land* took a similar pasting.

imitative and embarrassingly fulsome. But that is a small part of the total work; in most cases Bradbury carries his story off with guts and beauty and *panache*.

And it might be worth remembering that Theodore Dreiser, the author of *Sister Carrie* and *An American Tragedy*, was, like Bradbury, sometimes his own worst enemy ... mostly because Dreiser never knew when to stop. "When you open your mouth, Stevie," my grandfather once said to me in despair, "all your guts fall out." I had no reply to that then, but I suppose if he were alive today, I would reply: That's 'cause I want to be Theodore Dreiser when I grow up. Well, Dreiser was a great writer, and Bradbury seems to be the fantasy genre's version of Dreiser, although Bradbury's line-by-line writing is better and his touch is lighter. Still, the two of them share a remarkable commonality.

On the minus side, both show a tendency to not so much write about a subject as to bulldoze it into the ground ... and once so bulldozed, both have a tendency to bludgeon the subject until all signs of movement have ceased. On the plus side, both Dreiser and Bradbury are American naturalists of a dark persuasion, and in a crazy sort of way they seem to bookend Sherwood Anderson, the American champ of naturalism. Both of them wrote of American people living in the heartland (although Dreiser's heartland people come to the city while Bradbury's stay to home), of innocence coming heartbreakingly to experience (although Dreiser's people usually break, while Bradbury's people remain, although changed, whole), and both speak in voices which are uniquely, even startlingly American. Both narrate in a clear English which remains informal while mostly eschewing idiom—when Bradbury lapses occasionally into slang it startles us so much that he seems almost vulgar. Their voices are unmistakably American voices.

The easiest difference to point out, and maybe the most unimportant, is that Dreiser is called a realist while Bradbury is known as a fantasist. Even worse, Bradbury's paperback publisher insists tiresomely on calling him "The World's Greatest Living Science Fiction Writer" (making him sound like one of the freaks in the shows he writes about so often), when Bradbury has never written anything but the most nominal science fiction. Even in his space stories, he is not interested in negative-ion drives or relativity converters. There are rockets, he says in the connected stories which form *The Martian Chronicles, R Is for Rocket,* and *S Is for Space.* That is all you need to know and is, therefore, all I am going to tell you.

To this I would add that if you want to know how the rockets are going to work in any hypothetical future, turn to Larry Niven or Robert Heinlein; if you want literature—*stories,* to use Jack Finney's word—about what the future might hold, you must go to Ray Bradbury or perhaps to Kurt Vonnegut. What powers the rockets is *Popular Mechanics* stuff. The province of the writer is what powers the people.

All that said, it is impossible to talk of *Something Wicked This Way Comes,* which is most certainly not science fiction, without putting Bradbury's lifework in some sort of perspective. His best work, from the beginning, has been his fantasy . . . and his best fantasy has been his horror stories. As previously mentioned, the best of the early Bradbury was collected in the marvelous Arkham House collection *Dark Carnival.* No easily obtainable edition of this work, the *Dubliners* of American fantasy fiction, is available. Many of the stories originally published in *Dark Carnival* can be found in a later collection, *The October Country,* which is available in paper. Included are such short Bradbury classics of gut-chilling horror as "The Jar," "The Crowd," and the unforgettable "Small Assassin." Other Bradbury stories published in the forties were so horrible that the author now repudiates them (some were adapted as comics stories and published, with a younger Bradbury's permission, in the E.C. horror comics). One of these involves an undertaker who performs hideous but curiously moral atrocities upon his "clients"—for instance, when three old biddies who loved to gossip maliciously are killed in an accident, the undertaker chops off their heads and buries these three heads together, mouth to ear and ear to mouth, so they can enjoy a hideous *kaffeeklatsch* throughout eternity.

Of how his own life influenced the writing of *Something Wicked This Way Comes,* Bradbury says: "[*Something Wicked This Way Comes*] sums up my entire life of loving Lon Chaney and the magicians and grotesques he played in the twenties films. My mom took me to see *Hunchback* in 1923 when I was three. It marked me forever. *Phantom* [*of the Opera*] when I was six. Same thing. *West of Zanzibar* when I was about eight. Magician turns himself into a skeleton in front of black natives! Incredible! *The Unholy Three* ditto! Chaney took over my life. I was a raving film maniac long before I hit my eighth year. I became a full-time magician after seeing Blackstone on stage in Waukegan, my home town in upper Illinois, when I was nine. When I was twelve, MR. ELECTRICO and his traveling Electric Chair arrived with the Dill Brothers Sideshows and Carnival. That was his 'real' name. I got to know him. Sat by the lakeshore and talked grand philosophies . . . he his small ones, me my grandiose supersized ones about futures and magic. We corresponded several times. He lived in Cairo, Illinois, and was, he said, a defrocked Presbyterian minister. I wish I could remember his Christian name. But his letters have long since been lost in the years, though small magic tricks he gave me I still have. Anyway, magic and magicians and Chaney and libraries have filled my life. Libraries are the real birthing places of the universe for me. I lived in my home-town library move than I did at home. I loved it at night, prowling the slacks on my fat panther feet. All of that went into *Something Wicked,* which began as a short story in *Weird Tales* called "Black Ferris" in May, 1948, and just *grew* like Topsy . . ."

Bradbury has continued to publish fantasy throughout his career, and although the *Christian Science Monitor* called *Something Wicked This Way Comes* a "nightmarish allegory," Bradbury really settles for allegory only in his science fiction. In his fantasy, his preoccupation has been with theme, character, symbol . . . and that fantastic rush that comes to the writer of fantasy when he puts the pedal to the metal, yanks back on the steering wheel, and drives his jalopy straight up into the black night of unreality.

Bradbury relates it this way: "['Black Ferris' became] a screenplay in 1958 the night I saw Gene Kelly's *Invitation to the Dance* and so much wanted to work for and with him [that] I rushed home, finished up an outline of *Dark Carnival* (its then title) and ran it over to his house. Kelly flipped, said he would direct it, went off to Europe to find money, never found any, came back discouraged, gave me back my screen treatment, some eighty pages or more, and told me Good Luck. I said to hell with it and sat down and spent two years, off and on, finishing *Something Wicked*. Along the way, I said all and everything, just about, that I would ever want to say about my younger self and how I felt about that terrifying thing: Life, and that other terror. Death, and the exhilaration of both.

"But, above all, I did a loving thing without knowing it. I wrote a paean to my father. I didn't realize it until one night in 1965, a few years after the novel had been published. Sleepless, I got up and prowled my library, found the novel, reread certain portions, burst into tears. My father was locked into the novel, forever, as the father in the book! I wish he had lived to read himself there and be proud of his bravery in behalf of his loving son.

"Even writing this, I am touched again to remember with what a burst of joy and agony I found that my Dad was there, forever, forever for me anyway, locked on paper, kept in print, and beautiful to behold.

"I don't know what else to say. I loved every minute of writing it. I took six months off between drafts. I never tire myself. I just let my subconscious throw up when it feels like it.

"I love the book best of all the things I have ever written. I will love it, and the people in it, Dad and Mr. Electrico, and Will and Jim, the two halves of myself sorely tired and tempted, until the end of my days."

Maybe the first thing we notice in *Something Wicked This*

Way Comes is Bradbury's splitting of those two halves of himself. Will Halloway, the "good" boy (well, both of them are good, but Will's friend Jim goes astray for awhile), is born on October 30, a minute before midnight. Jim Nightshade is born two minutes later . . . a minute past midnight on Halloween morning. Will is Apollonian, a creature of reason and plan, a believer (mostly) in the status quo and the norm. Jim Nightshade, as his name implies, is the Dionysian half, a creature of emotion, something of a nihilist, hellbent for destruction, ready to spit in the devil's face just to see if the spittle will steam and sizzle running down the Dark Lord's cheek. When the lightning rod salesman comes to town at the beginning of Bradbury's fabulous tale ("running just ahead of the storm") and tells the boys that lightning will strike Jim's house, Will has to persuade Jim to put the lightning rod up. Jim's initial reaction is "Why spoil the fun?"

The symbolism of the times of birth is large, crude, and apparent; so is the symbolism of the lightning rod salesman, who arrives as a harbinger of bad times. Bradbury pulls it off nonetheless, mostly out of sheer fearlessness. He deals his archetypes large, like those bridge-sized cards.

In Bradbury's story an ancient carnival, marvelously named Cooger and Dark's Pandemonium Shadow Show, arrives in Green Town, bringing misery and horror under the guise of pleasure and wonder. Will Halloway and Jim Nightshade—and later, Will's father, Charles, as well—wise up to exactly what this particular carnival is all about. The tale eventually narrows down to the struggle for a single soul, that of Jim Nightshade. To call it an allegory would be wrong, but to call it a moral horror tale—much in the manner of those E.C. horror tales which foreran it—would be exactly right. In effect, what happens to Jim and Will is not so much different from Pinocchio's scary encounter on Pleasure Island, where boys who indulge their baser desires (smoking cigars and shooting snooker, for instance) are turned into donkeys. Bradbury in writing here of carnal enticements—not just sexual carnality, but carnality in its broadest forms and manifestations—the pleasures of the flesh run as wild as the tattooed illustrations which cover Mr. Dark's body.*

What saves Bradbury's novel from being merely a "nightmarish allegory" or a simplistic fairy story is its grasp of story and style. Bradbury's style, so attractive to me as an adolescent, now seems a bit oversweet. But it still wields a considerable power. Here is one of the passages which seems oversweet to me—

> And Will? Why, he's the last peach, high on a summer tree. Some boys walk by and you cry, seeing them. They feel good, they look good, they are good. Oh, they're not above peeing off a bridge, or stealing an occasional dimestore pencil-sharpener; it's not that. It's just, you know, seeing them pass, that's how they'll be all their life; they'll get hit, hurt, cut, bruised, and always wonder why, why does it happen?

—and one that seems just right:

> The wails of a lifetime were garnered in [that trainwhistle] from other nights in other slumbering years; the howls of moon-dreamed dogs, the sleep of river-cold winds through January porch screens which stopped the blood, a thousand fire-sirens weeping, or worse! the outgone shreds

---

* The one reference to sexual carnality here occurs during the business of the Theater, which Bradbury declined to discuss in his letter to me, although I asked him if he would be so kind as to elaborate a bit. It remains one of the book's most tantalizing episodes. Jim and Will discover the Theater, Bradbury says, on the upper floor of a house "while they were monkey-climbing for the sourest apples." Bradbury tells us that looking into the Theater changed everything, including the taste of the fruit, and while I have a tendency to bolt at the first stench of graduate-school analysis like a horse smelling good water polluted with alkali, the apple-and-Eden metaphor here is too strong to be denied. What exactly is going on in this second- or third-floor room, this "Theater" that changed the taste of the apples, that so fascinates Jim of the dark name and his friend, whose Christian name is so associated with our supposed ability (our supposed *Christian* ability) to consciously command goodness in any given situation? Bradbury suggests that the Theater is one room in a whorehouse. The people inside are naked; they "let fall clothes to the rug, stood raw and animal-crazy, naked, like shivering horses . . ." If so, it is the book's most telling foreshadowing of the carnal deviation from the norm which so strongly attracts Jim Nightshade as he stands on the threshold of adolescence.

of breath, the protests of a billion people dead or dying, not wanting to be dead, their groans, their sighing, burst over the earth!

Man, that's a train whistle! I want to tell you!

More clearly than any other book discussed here, *Something Wicked This Way Comes* reflects the differences between the Apollonian life and the Dionysian. Bradbury's carnival, which creeps inside the town limits and sets up shop in a meadow at three o'clock in the morning (Fitzgerald's dark night of the soul, if you like), is a symbol of everything that is abnormal, mutated, monstrous . . . Dionysian. I've always wondered if the appeal of the vampire myth for children doesn't lie partly in the simple fact that vampires get to sleep all day and stay up all night (vampires never have to miss Creature Features at midnight because of school the next day). Similarly, we know that part of this carnival's attraction for Jim and Will (sure, Will feels its pull too, although not as strongly as his friend Jim feels it; even Will's father is not entirely immune from its deadly siren song) is that there will be no set bedtimes, no rules and regulations, no dull and boring small town day after day, no "eat your broccoli, think of the people starving in China," no school. The carnival is chaos, it is the taboo land made magically portable, traveling from place to place and even from time to time with its freight of freaks and its glamorous attractions.

The boys (sure, Jim too) represent just the opposite. They are normal, not mutated, not monstrous. They live their lives by the rules of the sunlit world, Will willingly, Jim impatiently. Which is exactly why the carnival wants them. The essence of evil, Bradbury suggests, is its need to compromise and corrupt that delicate passage from innocence to experience that all children must make. In the rigid moral world of Bradbury's fiction, the freaks who populate the carnival have taken on the outward shapes of their inward vices. Mr. Cooger, who has lived for thousands of years, pays for his life of dark degeneracy by becoming a Thing even more ancient, ancient almost beyond our ability to comprehend, kept alive by a steady flow of electricity. The Human Skeleton is paying for miserliness of feeling; the fat lady for physical or emotional gluttony; the dust witch for her gossipy meddling in the lives of others. The carnival has done to them what the undertaker in that old Bradbury horror story did to his victims after they had died.

On its Apollonian side, the book asks us to recall and re-examine the facts and myths of our own childhoods, most specifically our small-town American childhoods. Written in a semipoetic style that seems to suit such concerns perfectly, Bradbury examines these childhood concerns and comes to the conclusion that only children are equipped to deal with childhood's myths and terrors and exhalations. In his midfifties story "The Playground," a man who returns magically to childhood is propelled into a world of lunatic horror which is only, after all, the corner playground with its sandboxes and its slippery slide.

In *Something Wicked This Way Comes,* Bradbury interconnects this small-town American boyhood motif with most of the ideas of the new American gothic which we have already discussed to some extent. Will and Jim are essentially okay, essentially Apollonian, riding easy in their childhoods and used to looking at the world from their shorter height. But when their teacher, Miss Foley, returns to childhood—the first of the carnival's Green town victims—she enters a world of monotonous, unending horror which is not much different from that experienced by the protagonist of "The Playground." The boys discover Miss Foley—or what remains of her—under a tree.

> . . . and there was the little girl, crouched, face buried in her hands, weeping as if the town were gone and the people in it and herself lost in a terrible woods.
>
> And at last Jim came edging up and stood at the edge of the shadow and said, "Who is it?"
>
> "I don't know." But Will felt tears start to his eyes, as if some part of him guessed.
>
> "It's not Jenny Holdridge, is it?"
>
> "No."

"Jane Franklin?"

"No." His mouth felt full of novocaine, his tongue merely stirred in his numb lips. ". . . no . . ."

The little girl wept feeling them near, but not looking up yet.

" . . . me . . . help me . . . nobody'll help me . . . me . . . me . . . I don't *like* this . . . somebody must help me . . . someone must help *her* . . ." she mourned as for one dead, ". . . someone must help her . . . nobody will . . . nobody has . . . terrible . . . terrible . . ."

The carnival "attraction" which has accomplished this malign trick is one that both Narcissus and Eleanor Vance could relate to: Miss Foley has been trapped in the carnival's mirror maze, imprisoned by her own reflection. Forty or fifty years have been jerked out from under her and she has been tumbled back into her own childhood . . . just what she thought she wanted. She had not considered the possibility of the nameless little girl weeping under the tree.

Jim and Will avoid this fate—barely—and even manage to rescue Miss Foley on her first foray into the mirror maze. One supposes it is not the maze itself but the carousel that has actually accomplished her doubling back in time; the mirrors in the maze show you a time of life you think you'd like to have again, and the carousel actually accomplishes it. The carousel can add a year to your age each time you go around forward or make you a year younger for every circle you make on it going backward. The carousel is Bradbury's interesting and workable metaphor for *all* of life's passages, and the fact that he darkens this ride, which is often associated with the sunniest pleasure we know as children, to fit the motif of this particular black carnival, causes other uneasy associations to come to mind. When we see the innocent merry-go-round with its prancing horses in this nether light, it may suggest to us that if time's passages are to be compared to a merry-go-round ride, then we see that each year's revolution is essentially the same as the last; it perhaps causes us to remember how fleeting and ephemeral such a ride is; and most of all it reminds us that the brass ring, which we have all tried so hard and fruitlessly to catch, is kept deliberately, tauntingly, out of reach.

In terms of the new American gothic, we can see that the mirror maze is the catch-trap, the place where too much self-examination and morbid introspection persuades Miss Foley to step over the line into abnormality. In Bradbury's world—the world of Cooger and Dark's Pandemonium Shadow Show—there are no options: first caught in the glass of Narcissus, you then find yourself riding a dangerous carousel charger backwards into an untenable past or forward into an untenable future. Shirley Jackson uses the conventions of the new American gothic to examine character under extreme psychological—or perhaps occult—pressure; Peter Straub uses them to examine the effects of an evil past upon the present; Anne Rivers Siddons uses them to examine social codes and social pressures; Bradbury uses these self-same conventions in order to offer us a moral judgment. In describing Miss Foley's terror and grief in attaining the childhood she so desired, Bradbury goes far toward defusing the potential flood of sticky-sweet romanticism that might have destroyed his tale . . . and I think this defusing reinforces the moral judgments he makes. In spite of imagery that sometimes swamps us instead of uplifting us, he manages to retain his own clear point of view.

This isn't to say Bradbury doesn't make a romantic myth of childhood, because he sure does. Childhood itself is a myth for almost all of us. We think we remember what happened to us when we were kids, but we don't. The reason is simple: we were crazy then. Looking back into this well of sanity as adults who are, if not totally insane, then at least neurotic instead of out-and-out psychotic, we attempt to make sense of things which made no sense, read importance into things which had no importance, and remember motivations which simply didn't exist. This is where the process of myth making begins.*

---

* The only novels I can think of that avoid making childhood into a myth or a fairy tale and still succeed wonderfully as stories are William Golding's *Lord of the Flies* and *A High Wind in Jamaica*, by Richard Hughes. Someone will write me a letter and suggest that I should have

Rather than trying to row against this strong current (as Golding and Hughes do), Bradbury uses it in *Something Wicked This Way Comes;* blending the myth of childhood with the myth of the dream-father, whose part is played here by Will's dad, Charles Halloway . . . and, if Bradbury himself is to be believed, who is also played by that Illinois power-linesman who was Ray Bradbury's dad. Halloway is a librarian who lives his own life of dreams, who is enough boy to understand Will and Jim, but who is also enough adult to provide, in the end, what the boys cannot provide for themselves, that final ingredient in our perception of Apollonian morality, normality, and rectitude: simple accountability.

Childhood is the time, Bradbury insists, when you are still able to believe in things you know cannot be true:

> "It's not true anyway," Will gasped. "Carnivals don't come this late in the year. Silly darn-sounding thing. Who'd go to it?"
> "Me." Jim stood quiet in the dark.
> Me, thought Will, seeing the guillotine flash, the Egyptian minors unfold accordions of light, and the sulphur-skinned devil-man sipping lava, like gunpowder tea.

They simply believe; their hearts are still capable of overruling their heads. They are still sure that they will be able to sell enough boxes of greeting cards or tins of Cloverine Salve to get a bike or a stereo, that the toy will really do all the things you saw it do on TV and that "you can put it together in just a matter of minutes with a few simple tools," or that the monster picture going on inside the theater will be as scary and wonderful as the posters and stills outside. That's okay; in Bradbury's world the myth is ultimately stronger than the reality, and the heart stronger than the head. Will and Jim stand revealed, not as the sordid, dirty, frightened boys of *Lord of the Flies,* but as

---

added either Ian McEwan's *The Cement Garden* or Beryl Bainbridge's *Harriet Said,* but I think that, in their differing ways (but uniquely British outlook), both of these short novels romanticize childhood as thoroughly as Bradbury ever did.

creatures built almost entirely of myth, a dream of childhood which becomes more believable than reality in Bradbury's hand.

> Through noon after noon, they had screamed up half the rides, knocked over dirty milk bottles, smashed kewpie-doll-winning plates, smelling, listening, looking their way through the autumn crowd trampling the leafy sawdust . . .

Where did they come by the wherewithal for their day at the fair? Most kids in a similiar situation have to count their finances and then go through an agonizing process of picking and choosing; Jim and Will apparently do everything. But once again, it's okay. They are our representatives in the forgotten land of childhood, and their apparently endless supply of cash (plus their dead-eye aim at the china plates and pyramids of milk bottles) are accepted with delight and little or no rational hesitation. We believe as we once believed that Pecos Bill dug the Grand Canyon one day when he came home tired, thus dragging his pick and shovel behind him instead of carrying them over his shoulder. They are in terror, but it is the unique ability of these myth-children to enjoy their terror. "They both stopped to enjoy the swift pound of each other's heart," Bradbury relates.

Cooger and Dark become Bradbury's myth of evil, threatening these children not as gangsters or kidnappers or any realistic bad guys; Cooger is more like Old Pew returned from *Treasure Island,* his blindness exchanged for a hideous fall of years that has been dropped upon him when the carousel goes wild. When he hisses at Will and Jim, "A . . . sssshort . . . sad life . . . for you both!" we feel the sort of comfortable chill we felt when the Black Spot was first passed at the Admiral Benbow.

Their hiding from the emissaries of the carnival, who come into town looking for them under the pretense of a free parade, becomes Bradbury's best summation of this childhood remembered in myth; the childhood that might really have existed in short bursts between long stretches of boredom and such cheesy chores as carrying wood, doing dishes, putting out the trash, or sitting baby brother or sister (and it's probably significant to this idea of the dream-child that both Jim and Will are only children).

> They ... hid in old garages, they ... hid in old barns ... in the highest trees they could climb and got bored and boredom was worse than fear so they came down and reported in to the Police Chief and had a fine chat which gave them twenty safe minutes right in the station and Will got the idea of touring churches and they climbed all the steeples in town and scared pigeons off the belfries. . . . But there again they began to get starchy with boredom and fatigued with sameness, and were almost on the point of giving themselves up to the carnival in order to have something to do, when quite fortunately the sun went down.

The only effective foil for Bradbury's dream-children is Charles Halloway, the dream-father. In the character of Charles Halloway we find attractions which only fantasy, with its strong myth-making abilities, can give us. Three points about him are worth mentioning, I think.

First, Charles Halloway understands the myth of childhood the two boys are living; for all of us who grew up and parted with some bitterness from our parents because we felt they didn't understand our youth, Bradbury gives us a portrait of the sort of parent we felt we deserved. His reactions are those which few real parents can ever afford to have. His parenting instincts are apparently supernaturally alert. Early on, he sees the boys running home from watching the carnival set up, and calls their names softly under his breath . . . but does no more. Nor does he mention it to Will later, although the two boys have been out at three o'clock in the morning. He's not worried that they've been out scoring dope or mugging old ladies or *shtupping* their girlfriends. He knows they have been out on boys' business, walking the night as boys sometimes will . . . and he lets it go.

Second, Charles Halloway comes by his understanding legitimately; he is still living the myth himself. Your father cannot be your pal very successfully, the psychology texts tell us, but there are few fathers, I think, who have not longed to be buddies with their sons, and few sons who have not wished for a buddy in their fathers. When Charles Halloway discovers that Jim and Will have nailed rungs under the climbing ivy on their respective houses so they can escape and reenter their bedrooms after bedtime, he does not demand that the rungs be torn down; his response is admiring laughter and an admonition that the boys not use the rungs unless they really have to. When Will tells his father in agony that no one will believe them if they try to explain what really happened in Miss Foley's house, where the evil nephew Robert (who is really Mr. Cooger, looking much younger since he has been reissued) framed them for a robbery, Halloway says simply, "I'll believe." He will believe because he is really just one of the boys and the sense of wonder has not died within him. Much later, while rummaging through his pockets, Charles Halloway almost seems like the world's oldest Tom Sawyer:

> And Will's father stood up, stuffed his pipe with tobacco, rummaged his pockets for matches, brought out a battered harmonica, a penknife, a cigarette lighter that wouldn't work, and a memo pad he had always meant to write great thoughts down on but had never got around to. . . .

Almost everything, in fact, except a dead rat and a string to swing it on.

Third, Charles Halloway is the dream-father because he is, in the end, accountable. He can switch hats, in the blink of an eye, from that of the child to that of the adult. He proves his accountability and responsibility by a simple symbolic act: when Mr. Dark asks, Halloway gives him his name.

> "A fine day to you, sir!"
> No. Dad! thought Will.
> The Illustrated Man came back.
> "Your name, sir?" he asked directly.
> Don't tell him! thought Will.
> Will's father debated a moment, took the cigar from his mouth, tapped ash and said quietly:
> "Halloway. Work in the library. Drop by sometime."
> "You can be sure, Mr. Halloway. I win."

> . . . [Halloway] was also gazing with surprise at himself, accepting the surprise, the new purpose, which was half despair, half serenity, now that the incredible deed was done. Let no one ask why he had given his true name; even he could not assay and give its real weight. . . .

But isn't it most likely that he has given his true name because the boys cannot? He must front for them—which he does admirably. And when Jim's dark wishes finally lead him into what seems utter ruin, it is Halloway who emerges, first destroying the fearsome Dust Witch, then Mr. Dark himself, and finally leading the fight for Jim's life and soul.

Something Wicked This Way Comes is probably not Bradbury's best work overall—I believe he has always found the novel a difficult form to work in—but its mythic interests are so well suited to Bradbury's dreamy, semipoetic prose that it succeeds wonderfully and becomes one of those books about childhood (like Hughes's *A High Wind in Jamaica*, Stevenson's *Treasure Island*, Cormier's *The Chocolate War*, and Thomas Williams's *Tsuga's Children*, to name just a few) that adults should take down once in awhile . . . not just to give to their own children, but in order to touch base again themselves with childhood's brighter perspectives and darker dreams. Bradbury has introduced his novel with a quotation from Yeats: "Man is in love, and loves what vanishes." He adds others, but we will perhaps agree that the line from Yeats is text enough . . . but let Bradbury himself have the final word, concerning one of Green Town's fascinations for the two dream-children of whom he has written:

> "As for my gravestone? I would like to borrow that great barber-pole from out front of the town shoppe, and have it run at midnight if you happened to drop by my mound to say hello. And there the old barber-pole would be, lit, its bright ribbons twining up out of mystery, turning, and twining away up into further mysteries, forever. And if you come to visit, leave an apple for the ghosts."

An apple . . . or maybe a dead rat and a string to swing it on.

7

Richard Matheson's *The Shrinking Man* (1956) is another case of a fantasy novel packaged as science fiction in a rationalistic decade when even dreams had to have some sort of basis in reality—and this mislabeling of the book has continued right up to the present, for no good reason other than this is how publishers do things. "One of the most incredible Science Fiction classics of all time!" booms the cover of the recent Berkley reissue, ignoring the fact that a story in which a man shrinks at the steady rate of one-seventh of an inch a day has really gone beyond even the furthest realms of science fiction.

Matheson, like Bradbury, has no real interest in hard science fiction. He brings forth an obligatory amount of mumbo-jumbo (my favorite is when a doctor exclaims over Scott Carey's "incredible catabolism") and then drops it. We know that the process which eventually results in Scott Carey's being chased through his own basement by a black widow spider begins when he is doused by a curtain of sparkling radioactive spray;

the radioactivity interacts with some bug spray he had ingested into his system a few days earlier. It is this double play that has caused the shrinking process to begin. It is the most minimal nod at rationality, a mid-twentieth-century version of pentagrams, mystic passes, and evil spells. Luckily for us, Matheson, like Bradbury, is more interested in Scott Carey's heart and mind than in his incredible catabolism.

It's worth noting that in *The Shrinking Man* we're back to the old radioactive blues again, and to the idea that horror fiction helps us to externalize in symbolic form whatever is really troubling us. It is impossible to see *The Shrinking Man* separated from its background of A-bomb tests, ICBMs, the "missile gap," and strontium-90 in the milk. If we look at it this way, Matheson's novel (his second published book, according to John Brosnan and John Clute, who collaborated on Matheson's entry in *The Science Fiction Encyclopedia,* citing Matheson's *I Am Legend* as the first; I believe they may have overlooked two other Richard Matheson novels, *Someone Is Bleeding* and *Fury on Sunday*), is no more science fiction than such Big Bug movies as *The Deadly Mantis* or *Beginning of the End.* But Matheson is doing more in *The Shrinking Man* than having radioactive nightmares; the title of Matheson's novel alone suggests bad dreams of a more Freudian nature. Concerning *The Body Snatchers,* we'll remember Richard Gid Powers saying that Miles Bennell's victory over the pods is a direct result of Miles's resistance against depersonalization, his fierce individualism, and his defense of more traditional America values. These same things can be said about the Matheson novel,[*] with one important variation. It seems to me that while Powers is right in suggesting that *The Body Snatchers* is in large part about the depersonalization, even the annihilation of the free

---

[*] Nor is this the only time that these two very different writers have taken up a similar theme. Both have written time-travel stories of men who are driven to escape a terrible present for a friendlier past: Finney's *Time and Again* (1970), in which the hero returns to turn-of-the-century times on America's east coast, and Matheson's *Bid Time Return* (1975), in which the hero returns to turn-of-the century times on America's west coast. In both cases, their desire to escape what Powers calls "cultural depersonalization" is a factor, but more different treatments of the idea—and different outcomes—cannot be imagined.

personality in our society, *The Shrinking Man* is story about the free personality's loss of power and growing impotency in a world increasingly controlled by machines, red tape, and a balance of terror where future wars are planned with one eye always cocked toward an "acceptable kill ratio." In Scott Carey we see one of the most inspired and original symbols of this modern devaluation of human currency ever created. Carey muses at one point that he is not shrinking at all; that instead, the world is growing larger. But seen either way—devaluation of the individual or inflation of the environment—the result is the same: as Scott shrinks, he retains his essential individuality but gradually loses more and more control over his world anyway. Also like Finney, Matheson sees his work as "just a story," and one he is not even particularly in touch with anymore. His comments:

"I started working on the book in 1955. It was the only book I ever wrote back east—if you exclude a novel I wrote when I was sixteen and living in Brooklyn. Things had been going badly out here [in California] and I thought it might be a good idea to be back east and close to editors for the sake of my career; I had given up on the idea of getting into movies. Actually, there was nothing rational in the move. I was just fed up out here on the coast and talked myself into going back east. My family was there. My brother had a business there and I knew I could get some work for us to live on if I couldn't sell any writing.* So we went. We were renting a house at Sound Beach on Long Island when I wrote the book. I had gotten the idea several years earlier while attending a movie in a Redondo Beach theater. It was a silly comedy with Ray Milland and Jane Wyman and Aldo Ray and, in this particular scene, Ray Milland, leaving Jane's apartment in a huff, accidentally put on

* In *The Shrinking Man,* Scott Carey's life becomes an ever-louder, ever more discordant medley of anxieties; one of the greatest is the shrinking money supply and his inability to support his family as he always has. I won't say that Matheson has done anything so simple as transferring his own feelings at the time to his character, but I will suggest that perhaps Matheson's own frustrations at the time enabled him to write Carey's character that much more convincingly.

Aldo Ray's hat, which sank down around his ears. Something in me asked, 'What would happen if a man put on a hat which he knew was his and the same thing happened?' Thus the notion came.

"The entire novel was written in the cellar of the rented house on Long Island. I did a shrewd thing in that. I didn't alter the cellar at all. There was a rocking chair down there and, every morning, I would go down into the cellar with my pad and pencil and I would imagine what my hero was up to that day.* I didn't have to keep the environment in my mind or keep notes. I had it all there, frozen. It was intriguing, when I watched them shoot the film, to see the cellar set because it reminded me a good deal of the cellar in Sound Beach and I had a momentary, enjoyable sense of *déjà vu*.

"It took me about two and a half months to write the novel. I originally used the structure the movie did, starting with the beginning of the shrinking process. This didn't work as it took too long to get to 'the good stuff.' So I recast the storyline to get the reader into the cellar immediately. Recently, when I thought they were going to do a remake of the film and I thought they wanted me to do it, I decided I would revert to the original structure because, in [the film], as in my original manuscript, 'the good stuff' took awhile to get to. But it turned out they were going to make it into a comedy with Lily Tomlin and I wasn't going to write it anyway. John Landis was going to direct it at the time and he wanted all the science-fantasy people out here to play minor parts in the film. He wanted me to play a pharmacist who . . . won't give a prescription to Lily Tomlin who is so small at the time that she is sitting on the shoulder of an intelligent gorilla (shows you how they changed the original idea). I demurred. As a matter of fact, the open-

---

* Matheson's hero, Scott Carey, also goes down into the cellar every day with his pad and pencil; he too is writing a book (these days, isn't everybody?). Scott's book is about his experiences as the world's only shrinking man, and it provides for his family quite adequately . . . as Matheson's own book and the subsequent film made from it did for Matheson's own family, one supposes.

ing of the script is almost like my original one to the point of actual dialogue. Later, it deviates wildly. . . .

"I don't think the book means anything to me at this time. None of my work does from this distant past. I think I prefer *I Am Legend* if I had to choose but they are both too far from me to have any significance in particular. . . . Accordingly, I wouldn't change anything about *The Shrinking Man*. It is a part of my history. I have no reason to change it, only to look at it without much interest and be pleased at whatever stir it made. I just read the first story I ever sold the other day— 'Born of Man and Woman'—[and] I cannot relate to the story at all. I remember writing certain phrases but it was someone else who wrote them. I'm sure you feel that way about the early stuff you wrote.*

"*The Shrinking Man* only recently had a hardcover edition. Now it is being printed by the Science Fiction Book Club too. Up to then it was strictly softcover. . . . Actually, *I Am Legend* is much more science fiction than *The Shrinking Man*. It has a lot of research in it. The science in *The Shrinking Man* is strictly gobbledegook. Well, I did *some* asking around and reading but I hardly had a great rationale for Scott Carey's shrinking. And I wince daily . . . that I made him shrink ⅐" a day instead of geometrically and that I had him worry about falling from heights when it wouldn't have hurt him. Well, to hell with it. I wouldn't have written 'Born of Man and Woman' a few years later either because it is so illogical. What difference does it make really?

"As I said, I enjoyed writing the book . . . because I was like Scott Carey's Boswell, watching him each day as he made his way around the cellar. I had a piece of cake with my coffee the first few days of writing and I laid it on the shelf and soon it became a part of the story. I think that some of the incidents

---

* As a matter of fact, I do. My first novel, *Carrie,* was written under difficult personal circumstances, and the book dealt with characters to unpleasant and so alien to my own outlook at to seem almost like Martians. When I pick up the book now—which it seldom—it does not seem as if someone else had written it, but I do get a peculiar sort of feeling from it . . . as if I had written it while suffering from a bad case of mental and emotional flu.

during his shrinking period are pretty good—the man who picks him up when he hitchhikes, the midget, the boys chasing him, his deteriorating marriage relationship."

A summary of *The Shrinking Man* is easy to render if we view it in the linear fashion Matheson suggests. After going through the sparkling cloud of radioactivity, Cary begins to lose a seventh of an inch a day, or roughly one foot per season. As Matheson suggests, this smacks of expediency, but as he also suggests, what does it matter as long as we realize that this is not hard science fiction and that it bears no resemblance to novels and stories by writers such as Arthur C. Clarke, Isaac Asimov, or Larry Niven? It is not exactly sensible that the children in the C. S. Lewis tale should be able to reach another world by going through a bedroom closet, either, but that is exactly what happens in the Narnia stories. It is not the techicalities of shrinking that we are interested in, and the inch-per-week pattern at least enables us to keep our own mental yardstick on Scott Carey.

We are given Scott's adventures in flashbacks as he shrinks; the main action takes place in what Scott assumes is his last week of life, as he shrinks from one inch down to nothing. He has gotten trapped in the cellar while trying to escape his own housecat and a garden sparrow. There's something particularly chilling in Scott's desperate duel with Puss; does anyone have the slightest doubt about what would happen if we were suddenly changed to a height of seven inches tall by malign magic and yon kitty curled up by the fire woke up and happened to see us skittering across the floor? Cats, those amoral gunslingers of the animal world, are maybe the scariest mammals going. I wouldn't want to be up against one in a situation like that.

Perhaps above all else, Matheson excels at the depiction of one man alone, locked in a desperate struggle against a force or forces bigger than himself. Here is the conclusion of Scott's battle with the bird that knocks him into his cellar prison:

> He stood up, flinging more snow at the bird, seeing the
> snow splatter off its dark, flaring beak. The bird flapped

back. Scott turned and struggled a few more strides, then the bird was on him again, wet wings pounding at his head. He slapped wildly at it and felt his hands strike the bony sides of its beak. It flew off again. . . .

Until, finally, cold and dripping, he stood with his back to the cellar window, hurling snow at the bird in the desperate hope that it would give up and he wouldn't have to jump into the imprisoning cellar.

But the bird kept coming, diving at him, hovering before him, the sound of its wings like wet sheets flapping in a heavy wind. Suddenly the jabbing beak was hammering at his skull, slashing skin, knocking him back against the house. . . . He picked up snow and threw it, missing. The wings were still beating at his face; the beak gashed his face again.

With a stricken cry, Scott whirled and leaped for the open square. He crawled across it dizzily. The leaping bird knocked him through.

When the bird knocks Scott into the cellar, the man is seven inches tall. Matheson has made it clear that the novel is, to a large extent, a simple comparison of the macrocosm and the microcosm, and his hero's seven weeks in this lower world are a tiny capsule of experience which exactly mimes what he has already been through in a larger world. When he falls into the cellar, he is its king; he is able to exert his own human power over the environment with no real trouble. But as he continues to shrink, his power begins to wane once again . . . and the Nemesis appears.

The spider rushed at him across the shadowed sands, scrabbling wildly on its stalklike legs. Its body was a giant, glossy egg that trembled blackly as it charged across the windless mounds, its wake a score of sand-trickling scratches . . . the spider was gaining on him, its pulsing egg of a body perched on running legs—an egg whose yolk swam with killing poisons. He raced on, breathless, terror in his veins.

In Matheson's view, *macrocosm* and *microcosm* are terms which are ultimately interchangeable, and all of Scott's problems throughout the shrinking process become symbolized in the black widow spider which also shares Scott's cellar world. When Scott discovers the one thing in his life which has not shrunk, his ability to think and plan, he also discovers a source of power which is immutable no matter which *-cosm* it happens to exist in. His escape from a cellar, which Matheson succeeds in making as strange and frightening as any alien world, follows . . . and his final heartening discovery "that to nature there was no zero," and that there is a place where the macrocosm and the microcosm eventually meet.

The Shrinking Man can be read simply enough as a great adventure story—it is certainly one of that select handful that I have given to people, envying them the experience of the first reading (others would include Bloch's *The Scarf,* Tolkien's *The Hobbit,* Berton Rouché's *Feral*). But there's more going on in Matheson's novel than just adventure, a kind of surreal Outward Bound program for little people. On a more thoughtful level, it is a short novel which deals in a thought-provoking way with concepts of power—power lost and power found.

Let me pull back from the Matheson book briefly—like Douglas MacArthur, I shall return—and make the following wild statement: all fantasy fiction is essentially about the concept of power; great fantasy fiction is about people who find it at great cost or lose it tragically; mediocre fantasy fiction is about people who have it and never lose it but simply wield it. Mediocre fantasy fiction generally appeals to people who feel a decided shortage of power in their own lives and obtain a vicarious shot of it by reading stories of strong-thewed barbarians whose extraordinary prowess at fighting is only excelled by their extraordinary prowess at fucking; in these stories we are apt to encounter a seven-foot-tall hero fighting his way up the alabaster stairs of some ruined temple, a flashing sword in one hand and a scantily clad beauty lolling over his free arm.

This sort of fiction, commonly called "sword and sorcery" by its fans, is not fantasy at its lowest, but it still has a pretty tacky feel; mostly it's the Hardy Boys dressed up in animal skins and rated R (and with cover art by Jeff Jones, as likely as not). Sword and sorcery novels and stories are tales of power for the powerless. The fellow who is afraid of being rousted by those young punks who hang around his bus stop can go home at night and imagine himself wielding a sword, his potbelly miraculously gone, his slack muscles magically transmuted into those "iron thews" which have been sung and storied in the pulps for the last fifty years.

The only writer who really got away with this sort of stuff was Robert E. Howard, a peculiar genius who lived and died in rural Texas (Howard committed suicide as his mother lay comatose and terminally ill, apparently unable to face life without her). Howard overcame the limitations of his puerile material by the force and fury of his writing and by his imagination, which was powerful beyond his hero Conan's wildest dreams of power. In his best work, Howard's writing seems so highly charged with energy that it nearly gives off sparks. Stories such as "The People of the Black Circle" glow with the fierce and eldritch light of his frenzied intensity. At his best, Howard was the Thomas Wolfe of fantasy, and most of his Conan tales seem to almost fall over themselves in their need to get out. Yet his other work was either unremarkable or just abysmal. . . . The word will hurt and anger his legion of fans, but I don't believe any other word fits. Robert Bloch, one of Howard's contemporaries, suggested in his first letter to *Weird Tales* that even Conan wasn't that much shakes. Bloch's idea was that Conan should be banished to the outer darkness where he could use his sword to cut out paper dolls. Needless to say, this suggestion did not go over well with the marching hordes of Conan fans; they probably would have lynched poor Bob Bloch on the spot, had they caught up with him back there in Milwaukee.

Even below the sword and sorcery stories are the superheroes who populate the comic magazines of the only two remaining giants in the field—although "giants" is almost too strong a word; according to a survey published in a 1978 issue of Warren's *Creepy* magazine, comic readership has gone into what may be an irrecoverable skid. These characters (traditionally called "long-underwear heroes" by the bullpen artists who draw them) are invincible. Blood never flows from their magical bodies; they are somehow able to bring such colorful villains as Lex Luthor and the Sandman to justice without ever having to remove their masks and testify against them in open court; they are sometimes down but never out.*

At the other end of the spectrum are the characters of fantasy who are either powerless and discover power within themselves (as Thomas Covenant discovers it in Stephen Donaldson's remarkable *Thomas Covenant the Unbeliever* trilogy, or as Frodo discovers it in Tolkien's epic tale of the Rings), or characters who lose power and then find it again, as Scott Carey does in *The Shrinking Man.*

Horror fiction, as we've said before, is one small circular area in the larger circle of fantasy, and what is fantasy fiction but tales of magic? And what are tales of magic but stories of power? One word nearly defines the other. Power is magic; power is potency. The opposite of potency is impotence, and impotence is the loss of the magic. There is no impotence in the stories of the sword and sorcery genre, nor in those stories of Batman and Superman and Captain Marvel which we read as children and then—hopefully—gave up as we moved on to more challenging literature and wider views of what the life experience

---

* One reason for the success of Marvel's Spider-Man when he burst on the comics scene in the early sixties may have been his vulnerability; he was and is an engaging exception to the standard comic-book formula. There is something winning in his vulnerability as Peter Parker and in his frequent klutziness as Spider-Man. After being bitten by that radioactive spider, Peter originally felt no holy desire to fight crime; he decided instead to make a bundle in showbiz. Before long, however, he discovers a truth which is bitter to him and amusing to the reader: no matter how great you looked on the Sullivan show, Marine Midland Bank still won't cash a check made out to The Amazing Spider-Man. Such touches of realism laced with rue can be traced to Stan Lee, Spider-Man's creator and the man probably most responsible for keeping the comic book from going the way of the pulps and the dime novels in the sixties and seventies.

really is. The great theme of fantasy fiction is not holding the magic and wielding it (if so, Sauron, not Frodo, would have been the hero of Tolkien's Rings cycle); it is—or so it seems to me—finding the magic and discovering how it works.

And getting back to the Matheson novel, shrinking itself is an oddly arresting concept, isn't it? Tons of symbolism come immediately to mind, most of it revolving around the potency/ impotency thing . . . sexual and otherwise. In Matheson's book, shrinking is most important because Scott Carey begins by perceiving size as power, size as potency . . . size as magic. When he begins to shrink, he begins to lose all three—or so he believes until his perceptions change. His reaction to his loss of power, potency, and magic is most commonly a blind, bellowing rage:

> "What do you think I'm going to do?" he burst out. "Go on letting them *play* with me? Oh, you haven't *been* there, you haven't *seen*. They're like kids with a new toy. A shrinking man. Godawmighty, a shrinking man! It makes their damn eyes light up . . ."

Like Thomas Covenant's constant cries of "By hell!" in the Donaldson trilogy, Scott's rage does not hide his impotency but highlights it, and it is Scott's fury which in a large part makes him such an interesting, believable character. He is not Conan or Superman (Scott bleeds plenty before escaping his cellar prison, and as we watch him go ever more frantically about the task of trying to escape, we suspect at times that he is more than half-mad) or Doc Savage. Scott doesn't always know what to do. He fumbles the ball frequently, and when he does, he goes on to do what most of us would probably do under the circumstances: he has the adult equivalent of a tantrum.

In fact, if we regard Scott's shrinking as a symbol for any incurable disease (and the progress of any incurable disease entails a kind of power loss which is analogous to shrinking), we see a pattern which psychologists would outline pretty much as Matheson wrote it . . . only the outline came years later. Scott follows this course, from disbelief to rage to depression to final acceptance, almost exactly. As with cancer patients, the final trick seems to be to accept the inevitable, perhaps to find fresh lines of power leading back into the magic. In Scott's case, in the case of many terminal patients, the final outward sign of this is an admission of the inevitable, followed by a kind of euphoria.

We can understand Matheson's decision to use flashbacks in order to get to "the good stuff" early on, but one wonders what might have happened if he had given us the story in a straight line. We see Scott's loss of power in several widely spaced episodes: he is chased by teenagers at one point—they think, and why not, that he is just a little kid—and at another he hitches a ride with a man who turns out to be a homosexual. He begins to feel an increasing disrespect from his daughter Beth, partly because of the "might makes right" idea that works unobtrusively but powerfully in even the most enlightened parent-child relationships (or, we could say, might makes power . . . or might makes magic), but perhaps mostly because his steady shrinking causes Beth to have to constantly restructure her feelings about her father, who ends up living in a dollhouse before his fall into the cellar. We can even blackly visualize Beth, who doesn't really understand what's happening, inviting her friends in on a rainy day to play with her daddy.

But Scott's most painful problems are with Lou, his wife. They are both personal and sexual, and I think that most men, even today, tend to identify the magic most strongly with sexual potency. A woman may not want to but she can; a man may want to and find he cannot. Bad news. And when Scott is 4'1" tall, he comes home from the medical center where be has been undergoing tests and walks straight into a situation where the loss of sexual magic becomes painfully evident:

> Louise looked up, smiling. "You look so nice and clean," she said.
>
> It was not the words or the look on her face; but suddenly he was terribly conscious of his size. Lips twitching into the semblance of a smile, he walked over to the couch and sat down beside her, instantly sorry that he had.

She sniffed. "Mmmmm, you smell nice," she said . . .

"You *look* nice," he said. "Beautiful."

"Beautiful!" She scoffed. "Not me."

He leaned over abruptly and kissed her warm throat. She raised her left hand and stroked his cheek slowly.

"So nice and smooth," she murmured.

He swallowed . . . was she actually talking to him as if he were a boy?

And a few minutes later:

He let breath trickle slowly from his nostrils.

"I guess it . . . would be rather grotesque anyway. . . . It'd be like . . ."

"Honey, please." She wouldn't let him finish. "You're making it worse than it is."

"Look at me," he said. "How much worse can it get?"

Later on, in another flashback, we see Scott as a voyeur, spying on the babysitter Louise has hired to care for Beth. In a series of comic-horrible scenes, Scott turns the pimply, overweight babysitter into a kind of masturbatory dream goddess. In his doubling back to powerless early adolescence, Matheson is able to show us just how much of the sexual magic Scott has lost.

But at a carnival some weeks later—Scott is a foot and a half tall at this point—he meets Clarice, a sideshow midget. And in his encounter with Clarice, we have our clearest indication of Matheson's belief that the lost magic can be found again; that the magic exists on many levels and thus becomes the unifying force that makes macrocosm and microcosm one and the same. When he first meets Clarice, Scott is a bit taller than she, and in her trailer he finds a world which is once more in perspective. It is an environment where he can reassert his own power:

Breath stopped. It was his world, his very own world— chairs and a couch he could sit on without being engulfed;

tables he could stand beside and reach across instead of walk under; lamps he could switch on and off, not stand futilely beneath as if they were trees.

And—almost needless to relate—he also rediscovers the sexual magic with Clarice in an episode which is both pathetic and touching. We understand he will lose this magic as well, sinking away from Clarice's level until she is also a giant to him, and while these episodes are somewhat softened by the flashback form, the point is nevertheless made: what can be found once can be found again, and the incident of Clarice most clearly justifies the novel's odd but strangely powerful ending: ". . . he thought: If nature existed on endless levels, so also might intelligence . . . Scott Carey ran into his new world, searching."

Not, we devoutly hope, to be eaten by the first garden slug or amoeba to cross his path.

In the movie version, which Matheson also wrote, Scott's final line is a triumphant "I still exist!" accompanied by shots of nebulae and exploding galaxies. I asked him if this had religious connotations, or perhaps reflected an early interest in life after death (a subject which has become more and more important in Matheson's later work; see *Hell House* and *What Dreams May Come*). Matheson comments: "Scott Carey's 'I still exist,' I think, only implied a continuum between macroscopic and microscopic, not between life and life after death. Interestingly, I was on the verge of doing a rewrite of *The Fantastic Voyage*, which Columbia is supposed to be making. I couldn't get involved in it because it was so technical and I would rather be involved with character now, but it was like a small continuation of the end of *The Shrinking Man*—into the microscopic world with rod and gun."

Overall, we can say that *The Shrinking Man* is a classic survival story; there is really only one character, and the questions here are elemental: food, shelter, survival, destruction of the Nemesis (the Dionysian force in Scott's mostly Apollonian cellar world). It is by no means a tremendously sexy book, but sex is at least dealt with on a level more thoughtful than the Shell Scott wham-bam-thank-you-ma'am level that was the common one for paperback originals in the fifties. Matheson was an important figure in pioneering the right of science fiction and fantasy writers to deal with sexual problems in a realistic and sensitive way; others involved in the same struggle (and it *was* a struggle) would have included Philip José Farmer, Harlan Ellison, and, perhaps most importantly of all, Theodore Sturgeon. It is hard to believe now what a furor was caused by the concluding pages of Sturgeon's *Some of Your Blood,* when it is revealed exactly how the vampire has been obtaining his supply ("The moon, is full," he writes both wistfully and chillingly to his girlfriend in the book's final paragraph, "and I wish I had some of your blood."), but the furor happened. We may wish that Matheson had dealt with the sexual angle a little less solemnly, but in light of the times, I think we can applaud the fact that he dealt with the sexual angle at all.

And as a fable of losing power and finding it, *The Shrinking Man* ranks as one of the finest fantasies of the period we've been discussing. And I don't want to leave you with the impression that I'm only talking here about sexual power and sexual potency. There are tiresome critics—the half-baked Freudians, mostly—who want to relate all of fantasy and horror fiction back to sex; one explanation for the conclusion of *The Shrinking Man* which I heard at a party in the fall of 1978—I'll not mention the name of the woman whose theory this was, but if you read science fiction, you'd know the name—maybe bears repeating, since we're on this. In symbolic terms, this woman said, spiders represent the vagina. Scott finally kills his Nemesis, the black widow (the most vaginal of all spiders) by impaling it on a pin (the phallic symbol, get it, get it?). Thus, this critic went on, after failing at sex with his wife, succeeding at first with the carnival midget Clarice and then losing her, Scott symbolically kills his own sex drive by impaling the spider. This is his last sexual act before escaping the cellar and achieving a wider freedom.

All of this was well-meaning bullshit, but bullshit is still bullshit and will never be mistaken for McDonald's Secret Sauce. I bring it up only to point out that it is the sort of bullshit that a lot of fantasy and horror writers have had to labor under . . . most of it spread by people who believe either secretly or openly that the horror writer must be suffering from madness to a greater or a lesser degree. The further view of such folks is that the writer's books are Rorschach inkblots that will eventually reveal the author's anal, oral, or genital fixation. In writing about the largely scoffing reaction that Leslie Fiedler's *Love and Death in the American Novel* received when it was published in 1960, Wilfrid Sheed adds, "Freudian interpretations [are] always greeted by guffaws." Not much bad news at that, when you remember that even the most staid novelists are regarded as a bit peculiar by their neighbors . . . but the horror novelist is always going to have to face what I think of as the couch questions, I guess. And most of us are perfectly normal. Heh-heh-heh.

Freudian huggermugger set aside, *The Shrinking Man* can be seen as just a pretty good story which happens to deal with the interior politics of power . . . or, if you like (and I do), the interior politics of magic. And Scott's killing of the spider is meant to show us that the magic is not dependent on size but upon mind and heart. If it stands considerably taller than other books in the genre (small pun much intended), and far above other books where tiny people battle beetles and praying mantises and such (Lindsay Gutteridge's *Cold War in a Country Garden* comes to mind), it is because Matheson couches his story in such intimate and riveting terms—and because he is ultimately so persuasive.*

---

* This examination of lives in microcosm continues to hold a fascination for writers and readers; early this year, Macmillan published *Small World* by Tabitha King, a malign comedy of manners revolving around a fabulously expensive presidential dollhouse, a nymphomaniacal presidential daughter, and an overweight mad scientist who is at pitiable as he it frightening. Published in 1981, it lies outside the temporal borders of this book, which is probably just as well; the lady is my wife, and my view would be prejudiced. So I'll only add that my prejudiced view is that *Small World* is a wonderful addition to this HO-scale subgenre.

8

It wouldn't be right to wind up even so brief a discussion of the modern horror novel as this one without mentioning two young British writers, Ramsey Campbell and James Herbert. They are a part of a whole new generation of British fantasy writers who seem to be revitalizing the genre by cross-fertilization much as British poets helped to revitalize American poetry during the early sixties. Besides Campbell and Herbert, the two who are perhaps best known over here, there is Robert Aickman (who could hardly be called a young Turk—but since such books as *Cold Hand in Mine* have brought him to a wider American audience, it seems fair enough to classify him as part of the British new wave), Nick Sharman, Thomas Tessier, an American living in London, who has recently published a novel called *The Nightwalker*, perhaps the finest werewolf novel of the last twenty years, and a score of others.

As Paul Theroux—another expatriate American living in London—has pointed out, there is something uniquely British about the tale of horror (perhaps particularly those which deal with the archetype of the Ghost). Theroux, who has written his own low-key horror tale, *The Black House,* favors the mannered but grisly tales of M. R. James, and they do seem to summarize everything that is best in the classic British horror story. Ramsey Campbell and James Herbert are both modernists, and while this family is really too small to avoid a certain resemblance even in cousins twice removed, it seems to me that both of these men, who are worlds apart in terms of style, point of view, and method of attack, are doing things that are exciting and worthy of mention.

Campbell, a Liverpudlian ("You talk just like one of the Beatles," a woman marvels to a writer from Liverpool in Campbell's new novel, *The Parasite*), writes a cool, almost icy prose line, and his perspective on his native Liverpool is always a trifle offbeat, a trifle unsettling. In a Campbell novel or story, one seems to view the world through the thin and shifting perceptual haze of an LSD trip that is just ending . . . or just beginning. The polish of his writing and his mannered turns of phrase and image make him seem something like the genre's Joyce Carol Oates (and like Oates, he is prolific, turning out good short stories, novels, and essays at an amazing clip), and there is also something Oatesian in the way his characters view the world—as when one is journeying on mild LSD, there is something chilly and faintly schizophrenic in the way his characters see things . . . and in the things they see. These are the perceptions of Rose as she shops in a Liverpool department store in *The Parasite:*

> A group of toddlers watched her pass, their eyes painted into their sockets. On the ground floor, red and pink and yellow hands on stalks reached for her from the glove counter. Blind mauve faces craned on necks as long as arms; wigs roosted on their heads.
> . . . The bald man was still staring at her. His head, which looked perched on top of a bookcase, shone like plastic beneath the fluorescent lights. His eyes were bright, flat, expressionless as glass; she thought of a display head stripped of its wig. When a fat pink tongue squeezed out between his lips, it was as if a plastic head had come to life.

Good stuff. But strange; so uniquely Campbell that it might as well be trademarked. Good horror novels are not a dime a dozen—by no means—but there never seems to be any serious shortage of good ones, either. And by that I mean that you seem to be able to count on a really good novel of horror and/or the supernatural (or at least a really interesting one) every year or so—and much the same could be said for the horror films. A vintage year may produce as many as three amid the paperback-original dreck about hateful, paranormal children and presidential candidates from hell and the too-large collection of hardcover boners, such as the recent *Virgin,* by James Petersen. But, maybe paradoxically, maybe not, good horror *writers* are quite rare . . . and Campbell is better than just good.

That's one reason fans of the genre will greet *The Parasite* with such pleasure and relief; it is even better than his first novel, of which I want to treat briefly here. Campbell has been turning out his own patented brand of short horror tale for some years now (like Bradbury and Robert Bloch, Arkham House published Ramsey Campbell's first book, *The Inhabitant of the Lake,* which was a Lovecraft clone). Several collections of his stories are available, the best of them probably being *The Height of the Scream.* A story you will not find in that book, unfortunately, is "The Companion," in which a lonely man who tours "funfairs" on his holidays encounters a horror beyond my ability to describe while riding a Ghost Train into its tunnel. "The Companion" may be the best horror tale to be written in English in the last thirty years; it is surely one of half a dozen or so which will still be in print and commonly read a hundred years from now. Campbell is literate in a field which has attracted too many comic-book intellects, cool in a field where too many writers—myself included—tend toward panting melodrama, fluid in a field where many of the best practitioners often fall prey to cant and stupid "rules" of fantasy composition.

But not all good short-story writers in this field are able to make the jump to the novel (Poe tried with *The Narrative of Arthur Gordon Pym* and made a conditional success of the job; Lovecraft failed ambitiously twice, with *The Strange Case of Charles Dexter Ward* and the rather more interesting *At the Mountains of Madness,* whose plot is remarkably *Pym*-like). Campbell made the jump almost effortlessly, with a novel as good as its title was off-putting: *The Doll Who Ate His Mother.* The book was published with absolutely no fanfare in 1977 in hardcover, and then with an even greater lack of fanfare a year later in paperback . . . one of those cases that make a writer wonder if publishers don't practice their own sort of voodoo, singling certain books out to be ritually slaughtered in the marketplace.

Well, never mind that. Concerning the jump from the short story to the novel—writing the latter is much like long-distance running, and you can almost feel some would-be novelists getting tired. You sense they're starting to breathe a trifle hard by page one hundred, to puff and blow by page two hundred, and to finally limp over the finish line with little to recommend them beyond the bare fact that they have finished. But Campbell runs well.

He is personally an amusing, even a jolly man (at the 1979 World Fantasy Convention he presented Stephen R. Donaldson with the British Fantasy Award, a modernistic little statuette, for his Thomas Covenant trilogy; Campbell, in that marvelously broad and calm Liverpool accent, referred to it as "the skeletal dildo." The audience broke up, and someone at my table marveled, "He sounds just like one of the Beatles."). As with Robert Bloch, the last thing you would suspect is that he is a writer of horror fiction, particularly of the grim brand he turns out. Of *The Doll Who Ate His Mother* he has this to say— some of it bearing directly on the difference in the amount of endurance needed to do a novel: "What I wanted to do with *The Doll* was to invent a new monster, if that is possible, but perhaps the big thing was to actually write the novel, since previously I'd been doing short stories. In 1961 or '62 I made notes for a story about a black magician who was going to take revenge on his town or village for some real or imagined wrong it had done him. He was going to do this by using voodoo dolls to deform the babies—you'd have the standard pulp-magazine scene of the white-faced doctor coming out of the delivery room saying, 'My God, it's not human . . . ! ' And the twist was going to be that, after all these deformed infants had died, the black magician would use the voodoo dolls to bring them back to life. An amazingly tasteless idea. At about the same time the Thalidomide tragedy occurred, making the story idea a little too 'topically tasteless' for me, and I dropped it.

"It resurfaced, I suppose, in *The Doll Who Ate His Mother*, which eats its way out of its mother's womb.

"How does writing novels differ from writing short stories? I think a novel gathers its own impetus. I have to creep up on it unawares, thinking to myself, 'Maybe I'll start it next week, maybe I'll start it next month.' Then one day I sat down, began to write, and looked up at noon, thinking: 'My God! I've started a novel! I don't believe it!'

"Kirby [McCauley] said, when I asked him how long the novel should be, that 70,000 words or so would be about right, and I took him almost literally. When I got up around the 63,000 word mark, I thought: 'Only 7,000 words left—time to wrap this up.' That's why many of the later chapters seem terse."

Campbell's novel begins with Clare Frayn's brother Rob losing an arm and his life in a Liverpool car accident. The arm, torn off in the accident, is important because somebody makes off with it . . . and eats it. This muncher of arms, we are led to suppose, is a shadowy young man named Chris Kelly. Clare—who embodies many of the ideas already labeled as "new American gothic" (sure, Campbell is British, but many of his influences—both literary and cinematic—are American)—meets a crime reporter named Edmund Hall who believes that the man who caused Rob Frayn's death was the grown-up version of a boy he knew in school, a boy fascinated with death and cannibalism. In dealing with archetypes, I've not suggested that we deal out a Tarot card for the Ghoul, one of the more grisly creatures in monsterdom, believing that the eating of dead flesh and the drinking of blood are really parts of the same archetype.* Is there really such a thing as a "new monster"? In light of the genre's strictness, I think not, and Campbell must be content instead with a fresh perspective . . . no mean feat in itself. In Chris Kelly I believe the face we see is that of our old friend the Vampire . . . as we see it in a movie

---

* Stories of ghouls and cannibalism venture into genuine taboo territory, I think—witness the strong public reactions to George Romero's *Night of the Living Dead* and *Dawn of the Dead*. Something rather more important than a harmless roller-coaster ride is going on here, I think; here's a chance to really grab people by the gag reflex and throttle them. I wrote a story four years ago called "Survivor Type," which I still have not been able to sell (gee, and people told me that when I got successful I'd be able to sell my laundry list if I wanted to!). It deals with a surgeon who is washed up on an uninhabited island—little more than a scratch of coral above the surface of the Pacific—and eats himself, a piece at a time, to stay alive. "I did everything according to Hoyle," he writes in his diary after amputating his foot. "I washed it before I ate it." Not even the men's magazines would consider that one, and it sits in my file cabinet to this day, waiting for a good home. It will probably never find one, though.

which resembles Campbell's novel by turns, the brilliant Canadian director David Cronenberg's *They Came from Within.*

Clare, Edmund Hall, and George Pugh, a cinema owner whose elderly mother has also been victimized by Kelly, join together in a strange and reluctant three-way partnership to track this supernatural cannibal down. Here again we feel echoes of the classic tale of the Vampire, Stoker's *Dracula.* And perhaps we never feel the changes of the nearly eighty years which lie between the two books so strongly as we do in the contrast between the group of six which forms to track down Count Dracula and the group of three which forms to track down "Chris Kelly." There is no sense of self-righteousness in Clare, Edmund, and George—they are truly little people, afraid, confused, often depressed; they turn inward to themselves rather than outward toward each other, and while we sense their fright very strongly, there is no feeling about the book that Clare, Edmund, and George must prevail because their cause is just. They somehow symbolize the glum and rather drab place England has become in the second half of the twentieth century, and we feel that if some or all of them do muddle through, it will be due more to impersonal luck than to any action of their own.

And the three of them do track Kelly down . . . after a fashion. The climax of the hunt takes place in the rotting cellar of a slum building marked for demolition, and here Campbell has created one of the dreamiest and most effective sequences in all of modern horror fiction. In its surreal and nightmarish evocation of ancient evil, in the glimpses it gives us of "absolute power," it is finally a voice from the latter part of the twentieth century which speaks powerfully in the language which Lovecraft can be said to have invented. Here is nothing so pallid or so imitative as a Lovecraft "pastiche," but a viable, believable version of those Lovecraftian Elder Gods that so haunted Dunwich, Arkham, Providence, Central Falls . . . and the pages of *Weird Tales* magazine.

Campbell is good, if rather unsympathetic, with character (his lack of emotion has the effect of chilling his prose even further, and some readers will be put off by the tone of this novel; they may feel that Campbell has not so much written a novel as grown one in a Petrie dish): Clare Frayn with her stumpy legs and her dreams of grace, Edmund with his baleful thoughts of glory yet to come, and best of all, because here Campbell does seem to kindle real feelings of emotion and kindliness, George Pugh holding on to the last of his cinemas and scolding two teenage girls who walk out before the playing of the National Anthem has finished.

But perhaps the central character here is Liverpool itself, with its orange sodium lights, its slums and docks, its cinemas converted into HALF A MILE OF FURNITURE. Campbell's short stories live and breathe Liverpool in what seems to be equal amounts of attraction and repulsion, and that sense of place is one of the most remarkable things about *The Doll* as well. This locale is as richly textured as Raymond Chandler's Los Angeles of the forties and fifties or Larry McMurtry's Houston of the sixties. "Children were playing ball against the church," Campbell writes. "Christ held up His arms for a catch." It is a small line, understated and almost thrown away (like all those creepy, reaching gloves in *The Parasite*), but this sort of thing is cumulative, and at least suggests Campbell's commitment to the idea that horror exists in point of view as well as in incident.

The Doll Who Ate His Mother is not the greatest of the novels discussed here—I suppose that would have to be either *The Haunting of Hill House* or Straub's *Ghost Story*—and it is not as good as Campbell's *The Parasite* . . . but it is remarkably good. Campbell keeps a tight rein on his potentially tabloid-style material, even playing off it occasionally (a dull and almost viciously insensitive teacher sits in the faculty room of his school reading a paper with a headline which blares HE CUT UP YOUNG VIRGINS AND LAUGHED—the story's blackly hilarious subhead informs us that *His Potency Came From Not Having Orgasms*). He carries us inexorably past levels of abnormal psychology into something that is much, much worse.

Campbell is extremely conscious of his literary roots—he mentions Lovecraft (adding "of course" almost unconsciously),

Robert Bloch (he compares *The Doll*'s climax in the abandoned cellar to the climax of *Psycho*, where Lila Crane must face Norman Bates's "mother" in a similar basement), and Fritz Leiber's stories of urban horror (such as "Smoke Ghost") and more notably, Leiber's eerie novel of San Francisco, *Our Lady of Darkness* (winner of the Best Novel award at the 1978 World Fantasy Convention). In *Our Lady of Darkness*, Leiber adopts as his thesis the idea that when a city becomes complex enough, it may take on a tenebrous life of its own, quite apart from the lives of the people who live and work there—an evil sentience linked, in some unstated way, to the Elder Ones of Lovecraft and, more importantly in terms of the Leiber novel, Clark Ashton Smith. Amusingly, one of the characters in *Our Lady of Darkness* suggests that San Francisco did not become truly sentient until the Transamerica Pyramid was finished and occupied.

While Campbell's Liverpool does not have this kind of conscious evil life, the picture he draws of it gives the reader the feeling that he is observing a slumbering, semisentient monster that *might* awake at any moment. His debt to Leiber seems clearer here than that to Lovecraft, in fact. Either way, Ramsey Campbell has succeeded in forging something uniquely his own in *The Doll Who Ate His Mother*.

James Herbert, on the other hand, comes from an older tradition—the same sort of pulp horror-fiction that we associate with writers such as Robert E. Howard, Seabury Quinn, the early Sturgeon, the early Henry Kuttner, and, on the English side of the Atlantic, Guy N. Smith. Smith, the author of paperback originals beyond counting, has written a novel whose title is my nominee for the all-time pulp horror classic: *The Sucking Pit*.

This sounds as if I were getting ready to knock Herbert, but this isn't the case. It's true that he is held in remarkably low esteem by writers in the genre on both sides of the Atlantic; when I've mentioned his name in the past, noses have automatically wrinkled (it's a little like ringing a bell in order to watch conditioned dogs salivate), but when you inquire more closely, you find that remarkably few people in the field have actually read Herbert—and the fact is that James Herbert is probably the best writer of pulp horror to come along since the death of Robert E. Howard, and I believe that Conan's creator would have responded to Herbert's work with immediate enthusiasm, although the two men were opposites in many ways. Howard was big and broad shouldered; the face in those pictures which remain to us is expressionless with, we might think, undertones of either shyness or suspicion. James Herbert is of medium height, slim, quick to smile or frown, open and frank. Of course the biggest difference may be that Howard is dead and Herbert ain't, ha-ha.

Howard's best work—his stories of Conan the Barbarian—are in the mythic country of Cimmeria, far in a similarly mythic past inhabited by monsters and beautiful, sexy maidens in need of rescue. And Conan will be happy to effect said rescue . . . if the price is right. Herbert's work is set firmly in England's present, most commonly against the backdrop of London or the southern counties which surround it. Howard was brought up in rural circumstances (he lived and died in a small sagebrush town called Cross Plains, Texas); Herbert was born in London's East End, the son of street traders, and his work reflects a checkered career as a rock and roll singer, artist, and ad executive.

It is in the elusive matter of style—a confusing word that may be most accurately defined as "plan or method of attack"—that Herbert strongly recalls the Howard that was. In his novels of horror—*The Rats, The Fog, The Survivor, The Spear, The Lair,* and *The Dark*—Herbert does not just write; as Robert E. Howard did, he puts on his combat boots and goes out to assault the reader with horror.

Let me also take a moment to point out one similarity that James Herbert and Ramsey Campbell do share, simply by virtue of their Englishness: they both write that clear, lucid, grammatical prose that only those educated in England seem able to produce. You'd think that the ability to write lucid prose would be the bottom line for any publishing novelist, but it is not so. If you don't believe me, go check out the paperback originals rack at your local bookstore. I promise you such a carnival of dangling participles, misplaced modifiers, and even lack of agreement between subject and verb that your hair may turn white. You would expect that proofreaders and copy editors would pick this sort of stuff up even if the writers of such embarrassing English do not, but many of them seem as illiterate as the writers they are trying to bail out.

Worse than the mechanical errors, many writers of fiction seem totally unable to explain simple operations or actions clearly enough for the reader to be able to see them in his or her mind's eye. Some of this is a failure on the writer's part to visualize well and completely; his or her own mind's eye seems bleared half-shut. More of it is a simple failure of that most basic writer's tool, the working vocabulary. If you're writing a haunted-house story and you don't know the difference between a gable and a gambrel, a cupola and a turret, paneling and wain-scotting, you, sir or madam, are in trouble.

Now don't get me wrong here; I thought Edwin Newman's book on the degeneration of the English language was moderately entertaining but also often tiresome and amazingly prissy, the book of a man who would like to put language inside a hermetically sealed bell-jar (like a carefully groomed corpse inside a glass coffin) instead of sending it out into the streets to jive with the people. But language has its own point and reason for being. Parapsychologists may argue over extrasensory perception; psychologists and neurologists may claim there is no such thing; but those who love books and love the language know that the printed word really is a kind of telepathy. In most cases the writer does her or his work silently, couching thoughts in symbols composed of letters in groups set off one from the next by white space, and in most cases the reader does her or his work silently, reading the symbols and reintegrating them as thoughts and images. Louis Zukofsky, the poet (*A*, among other books), claimed that even the look of words on the page—the indents, the punctuation, the place on the line where the paragraph ends—has its own story to tell. "Prose," Zukofsky said, "is poetry."

It's probably true that the writer's thoughts and the reader's thoughts never tally exactly, that the image the writer sees and the image the reader sees are never 100 percent the same. We are, after all, not angels but were made a little less than the angels, and our language is maddeningly hobbled, a fact to which any poet or novelist will attest. There is no creative writer, I think, who has not suffered that frustrating crash off the walls which stand at the limits of language, who has not cursed the word that just doesn't exist. Emotions such as grief and romantic love are particularly hard to deal with, but even such a simple operation as starting up a car with a manual transmission and driving it to the end of the block can present nearly insurmountable problems if you try to write the process down instead of simply *doing* it. And if you don't believe this is so, write down such instructions and try them on a nondriving friend . . . but check your auto insurance policy first.

Different languages seem particularly suited to different purposes; the French may have gotten a reputation for being great lovers because the French language seems particularly well suited to the expression of emotion (there is no nicer way to say it than *Je t'aime* . . . and no better language in which to sound really jacked off at someone). German is the language of explanation and clarification (but it is a cold language for all that; the sound of many people speaking German is the sound of large machines running in a factory). English serves very well to express thought and moderately well to express image, but there is nothing inherently lovely about it (although as someone has pointed out, it has its queerly perverse moments; think of the lovely and euphonious sound of the words "proctological examination"). It has always seemed to me ill suited to the expression of feeling, though. Neither "Why don't we go to bed together" or the cheerful but undeniably crude "Baby, let's fuck" can touch *"Voulez-vous coucher avec moi ce soir?"* But we must do the best we can with what we have . . . and as readers of Shakespeare and Faulkner will attest, the best we can do is often remarkably good.

American writers are more apt to mangle the language than our British cousins (although I'd argue with anyone that English English is much more bloodless than American English—many British writers have the unhappy habit of droning; droning in perfectly grammatical English, but a drone is still a drone for a' that and a' that), often because they were subjected to poor or erratic teaching methods as children, but the best American work is striking in a way that British prose and poetry rarely is anymore: see, for instance, such disparate writers as James Dickey, Harry Crews, Joan Didion, Ross Mac-Donald, John Irving.

Both Campbell and Herbert write that unmistakable, impeccable English line; their stories go out into the world with their pants buttoned, their zippers zipped, and their braces in their places—but to what a different ultimate effect!

James Herbert comes at us with both hands, not willing to simply engage our attention; he seizes us by the lapels and begins to scream in our faces. It is not a tremendously artistic method of attack, and no one is ever going to compare him to Doris Letting or V. S. Naipaul . . . but it works.

The Fog (no relation to the film of the same name by John Carpenter) is a multiple-viewpoint story about what happens when an underground explosion breaches a steel cannister that has been buried by the British Ministry of Defense. The cannister contains a living organism called a mycoplasma (an ominous protoplasm that may remind readers of an obscure Japanese horror film from the fifties titled *The H-Man*) which resembles a smoggy yellow-green mist. Like rabies, it attacks the brains of the humans and animals it envelops, turning them into raving maniacs. Some of the incidents involving animals are particularly grisly; a farmer is trampled to death by his own cows in a foggy pasture, and a drunken shopkeeper who seems to loathe everything but his racing pigeons (and one battered old campaigner in particular, a pigeon named Claude) has his eyes pecked out by his birds, who have flown back to their London coop through the fog. The shopkeeper, clutching the remains of his face, staggers off the rooftop where the birds are quartered and falls to his death.

Herbert rarely finesses and never pulls back from the crunch; instead he seems to race eagerly, zestfully, toward each new horror. In one scene a crazed bus driver castrates the teacher who has been his nemesis with a pair of garden shears; in another, an elderly poacher who has been previously caught and "thrashed" by the local large landowner suffers the effects of the fog, goes after the landowner, and nails him to his own dining room table before finishing him off with an ax. A snotty bank manager is locked in his own vault, a gym teacher is beaten to death by his phys ed students, and in the book's most effective scene, almost a hundred and fifty thousand residents and holiday-makers at Bournemouth walk into the ocean in a massive, lemminglike group suicide.

The Fog was published in 1975, three years before the gruesome events at Jonestown, Guyana, and in many of the book's episodes—particularly in the Bournemouth episode—Herbert seems to have forecast it. We see the event through the eyes of a young woman named Mavis Evers. Her lesbian lover has just left her, having discovered the joys of going hetero, and Mavis has gone to Bournemouth to commit suicide . . . a little irony worthy of E.C. comics at their best. She wades breast-deep into the water, becomes frightened, and decides she will try living a little longer. The undertow nearly gets her, but following a short, tense struggle, she is able to get to shallow water again. Turning to face the shore, Mavis is greeted by this nightmare:

> There were hundreds—could it be thousands—of people climbing down the steps to the beach and walking toward her, toward the sea!
>
> Was she dreaming? . . . The people of the town were marching in a solid wall out to the sea, making no sound, staring toward the horizon as though something was beckoning to them. Their faces were white, trancelike, barely human. And there were children among them; some

walked along on their own, seeming to belong to no one; those that couldn't walk were being carried. Most of the people were in their nightclothes, some were naked, having risen from their beds as though answering a call that Mavis neither heard nor saw. . . .

This was written *before* the Jonestown tragedy, remember.

In the aftermath of that, I recall one commentator intoning with dark and solemn sonorousness, "It was an event that not even the most darkly fertile imagination could have envisioned." I flashed on the Bournemouth scene from *The Fog* and thought, "You're wrong. James Herbert envisioned it."

> . . . still they came on, oblivious to her cries, unseeing. She realized her danger and ran toward them in a vain attempt to break through, but they forced her back, heedless of her pleas as she strained against them. She managed to push a short path through them, but the great numbers before her were unconquerable, pushing her back, back into the waiting sea. . . .

Well, as you've probably guessed, poor old Mavis gets her suicide whether she wants it or not. And in point of fact, it is explicit scenes of horror and violence like the one just described which have made Herbert the focus of a great deal of criticism in his native England. He told me that he finally got sick enough of the "Do you write violence for the sake of violence?" question to finally blow up at a reporter. "That's right," he said. "I write violence for the sake of violence, just as Harold Robbins writes sex for the sake of sex, and Robert Heinlein writes science fiction for the sake of science fiction, and Margaret Drabble writes literature for the sake of literature. Except no one ever asks them, do they?"

As to how Herbert came to write *The Fog*, he replies: "It's about impossible to remember where any idea comes from—I mean a single idea may come from many sources. But as clearly as I can recall, the kernel came during a business meeting. I was with an advertising firm then, and sitting in the office of my creative director, who was a rather dull man. And all of a sudden it occurred to me: 'What would happen if this man just turned, walked to the window, opened it, and stepped out?' "

Herbert turned the idea over in his mind for some time and finally sat down to do the novel, spending about eight months' worth of weekends and late nights getting it together. "The thing I like best about it," he says, "is that it had no limits of structure or place. It could simply go on and on until the thing resolved itself. I liked working with my main characters, but I also liked the vignettes because when I got tired of what my heroes were up to, I could go off on just about any tangent I liked. My feeling throughout the writing was, 'I'm just going to enjoy myself. I'm going to try to go over the top; to see how much I can get away with.' "

In its construction, *The Fog* shows the effect of those apocalyptic Big Bug movies of the late fifties and early sixties. All the ingredients are there: we have a mad scientist who was screwing around with something he didn't understand and was killed by the mycoplasma he invented; the military testing secret weapons and unleashing the horror, the "young scientist" hero, John Holman, who we first meet bravely rescuing a little girl from the fissure that has Unleashed the Fog on an Unsuspecting World; the beautiful girlfriend, Casey; the obligatory gathering of scientists, who natter about "the F100 method of fog dispersion" and lament the fact that carbon dioxide can't be used to disperse the fog because "the organism thrives on it" and who inform us that the fog is really "a pleuro-pneumonia-like organism."

We will recognize these obligatory trappings of science fiction from such movies as *Tarantula, The Deadly Mantis, Them!*, and a dozen others; yet we will also recognize that trappings are all they are, and the heart of Herbert's novel lies not in the fog's origin or composition but in its decidedly Dionysian effects—murder, suicide, sexual aberrations, and all manner of deviant behavior. Holman, the hero, is our representative from a saner Apollonian world, and to do Herbert full justice, he manages to make Holman a good deal more interesting than the zero-heroes played by William Hopper, Craig Stevens, and Peter Graves in various of the Big Bug films . . . or consider, if you will, poor old Hugh Marlowe in *Earth vs. the Flying Saucers,* whose entire set of lines during the last third of the movie seems to consist of, "Keep firing at saucer!" and "Fire at saucer until it crashes!"

Nonetheless, our interest in Holman's adventures and whether or not his girlfriend Casey will recover from the effects of her own bout with the fog (and what will be her reaction to the information that she plunged a scissors into her father's stomach while under the influence?) seems pallid when compared to our morbid let's-slow-down-and-look-at-the-accident interest in the old lady who is eaten alive by her pet cats or the crazed pilot who crashes his loaded jumbo jet into the London skyscraper where his wife's lover works.

I suppose that popular fiction divides itself quite naturally into two halves: what we call "mainstream fiction" and that which I would call "pulp fiction." The pulps, including the so-called "shudder-pulps," of which *Weird Tales* was the finest exponent, have been long gone from the scene, but they live on in the novel and do a brisk business on paperback racks everywhere. Many of these modern pulps would have been printed as multipart serials in the pulp magazines that existed roughly from 1910 until about 1950, had they been written during that period. But I wouldn't restrict the label "pulp" simply to genre works of horror, fantasy, science fiction, detective, and western; Arthur Hailey, for instance, seems to me to be writing modern-day pulp. The ingredients are all there, from the inevitable violence to the inevitable maiden in distress. The critics who have regularly toasted Hailey over the coals are the same critics who—infuriatingly enough—see the novel as divisible only into two categories: "literature," which may either succeed or fail upon its merits, and "popular fiction," which always fails, no matter how good it may be (every now and then a writer such as John D. MacDonald may be elevated in the critical mind from a writer of "popular fiction" to a writer of "literature," at which point his body of work may be safely reevaluated).

My own idea is that fiction actually falls into three main categories: literature, mainstream fiction, and pulp fiction—and that to categorize does not end the critic's job but only gives him or her a place to set his or her feet. To label a novel "pulp" is not the same as saying it's a bad novel, or will give the reader no pleasure. Of course we will readily accept that most pulp fiction is indeed bad; there is not a great deal one can say in defense of such brass oldies from the pulp era as William Shelton's "Seven Heads of Bushongo" or "Satan's Virgin," by Ray Cummings.* On the other hand, though, Dashiell Hammett published extensively in the pulps (most notably in the highly regarded *Black Mask,* where contemporaries Raymond Chandler, James M. Cain, and Cornell Woolrich also published); Tennessee Williams's first published wok, a vaguely Lovecraftian tale titled "The Vengeance of Nitocris," appeared in an early issue of *Weird Tales;* Bradbury broke in by way of the same market; so did MacKinlay Kantor, who would go on to write *Andersonville.*

To condemn pulp writing out of hand is like condemning a girl as loose simply because she comes from unpleasant family circumstances. The fact that supposedly reputable critics both in the genre and outside it continue to do so makes me both sad and angry. James Herbert is not a nascent Tennessee Williams only waiting for the right time to spin a cocoon and emerge as a great figure of modern literature; he is what he is and that's all that he is, as Popeye would say. My point is simply that what he is, is good enough. I loved John Jakes's comment

---

* And there's a wonderful story about Erle Stanley Gardner's days in what Frank Gruber used to call the pulp jungle. At that time the Depression was in full swing and Gardner was writing westerns for a penny a word, selling to such publications as *Western Round-Up, West Weekly,* and *Western Tales* (whose slogan was "Fifteen Stories, Fifteen Cents"). Gardner admitted that he made a habit of stretching the final shoot-out as far as it would go. Of course the bad guy finally bit the dust and the good guy strode into the saloon, .44s smoking and spurs jingling, for a cold sarsaparilla before moving on, but in the meantime, each time Gardner wrote "Bang!" he made another penny . . . and in those days, two bangs would buy you the daily newspaper.

on his Bicentennial/Kent Family saga some years back. He said that Gore Vidal was the Rolls-Royce of historical novelists; that he himself was more in the Chevrolet Vega class. What Jakes so modestly left unstated was that both vehicles will get you where you want to go quite adequately; how you feel about style is between you and you.

James Herbert is the only writer discussed in these pages who is squarely in the pulp tradition. He specializes in violent death, bloody confrontation, explicit and in some cases kinky sex, strong and virile young heroes possessed of beautiful girl-friends. The problem which needs to be solved is in most cases apparent, and the story's emphasis is put squarely on solving that problem. But Herbert works effectively within his chosen genre. He has consistently refused, from the very first, to be satisfied with characters who are nothing more than cardboard cutouts which he moves around the playing-field of his novel; in most cases we are given motivations we can identify with and believe in, as in the case of poor, suicide-bound Mavis. Mavis reflects with a kind of pitiful, deranged defiance that "She wanted them to know she had taken her own life; her death, unlike her life, had to have some meaning. Even if it was only Ronnie who fully understood that reason." This is hardly stunning character insight, but it is fully adequate to Herbert's purposes, and if the ironic outcome is similar to the ironic outcome of the tales in E.C.'s series of horror comics, we are able to see more and thus believe more, a victory for Herbert which the reader can share. Further, Herbert has continued to improve. *The Fog* is his second novel; those that follow show a gratifying development in the writer, culminating perhaps in *The Spear*, which shows us a writer who has stepped out of the pulp arena altogether and has entered the wider field of the mainstream novel.

9

Which brings us to Harlan Ellison . . . and all kinds of problems. Because here it is impossible to separate the man from the work. I've decided to close this brief review of some of the elements in modern horror fiction by discussing Ellison's work because, although he repudiates the label "horror writer," he sums up, for me, the finest elements of the term. Closing with Ellison is perhaps almost mandatory because in his short stories of fantasy and horror, he strikes closest to all those things which horrify and amuse us (sometimes both at the same time) in our present lives. Ellison is haunted by the death of Kitty Genovese—a murder that comes up in his "The Whimper of Whipped Dogs" and in several of his essays—the mass suicides in Jonestown; and he is convinced that Iran's Ayatollah has created a senile dream of power in which we are now all living (like men and women in a fantasy tale who ultimately come to realize they are living in a psychotic's hallucinations). Most of all, it seems to me that Ellison's work is the proper place to conclude because he never looks back; he has been the field's point-man for fifteen years now, and if there is such a thing as a fantasist for the 1980s (always assuming there *are* a 1980s, ha-ha), then Harlan Ellison is almost surely that writer. He has quite deliberately provoked a storm of controversy over his own work—one writer in the field whom I know considers him to be a modern incarnation of Jonathan Swift, and another regularly refers to him as "that no-talent son of a bitch." It is a storm that Ellison lives in quite contentedly.

"You're not a writer at all," an interviewer once told me in slightly wounded tones. "You're a goddamn industry. How do you ever expect serious people to take you seriously if you keep turning out a book a year?" Well, in point of fact, I'm not "a goddamn industry" (unless it's a cottage industry); I work steadily, that's all. Any writer who only produces a book every seven years is not thinking Deep Thoughts; even a long book takes at most three years to think and write. No, a writer who only produces one book every seven years is simply dicking off. But my own fecundity—however fecund that may be—pales before Ellison's, who has written at a ferocious clip; at this point he has published just over one thousand short stories. In addition to all the stories published under his own name, Ellison has written as Nalrah Nosille, Sley Harson, Landon Ellis, Deny Tiger, Price Curtis, Paul Merchant, Lee Archer, E. K. Jarvis, Ivar Jorgensen, Clyde Mitchell, Ellis Hart, Jay Solo, Jay Charby, Wallace Edmondson—and Cordwainer Bird.*

The Cordwainer Bird name is a good example of Ellison's restless wit and his anger at work he feels to be substandard dreck. Since the early sixties he has done many TV scripts, including produced scripts for *Alfred Hitchcock Presents, The Man from U.N.C.L.E., The Young Lawyers, The Outer Limits,* and what many fans reel may have been the best *Star Trek* episode of them all, "The City on the Edge of Forever." † At the same

---

* All quoted in the Ellison entry by John Clute and Peter Nicholls in *The Science Fiction Encyclopedia.* To point out the obvious, "Nalrah Nosille" is Harlan Ellison spelled backwards. Other names Ellison used—E. K. Jarvis, Ivar Jorgensen, and Clyde Mitchell—were so-called house names. In pulp terminology, a "house name" was the name of a totally fictional writer who was, nevertheless, extremely prolific . . . mostly because several (sometimes dozens) of writers published works under that name when they had another story in the same magazine. Thus, "Ivar Jorgensen" wrote Ellison-style fantasy when he was Ellison and sexy, pulp-style horror, as in the Jorgensen novel *Rest in Agony,* when he was someone else (in this case, Paul Fairman). To this should be added that Ellison has since acknowledged all of his pseudonomous work, and has published only under his own name since 1965. He has, he says, a "lemming-like urge to be up front."

† This may be the longest footnote in history, but I really must pause and tell two more Harlan stories, one apocryphal, the other Harlan's version of the same incident.

The apocryphal, which I first heard at a science fiction bookstore, and later at several different fantasy and science fiction conventions: It was told that Paramount Pictures had a preproduction conference of Big Name Science Fiction Writers prior to shooting on *Star Trek: The Movie.* The purpose of the conference was to toss around ideas for a mission that would be big enough to fly the Starship *Enterprise* from the cathode tube to the Silver Screen . . . and BIG was the word that the exec in charge of the conference kept emphasizing. One writer suggested that the *Enterprise* might be sucked into a black hole (the Disney people scoffed that idea up about three months later). The Paramount exec didn't think that was big enough. Another suggested that Kirk, Spock, and company might discover a pulsar that was in fact a living organism. Still not big enough, the writer was admonished; the writers were again reminded that they should think BIG. According to the tale, Ellison sat silent, doing a slow burn . . . only with Harlan, a slow burn lasts only about five seconds. Finally, he spoke up. "The *Enterprise,*" he said, "goes through an interstellar warp, the great-granddaddy of all interstellar warps. It's transported over a googol of light-years in the space of seconds and comes out at a huge gray wall. The wall marks the edge of the entire universe. Scotty rigs full-charge ion blasters which breach the wall so they can see what's beyond the edge of everything. Peering through at them, bathed in an incredible while light, is the face of God Himself."

time he was writing these scripts for television—and winning an unprecedented three Writers Guild of America awards for best dramatic television scripts in the process—Ellison was engaging in a bitter running battle, a kind of creative guerilla warfare, with other TV producers over what he regarded as a deliberate effort to degrade his work and to degrade the

---

A brief period of silence followed this. Then the exec said, "It's not big enough. Didn't I just tell you guys to think really BIG?"

In response, Ellison is supposed to have flipped the guy the bird (the *Cordwainer* Bird, one assumes) and walked out.

Here is Harlan Ellison's recitation of the True Facts:

"Paramount had been trying to get a *Star Trek* film in work for some time. Roddenberry was determined that his name would be on the writing credits somehow. . . . The trouble is, he can't write for sour owl poop. His one idea, done six or seven times in the series and again in the feature film, is that the crew of the *Enterprise* goes into deepest space, finds God, and God turns out to be insane, or a child, or both. I'd been called in twice, prior to 1975, to discuss the story. Other writers had also been milked. Paramount couldn't make up their minds and had even kicked Gene off the project a few times, until he brought in lawyers. Then the palace guard changed again at Paramount and Diller and Eisner came over from ABC and brought a cadre of their . . . buddies. One of them was an ex-set designer . . . named Mark Trabulus.

"Roddenberry suggested me as the scenarist for the film with this Trabulus, the latest . . . of the know-nothing duds Paramount had assigned to the troublesome project. I had a talk with Gene . . . about a storyline. He told me they kept wanting bigger and bigger stories and no matter what was suggested, it wasn't big enough. I devised a storyline and Gene liked it, and set up a meeting with Trabulus for 11 December (1975). That meeting was canceled . . . but we finally got together on 15 December. It was just Gene (Roddenberry) and Trabulus and me in Gene's office on the Paramount lot.

"I told them the story. It involved going to the end of the known universe to slip back through time to the Pleistocene period when Man first emerged. I postulated a parallel development of reptile life that might have developed into the dominant species on Earth had not mammals prevailed. I postulated an alien intelligence from a far galaxy where the snakes *had* become the dominant life form, and a snake-creature who had come to Earth in the *Star Trek* future, had seen its ancestors wiped out, and who had gone back into the far past of Earth to set up distortions in the time-flow so the reptiles could beat the humans. The *Enterprise* goes back to set time right, finds the snake-alien, and the human crew is confronted with the moral dilemma of whether it had the right to wipe out an entire life form just to ensure its own territorial imperative in our present and future. The story, in short, spanned all of time and all of space, with a moral and ethical problem.

"Trabulus listened to all this and sat silently for a few minutes. Then he said, 'You know, I was reading this book by a guy named Von Daniken and he proved that the Maya calendar was exactly like ours, so it must have come from aliens. Could you put in some Mayans?'

"I looked at Gene; Gene looked at me; he said nothing. I looked at Trabulus and said, 'There weren't any Mayans at the dawn of time.' And he said, 'Well, who's to know the difference?' And I said, '*I'm* to know the difference. It's a dumb suggestion.' So Trabulus got very uptight and said he liked Mayans a lot and why didn't I do it if I wanted to write this picture. So *I* said, 'I'm a writer. I don't know *what* the fuck *you* are!' And I got up and walked out. And that was the end of my association with the *Star Trek* movie."

Which leaves the rest of us mortals, who can never find exactly the right word at exactly the right time, with nothing to say but "Right on, Harlan!"

medium itself ("to Cuisinart it," in Ellison's own words). In cases where he felt his work had become so watered down that he no longer wanted his name on the credits, he would substitute the name of Cordwainer Bird—a name that comes up again in "The New York Review of Bird" in *Strange Wine*, a madly amusing story that might well be subtitled "The Chicago Seven Visit Brentano's."

Cordwainer is an archaic English word for "shoemaker"; so the literal meaning of Ellison's pen name for scripts which he feels have been perverted beyond any kind of useful life is "one who makes shoes for birds." It is, I think, as good an explanation as any for the work that television is engaged in, and suggests quite well the nature of its usefulness.

It is not the purpose of this book to talk about people *per se*, nor is it the purpose of this chapter on horror fiction to fulfill a "personal glimpse of the writer" sort of function; that is the job of the Out of the Pages section in *People* magazine (which my youngest son, with unknowing critical acuity, insists on calling *Pimple*). But in the case of Harlan Ellison, the man and his work have become so entwined that it is impossible to pull them completely apart.

The book I want to talk about here is Ellison's collection of short fiction, *Strange Wine* (1978). But each Ellison collection seems built on the collections which have preceded it—each seems to be Ellison's report to the outside world on the subject This Is Where Harlan Is Now. And so it becomes necessary to discuss this book in a more personal way. He demands it of himself, and while that doesn't specially matter, his work also demands it . . . and that does matter.

Ellison's fiction is and always has been a nervous bundle of contradictions. He's not a novelist, he says, but he has written at least two novels, and one of them, *Rockabilly* (later retitled *Spider Kiss*), remains one of the two or three best novels ever to be published about the cannibalistic world of rock and roll music. He says he's not a fantasist, but nearly all of his stories are fantasies. In the course of *Strange Wine*, for instance, we meet a writer whose work is done for him by gremlins after the writer himself has gone dry; we also meet a nice Jewish boy who is haunted by his mother after she dies ("Mom, why don't you get off my case?" Lance, the nice Jewish boy in question, asks the ghost desperately at one point; "I saw you playing with yourself last night," the shade of Mom returns sadly).

In the introduction to the book's most frightening story, "Croatoan," Ellison says he is pro-choice when it comes to abortion, just as he has said in both his fiction and in his essays over the last twenty years that he is an affirmed liberal and free-thinker,* but "Croatoan"—and most of Ellison's short stories—are as sternly moralistic as the words of an Old Testament prophet. In many of the out-and-out horror tales there is more than a whiff of those *Tales from the Vault/Vault of Horror* ghastlies where the climax so often involves the evildoer having his crimes revisited upon himself . . . only raised to the tenth power. But the irony cuts with a keener blade in Ellison's work, and we have less feeling that rough justice has been meted out and the balance restored. In Ellison's stories, we have little sense of winners and losers. Sometimes there are survivors. Sometimes there are no survivors.

"Croatoan" uses that myth of alligators under the streets of New York as its starting point—see also Thomas Pynchon's *V.* and a funny-horrible novel called *Death Tour* by David J. Michael; this is an oddly pervasive urban nightmare. But Ellison's story is really about abortion. He may not be antiabortion (nowhere in his intro to this story does he say he's *pro*-abortion, however), but the story is certainly more sharply honed and unsettling than that tattered piece of yellow journalism which all right-to-lifers apparently keep in their wallets or purses so they can wave it under your nose at the drop of an opinion—this is the one which purports to have been written by a baby

---

* Ellison Anecdote #2: My wife and I attended a lecture that Harlan gave at the University of Colorado in the fall of 1974. He had at that time just finished "Croatoan," the skin-freezer which leads off *Strange Wine*, and he'd had a vasectomy two days before. "I'm still bleeding," he told the audience, "and my lady can attest that I'm telling the truth." The lady did to attest, and an elderly couple began to make their way out of the auditorium, looking a bit shocked. Harlan waved a cheery goodbye to them from the podium. "Night, folks," he called. "Sorry it wasn't what you wanted."

while *in utero*. "I can't wait to see the sun and the flowers," the fetus gushes. "I can't wait to see my mother's face, smiling down at me . . ." It ends, of course, with the fetus saying, "Last night my mother killed me."

"Croatoan" begins with the protagonist flushing the aborted fetus down the toilet. The ladies who have done the deed to the protagonist's girlfriend have packed their d & c tools and left. Carol, the woman who has had the abortion, flips out and demands that the protagonist go and find the fetus. Trying to placate her, he goes out into the street with a crowbar, levers up a manhole cover . . . and descends into a different world.

The alligator story began, of course, as a result of the give-a-kid-a-baby-alligator-aren't-they-just-the-*cutest*-little-things craze of the mid-fifties. The kid who got the gator would keep it for a few weeks, then the tiny alligator would all of a sudden not be so tiny anymore. It would nip, perhaps draw blood, and down the toilet it went. It was not so farfetched to believe that they might all be down there on the black underside of our society, feeding, growing bigger, waiting to gobble up the first unwary sewer repairman to come sloshing along in his hipwaders. As David Michael points out in *Death Tour,* the problem is that most sewers are much too cold to sustain life in fully grown alligators, let alone in those still small enough to flush away. Such a dull fact, however, is hardly enough to kill such a powerful image . . . and I understand that a movie which takes this image as its text is on the way.

Ellison has always been a sociological sort of writer, and we can almost feel him seizing upon the symbolic possibilities of such an idea, and when the protagonist descends deep enough into this purgatorial world, he discovers a mystery of cryptic, Lovecraftian proportions:

> At the entrance of their land someone—not the children, they couldn't have done it—long ago built a road sign. It is a rotted log on which has been placed, carved from fine cherrywood, a book and a hand. The book is open, and the hand rests on the book, one finger touching

the single word carved in the open pages. The word is
CROATOAN.

Further along, the secret is revealed. Like the alligators of
the myth, the fetuses have not died. The sin is not so easily gotten rid of. Used to swimming in placental waters, in their own
way as primitive and reptilian as alligators themselves, the fetuses have survived the flush and live here in the dark, symbolically existing in the filth and the shit dropped down on them
from the society of our overworld. They are the embodiment of
such Old Testament maxims as "Sin never dies" and "Be sure
your sin will find you out."

> Down here in this land beneath the city live the chil-
> dren. They live easily and in strange ways. I am only now
> coming to know the incredible manner of their existence.
> How they eat, what they eat, bow they manage to sur-
> vive, and have managed for hundreds of years, these are
> all things I learn day by day, with wonder surmounting
> wonder.
> I am the only adult here.
> They have been waiting for me.
> They call me father.

At its simplest, "Croatoan" is a tale of the Just Revenge. The
protagonist is a rotter who has casually impregnated a number
of women; the abortion on Carol is not the first one his friends
Denise and Joanna have performed for this irresponsible Don
Juan (although they swear it will be the last). The Just Revenge
is that he finds his dodged responsibilities have been waiting
for him all along, as implacable as the rotting corpse which
to often returned from the dead to hunt down its killer in the
archetypical *Haunt of Fear* story (the Graham Ingles classic
"Horror We? How's Bayou?" for instance).

But Ellison's prose style is arresting, his grasp of this myth-
image of the lost alligators seems solid and complete, and his
evocation of this unsuspected underworld is marvelous. Most

of all, we sense outrage and anger—as with the best Ellison stories, we sense personal involvement, and have a feeling that Ellison is not so much telling the tale as he is jabbing it viciously out of its hiding place. It is the feeling that we are walking over a lot of jagged glass in thin shoes, or running across a minefield in the company of a lunatic. Accompanying these feelings is the feeling that Ellison is preaching to us . . . not in any lackluster, ho-hum way, but in a large, bellowing voice that may make us think of Jonathan Edwards's "Sinners in the Hands of an Angry God." His best stories seem strong enough to contain morals as well as themes, and the most surprising and gratifying thing about his short fiction is that he gets away with the moralizing; we find he rarely sells his birthright for a plot of message. It should not be so, but in his fury, Ellison manages to carry everything, not at a stagger but at a sprint.

In "Hitler Painted Roses," we have Margaret Thrushwood, whose sufferings make Job's look like a bad case of athlete's foot. In this fantasy, Ellison supposes—much as Stanley Elkin does in *The Living End*—that the reality we experience in the afterlife depends on politics: namely, on what people back here think of us. Further, it posits a universe where God (a multiple God here, referred to as They) is an image-conscious poseur with no real interest in right or wrong.

Margaret's lover, a Mr. Milquetoast veterinarian named Doc Thomas, murders the entire Ramsdell family in 1935 when he discovers that the hypocritical Ramsdell ("I'll have no whores in my house," Ramsdell says when he catches Margaret in the kip with Doc) has been helping himself to a bit of Margaret every now and then; Ramsdell's definition of "whore" apparently begins when Margaret's sex partner stops being him.

Only Margaret survives Doc's berserk rage, and when she is discovered alive by the townspeople, she is immediately assumed guilty, carried to the Ramsdell well naked, and pitched in. Margaret is sent to hell for the crime she is presumed to have committed, while Doc Thomas, who dies peacefully in bed twenty-six years later, goes to heaven. Ellison's vision of heaven also resembles Stanley Elkin's in *The Living End*. "Paradise,"

Elkin tells us, resembles "a small theme-park." Ellison sees it as a place where moderate beauty balances off—but just barely—moderate tackiness. There are other similarities; in both cases good—nay, *saintly!*—people are sent to hell because of what amounts to a clerical error, and in this desperate view of the modern condition, even the gods are existential. The only horror we are spared is a vision of the Almighty in Adidas sneakers with a Head tennis racket over His shoulder and a golden coke-spoon around His neck. All of this comes next year, no doubt.

Before we leave the comparison entirely, let me point out that while Elkin's novel was heavily and for the most part favorably reviewed, Ellison's story, originally published in *Penthouse* (a magazine not regularly purchased by seekers after literary excellence), is almost unknown. *Strange Wine* itself is almost unknown, in fact. Most critics ignore fantasy fiction because they don't know what to do with it unless it is out-and-out allegory. "I do not choose to review fantasy," a sometime-critic for no less an organ than the *New York Times Book Review* once told me. "I have no interest in the hallucinations of the mad." It's always good to be in contact with such an open mind. It broadens one.

Margaret Thrushwood escapes hell through a fluke, and in his heroically overblown description of the auguries which foreshadow this supernatural belch, Ellison has an amusing whack at rewriting Act I of Shakespeare's *Julius Caesar*. Humor and horror are the original Chang and Eng of literature, and Ellison knows it. We laugh . . . but there is still that undercurrent of unease.

> As the smoldering sun passed the celestial equator going north to south, numberless portents revealed themselves: a two-headed calf was born in Dorset near the little town of Blandford; wrecked ships rose from the depths of the Marianas Trench; everywhere, children's eyes grew old and very wise; over the Indian state of Maharashtra clouds assumed the shapes of warring armies; leprous moss quickly grew on the south side of Celtic megaliths and then died

away in minutes; in Greece the pretty little gilly-flowers began to bleed and the earth around their clusters gave off a putrescent smell; all sixteen of the ominous *dirae* designated by Julius Caesar in the first century B.C., including the spilling of salt and wine, stumbling, sneezing, and the creaking of chairs, made themselves apparent; the aurora australis appeared to the Maori; a horned horse was seen by Basques as it ran through the streets of Vizcaya. Numberless other auguries.

And the doorway to Hell opened.

The best thing about the passage quoted above is that we can feel Ellison taking off, pleased with the effect and balance of the language and the particulars described, pushing it, having fun with it. Among those who escape hell during the brief period that the door stands open are Jack the Ripper, Caligula, Charlotte Corday, Edward Teach ("beard still bristling but with the ribbons therein charred and colorless . . . laughing hideously"), Burke and Hare, and George Armstrong Custer.

All are sucked back except for Ellison's Lizzie Borden lookalike, Margaret Thrushwood. She makes her way to heaven, confronts Doc . . . and is sent back by God when her realization of the hypocrisy at work causes heaven to begin cracking and peeling around the edges. The pool of water Doc is soaking his feet in when Margaret drags her blackened, blistered body over to him begins to fill up with lava.

Margaret returns to hell, realizing that she can take it, while poor Doc, who she still manages somehow to love, could not. "There are some people who just shouldn't be allowed to fool around with love," she tells God in the story's best line. Hitler, meanwhile, is still painting his roses just inside the portal to hell (he has been too absorbed to even think about escape when the door opened). God takes one look, Ellison tells us, and "could not wait to get back to find Michelangelo, to tell him about the grandeur They had beheld, there in that most unlikely of places."

The grandeur Ellison wants us to see, of course, is not

Hitler's roses but Margaret's ability to love and to go on believing (if only in herself) in a world where the innocent are punished and the guilty rewarded. As in most of Ellison's fiction, the horror revolves around some smelly injustice; its antidote lies most frequently in the human ability of his protagonists to surmount the unfair situation, or, lacking that, at least to reach a *modus vivendi* with it.

Most of these stories are fables—an uneasy word in a period of literature when the concept of literature is seen to be a simplistic one—and Ellison uses the word frankly in several of his introductions to individual stories. In a letter to me, dated December 28, 1979, he discusses the use of the fable in fantasy fiction that has been deliberately laid against the backdrop of the modern world:

"*Strange Wine* continues—as I see it in retrospect—my perception that reality and fantasy have exchanged positions in contemporary society. If there is a unified theme in the stories, it is that. Continued from the work I have done in the previous two books. *Approaching Oblivion* (1974) and *Deathbird Stories* (1975), it tries to provide a kind of superimposed precontinuum by the use and understanding of which the reader who leads even a lightly examined existence can grasp hold of his/her life and transcend his/her fate by understanding it.

"That's all pretty high-flown stuff; but what I mean, simply put, is that the workaday events that command our attention are so big, so fantastic, so improbable that no one who isn't walking the parapet of madness can cope with what's coming down.*

"The Teheran hostages, the Patty Hearst kidnapping, the

---

* Which reminds me of something that happened at the 1979 World Fantasy Conversation. A UPI reporter asked me the eternal question: "Why do people read this horror stuff?" My reply was essentially Harlan's; you try to catch the madness in a bell-jar so you can cope with it a little better. People who read horror fiction are warped, I told the reporter; but if you don't have a few warps in your record, you're going to find it impossible to cope with life in the last quarter of the twentieth century. The headline on the UPI squib that came down the wire and into newspaper coast to coast was predictable enough, I suppose, and exactly what I deserved for presuming to speak metaphorically to a newspaperman: KING SAYS HIS FANS ARE WARPED. Open mouth; insert foot; close mouth.

Howard Hughes fake biography and subsequent death, the Entebbe raid, the murder of Kitty Genovese, the Jonestown massacre, the H-bomb alert in Los Angeles several years ago, Watergate, the Hillside Strangler, the Manson Family, the oil conspiracy: all of them are melodramatic and excessive beyond the ability of a writer of mimetic fiction to capture in fiction without being ridiculous. Yet all of them happened. If you or I were to attempt writing a novel about such things, before the fact, we'd be laughed out of the critical esteem of even the lowliest reviewer.

"I'm not paraphrasing the old saw that truth is stranger than fiction, because I don't see *any* of these events as mirroring 'truth' or 'reality.' Twenty years ago the very *idea* of international terrorism would have been inconceivable. Today it's a given. So commonplace that we're unmanned and helpless in the face of Khomeini's audacity. In one fell swoop the man has become the most important public figure of our time. In short, he has manipulated reality simply by being bold. How precise a paradigm he has become for the copelessness of our times. In this madman we have an example of one who understands— even if subcutaneously—that the real world is infinitely manipulable. He has dreamed, and forced the rest of the world to live in that dream. That it is a nightmare for the rest of us is of no concern to the dreamer. One man's Utopia . . .

"But his example, I suppose, in cathexian terms, is endlessly replicable. And what he has done is what I try to do in my stories. To alter everyday existence in a stretch of fiction. . . . And by the altering, by an insertion of a paradigmatic fantasy element, to permit the reader to perceive what she/he takes for granted in the surrounding precept in a slightly altered way. My hope is that the *frisson,* the tiny shock of new awareness, the little spark of seeing the accepted from an uncomfortable angle, will convince them that there is room enough and time enough, if one only has courage enough, to alter one's existence.

"My message is always the same: we are the finest, most ingenious, potentially the most godlike construct the Universe has ever created. And every man or woman has the ability within him or her to reorder the perceived universe to his or her own design. My stories all speak of courage and ethic and friendship and toughness. Sometimes they do it with love, sometimes with violence, sometimes with pain or sorrow or joy. But they all present the same message: the more you know, the more you can do. Or as Pasteur put it, 'Chance favors the prepared mind.'

"I am antientropy. My work is foursquare for chaos. I spend my life personally, and my work professionally, keeping the soup boiling. Gadfly is what they call you when you are no longer dangerous; I much prefer troublemaker, malcontent, desperado. I see myself as a combination of Zorro and Jiminy Cricket. My stories go out from here and raise hell. From time to time some denigrator or critic with umbrage will say of my work, 'He only wrote that to shock.'

"I smile and nod. Precisely."

So we find that Ellison's effort to "see" the world through a glass of fantasy is not really much different from Kurt Vonnegut's efforts to "see" it through a glass of satire, semi-science-fiction, and a kind of existential vapidity ("Hi-ho . . . so it goes . . . how about that"); or Heller's efforts to "see" it as an endless tragicomedy played out in an open-air madhouse; or Pynchon's effort to "see" it as the longest-running Absurdist play in creation (the epigram heading the second section of *Gravity's Rainbow* is from *The Wizard of Oz*—"I don't think we're in Kansas anymore, Toto . . ."; and I think that Harlan Ellison would agree that this sums up postwar life in America as well as anything else). The essential similarity of these writers is that they are *all* writing fables. In spite of varying styles and points of view, the point in all cases is that these are moral tales.

In the late fifties Richard Matheson wrote a terrifying and utterly convincing tale of a modern-day succubus (a female sexual vampire). In terms of shock and effect, it is one of the best tales I've ever read. There is also a succubus tale in *Strange*

Wine, but in "Lonely Women Are the Vessels of Time," the succubus is *more* than a sexual vampire; she is an agent of moral forces, come to set things back in balance by stealing the self-confidence of a wretched man who likes to pick up lonely women in singles bars because they're easy lays. She exchanges her own loneliness for Mitch's potency and when the sexual encounter is done, she tells him: "Get up and get dressed and get out of here." The story cannot even be described as socio-logical, although it has a patina of sociology; it is a moral tale, pure and simple.

In "Emissary from Hamelin," a child piper returns on the 700th anniversary of the abduction of the children from that medieval town and pipes *finis* for all of mankind. Here Elli-son's basic idea, that progress is progressing in an immoral way, seems a bit shrill and tiresome, an unsurprising mating of the *Twilight Zone* moral stance with that of the Woodstock Nation (we can almost hear PA systems blaring, "And don't forget to pick up the garbage."). The child's explanation for his return is simple and direct: "We want everyone to stop what they are doing to make this a bad place, or we will take this place away from you." But the words Ellison puts into his newspaperman-narrator's mouth to amplify the thought smacks a little bit too much of Woodsy Owl for me: "Stop paving over the green lands with plastic, stop fighting, stop killing friendship, have courage, don't lie, stop brutalizing each other . . ." These are Ellison's own thoughts, and fine thoughts they are, but I like my stories without billboards.

I suppose this sort of misstep—a story with a commercial embedded in its center—is the risk that all "fable fiction" runs. And perhaps the writer of short stories runs a higher risk of falling into the pit than the novelist (although when a novel falls into this pit, the results are even more awful; go down to your local library sometimes, get a stack permit, and look up some of the reporter Tom Wicker's novels from the fifties and sixties—your hair will turn white). In most cases Ellison goes around the pit, jumps over it . . . or jumps right into it, on purpose, avoiding major injury either by his own talent, the grace of God, or a combination of the two.

Some of the stories in *Strange Wine* don't fit so comfortably into the fable category, and Ellison is perhaps at his best when he is simply goofing with the language, not playing whole songs but simply producing runs of melody and feeling. "From A to Z, in the Chocolate Alphabet" is such a story (except it is not really a story at all; it is a series of fragments, some narrative, some not, that reads more like beat poetry). It was written in the window of the Change of Hobbit bookstore in Los Angeles, under circumstances so confusing that Ellison's introduction to the piece does not even really do it justice. The individual pieces produce individual little ripples of feeling, as good short poems do, and reveal an inspired playfulness with the language that is as good a place to conclude all this as anywhere else, I suppose.

Language *is* play to most writers, thoughts are play. Stories are fun, the equivalent of a child's tug-me-push-me car that makes such an entrancing sound when you roll it across the floor. So, to close, "From A to Z, in the Chocolate Alphabet," Harlan Ellison's version of the sound of one hand clapping . . . a sound which only the best fantasy-horror fiction can provide. And set against it, a little something from the work of Clark Ashton Smith, contemporary of Lovecraft and something much closer to a true poet than Lovecraft could ever hope to be; although Lovecraft desperately wanted to be a poet, I think the best we can say about his poetry is that he was a competent enough versifier, and no one would ever mistake one of his moody staves for the work of Rod McKuen. George F. Haas, Smith's biographer, suggests that Smith's finest work may have been *Ebony and Crystal,* and this general reader is inclined to agree, although few readers of modern poetry will find much to like in Smith's conventional treatment of his unconventional subject matter. I suspect, though, that Clark Ashton Smith would have liked what Ellison is doing in "From A to Z, in the Chocolate Alphabet." Here, preceding two selections from the Ellison piece, is a selection from Smith's idea notebook, published by Arkham House two years ago as *The Black Book of Clark Ashton Smith:*

> *The Face from Infinity*
> A man who fears the sky for some indefinable reason, and tries to avoid the open as much as possible. Dying at last in a room with short, curtained windows, he finds himself suddenly on a vast, bare plain beneath . . . a void heaven. Into this heaven, slowly, there arises a dreadful, infinite face, from which he can find no refuge, since all his senses have apparently been merged in the one sense of sight. Death, for him, is the eternal moment in which he confronts the face, and knows why he has always feared the sky.

Now, the ominous jocularity of Harlan Ellison:

> E is for ELEVATOR PEOPLE
> They never speak, and they cannot meet your gaze. There are five hundred buildings in the United States whose elevators go deeper than the basement. When you have pressed the basement button and reached the bottom, you must press the basement button twice more. The elevator doors will close and you will hear the sound of special relays being thrown, and the elevator will descend. Into the caverns. Chance has not looked favorably on occasional voyagers in those five hundred cages. They have pressed the wrong button, too many times. They have been seized by those who shuffle through the caverns, and they have been . . . treated. Now they ride the cages. They never speak, and they cannot meet your gaze. They stare up at the numbers as they light and then go off, riding up and down even after night has fallen. Their clothes are clean. There is a special dry cleaner who does the work. Once you saw one of them, and her eyes were filled with screams. London is a city filled with narrow, secure stairways.

And, finally:

H is for HAMADRYAD

The Oxford English Dictionary has three definitions of hamadryad. The first is: a wood nymph that lives and dies in her tree. The second is: a venemous, hooded serpent of India. The third definition is improbable. None of them mentions the mythic origins of the word. The tree in which the Serpent lived was the hamadryad. Eve was poisoned. The wood of which the cross was made was the hamadryad. Jesus did not rise, he never died. The ark was composed of cubits of lumber cut from the hamadryad. You will find no sign of the vessel on top of Mt. Ararat. It sank. Toothpicks in Chinese restaurants should be avoided at all costs.

So now . . . tell me. Did you hear it? The sound of one hand clapping in thin air?

10

I began this chapter—one hundred and twenty-four manuscript pages and two months ago—by saying that it would be impossible to effect an overview of horror fiction during the last thirty years without writing a whole book on the subject, and that is as true now as it was two months and all those pages ago. All I've been able to do here is to mention some books in the genre that I like, and hopefully draw short arrows in the direction these novels and stories seem to point. I haven't discussed *I Am Legend,* but if you should be intrigued enough to read *The Shrinking Man* as a result of what I've said here, you'll probably get to it, and find Matheson's unmistakable trademarks on that book as well: his interest in restricting character to a single person under pressure so that character can be fully examined, his emphasis on courage in adversity, his mastery of terror against what appears to be a normal, everyday backdrop. I haven't discussed the work of Roald Dahl or John Collier or

Jorge Luis Borges, but if you exhaust Harlan Ellison's current stock of offbeat, jivey fantasy, you will find these others, and in them you will find many of Ellison's interests repeated, particularly his examination of man at his wont, most venal . . . and his best, most courageous and true. To read Anne Rivers Siddons's novel of domicile possession may lead you to my novel on the same subject, *The Shining*, or Robert Marasco's brilliant *Burnt Offerings*.

But a few short arrows is all I can possibly draw. To enter the world of horror fiction is to venture, small as a hobbit, through certain mountain passes (where the only trees which will grow are undoubtedly hamadryads) and into the equivalent of the Land of Mordor. This is the fuming, volcanic country of the Dark Lord, and if the critics who have seen it firsthand are few, the cartographers are fewer. This Land is mostly white space on the map . . . which is how it should be; I'll leave more detailed map making to those graduate students and English teachers who feel that every goose which lays gold must be dissected so that all of its quite ordinary guts can be labelled; to those figurative engineers of the imagination who cannot feel comfortable with the comfortably overgrown (and possibly dangerous) literary wilderness until they have built a freeway composed of Cliff's Notes through it—and listen to me, you people: every English teacher who ever did a Monarch or Cliff's Notes ought to be dragged out of his or her quad, drawn and quartered, then cut up into tiny pieces, said pieces to be dried and shrunk in the sun and then sold in the college bookstore as bookmarks. I'll leave the longer arrows to those pharmacists of creativity who cannot feel totally at ease until each tale, created to hold some reader spellbound as each of us was at one time held spellbound by the story of Hansel and Gretel, Little Red Riding Hood, or The Hook, has been neatly dehydrated and poured into a gel capsule to be swallowed. That is their job—the job of dissectors, engineers, and pharmacists—and I leave it to them, along with the fervent wish that Shelob may catch them and eat them as they enter the Dark Lord's land, or that the faces in the Marsh of the Dead will first hypnotize them and then drive them mad by quoting Cleanth Brooks to them eternally in mud-choked voices, or that the Dark Lord himself will take them up to his Tower forever or cast them into the Cracks of Doom, where crocodiles of living obsidian wait to crunch up their bodies and silence their quacking, droning voices forever.

And if they avoid all that, I hope they catch poison oak.

My job is done, I think. My grandfather told me once that the best map is one that points to which way is north and shows you how much water is in your way. That's the sort of map I've tried to provide here. Literary criticism and rhetoric aren't forms I'm comfortable with, but I'd just as soon talk books for . . . well, for two months at a time is the way it looks. Somewhere in the middle of "Alice's Restaurant," Arlo Guthrie tells his audience, "I could play all night. I'm not proud . . . *or* tired . . ." I could say much the same thing. I haven't talked about Charles Grant's Oxrun Station books, or Manley Wade Wellman's Appalachian bard John, he of the silver-stringed guitar. I've had only a chance to touch briefly on Fritz Leiber's *Our Lady of Darkness* (but gentle reader, there is a pale brown dung in that book that will haunt your dreams). There are dozens of others. No, I take that back. There are *hundreds*.

If you need a slightly longer arrow—or if you're just not tired of talking about books yet—glance at Appendix II, where there is a list of roughly one hundred books issued during the thirty years we've been jawing over here, all of them horror, all of them excellent in one way or another. If you're new to the field, you'll find enough stuff to keep you quaking in your boots for the next year and a half. If you're not, you'll find you've read many of them already . . . but they'll give you my own hazy conception of where north lies, at least.

CHAPTER X

The Last Waltz—Horror and Morality, Horror and Magic

1

"Yes, but how do you justify earning a living by feeding off people's worst fears?"

2

The police have been summoned by a neighbor who has heard a commotion of some kind. What they find is a bloodbath—and something worse. The young man admits, quite calmly, that he has murdered his grandmother with a pipe, and then cut her throat.

"I needed her blood," the young man tells the police calmly. "I'm a vampire. Without her blood, I would have died."

In his room the police find magazine articles about vampires, vampire comic books, stories, novels.

3

We'd been having a pretty nice lunch, this reporter from the *Washington Post* and I, something I was grateful for. I'd just started a twelve-city tour for my novel *The Dead Zone* the day before in New York with a kick-off party thrown by the Viking Press at Tavern on the Green, a huge, rococo eating and drinking establishment on the edge of Central Park. I had tried to take it easy at the party, but I still managed to put away about eight beers there, and another six or so at a smaller, more relaxed party with some friends from Maine later on. Nevertheless I was up the next morning at quarter of five to make the six o'clock Eastern shuttle to Washington so I could, in turn, make a seven o'clock TV appearance to plug my novel. Welcome to touring, friends and neighbors.

I made the shuttle handily, telling invisible beads as it took off in a pouring rainstorm (sitting next to an overweight businessman who read the *Wall Street Journal* through the entire flight and ate Tums one after another, deliberately and reflectively, as if enjoying them) and made *A.M. Washington* with at least ten minutes to spare. The television lights intensifed the mild hangover I'd gotten up with, and I was grateful for what had been a fairly laid-back lunch with the *Post* reporter, whose questions had been interesting and relatively unthreatening. Then this spitball about feeding off people's fears comes out of nowhere. The reporter, a young, lanky guy, was looking at me over his sandwich, eyes bright.

<u>4</u>

It's 1960, and a lonely Ohio youth has left the movie theater where he has just seen Psycho *for the fifth time. This young man goes home and stabs his grandmother to death. The pathologist would later count over forty separate stab wounds.*

Why? the police asked.

Voices, the young man replies. Voices told me to do it.

<u>5</u>

"Look," I said, putting my own sandwich down. "You take any big-city psychiatrist. He's got a marvelous home in the suburbs, a hundred thousand dollars' worth of house at the very least. He drives a Mercedes-Benz, either tobacco-brown or silver-gray. His wife has got a Country Squire wagon. His kids go to private schools during the academic year and to good summer camps in New England or in the northwest every summer.

Sonny has got Harvard if he can make the grades—money is certainly no problem—and his daughter can go to some reet and compleet girls' school where the sorority motto is 'We don't conjugate, we decline.' And how is he making the money that produces all of these wonders? He is listening to women weep over their frigidity, he is listening to men with suicidal impulses, he is dealing with paranoia both high and low, he's maybe striking on the occasional true schizophrenic. He's dealing with people who most of all are scared shitless that their lives have somehow gotten out of control and that things are falling apart . . . and if that isn't earning a living by feeding off people's fears, I don't know what is."

I picked up my sandwich again and bit into it, convinced that if I hadn't hit the spitter he had thrown me, I'd at least managed to foul it back and stay alive at the plate. When I looked up from my Reuben, the little half-smile on the reporter's face was gone.

"I," he said softly, "happen to be in analysis."

6

January of 1980. The woman and her mother are having a worried conference over the woman's three-month-old baby. The baby won't stop crying. It always cries. They agree on the source of the problem: the baby has been possessed by a demon, like that little girl in The Exorcist. *They pour gasoline on the baby as it lies crying in its crib and then light the child on fire to drive the demon out. The baby lingers in a burn ward for three days. Then it dies.*

7

The reporter's article was clean and fair for all of that; he was unkind about my physical appearance and I suppose he had some cause—I was in the slobbiest shape I've been in for ten years during that late summer of 1979—but other than that, I felt I got a pretty square shake. But even in the piece he wrote, you can feel the place where his path and mine diverged; there is that quiet snap which is the sound of ideas suddenly going off in two completely different directions.

"You get the impression that King likes this sort of sparring," he wrote.

8

Boston, 1977. A woman is killed by a young man who uses a number of kitchen implements to effect the murder. Police speculate that he might have gotten the idea from a movie—Brian De Palma's Carrie, *from the novel by Stephen King. In the film version, Carrie kills her mother by causing all sorts of kitchen implements—including a corkscrew and a potato peeler—to fly across the room and literally nail the woman to the wall.*

9

Prime-time television survived the call by pressure groups to end the excessive, graphic depiction of violence on the tube for over ten years and House and Senate subcommittees almost without number which were convened to discuss the subject. Private eyes went on shooting bad guys and getting clopped over the head after the assassinations of John F. Kennedy, Robert F. Kennedy, Martin Luther King; you could order up a dose of carnage at the twist of the channel selector on any night of the week, including Sundays. The undeclared war in Vietnam was heating up quite nicely, thank you; body counts were spiralling into the stratosphere. Child psychologists testified that after watching two hours of violent prime-time TV, groups of children in the test group showed a marked increase in play aggressiveness—beating the toy truck against the floor rather than rolling it back and forth, for instance.

10

Los Angeles, 1969. Janis Joplin, who will latter die of a drug overdose, is belting out "Ball and Chain." Jim Morrison, who will die of a heart attack in a bathtub, is chanting "Kill, kill, kill, kill" at the end of a song titled "The End"—Francis Ford Coppola will use the song ten years later to fade in the prologue of Apocalypse Now. Newsweek *publishes a picture of a shyly smiling U.S. soldier holding up a severed human ear. And in a Los Angeles suburb, a young boy puts out his brother's eyes with his fingers. He was, he explained, only trying to imitate the old Three Stooges two-fingered* boinnng! *When they do it on TV, the weeping child explains, no one gets hurt.*

11

Television's make-believe violence rolled on nevertheless, through the sixties, past Charles Whitman up on the Texas Tower ("There was a rumor/about a tumor," Kinky Friedman and the Texas Jewboys sang gleefully, "nestled at the base of his braiyyyyn . . ."), and what finally killed it and ushered in the Sitcom Seventies was a seemingly unimportant event when compared to the deaths of a President, a Senator, a great civil rights leader. Television execs were finally forced to rethink their position because a young girl ran out of gas in Roxbury.

She had a gas can in her trunk, unfortunately. She got it filled at a gas station, and while walking back to her beached car, she was set upon by a gang of black youths who took her gas can away from her, doused her with the gas, and then—like the woman and her mother trying to drive the demon out of the baby—lit her on fire. Days later she died. The youths were caught, and someone finally asked them the sixty-four-dollar question: Where did you get such a horrible idea?

From TV, came the response. From *The ABC Movie of the Week.*

Near the end of the sixties, Ed McBain (in reality novelist Evan Hunter) wrote one of his finest 87th Precinct novels of the policeman's lot. It was called *Fuzz*, and dealt in part with a gang of teenagers who went around dousing winos with gasoline and lighting them up. The film version, which is described by Steven Scheuer in his invaluable tubeside companion *Movies on TV* as a "scatterbrained comedy," starring Burt Reynolds and Raquel Welch. The biggest yocks in the movie came when several cops on stakeout dress up as nuns and then chase after a suspect, holding their habits up to reveal big, clunky work-shoes. Pretty funny, right, gang? A real gut-buster.

McBain's novel isn't a gut-buster. It's grim and almost beau-tiful. Certainly he has never come any closer to defining exactly what the policeman's lot may be than near the end of the novel when Steve Cardella, masquerading as a wino, is lit on fire himself. The producers of the movie apparently saw something between *M*A*S*H* and *Naked City* in this, and the misbegot-ten result is in most respects as forgettable as a Tracy Stallard fastball . . . except that one of Stallard's fastballs went out of Fenway Park to become Roger Maris's record-breaking sixty-first home run. And *Fuzz*, a poorly executed comedy-drama, effectively ended TV violence.

The message? You are responsible. And network TV ac-cepted the message.

12

"How do you justify the violence of the shower scene in Psycho?" *a critic once asked Sir Alfred Hitchcock.*

"How do you justify the opening scene in Hiroshima, Mon Amour?" *Hitchcock is reputed to have replied. In that opening scene, which was certainly scandalous by American standards in 1959, we see Emmanuele Riva and Eliji Okada in a naked em-brace.*

"The opening scene was necessary to the integrity of the film," the critic answered.

"So was the shower scene in Psycho," *Hitchcock said.*

13

What sort of burden does the writer—particularly the writer of horror fiction—have to bear in all of this? Certainly there has never been a writer in the field (with the possible exception of Shirley Jackson) who has not been regarded with more than a degree of critical caution. The morality of horror fiction has been called into question for a hundred years. One of the blood-spattered forerunners of *Dracula, Varney the Vampyre,* was referred to as a "penny dreadful." Later on, inflation turned the penny dreadfuls into dime dreadfuls. In the 1930s there were cries that pulps such as *Weird Tales* and *Spicy Stories* (which regularly served up lip-smacking S & M covers on which lovely ladies were tied down, always in their "small clothes," and menaced by some beastly—but identifiably male—creature of the night) were ruining the morals of the youth of America. Similarly in the fifties, the comics industry choked off such outlaw growths as E.C.'s *Tales from the Crypt* and instituted a Comics Code when it became clear that Congress intended to clean their house for them if they would not clean it for themselves. There would be no more tales of dismemberment, corpses come back from the dead, and premature burials—or at least not for the next ten years. The return was signalled by the unpretentious birth of *Creepy,* a Warren Group magazine which was a complete throwback to the salad days of Bill Gaines's E.C. horror comics. Uncle Creepy, and his buddy Cousin Eerie, who came along two years or so later, were really interchangeable with the Old Witch and the Cryp-Keeper. Even some of the old artists were back—Joe Orlando, who made his debut as an E.C. artist, was also represented in the premiere issue of *Creepy,* if memory serves.

I would suggest that there has been a great tendency, particularly when it comes to such popular forms as movies, television, and mainstream fiction, to kill the messenger for the message. I do not now and never have doubted that the youths who burned the lady in Roxbury got the idea from the telecast of *Fuzz* one Sunday night on ABC; if it had not been shown, stupidity and lack of imagination might well have reduced them to murdering her in some more mundane way. The same holds true with many of the other cases mentioned here.

The danse macabre is a waltz with death. This is a truth we cannot afford to shy away from. Like the rides in the amusement park which mimic violent death, the tale of horror is a chance to examine what's going on behind doors which we usually keep double-locked. Yet the human imagination is not content with locked doors. Somewhere there is another dancing partner, the imagination whispers in the night—a partner in a rotting ball gown, a partner with empty eye sockets, green mold growing on her elbow-length gloves, maggots squirming in the thin remains of her hair. To hold such a creature in our arms? Who, you ask me, would be so mad? Well . . . ?

"You will not want to open this door," Bluebeard tells his wife in that most horrible of all horror stories, "because your husband has forbidden it." But this, of course, only makes her all the more curious . . . and at last, her curiosity is satisfied.

"You may go anywhere you wish in the castle," Count Dracula tells Jonathan Harker, "except where the doors are locked, where of course you will not wish to go." But Harker goes soon enough.

And so do we all. Perhaps we go to the forbidden door or window willingly because we understand that a time comes when we must go whether we want to or not . . . and not just to look, but to be pushed through. Forever.

14

Baltimore, 1980. The woman is reading a book and waiting for her bus to arrive. The demobbed soldier who approaches her is a Vietnam vet, a sometime dope addict. He has a history of mental problems which seem to date from his period of service. The woman has noticed him on the bus before, sometimes weaving, sometimes staggering, sometimes calling loudly and wildly to people who are not there. "That's right, Captain!" she has heard him say. "That's right, that's right!"

He attacks the woman as she waits for her bus; later, the police will theorize he was after drug money. No matter. He will be just as dead, no matter what he was after. The neighborhood is a tough one. The woman has a knife secreted upon her person. In the struggle, she uses it. When the bus comes, the black ex-soldier lies dying in the gutter.

What were you reading? a reporter asks her later; she shows him The Stand, *by Stephen King.*

15

With its disguise of semantics carefully removed and laid aside, what those who criticize the tale of horror (or who simply feel uneasy about it and their liking for it) seem to be saying is this: you are selling death and disfigurement and monstrosity; you are trading upon hate and violence, morbidity and loathing; you are just another representative of those forces of chaos which so endanger the world today.

You are, in short, immoral.

A critic asked George Romero, following the release of *Dawn of the Dead,* if he felt such a movie, with its scenes of gore, cannibalism, and gaudy pop violence, was a sign of a healthy society. Romero's reply, worthy of the Hitchcock anecdote related earlier, was to ask the critic if he felt the DC-10 engine-mount assembly was a healthy thing for society. His response was dismissed as a quibble ("You get the impression Romero likes this kind of sparring," I can almost hear the critic thinking).

Well, let's see if the quibble really is a quibble—and let's go one layer deeper than we have yet gone. The hour has grown late, the last waltz is playing, and if we don't say certain things now, I suppose we never will.

I've tried to suggest throughout this book that the horror story, beneath its fangs and fright wig, is really as conservative as an Illinois Republican in a three-piece pinstriped suit; that its main purpose is to reaffirm the virtues of the norm by showing us what awful things happen to people who venture into taboo lands. Within the framework of most horror tales we find a moral code so strong it would make a Puritan smile. In the old E.C. comics, adulterers inevitably came to bad ends and murderers suffered fates that would make the rack and the boot look like kiddy rides at the carnival.* Modern horror stories are not much different from the morality plays of the fifteenth, sixteenth, and seventeenth centuries, when we get right down to it. The horror story most generally not only stands foursquare for the Ten Commandments, it blows them up to tabloid size. We have the comforting knowledge when the lights go down in the theater or when we open the book that the evildoers will almost certainly be punished, and measure will be returned for measure.

Further, I've used one pompously academic metaphor, suggesting that the horror tale generally details the outbreak of some Dionysian madness in an Apollonian existence, and that the horror will continue until the Dionysian forces have been repelled and the Apollonian norm restored again. Excluding a powerful if puzzling prologue set in Iraq, William Friedkin's film *The Exorcist* actually begins in Georgetown, an Apollonian suburb if ever there was one. In the first scene, Ellen Burstyn is awakened by a crashing, roaring sound in the attic— it sounds like maybe someone let a lion loose up there. It is the first crack in the Apollonian world; soon everything else will pour through in a nightmare torrent. But this disturbing crack between our normal world and a chaos where demons are allowed to prey on innocent children is finally closed again at the end of the film. When Burstyn leads the pallid but obviously okay Linda Blair to the car in the film's final scene, we understand that the nightmare is over. Steady state has been restored. We have watched for the mutant and repulsed it. Equilibrium never felt so good.

Those are some of the things we've talked about in this book . . . but suppose all of that is only a sham and a false front?

---

* My all-time favorite (he said affectionately): A crazed husband stuffs the hose of an air compressor down his skinny wife's throat and blows her up like a balloon until she bursts. "Fat at last," he tells her happily just moments before the pop. But later on the husband, who is roughly the size of Jackie Gleason, trips a booby-trap she has set for him and is squashed to a shadow when a huge safe falls on him. This ingenious reworking of the old story of Jack Sprat and his wife is not only gruesomely funny; it offers us a delicious example of the Old Testament eye-for-an-eye theory. Or, as the Spanish say, revenge is a dish best eaten cold.

I don't say that it is, but perhaps (since this *is* the last dance) we ought to discuss the possibility, at least.

In our discussion of archetypes, we've had occasion to discuss the Werewolf, that fellow who is sometimes hairy and who is sometimes deceptively smooth. Suppose there was a double werewolf? Suppose that the creator of the horror story was, under his/her fright wig and plastic fangs, a Republican in a three-button suit, as we have said . . . ah, but suppose below *that* there is a *real* monster, with real fangs and a squirming Medusa-tangle of snakes for hair? Suppose it's all a self-serving lie and that when the creator of horror is finally stripped all the way to his or her core of being we find not an agent of the norm but a friend—a capering, gleeful, red-eyed agent of chaos?

What about *that* possibility, friends and neighbors?

16

About five years ago I finished *The Shining*, took a month off, and then set about writing a new novel, the working title of which was *The House on Value Street*. It was going to be a *roman à clef* about the kidnapping of Patty Hearst, her brainwashing (or her sociopolitical awakening, depending on your point of view, I guess), her participation in the bank robbery, the shootout at the SLA hideout in Los Angeles—in my book, the hideout was on Value Street, natch—the fugitive run across the country, the whole ball of wax. It seemed to me to be a highly potent subject, and while I was aware that lots of nonfiction books were sure to be written on the subject, it seemed to me that only a novel might really succeed in explaining all the contradictions. The novelist is, after all, God's liar, and if he does his job well, keeps his head and his courage, he can sometimes find the truth that lives at the center of the lie.

Well, I never wrote that book. I gathered my research materials, such as they were, to hand (Patty was still at large then, which was another attraction the idea had for me; I could make up my own ending), and then I attacked the novel. I attacked it from one side and nothing happened. I tried it from another side and felt it was going pretty well until I discovered all my characters sounded as if they had just stepped whole and sweaty from the dance marathon in Horace McCoy's *They Shoot Horses, Don't They?* I tried it *in medias res*. I tried to imagine it as a stage play, a trick that sometimes works for me when I'm badly stuck. It didn't work this time.

In his marvelous novel *The Hair of Harold Roux*, Thomas Williams tells us that writing a long work of fiction is like gathering characters together on a great black plain. They stand around the small fire of the writer's invention, warming their hands at the blaze, hoping the fire will grow into a blaze which will provide light as well as heat. But often it goes out, all light is extinguished, and the characters are smothered in black. It's a lovely metaphor for the fiction-making process, but it's not mine . . . maybe it's too gentle to be mine. I've always seen the novel as a large black castle to be attacked, a bastion to be taken by force or by trick. The thing about this castle is, it appears to be open. It doesn't look buttoned up for siege at all. The drawbridge is down. The gates are open. There are no bowmen on the turrets. Trouble is, there's really only one safe way in; every other attempt at entry results in sudden annihilation from some hidden source.

With my Patty Hearst book, I never found the right way in . . . and during that entire six-week period, something else was nagging very quietly at the back of my mind. It was a news story I had read about an accidental CBW spill in Utah. All the bad nasty bugs got out of their cannister and killed a bunch of sheep. But, the news article stated, if the wind had been blowing the other way, the good people of Salt Lake City might have gotten a very nasty surprise. This article called up memories of a novel called *Earth Abides*, by George R. Stewart. In Stewart's book, a plague wipes out most of mankind, and the protagonist, who has been made immune by virtue of a well-timed snakebite, witnesses the ecological changes which the passing of man causes. The first half of Stewart's long book is riveting; the second half is more of an uphill push—too much ecology, not enough story.

We were living in Boulder, Colorado, at the time, and I used to listen to the Bible-thumping station which broadcast out of Arvada quite regularly. One day I heard a preacher dilating upon the text. "Once in every generation the plague will fall among them." I liked the sound of the phrase—which sounds like a biblical quotation but is not—so well that I wrote it down and tacked it over my typewriter: *Once in every generation the plague will fall among them.*

This phrase and the story about the CBW spill in Utah and my memories of Stewart's fine book all became entwined in my thoughts about Patty Hearst and the SLA, and one day while sitting at my typewriter, my eyes traveling back and forth between that creepy homily on the wall to the maddeningly blank sheet of paper in the machine, I wrote—just to write something: *The world comes to an end but everybody in the SLA is somehow immune. Snake bit them.* I looked at that for a while and then typed: *No more gas shortages.* That was sort of cheerful, in a horrible sort of way. No more people, no more gas lines. Below *No more gas shortages* I wrote in rapid order: *No more cold war. No more pollution. No more alligator handbags. No more crime. A season of rest.* I liked that last; it sounded like something that should be written down. I underlined it. I sat there for another fifteen minutes or so, listening to the Eagles on my little cassette player, and then I wrote: *Donald DeFreeze is a dark man.* I did not mean that DeFreeze was black; it had suddenly occurred to me that, in the photos taken during the bank robbery in which Patty Hearst participated, you could barely see DeFreeze's face. He was wearing a big badass hat, and what he looked like was mostly guesswork. I wrote *A dark man with no face* and then glanced up and saw that grisly little motto again: *Once in every generation the plague will fall among them.* And that was that. I spent the next two years writing an apparently endless book called *The Stand.* It got to the point where I began describing it to friends as my own little Vietnam, because I kept telling myself that in another hundred pages or so I would begin to see light at the end of the tunnel. The finished manuscript was over twelve hundred pages long and weighed twelve pounds, the same weight as the sort of bowling ball I favor. I carried it thirty blocks from the U.N. Plaza Hotel to my editor's apartment one warm night in July. My wife had wrapped the entire block of pages in Saran Wrap for some reason known only to her, and after I'd switched it from one arm to the other for the third or fourth time, I had a sudden premonition: I was going to die, right there on Third Avenue. The Rescue Unit would find me sprawled in the gutter, dead of a heart attack, my monster manuscript, triumphantly encased in Saran Wrap, resting by my outstretched hands, the victor.

There were times when I actively hated *The Stand,* but there was never a time when I did not feel compelled to go on with it. Even when things were going bad with my guys in Boulder, there was a crazy, joyful feeling about the book. I couldn't wait to sit down in front of the typewriter every morning and slip back into that world where Randy Flagg could sometimes become a crow, sometimes a wolf, and where the big battle was not for gasoline allocations but for human souls. There was a feeling—I must admit it—that I was doing a fast, happy tapdance on the grave of the whole world. Its writing came during a troubled period for the world in general and America in particular; we were suffering from our first gas pains in history, we had just witnessed the sorry end of the Nixon administration and the first presidential resignation in history, we had been resoundingly defeated in Southeast Asia, and we were grappling with a host of domestic problems, from the troubling question of abortion-on-demand to an inflation rate that was beginning to spiral upward in a positively scary way.

Me? I was suffering from a really good case of career jet lag. Four years before, I had been running sheets in an industrial laundry for $1.60 an hour and writing *Carrie* in the furnace room of a trailer. My daughter, who was then almost a year old, was dressed mostly in scrounged clothes. The year before that, I had married my wife Tabitha in a borrowed suit that was too big for me. I left the laundry when a teaching position opened up at a nearby school, Hampden Academy, and my wife Tabby and I were dismayed to learn that my first-year salary of $6,400 was not going to take us much further than my laundry salary—and pretty soon I'd secured my laundry job back for the following summer.

Then *Carrie* sold to Doubleday, and Doubleday sold the reprint rights for a staggering sum of money which was, in those days, nearly a record-breaker. Life began to move at Concorde speed. *Carrie* was bought for films; *'Salem's Lot* was bought for a huge sum of money and then also bought for films; *The Shining* likewise. Suddenly all of my friends thought I was rich. That was bad enough, scary enough; what was worse was the fact that maybe I was. People began to talk to me about investments, about tax shelters, about moving to California. These were changes enough to try and cope with, but on top of them, the America I had grown up in seemed to be crumbling beneath my feet . . . it began to seem like an elaborate castle of sand unfortunately built well below the high-tide line.

The first wave to touch that castle (or the first one that I perceived) was that long-ago announcement that the Russians had beaten us into space . . . but now the tide was coming in for fair.

And so here, I think, is the face of the double werewolf, revealed at last. On the surface, *The Stand* pretty much conforms to those conventions we have already discussed: an Apollonian society is disrupted by a Dionysian force (in this case a deadly strain of superflu that kills almost everybody). Further, the survivors of this plague discover themselves in two camps: one, located in Boulder, Colorado, mimics the Apollonian society just destroyed (with a few significant changes); the other, located in Las Vegas, Nevada, is violently Dionysian.

The first Dionysian incursion in *The Exorcist* comes when Chris MacNeil (Ellen Burstyn) hears that lionlike roar in the attic. In *The Stand*, Dionysus announces himself with the crash of an old Chevy into the pumps of an out-of-the-way gas station in Texas. In *The Exorcist*, the Apollonian steady state is restored when we see a pallid Regan MacNeil being led to her mother's Mercedes-Benz; in *The Stand* I believe that this moment comes when the book's two main characters, Stu Redman and Frannie Goldsmith, look through a plate-glass window in the Boulder hospital at Frannie's obviously normal baby. As with *The Exorcist,* the return of equilibrium never felt so good.

But below all of this, hidden by the moral conventions of the horror tale (but perhaps not all that hidden), the face of the *real* Werewolf can be dimly seen. Much of the compulsion I felt while writing *The Stand* obviously came from envisioning an entire entrenched societal process destroyed at a stroke. I felt a bit like Alexander, lifting his sword over the Gordian knot and growling, "*Fuck* untying it; I've got a better way." And I felt a bit the way Johnny Rotten sounds at the beginning of that classic and electrifying Sex Pistols song, "Anarchy for the U.K." He utters a low, throaty chuckle that might have come from Randall Flagg's own throat and then intones, "Right . . . *NOW!*" We hear that voice, and our reaction is one of intense relief. The worst is now known; we are in the hands of an authentic madman.

In this frame of mind, the destruction of THE WORLD AS WE KNOW IT became an actual relief. No more Ronald McDonald! No more *Gong Show* or *Soap* on TV—just soothing snow! No more terrorists! *No more bullshit!* Only the Gordian knot unwinding there in the dust. I am suggesting that below the writer of the moral horror tale (whose feet, like those of Henry Jekyll, are "always treading the upward path") there lies another creature altogether. He lives, let us say, down there on Jack Finney's third level, and he is a capering nihilist who, to extend the Jekyll-Hyde metaphor, is not content to tread over the tender bones of one screaming little girl but in this case feels it necessary to do the funky chicken over the whole world. Yes, folks, in *The Stand* I got a chance to scrub the whole human race, and *it was fun!*

So where is morality now?

Well, I'll give you my idea. I think it lies where it has always lain: in the hearts and minds of men and women of good will. In the case of the writer, this may mean beginning with a nihilistic premise and gradually relearning old lessons of human values and human conduct. In the case of *The Stand,* this meant beginning with the glum premise that the human race carries a kind of germ with it—I began by seeing this germ symbolically visualized in the SLA, and ended by seeing it visualized in the superflu germ—which grows more and more virulent as technology grows in power. The superflu is unleashed by a single technological misstep (not such a far-fetched presumption, either, when you consider what happened at Three Mile Island last year or the fact that Loring AFB in my own state scrambled bombers and fighters ready to head over the pole toward Russia as the result of an amusing little computer foul-up which suggested that the Russians had launched their missiles and the Big Hot One was on). By simple agreement with myself to allow a few survivors—no survivors, no story, am I right?—I was able to envision a world in which all the nuclear stockpiles would simply rust away and some kind of normal moral, political, and ecological balance would return to the mad universe we call home.

But I don't think anyone knows what they really think—or perhaps even what they really know—until it's written down, and I came to realize that the survivors would be very likely to first take up all the old quarrels and then all the old weapons. Worse, all those deadly toys would be available to them, and things might well become a sprint to see which group of loonies could figure out how to launch them first. My own lesson in writing *The Stand* was that cutting the Gordian Knot simply destroys the riddle instead of solving it, and the book's last line is an admission that the riddle still remains.

The book also tries to celebrate brighter aspects of our lives: simple human courage, friendship, and love in a world which so often seems mostly loveless. In spite of its apocalyptic theme, *The Stand* is mostly a hopeful book that echoes Albert Camus's remark that "happiness, too, is inevitable."

More prosaically, my mother used to tell my brother David and me to "hope for the best and expect the worst," and that expresses the book I remember writing as well as anything.

So, in short, we hope for a fourth level (a triple Werewolf?), one that will bring us full circle again to the horror writer not just as writer but as human being, mortal man or woman, just another passenger in the boat, another pilgrim on the way to whatever there is. And we hope that if he sees another pilgrim fall down that he will write about it—but not before he or she has helped the fallen one off his or her feet, brushed off his or her clothes, and seen if he or she is all right, and able to go on. If such behavior is to be, it cannot be as a result of an intellectual moral stance; it is because there is such a thing as love, merely a practical fact, a practical force in human affairs.

Morality is, after all, a codification of those things which the heart understands to be true and those things which the heart understands to be the demands of a life lived among others . . . civilization, in a word. And if we remove the label "horror story" or "fantasy genre" or whatever, and replace it with "literature" or more simply still, "fiction," we may realize more easily that no such blanket accusations of immorality can be made. If we say that morality proceeds simply from a good heart—which has little to do with ridiculous posturings and happily-ever-afterings—and immorality proceeds from a lack of care, from shoddy observation, and from the prostitution of drama or melodrama for some sort of gain, monetary or otherwise, then we may realize that we have arrived at a critical stance which is both workable and humane. Fiction is the truth inside the lie, and in the tale of horror as in any other tale, the same rule applies now as when Aristophanes told his horror tale of the frogs: morality is telling the truth as your heart knows it. When asked if he was not ashamed of the rawness and sordidness of his turn-of-the-century novel *McTeague,* Frank Norris replied: "Why should I be? I did not lie. I did not truckle. I told them the truth."

Seen in that light, I think the horror tale may more often be adjudged innocent than guilty.

17

My, look at this . . . I do believe the sun is coming up. We have danced the night away, like lovers in some old MGM musical. But now the band has packed their melodies back inside their cases and has quitted the stage. The dancers have left, all but you and I, and I suppose we must go, as well. I cannot tell you how much I've enjoyed the evening, and if you sometimes found me a clumsy partner (or if I occasionally stepped on your toes), I do apologize. I feel as I suppose all lovers feel when the dance has finally ended, tired . . . but still gay.

As I walk you to the door, may I tell you one more thing? We'll stand here in the vestibule as they unroll the rug again and douse the lights. Let me help you with your coat; I'll not keep you long.

Questions of morality in the pursuit of horror may be begging the actual question. The Russians have a phrase, "the scream of the woodcock." The phrase is derisory because the woodcock is nature's ventriloquist, and if you fire your shotgun at the place where the sound came from, you'll go hungry. Shoot the woodcock, not the scream, the Russians say.

So let's see if we can't find a woodcock—just one—in all these screaming thickets. It might just be hiding in this item, truth rather than fiction, from *The Book of Lists*, the Wallace/Wallechinsky clan's attic full of fascinating rickrack and useful junk. As you get ready to leave, think about this . . . or brood upon it:

THE MYSTERY OF LITTLE MISS NOBODY

On July 6, 1944, the Ringling Brothers and Barnum & Bailey circus was giving a performance in Hartford, Connecticut, before 7,000 paid customers. A fire broke out; 168 persons died in the blaze and 487 were injured. One of the dead, a small girl thought to be six years old, was unidentified. Since no one came to claim her, and since her face was unmarred, a photograph was taken of her and distributed locally and then throughout the U.S. Days passed, weeks and months passed, but no relative, no playmate, no one in the nation came forward to identify her. She remains unknown to this day.

My idea of growing up is that the process consists mainly of developing a good case of mental tunnel vision and a gradual ossification of the imaginative faculty (what about Little Miss Nobody, you ask me—well, hang on; we'll get there). Children see everything, consider everything; the typical expression of the baby which is full, dry, and awake is a wide-eyed goggle at everything. Hello, pleased to meet you, freaked to be here. A child has not yet developed the obsessional behavior patterns which we approvingly call "good work habits." He or she has not yet internalized the idea that a straight line is the shortest distance between two points.

All of that comes later. Children believe in Santa Claus. It's no big deal; just a piece of stored information. They likewise believe in the bogeyman, the Trix Rabbit, McDonaldland (where hamburgers grow on trees and moderate thievery is approved behavior—witness the lovable Hamburglar), the Tooth Fairy who takes ivory and leaves silver . . . all of these things are taken as a matter of course. These are some of the popular myths; there are others which, while more specialized, seem just as *outré*. Grampa has gone to live with the angels. The stuff in the middle of the golf ball is the worst poison in the world. Step on a crack, break your mother's back. If you walk through holly bushes, your shadow can get caught and it will be left there forever, flapping on the sharp leaves.

The changes come gradually, as logic and rationalism assert themselves. The child begins to wonder how Santa can be at the Value House, on a downtown corner ringing a bell over a Salvation Army pot, and up at the North Pole generaling his troop of elves all at the same time. The child maybe realizes that although he's stepped on a hell of a lot of cracks, his or her mother's back is yet all right. Age begins to settle into that child's face. "Don't be a baby!" he or she is told impatiently. "Your head is always in the clouds!" And the kicker, of course: "Aren't you ever going to *grow up*?"

After awhile, the song says, Puff the magic dragon stopped trundling his way up the Cherry Lane to see his old good buddy Jackie Paper. Wendy and her brothers finally left Peter Pan and the Wild Boys to their fate. No more Magic Dust and only an occasional Happy Thought . . . but there was always something a little dangerous about Peter Pan, wasn't there? Something just a little too woodsy-wild? Something in his eyes that was . . . well, downright Dionysian.

Oh, the gods of childhood are immortal; the big kids don't really sacrifice them; they just pass them on to their bratty kid brothers and kid sisters. It's childhood itself that's mortal: man is in love, and loves what passes. And it's not just Puff and Tink and Peter Pan that are left behind in that rush for the driver's license, the high school and college diploma, in that mostly eager training to achieve "good work habits." We have each exiled the Tooth Fairy (or perhaps he exiles us when we are no longer able to provide the product he requires), murdered Santa Claus (only to reanimate the corpse for our own children), killed the giant that chased Jack down the beanstalk. And the poor old bogeyman! Laughed to death again and again, like Mr. Dark at the conclusion of *Something Wicked This Way Comes*.

Listen to me now: At eighteen or twenty or twenty-one, whatever the legal drinking age may be in your state, "getting carded" is something of an embarrassment. You have to fumble around for a driver's license or your State Liquor Card or maybe even a photostat of your birth certificate so you can get a simple fa' Chrissakes glass of beer. But you let ten years go past, get so you are looking the big three-o right in the eye, and there is something absurdly flattering about getting carded. It means you still look like you might not be old enough to buy a drink over the bar. You still look a little wet behind the ears. You still look *young*.

This got into my head a few years ago when I was in a bar called Benjaman's in Bangor, getting pleasantly loaded. I began to study the faces of entering patrons. The guy standing unobtrusively by the door let this one pass . . . and that one . . . and the next one. Then, bang! He stopped a guy in a U of M jacket and carded him. And I'll be damned if that guy didn't do a quick fade. The drinking age in Maine was then eighteen (booze-related accidents on the highways have since caused the lawmakers to move the age up to twenty), and all of those people had looked about eighteen to me. So I got up and asked the bouncer how he knew that last guy was underage. He shrugged. "You just know," he said. "It's mostly in their eyes."

For weeks after, my hobby was looking at the faces of adults and trying to decide exactly what it was that made them "adult faces." The face of a thirty-year-old is healthy, unwrinkled, and no bigger than the face of a seventeen-year-old. Yet you know that's no kid; you *know*. There seems to be some hidden yet overriding characteristic that makes what we all agree is the Adult Face. It isn't just the clothes or the stance, it isn't the fact that the thirty-year-old is toting a briefcase and the seventeen-year-old is toting a knapsack; if you put the head of each in one of those carnival cut-outs which show the body of a capering sailor or a prize-fighter, you could still pick out the adult ten tries out of ten.

I came to believe that the bouncer was right. It's in the eyes.

Not something that's there; something, rather, that has left.

Kids are bent. They think around corners. But starting at roughly age eight, when childhood's second great era begins, the kinks begin to straighten out, one by one. The boundaries of thought and vision begin to close down to a tunnel as we gear up to get along. At last, unable to grapple to any profit with Never-Never Land anymore, we may settle for the minor-league version available at the local disco . . . or for a trip to Disney World one February or March.

The imagination is an eye, a marvelous third eye that floats free. As children, that eye sees with 20/20 clarity. As we grow older, its vision begins to dim . . . and one day the guy at the door lets you into the bar without asking to see any ID and that's it for you, Cholly; your hat is over the windmill. It's in your eyes. Something in your eyes. Check them out in the mirror and tell me if I'm wrong.

The job of the fantasy writer, or the horror writer, is to bust the walk of that tunnel vision wide for a little while; to provide a single powerful spectacle for the third eye. The job of the fantasy-horror writer is to make you, for a little while, a child again.

And the horror writer himself/herself? Someone else looks

at that item about Little Miss Nobody (toldja we'd get back to her, and here she is, still unidentified, as mysterious as the Wolf Boy of Paris) and says, "Jeez, you never can tell, can you?" and goes on to something else. But the fantasist begins to play with it as a child would, speculating about children from other dimensions, about dööpplegangers, about God knows what. It's a child's toy, something bright and shiny and strange. Let us pull a lever and see what it does, let us push it across the floor and see if it goes *Rum-Rum-Rum* or *wacka-wacka-wacka*. Let us turn it over and see if it will magically right itself again. In short, let us have our Fortian rains of frogs and people who have mysteriously burned to death while sitting at home in their easy chairs; let us have our vampires and our werewolves. Let us have Little Miss Nobody, who perhaps slipped sideways through a crack in reality, only to be trampled to death in the rush from a burning circus tent.

And something of this is reflected in the eyes of those who write horror stories. Ray Bradbury has the dreamy eyes of a child. So, behind his thick glasses, does Jack Finney. The same look is in Lovecraft's eyes—they startle with their simple dark directness, especially in that narrow, pinched, and somehow eternal New England face. Harlan Ellison, in spite of his rapid jive-talking shoot-from-the-hip Nervous-Norvus mode of conversation (talking with Harlan can sometimes be like talking with an apocalyptic Saladmaster salesman who has just taken three large bennies), has those eyes. Every now and then he'll pause, looking away, looking at something else, and you know that it's true: Harlan is bent, and he just thought his way around a corner. Peter Straub, who dresses impeccably and who always seems to project the aura of some big company success, also has that look in his eyes. It is an indefinable look, but it's there.

"It's the best set of electric trains a boy ever had," Orson Welles once said of making movies; the same can be said of making books and stories. Here is a chance to bust that tunnel vision wide open, bricks flying everywhere so that, for a moment at least, a dreamscape of wonders and horrors stands forth as clearly and with all the magic reality of the first Ferris wheel you ever saw as a kid, turning and turning against the sky. Someone's dead son is on the late movie. Somewhere a foul man—bogeyman!—is slouching through the snowy night with shining yellow eyes. Boys are thundering through autumn leaves on their way home past the library at four in the morning, and somewhere else, in some other world, even as I write this, Frodo and Sam are making their way toward Mordor, where the shadows lie. I am quite sure of it.

Ready to go? Fine. I'll just grab my coat.

It's not a dance of death at all, not really. There is a third level here, as well. It is, at bottom, a dance of dreams. It's a way of awakening the child inside, who never dies but only sleeps ever more deeply. If the horror story is our rehearsal for death, then its strict moralities make it also a reaffirmation of life and good will and simple imagination—just one more pipeline to the infinite.

In his epic poem of a stewardess falling to her death from high above the fields of Kansas, James Dickey suggests a metaphor for the life of the rational being, who must grapple as best he/she can with the fact of his/her own mortality. We fall from womb to tomb, from one blackness and toward another, remembering little of the one and knowing nothing of the other . . . except through faith. That we retain our sanity in the face of these simple yet blinding mysteries is nearly divine. That we may turn the powerful intuition of our imaginations upon them and regard them in this glass of dreams—that we may, however timidly, place our hands within the hole which opens at the center of the column of truth—that is . . .

. . . well, it's magic, isn't it?

Yeah. I think maybe that's what I want to leave you with, in lieu of a goodnight kiss, that word which children respect instinctively, that word whose truth we only rediscover as adults in our stories . . . and in our dreams:

Magic.

Afterword

I n July of 1977, my wife and I hosted a gathering of my wife's entire family—a giant collection of sisters, brothers, aunts, uncles, and millions of kids. My wife spent most of that week cooking and of course what always happens at family gatherings happened at this one: everybody brought a casserole. Much food was eaten on the shores of Long Lake that sunny summer day; many cans of beer were consumed. And when the crowd of Spruces and Atwoods and LaBrees and Graveses and everyone else had departed, we were left with enough food to feed an army regiment.

So we ate leftovers.

Day in, day out, we ate leftovers. And when Tabby brought out the remains of the turkey for the fifth or sixth time (we had eaten turkey soup, turkey surprise, and turkey with noodles; this day it was something simpler, nice, nourishing turkey sandwiches), my son Joe, who was then five, looked at it and screamed: "Do we have to eat this shit *again?*"

I didn't know whether to laugh or clout him upside the head. As I recall, I did both.

I told you that story because people who have read a lot of my work will realize that they have eaten a few leftovers here. I have used material from my introduction to *Night Shift*, from my introduction to the New American Library's omnibus edition of *Frankenstein, Dracula,* and *Dr. Jekyll and Mr. Hyde,* from an article entitled "The Fright Report" originally published in *Oui* magazine, from an article called "The Third Eye" in *The Writer;* much of the material on Ramsey Campbell originally appeared in Stuart Schiff's *Whispers* magazine.

Now before you decide to clout me upside the head or to scream "Do we have to eat this shit again?" let me point out to you what my wife pointed out to my son on the day of the turkey sandwiches: there are hundreds of different recipes for turkey, but they all *taste* like turkey. And coupled with that, she said, it is a shame to waste good things.

This is not to say that my article in *Oui* was so paralyzingly great or that my thoughts on Ramsey Campbell were so deathless that they deserved to be preserved in a book; it is only to say that, while my thoughts and feelings on the genre I've spent most of my life working in may have evolved or shifted somewhat in perspective, they haven't really changed. That change may come, but since there has only been a passage of four years since I originally stated many of my feelings about horror and terror in the *Night Shift* introduction, it would be surprising—even suspect—if I were to suddenly deny everything I had written previous to this book.

In my own defense, I'll add that *Danse Macabre* gave me the space to develop some of these ideas in more detail than I had ever been given before, and for that I must thank Bill Thompson and Everest House. In no case did I simply reheat something I had written before; I tried as hard as I could to develop each idea as fully as possible without beating it into the ground. In some cases, I may have done just that, though, and all I can do in such cases is to beg your indulgence.

And I think that really is the end. Thank you again for coming with me, and rest you well. But, being who I am and what I am, I cannot find it in my heart to wish you pleasant dreams. . . .

The Films

Below is a list of roughly one hundred fantasy/horror films tied together by their time and their excellence. All were released during the period 1950–1980, and all of them seem to me to be particularly interesting in one way or another; if I may say so without sounding like an Academy Awards presenter, all of them have contributed something of value to the genre. You will find my own personal favorites marked with an asterisk (*). Special thanks are due to Kirby McCauley, who provided invaluable help with the list.

TITLE	DIRECTOR	YEAR
The Abominable Dr. Phibes	Robert Fuest	1971
*Alien	Ridley Scott	1979
Asylum	Roy Ward Baker	1972
The Bad Seed	Mervyn LeRoy	1956
The Birds	Alfred Hitchcock	1963
The Bird with the Crystal Plumage	Dario Argento	1969
*Black Sunday	Mario Bava	1961
*The Brood	David Cronenberg	1979
Burnt Offerings	Dan Curtis	1976
Burn Witch Burn	Sidney Hayers	1962
*Carrie	Brian De Palma	1976

The Conqueror Worm	Michael Reeves	1968
Creature from the Black Lagoon	Jack Arnold	1954
The Creeping Unknown	Val Guest	1955
Curse of the Demon	Jacques Tourneur	1957
The Day of the Triffids	Steve Sekely	1963
Dawn of the Dead	George A. Romero	1979
The Deadly Bees	Freddie Francis	1967
Deep Red	Dario Argento	1976
Deliverance	John Boorman	1972
Dementia-13	Francis Coppola	1963
Diabolique	Henri-Georges Clouzot	1955
Doctor Terror's House of Horrors	Freddie Francis	1965
Don't Look Now	Nicholas Roeg	1973
Duel	Steven Spielberg	1971
Enemy from Space	Val Guest	1957
Eraserhead	David Lynch	1976
The Exorcist	William Friedkin	1973
The Exterminating Angel	Luis Buñuel	1963
Eye of the Cat	David Lowell Rich	1969
The Fly	Kurt Neumann	1958
Frenzy	Alfred Hitchcock	1972
The Fury	Brian De Palma	1978
Gorgo	Eugene Lourie	1961
Halloween	John Carpenter	1978
The Haunting	Robert Wise	1963
The H-Man	Inoshiro Honda	1958

Horrors of the Black Museum	Arthur Crabtree	1959
Hour of the Wolf	Ingmar Bergman	1967
The House that Dripped Blood	Peter Duffell	1970
Hush . . . Hush, Sweet Charlotte	Robert Aldrich	1965
*I Bury the Living	Albert Band	1958
The Incredible Shrinking Man	Jack Arnold	1957
*Invasion of the Body Snatchers	Don Siegel	1956
Invasion of the Body Snatchers	Philip Kaufman	1978
I Saw What You Did	William Castle	1965
*It Came from Outer Space	Jack Arnold	1953
It! The Terror from Beyond Space	Edward L. Cahn	1958
*Jaws	Steven Spielberg	1975
The Killer Shrews	Ken Curtis	1959
*Lady in a Cage	Walter Graumann	1963
Last Summer	Frank Perry	1969
*Let's Scare Jessica to Death	John Hancock	1971
Macabre	William Castle	1958
*Martin	George A. Romero	1977
The Masque of the Red Death	Roger Corman	1964
Night Must Fall	Karel Reisz	1964
*The Night of the Hunter	Charles Laughton	1955
*Night of the Living Dead	George A. Romero	1968
Not of This Earth	Roger Corman	1956
No Way to Treat a Lady	Jack Smight	1968
Panic in the Year Zero	Ray Milland	1962
*Picnic at Hanging Rock	Peter Weir	1978

The Pit and the Pendulum	Roger Corman	1961
*Psycho	Alfred Hitchcock	1960
*Rabid	David Cronenberg	1977
Race with the Devil	Jack Starrett	1975
*Repulsion	Roman Polanski	1965
*Rituals	?	1978
*Rosemary's Baby	Roman Polanski	1968
'Salem's Lot	Tobe Hooper	1979
Seance on a Wet Afternoon	Bryan Forbes	1964
Seizure	Oliver Stone	1975
*The Seventh Seal	Ingmar Bergman	1956
*Sisters	Brian De Palma	1973
*The Shining	Stanley Kubrick	1980
The Shout	Jerzy Skolimowski	1979
Someone's Watching Me	John Carpenter	1978
The Stepford Wives	Bryan Forbes	1975
Strait-Jacket	William Castle	1964
Suddenly Last Summer	Joseph L. Mankiewicz	1960
*Suspiria	Dario Argento	1977
*The Texas Chainsaw Massacre	Tobe Hooper	1974
*Them!	Gordon Douglas	1954
They Came from Within	David Cronenberg	1975
*The Thing	Christian Nyby	1951
The Tomb of Ligeia	Roger Corman	1965
Trilogy of Terror	Dan Curtis	1975
Village of the Damned	Wolf Rilla	1960

Wait Until Dark	Terence Young	1967
What Ever Happened to Baby Jane?	Robert Aldrich	1961
When Michael Calls	Philip Leacock	1971
The Wicker Man	Robin Hardy	1973
Willard	Daniel Mann	1971
X—the Man with the X-Ray Eyes	Roger Corman	1963
X the Unknown	Leslie Norman	1956

The Books

Below is a list of roughly one hundred books—novels and collections—which span the period we have been discussing. They are listed alphabetically according to author. As with my list of films, you may not find all of these to your taste, but all seem—to me, at least—important to the genre we have been discussing. Thanks again to Kirby McCauley, who helped with the list, and a special tip of the hat to "Fast Eddie" Melder, who owns a pub in North Lovell and who put up with our wild talk until well past closing time.

Once again, I've marked with an asterisk (*) books which I felt were particularly important.

Richard Adams. *The Plague Dogs; Watership Down**
Robert Aickman. *Cold Hand in Mine; Painted Devils*
Marcel Ayme. *The Walker through Walls*
Beryl Bainbridge. *Harriet Said*
J. G. Ballard. *Concrete Island*; High Rise*
Charles Beaumont. *Hunger*; The Magic Man*
Robert Bloch. *Pleasant Dreams*; Psycho**
Ray Bradbury. *Dandelion Wine; Something Wicked This Way Comes*; The October Country*
Joseph Payne Brennan. *The Shapes of Midnight**
Frederic Brown. *Nightmares and Geezenstacks**
Edward Bryant. *Among the Dead*
Janet Caird. *The Loch*

Ramsey Campbell. *Demons By Daylight; The Doll Who Ate His Mother*; The Parasite**

Suzy McKee Charnas. *The Vampire Tapestry*

Julio Cortazar. *The End of the Game and Other Stories*

Harry Crews. *A Feast of Snakes*

Roald Dahl. *Kiss Kiss*; Someone Like You**

Les Daniels. *The Black Castle*

Stephen R. Donaldson. *The Thomas Covenant Trilogy (3 vols.)**

Daphne Du Maurier. *Don't Look Now*

Harlan Ellison. *Deathbird Stories*; Strange Wine**

John Farris. *All Heads Turn When the Hunt Goes By*

Charles G. Finney. *The Ghosts of Manacle*

Jack Finney. *The Body Snatchers*; I Love Galesburg in the Springtime; The Third Level*; Time and Again**

William Golding. *Lord of the Flies**

Edward Gorey. *Amphigorey: Amphigorey Too*

Charles L. Grant. *The Hour of the Oxrun Dead; The Sound of Midnight**

Davis Grubb. *Twelve Tales of Horror**

William H. Hallahan. *The Keeper of the Children; The Search for Joseph Tully*

James Herbert. *The Fog; The Spear*; The Survivor*

William Hjortsberg. *Falling Angel**

Shirley Jackson. *The Haunting of Hill House*; The Lottery and Others*; The Sundial*

Gerald Kersh. *Men Without Bones**

Russell Kirk. *The Princess of All Lands*

Nigel Kneale. *Tomato Caine*

William Kotzwinkle. *Dr. Rat**

Jerry Kozinski. *The Painted Bird**

Fritz Leiber. *Our Lady of Darkness**

Ursula LeGuin. *The Lathe of Heaven*; Orsinian Tales*

Ira Levin. *Rosemary's Baby*; The Stepford Wives*

John D. MacDonald. *The Girl, the Gold Watch, and Everything*

Bernard Malamud. *The Magic Barrel*; The Natural*

Robert Marasco. *Burnt Offerings**
Gabriel Maria Marquez. *One Hundred Years of Solitude*
Richard Matheson. *Hell House; I Am Legend**; *Shock II; The*
*Shrinking Man**; *A Stir of Echoes*
Michael McDowell. *The Amulet**; *Cold Moon Over Babylon**
Ian McEwen. *The Cement Garden*
John Metcalf. *The Feasting Dead*
Iris Murdoch. *The Unicorn*
Joyce Carol Oates. *Nightside**
Flannery O'Connor. *A Good Man Is Hard to Find**
Mervyn Peake. *The Gormenghast Trilogy (3 volumes)*
Thomas Pynchon. *V.**
Edogawa Rampo. *Tales of Mystery and Imagination*
Jean Ray. *Ghouls in My Grave*
Anne Rice. *Interview with the Vampire*
Philip Roth. *The Breast*
Ray Russell. *Sardonicus**
Joan Samson. *The Auctioneer**
William Sansom. *The Collected Stories of William Sansom*
Sarban. *Ringstones; The Sound of His Horn**
Anne Rivers Siddons. *The House Next Door**
Isaac Bashevis Singer. *The Seance and Other Stories**
Martin Cruz Smith. *Nightwing*
Peter Straub. *Ghost Story**; *If You Could See Me Now; Julia;*
*Shadowland**
Theodore Sturgeon. *Caviar; The Dreaming Jewels; Some of*
*Your Blood**
Thomas Tessier. *The Nightwalker*
Paul Theroux. *The Black House*
Thomas Tryon. *The Other**
Les Whitten. *Progeny of the Adder**
Thomas Williams. *Tsuga's Children**
Gahan Wilson. *I Paint What I See*
T. M. Wright. *Strange Seed**
John Wyndham. *The Chrysalids; The Day of the Triffids**

Index

Abbott and Costello Meet Frankenstein (film), 76

Abominable Dr. Phibes, The (film), 140

Adventures of Chickenman, The (radio series), 114

Aickman, Robert, 376

Alas, Babylon (book), 9

Alfred Hitchcock Presents (TV series), 237, 261

Alien (film), 16, 21–22, 192, 194–95, 198, 222

Aliens Are Coming, The (TV film), 236

Allegory, 9–10, 32–33, 41–43, 74, 155

Allen, Irwin, 219

Allen, Woody, 57

American-International Pictures, 31–32, 41–43

Amityville Horror, The (film), 145–53

Andromeda Strain, The (film), 169, 170

Anxiety, 108–9

Apollonian themes, 78–79, 166, 170

Approaching Oblivion (book), 404

Archer, Lee, *see* Ellison, Harlan

Argento, Dario, 200

Arkham House, 30, 266

Arkoff, Samuel Z., 31–32

Armadale (book), 51

Arnold, Jack, 111

Art, 137–39

Assault on a Queen (film), 259

Assault on Precinct 13 (film), 222

Attack of the Fifty-Foot Woman, The (film), 218–19

Attack of the Giant Leeches, The (film), 32

Avon Press, 100

Bad (film), 187

Bad Place (archetype), 278, 280–81

Bad Seed, The (film), 192

Ballard, J. G., 163*n*.

Beaumont, Charles, 254, 255

Beck, Calvin, 213

Beginning of the End (film), 65, 166

"Big Tall Wish, The" (TV show), 257

Bird, Cordwainer, 395–97
   see also Ellison, Harlan

Birds, The (film), 192, 198

Bissell, Whit, 45, 48

Black Book of Clark Ashton Smith, The (book), 409

Black comedy, 161–62

Black House, The (book), 376

Blatty, William Peter, 315
Blob, The (film), 219
Bloch, Robert, 30–31, 79, 127, 240, 286*n.*
Body Snatchers, The (book), 324–44, 361
Bonnie and Clyde (film), 58
"Boomerang" (TV show), 256
"Born of Man and Woman" (short story), 329
Boys from Brazil, The (book), 314
B-pictures, 139, 212
Bradbury, Ray, 11, 30, 124, 127, 257, 329*n.*–30*n.*, 344–45
Brennan, Joseph Payne, 23, 306
Bride of Frankenstein (film), 60
Brides of Dracula (film), 69
Brontë, Branwell, 40
Brood, The (film), 107, 139
Brooks, Mel, 30
Browning, Ricou, 103
Browning, Tod, 35–36
"Burial, The" (short story), 63
Byron, Lord, 62–63

Cain, James M., 79
Cain's Hundred (TV series), 237
Campbell, John W., 160
Campbell, Ramsey, 195*n.*, 376–78, 384
"Canavan's Back Yard" (short story), 306
Cannibalism, 81, 142, 379–80
Cantalupo, Michael, 195
Car, The (film), 173
Carlson, Richard, 7–8, 102
Carpenter, John, 21, 222–23
Carrie (book), 426–27
Carrie (film), 179–83, 226

Car Sinister (book), 174
Cartoons, 132
Disney movies, 106–7
Castle, William, 192*n.*, 196–97
Castle of Frankenstein, The (magazine), 213–14
Cat People (film), 120–22
Changeling, The (film), 109, 117, 153
Charby, Jay, *see* Ellison, Harlan
Chayefsky, Paddy, 251
"Cheaters, The" (short story), 240
Chermak, Cy, 249
"Chicken Heart That Ate the World" (radio program), 130
Children, 104–6
cruelty of, 207–8
fears of, 125–27
and horror, 107–8
Children of Cain (film), 219
"Children of the Kingdom" (short story), 265
China Syndrome, The (film), 164, 170
"Chopper" (TV show), 249
Chrysalids, The (book), 41
Clarke, Arthur C., 110*n.*
Cline, C. Terry, 315
Clockwork Orange, A (film), 162
Clone, The (book), 23*n.*
Close Encounters of the Third Kind (film), 17, 159
Cochran, Eddie, 44
Coleridge, S. T., 104
Collins, Wilkie, 50
Colossus (book), 162
Coma (film), 192, 199
Comeback, The (film), 212

Comics, 22–23, 36–37, 369, 419
"Companion, The" (short story), 378
Conqueror Worm, The (film), 206
Cook, Oscar, 256
Coppola, Francis, 226
Corman, Roger, 32, 202, 204
Creature from the Black Lagoon (film), 102, 109, 111
Creeping Unknown, The (film), 171
Crichton, Michael, 225
Crime, 79–80
"Croatoan" (short story), 398
Cronenberg, David, 107, 138n., 139, 222
Currey, L. W., 326
Curse of the Demon (film), 117
Curse of the Werewolf (film), 298
Curtis, Dan, 245–47
Curtis, Jamie Lee, 21
Curtis, Price, *see* Ellison, Harlan

Dahl, Roald, 261
Damon (book), 315
Dark Carnival (book), 346
Darkness, fear of, 193–99
Dark Shadows (TV series), 245–46
Dark Star (film), 222
Davis, Jack, 23
Dawn of the Dead (film), 81, 139, 216
"Day at the Dentist's, A" (short story), 134–36
Day the Earth Stood Still, The (film), 1
Deadbeat, The (book), 79
Death, 140, 205–6
Deathbed Stories (book), 404

Death Tour (book), 398
De Laurentiis, Dino, 62
Deliverance (film), 192, 199
Dementia-13 (film), 80, 192, 199, 228
"Demon with a Glass Hand" (TV show), 243
Denning, Richard, 102
De Palma, Brian, 179–82, 206, 229, 325
Derleth, August, 30, 266n.
Die, Monster, Die (film), 185
Dimension X (radio series), 124
Dionysian themes, 78–79, 166, 170
Dirty Harry (film), 57
Disbelief, suspension of, 128–29
Discrimination, 38–39
Disney, Walt, 106–7
Dr. Cook's Garden (TV film), 312n.
Dr. Doom, 37
Dr. Jekyll and Mr. Hyde (book), 50, 72–78, 83
Dr. Octopus, 36–37
Dr. Strangelove, or How I Learned to Stop Worrying and Love the Bomb (film), 162
Dog Soldiers (book), 78
Doll Who Ate His Mother, The (book), 378–79
Donovan's Brain (book), 17–19
Dracula (book), 26–27, 50, 63–68, 69, 82
Dracula (film), 70, 144
Dracula (TV drama), 261
Dreiser, Theodore, 345
Drop Dead! An Exercise in Horror (radio play), 136
Duel (short story, TV film), 173–74

Earth Abides (book), 424

Earth vs. The Flying Saucers (film), 2, 13, 158, 170

Easy Rider (film), 168

Edison, Thomas, 59

Edmundson, Wallace, *see* Ellison, Harlan

Edwards, Blake, 58

Elkin, Stanley, 401–2

Ellis, Landon, *see* Ellison, Harlan

Ellison, Harlan, 127, 231–33, 236, 243, 394–410

"Emissary from Hamelin" (short story), 407

Evictors, The (film), 223*n.*

Evil, 65

Exorcist, The (book), 273, 315, 330

Exorcist, The (film), 3, 139, 177–79, 422

"Eye of the Beholder" (TV show), 38, 260

Eye of the Cat (film), 242–43

Fairy tales, 109, 139, 186–87

Family Plot (film), 225

Fantasia (film), 106

Faulkner, William, 291–92

Fear, 5, 105–6, 126–27, 193, 204–5, 297

in children, 125–27

in film, 139

"Fever, The" (TV show), 259

Fiedler, Leslie, 375

Finney, Jack, 5, 258–59, 324–27

Five (film), 131

Fog, The (book), 387–90

Forbes, Bryan, 175

Forbin Project, The (film), 162

"Foul Play" (short story), 24–25

Frank, Pat, 9

Frankenheimer, John, 3, 214

Frankenstein (book), 50, 52–56, 59–60

Frankenstein: The True Story (TV film), 262

Freaks, 33–35, 38
  see also Monsters

Freaks (film), 35

Free will, 64

Freud, Sigmund, 74

Friedkin, William, 139, 214

Friedman, Lenemaja, 299, 301

"From A to Z, in the Chocolate Alphabet" (short story), 408

Frye, William, 240

Funerals, 140–42

Fury, The (film), 107, 206, 325

Fuzz (book), 417

Gaines, William M., 22

"Galaxy Being, The" (TV show), 243

Gardner, Erle Stanley, 392*n.*

Gargoyles (TV film), 262

Geeks, 35

Ghastly Ones, The (film), 138

Ghosts, 51, 265, 271

Ghost Story (book), 26, 266, 267–77

Giant Spider Invasion, The (film), 200, 201–2, 218

Gimmicks, 195–97

God, 64

Gog (film), 163

Goldman, William, 175*n.*, 314

"Good Man Is Hard to Find, A" (short story), 21

Gothic fiction, 271–72, 296–97, 300

Grant, Charles L., 306

"Graveyard Shift" (short story), 28*n.*

Gregg Press, 326

Guest, Val, 171, 172

Haas, George F., 408

Hailey, Arthur, 391

Hair of Harold Roux, The (book), 424

Halloween (film), 21, 192, 197

Hammer Films, 61, 69, 80

Hammett, Dashiell, 392

"Hansel and Gretel" (fairy tale), 109, 183–84, 187

"Harrison Bergeron" (short story), 234

Harryhausen, Ray, 2

Harson, Sley, *see* Ellison, Harlan

Hart, Ellis, *see* Ellison, Harlan

Hartwell, David, 326

Hatlen, Burton, 51, 52, xii

Haunted houses, 146, 277–80

"Haunter of the Dark, The" (short story), 119

Haunting, The (film), 25, 119, 192

Haunting of Hill House, The (book), 118, 282, 297, 298

Hawks, Howard, 81, 154

Height of the Scream, The (book), 378

Heinlein, Robert, 341

"He Lives" (TV show), 253

Herbert, James, 4, 212, 376, 383

Herrmann, Bernard, 260

Hitchcock, Alfred, 79, 225, 235–36

"Hitler Painted Roses" (short story), 401–4

Home Box Office, 223*n.*

Hooper, Tobe, 138

Horror of Party Beach, The (film), 164–65, 228

Horrors of the Black Museum (film), 140

Hour of the Oxrun Dead, The (book), 306

House Next Door, The (book), 262, 282, 283–96

House on Value Street, The (book), 423

Howard, Robert E., 71, 240, 368

Humor, 130

"Hungry Glass, The" (short story), 240

Hunter, Evan, 417

Hypnotism, 68

I Am Legend (book), 161

I Bury the Living (film), 192

If You Could See Me Now (book), 267

I Married a Monster from Outer Space (film), 221, 223–24

Immortality, 50

Incredible Hulk, The (TV series), 45, 59, 298

Incredible Shrinking Man, The (film), 4, 169

Independent films, 227

Inhabitants of the Lake, The (book), 378

Inner Sanctum (TV series), 116

Insanity, 185–86

"Invaders, The" (TV show), 260

Invasion of the Body Snatchers (film), 5, 139, 140

Invasion of the Saucer-Men (film), 220

Invasion of the Star Creatures (film), 221

Irish, William, *see* Woolrich, Cornell

"It Came Out of the Woodwork" (TV show), 243

I Was a Teenage Frankenstein (film), 45, 46, 48–49

I Was a Teenage Werewolf (film), 45–46

Jackson, Shirley, 33, 118, 282, 296, 297

Jack the Ripper (film), 197*n.*

Jakes, John, 392–93

James, Henry, 51

Jarvis, E. K., *see* Ellison, Harlan

Jaws (film), 206

Jewel of Seven Stars, The (book), 83

Job, 64

Jones, D. F., 162–63

Jong, Erica, 69

Jorgensen, Ivar, *see* Ellison, Harlan

Journey to the Unknown (TV series), 262

Jude the Obscure (book), 82

Julia (book), 267, 269–70

Juvenile delinquency, 43–44

Kael, Pauline, 325

Karloff, Boris, 53, 61, 238

Kaufman, Philip, 5*n.*, 6–7

King, Tabitha, 375*n.*

Kingdom of the Spiders (film), 4

King Kong (film), 61–62

Kipling, Rudyard, 74

Kiss Before Dying, A (book), 313

Klein, T. E. D., 265

Kolchak: The Night Stalker (TV series), 248, 249–50

Kolchak Tapes, The (book), 245

Kubrick, Stanley, 121, 122, 123, 162

Lady in a Cage (film), 81

Lair of the White Worm, The (book), 83

Landis, John, 363

Last Man on Earth, The (film), 161

Lederer, Charles, 160

Lee, Christopher, 61

Lee, Stan, 36

Left-handedness, 38–40

"Legacy of Terror" (TV show), 249

Leiber, Fritz, 174, 383

Leone, Sergio, 58

Levin, Ira, 174, 175, 311–17

Lewis, M. G., 51

Lighting techniques, 121–23, 198–99

see also Gimmicks

Lights Out (radio series), 129

Little Shop of Horrors, The (film), 202

Living End, The (book), 401–2

"Lonely Women Are the Vessels of Time" (short story), 407

Looking for Mr. Goodbar (film), 192, 197–98

"Lottery, The" (short story), 33

Love and Death in the American Novel (book), 375

Lovecraft, H. P., 30, 65, 79, 81, 100–102, 119–20, 203–4, 255–56, 378, 408

Lugosi, Bela, 61*n.*, 70, 224

Lurking Fear and Other Stories, The (book), 100

Lustig, William, 200

Macabre (film), 192

MacDonald, John D., 126

Malin, Irving, 296

Maniac (film), 200–201

Marriages (book), 267

"Mars Is Heaven" (short story), 124–25

Martian Chronicles (book), 11

Martin (film), 81 n.

Martin, Quinn, 262

Marvel Comics, 36–37

Matheson, Richard, 30, 161, 173, 247, 254, 260, 329, 360

McBain, Ed, 417

McCauley, Kirby, 222, xii

McTeague (book), 430

Merchant, Paul, *see* Ellison, Harlan

Mesmer, Franz, 68

MGM, 35, 225

Michael, David J., 398

Midnight Express (film), 192

"Miniature" (TV show), 255

Mitchell, Clyde, *see* Ellison, Harlan

Monk, The (book), 50–51

"Monkey's Paw, The" (short story), 22

Monsters, 32–43, 217–18

   see also Freaks

"Monsters Are Due on Maple Street, The" (TV show), 253

Motion pictures, *see* Movies

Movies, 57–58, 110–11, 137–211

   cartoons, 132

   Disney movies, 106–7

Munsters, The (TV series), 57

Music, 110

Mystery Playhouse Starring Boris Karloff (TV series), 238

Mythology, 52, 78–79

Narcissism, 296, 298

Narrative of Arthur Gordon Pym, The (book), 378

National Enquirer (newspaper), 34

National Lampoon (magazine), 34

"New Exhibit, The" (TV show), 255

Newman, Edwin, 385

Nicholson, James H., 31–32

"Nick of Time" (TV show), 259

Night Evelyn Came out of the Grave, The (film), 197 n.

Night Gallery (TV series), 252, 255–56

Nightmare (film), 80

"Nightmare at 20,000 Feet" (TV show), 260

Night of the Hunter, The (film), 192, 198

Night of the Lepus (film), 169

Night of the Living Dead (film), 33, 81, 142–43, 166, 170, 192, 198, 227, 228

Night Shift (book), 85, 241

Night Stalker, The (TV series), 245, 246–49

Night Strangler, The (TV series), 248

Nightwalker, The (book), 376

Night Watch (film), 192

1984 (film), 161

Nolan, William F., 116, 117

Norris, Frank, 430

Nosferatu (film), 68

Nosille, Nalrah, *see* Ellison, Harlan

Nyby, Christian, 154

Oates, Joyce Carol, 377

Oboler, Arch, 129, 131–35

O'Brien, Willis, 62

O'Connor, Flannery, 21
"Of Missing Persons" (short story), 259
Ogle, Charles, 59
Omega Man, The (film), 161
Omen, The (film), 192, 199, 201
Once Upon a Time in the West (film), 58
One Hundred and One Dalmatians (film), 106
Oral sex, 69
Orgasm, 68
Our Lady of Darkness (book), 383
Outer Limits (TV series), 80, 241–44

Pal, George, 161
Paranoia, 322, 326, 330–32
Parasite, The (book), 376
Park, John G., 296–97, 301–2
"Patterns" (short story), 252
"Perchance to Dream" (TV show), 254
Peter Gunn (TV series), 237
Phase IV (film), 149
Phobias, see Fear
Physical deformities, see Freaks; Monsters
Pierce, Jack, 60–61
"Pigeons from Hell" (short story), 240
Pimples, 46–47
Pit and the Pendulum, The (film), 143
Plan 9 from Outer Space (film), 224
Playden, Paul, 249
Pleasance, Donald, 21
Poe, E. A., 65, 378
Polanski, Roman, 311–12
Polidori, John, 62–63

Political subtexts, 154–61
Powers, Richard Gid, 342–44
"Prey" (short story), 247
"Printer's Devil" (TV show), 253n., 255
Prophecy (film), 3, 163, 214
Psycho (film), 79–80, 143, 192, 199, 235–36, 242
Puppet Masters, The (book), 341

Rabid (film), 222
Radio, 113–36
Rape, 67, 68–69
Rat (book), 4
Raven, The (film), 70
Rebirth (book), 41
Religion, 76, 320–21
Repulsion (film), 80
Rice, Jeff, 245
Riders to the Stars (film), 8
Right Stuff, The (book), 9
Ritual (film), 222
Robbins, Marty, 44
Robot Monster (film), 213–14
Rockabilly (book), 397
Rock and roll, 41, 43
Rocky Horror Picture Show, The (film), 228–29
Rodrigues, 34
Romero, George, 81, 143, 216, 421
Rose, Reginald, 251
Rosemary's Baby (book), 311–23
Ruby (film), 219
Russell, Ray, 202

'Salem's Lot (book), 26–27, 69–70, 87, 205, 280
'Salem's Lot (TV film), 215, 226, 239, 262

Sanctuary (book), 292

Sandman, The, 37

Sangster, Jimmy, 197*n.*

Scarf, The (book), 79

Scenery, *see* Set design

Science fiction, 16

Scorpion, The, 36

Search for Bridey Murphey (book), 149

"Sentry, The" (TV show), 249

Serling, Rod, 123, 250–60

Set design, 122–23

Sex, 68–72, 86, 297

Sexism, 70

Sexuality, 67

Sheed, Wilfrid, 375

Shelley, Mary, 53, 59–60, 62–63, 82, 83

Shelley, Percy, 62–63

"Shelter, The" (TV show), 253

Shining, The (film), 108, 122, 123, 226–27

Shrinking Man, The (book), 30, 360–68, 369–74

Siamese twins, 33–34

Siddons, Anne Rivers, 282

Siegel, Don, 5–6, 57, 139, 326

Singer, Isaac Bashevis, 128

Siodmak, Curt, 17–18

Sisters (film), 229

Sleeping Beauty (film), 106

"Slime" (short story), 23

Small World (book), 375*n.*

Smith, Clark Ashton, 383, 408–9

Smith, Guy N., 383

Snow White and the Seven Dwarfs (film), 106, 111

Social horror films, 174–83

Sohl, Jerry, 243

Solo, Jay, *see* Ellison, Harlan

Something Wicked This Way Comes (book), 344–60

Sorcerer (film), 214

Space travel themes, 170–71

"Spanish Moss Murders, The" (TV show), 249

Spicy Stories (magazine), 419

Spider Kiss (book), *see Rockabilly*

Spiderman, 369*n.*

Spielberg, Steven, 159, 173–74

Squirm (film), 200

Stand, The (book), 274, 425–28

Starring Boris Karloff (TV series), 238

Star Trek (film), 395*n.*–96*n.*

Star Trek (TV series), 395

Star Wars (film), 16

Stefano, Joseph, 80, 242

Stepford Wives, The (book), 313, 314

Stepford Wives, The (film), 33, 174–75

Stevens, Leslie, 242

Stevenson, R. L., 50, 72, 82

Stewart, George R., 424, 425

Stoker, Bram, 26–27, 64, 65, 82, 83

   see also Dracula (book)

Stone, Robert, 78

Straitjacket (film), 80

Strange Eons (book), 79

Strange Wine (book), 397, 404

Straub, Peter, 26, 266, 267

"Strawberry Spring" (short story), 241

Sucking Pit, The (book), 383

Sundial, The (book), 296, 297

Superheroes, 36–37

Survive (film), 109

"Survivor Type" (short story), 380*n.*

Suspense (radio series), 114

Suspension of disbelief, 128–29

Suspiria (film), 200

Swarm, The (film), 219

Symbolism, *see* Allegory

Taboos, 139–40, 142–43, 184, 293–94

Tales from the Crypt (comic), 22, 23

Tales of the Unexpected (TV series), 262

Tarantula (film), 4

Techno-horror films, 163–74

Teenage Monster (film), 218

Teenagers, 41–43, 46–47

Television, 132

"Tell-Tale Heart, The" (short story), 23, 65

Tessier, Thomas, 376

Texas Chainsaw Massacre, The (film), 43, 108, 138

Them! (film), 81, 149

Theroux, Paul, 376

They Came from Within (film), 139, 142, 222, 381

Thing, The (film), 81, 154–60

Thing Without a Name, 59, 81, 158

"Third from the Sun" (TV show), 254

Third Level, The (book), 258, 259

"Thirty-Fathom Grave, The" (TV show), 255

This Island Earth (film), 71

Thomas, Ted, 23*n.*

Thompson, Bill, 198, ix–xii

Thriller (TV series), 237–41

Tiger, Derry, *see* Ellison, Harlan

Time and Again (book), 258, 333

"Time Enough at Last" (TV show), 253

Tingler, The (film), 196–97

Tors, Ivan,

Tourist Trap (film), 223

Toys, 57

"Trevi Collection, The" (TV show), 249

Trilogy of Terror (film), 247

Turn of the Screw, The (book), 51

Tuttle, William, 260

Twilight Zone (TV series), 38, 242, 250–60

2001: A Space Odyssey (film), 162

Universal Pictures, 61

Untouchables, The (TV series), 237

Vampires, 26–27, 63–64, 68, 71, 81

see also Dracula

"Vampyre, The" (short story), 63–64

Vault of Horror, The (comic), 22

Violence, 133–34, 138, 143, 200–201

Vonnegut, Kurt, Jr., 163*n.*, 234

Wait Until Dark (film), 192, 195–96

War babies, 42

Warhol, Andy, 187

War of the Worlds, The (film), 161

War of the Worlds, The (radio program), 124

Weird Tales (magazine), 30, 31, 240

Welles, Orson, 124, 435

Werewolves, 72–78, 81, 166, 298
Westworld (film), 225–26
Whale, James, 60
What Ever Happened to Baby Jane? (film), 81, 192
When a Stranger Calls (film), 185
"Wig for Miss DeVore, A" (short story), 240
Wild Angels, The (film), 204
Wild Bunch, The (film), 207
Wild One, The (film), 44
Wilhelm, Kate, 23*n.*

Williams, Tennessee, 392
Wise, Robert, 25, 118–19, 120, 300
Wolfe, Tom, 9
Woolrich, Cornell, 392
Wyndham, John, 41

X—The Man with the X-Ray Eyes (film), 192, 202–3

Zombies, 166
Zukofsky, Louis, 385–86

About the Author

Stephen King is the author of more than fifty books, all of them worldwide bestsellers. Among his most recent are *Under the Dome*, the Dark Tower novels, *Cell, From a Buick 8, Everything's Eventual, Hearts in Atlantis, The Girl Who Loved Tom Gordon, Lisey's Story,* and *Bag of Bones.* His acclaimed nonfiction book *On Writing* was also a bestseller. He was the recipient of the 2003 National Book Foundation Medal for Distinguished Contribution to American Letters. He lives in Maine with his wife, novelist Tabitha King.